ANALYSIS
FOR MILITARY DECISIONS

ANALYSIS
FOR MILITARY DECISIONS

Edited by

E. S. QUADE

The RAND Corporation, Santa Monica, California

1966
RAND McNALLY & COMPANY – CHICAGO
NORTH-HOLLAND PUBLISHING COMPANY – AMSTERDAM

Published by:

RAND McNALLY & COMPANY – CHICAGO

Sole distributors outside North and Central America:

NORTH-HOLLAND PUBLISHING COMPANY – AMSTERDAM

1st edition 1964
2nd printing 1966

LC65003032

J16482.
Pwod Ewj.
c

PRINTED IN THE NETHERLANDS

PREFACE

The RAND Corporation is a private, nonprofit organization whose principal activity is scientific study and research on problems of national security. Working for the United States Air Force, RAND has played a leading role in developing an approach called "systems analysis," designed to help answer complex questions of choice in the face of uncertainty, such as occur in problems of national defense. This approach, rooted in the operations analysis techniques developed during World War II, is now applied to problems of development, disarmament, and deterrence, as well as to military operations proper. Yet its methodology is by no means fully developed, nor are its successes and failures yet completely understood.

During 1955, and again in 1959, RAND offered an intensive five-day course entitled "An Appreciation of Analysis for Military Decisions" to military officers and civilians associated with the armed forces. Designed primarily for decisionmakers and not for analysts, this course did not attempt to teach operations research but to point out the weaknesses and possible abuses, as well as the effectiveness, of an analytic approach to long-range military planning. It was based on the premise that a decision-maker can appreciate analysis and use its results with confidence without knowing how to perform it.

This book contains the lectures (some extensively revised) that were given in the course, plus some supplementary material. It is not a reference work on systems analysis; neither is it a treatment of how to carry out analyses for military decisions. It is little more than an attempt at a critical evaluation. The concepts and methodology discussed, however, should be useful to those concerned with the military aspects of national security and should be adaptable to planning and analysis in many nonmilitary fields as well.

ACKNOWLEDGMENTS

A work of this type reflects the efforts of many people not named in the table of contents. These are people who have worked on actual systems analyses, and then consciously thought about the methodology, developing the concepts and techniques and learning through experience.

The authors are indebted to various RAND staff members and consultants who criticized the original lectures and the present collection. Special recognition should be given to D. M. Fort, Herman Kahn, B. H. Klein, C. E. Lindblom, Irwin Mann, A. W. Marshall, L. J. Savage, and J. D. Williams. Many of their ideas and sometimes even their statements from various unpublished papers or oral communications appear in the lectures without special citation. Chapter 8 benefited, in particular, from comments by L. J. Savage, many of which are included almost verbatim.

To others at RAND we wish to make blanket acknowledgment, since the lists of individuals who have helped shape the ideas in these lectures would amount almost to a roster of personnel.

The views expressed here were those of the individual lecturers at the time of presentation and should not be interpreted as reflecting the views of The RAND Corporation or the official opinion of any sponsor.

CONTENTS

PREFACE V

ACKNOWLEDGMENTS VI

Part One: ORIENTATION 1

   1. Introduction, by E. S. Quade 2
   2. Analysis for Air Force Decisions, by C. J. Hitch 13
   3. The Selection and Use of Strategic Air Bases: A Case History, by
      E. S. Quade 24

Part Two: ELEMENTS AND METHODS 65

   4. The Why and How of Model Building, by R. D. Specht 66
   5. Criteria, by R. N. McKean 81
   6. The Relevance of Costs, by Malcolm W. Hoag 92
   7. Analysis and Design of Conflict Systems, by Albert Wohlstetter . . . 103
   8. Methods and Procedures, by E. S. Quade 149

Part Three: SPECIAL ASPECTS 177

   9. Technological Considerations, by R. Schamberg 179
  10. Assumptions about Enemy Behavior, by T. C. Schelling 199
  11. Gaming Methods and Applications, by M. G. Weiner 217
  12. Strategies for Development, by W. H. Meckling. 227
  13. Mathematics and Systems Analysis, by E. S. Quade 237
  14. The Use of Computers, by Paul Armer 250
  15. Costing Methods, by G. H. Fisher and the Staff of the RAND Cost
      Analysis Department 264
  16. Pitfalls in Systems Analysis, by E. S. Quade 300

Part Four: SUMMARY 317

  17. Recapitulation, by E. S. Quade 318

Appendixes 331

   A. An Introduction to the Lunar Base Problem, by E. W. Paxson . . 332
   B. A Missile Comparison, by E. S. Quade 345

BIBLIOGRAPHY 362

INDEX 365

Part One

ORIENTATION

As the correct solution of any problem depends primarily on a true under-standing of what the problem really is, and wherein lies its difficulty, we may profitably pause upon the threshold of our subject to consider first, in a more general way, its real nature; the causes which impede sound practice; the conditions on which success or failure depends; the directions in which error is most to be feared. Thus we shall more fully attain that great prerequisite for success in any work—a clear mental perspective, saving us from confusing the obvious with the important, and the obscure and remote with the un-important.

Arthur Mellen Wellington[1]

The chapters in this book are not presented in the same sequence as the lectures in the course but are grouped according to their subject matter. The first group is concerned with the origin and development of the systems analysis approach and its relation to national security planning. The chapters in Part Two treat the elements and methods common to all systems analyses, and those in Part Three deal with the special aspects. A summary chapter and two appendixes containing hypothetical examples conclude the book.

This first part contains an introduction, a survey of military systems analysis, and an example. Most of the points made here are treated again in later chapters in greater detail. The example presented is an adaptation from an actual study. It is used to illustrate the elements and language of analysis, to demonstrate how an analyst might approach a problem, and to point out some of the difficulties he might encounter.

---

[1] In *The Economic Theory of the Location of Railways,* John Wiley & Sons, New York, 1877.

Chapter 1

INTRODUCTION

E. S. QUADE

In past wars, the initial blow was seldom decisive. The United States always had time in which to manufacture its weapons, train its forces, and plan its strategies. Today the possession of nuclear weapons by a possible enemy denies any defender the luxury of a period after the start of hostilities in which to create or deploy his weapons, or even decide what to do with them. Survival may well depend on a nation's ability to solve the problems of modern warfare far in advance, and solve them in the knowledge that the lessons of previous wars can hardly offer reliable—indeed, relevant— experience from which to learn. Much that a future conflict might involve cannot be planned except by calculation; there is no other way to discover how many missiles are needed to destroy a target system or how to preserve a communication center from a 20-megaton near miss or how to disarm with security.

Systematic, quantitative studies, by physical and social scientists and engineers working in collaboration with the military, have become important in the formulation of defense policy. Their scope ranges upward from increasing the efficiency of routine commercial and industrial housekeeping operations in a military context (probably their most fruitful role!) to advising decisionmakers on the broadest issues of national security. The type of study appropriate to this latter role, called "systems analysis", is the subject of this book. It is to a description of the growth, nature, and uses of systems analysis that the rest of this chapter is devoted.

During the desperate military situation that arose in England in World War II, it occurred to the people responsible for the defense of the country that physicists, biologists, mathematicians, and other highly trained (and highly specialized) people might have something to contribute to what, historically, were almost universally considered strictly military problems. Involving these people was prompted not only by the depth of the crisis, but also by the introduction of new weapons based on technical know-how foreign to past military experience. These weapons and weapons systems (radar is the outstanding example) were so novel in concept and design that their exploitation could not be planned purely on the basis of traditional military experience.

2

New methods of analysis were required. These were developed during World War II and formed the beginnings of a body of knowledge called at that time operations analysis[2] and later, in its various extensions, operations research, systems engineering, management science, cost-effectiveness analysis, and systems analysis. The success of the small-scale but organized efforts in England provided the real impetus to the growth of activity of this type and, naturally enough, the use of scientists[3] to help solve problems that might ordinarily be thought of as lying outside their proper domain.

In its extensions, operations analysis is by no means limited exclusively to military questions. The names given the various extensions reflect to some extent the purpose of the analysis and the context in which it appears, but there is little consistent use. Operations research is the best known. It is used both narrowly to refer to analysis to increase the efficiency of organized man-machine systems and broadly to encompass almost all quantitative analysis. In particular, it is frequently applied to studies concerning national or institutional planning and policy where the idea of increasing efficiency is almost meaningless. It is even used this way in the following chapters. In such a use, it is identical (or should be!) with the body of knowledge and technique that we are calling systems analysis[4]. There is less confusion among the other extensions, but even here few of these names have a single, established referent. If the attention is on, say, the planning and design of new industrial or military systems to better perform existing operations or implement operations never before performed, the terms "systems research", "systems design", or "systems engineering" are frequently used. The attack on problems dealing with the efficient management and control of existing systems is called "management science". If the emphasis falls on finding the differences in costs or resource requirements among the available alternatives for carrying out some specified task, the analysis may be referred to as a "cost-effectiveness analysis". "Operations Research" is also used almost interchangeably with "management science", but is more likely to be applied to those studies in business and public administration that emphasize methodology more than application.

---

2 "Operational analysis" to the British, who deplore the use of nouns as adjectives.

3 The use of scientists to help solve military problems related to their field goes back, at least sporadically, to antiquity.

4 Similarly, and unfortunately, even the term "systems analysis" appears in certain contexts with much more restricted meanings than it does here. For example, it is used to refer to a phase of systems engineering (see A. D. Hall, *A Methodology for Systems Engineering*, D. van Nostrand Co., Inc., Princeton, N. J., 1962, p. 9). A common use of the term in the commercial world is in reference to the analysis of business office systems.

When used in a military context, the label "systems analysis" is applied very broadly to any systematic approach to the comparison of alternatives. Thus, although the character of an analysis addressed to such a problem as improving the operational characteristics of a radar network may be inherently different from one addressed to the problem of increasing the stability of the thermo-nuclear balance, both would be identified as instances of systems analysis. Although the term operations research or its military equivalent, present-day operations analysis, might reasonably be applied to the effort to increase efficiency in the radar network, a new name is needed for the type of study that might be usefully applied to the higher level problem. Incidentally, it was not the systematic character of these studies but rather the nature of the subjects being investigated that originally suggested the name. The first postwar military studies were primarily concerned with weapon systems. Evaluations undertaken to enable decisionmakers to choose among systems, to discover whether a given system would accomplish its objectives, or to set up a framework within which tests of a system could be prepared came naturally to be called "systems analysis".

In light of its origins and its present uses, systems analysis might be defined as inquiry to aid a decisionmaker choose a course of action by systematically investigating his proper objectives, comparing quantitatively where possible the costs, effectiveness, and risks associated with the alternative policies or strategies for achieving them, *and formulating additional alternatives if those examined are found wanting.* Systems analysis represents an approach to, or way of looking at, complex problems of choice under uncertainty, such as those associated with national security. In such problems, objectives are usually multiple, and possibly conflicting, and analysis designed to assist the decision-maker must necessarily involve a large element of judgment.

The concept of a systems analysis is by no means exclusively military, but one that is used extensively by managers and engineers of large industrial enterprises, such as telephone companies and producers and distributors of electric power. It offers a means of discovering how to design or to make effective use over time of a technologically complex structure in which the different components may have apparently conflicting objectives; that is, an approach to choosing a strategy that yields the best balance among risks, effec-tiveness, and costs. Its purpose is to place each element in its proper context so that in the end the system as a whole may achieve its aims with a minimal expenditure of resources.

In two respects, the normal business systems analysis is conceptually simpler. For one thing, in such analysis there is usually a single over-all objective—the maximization of profits—which can be measured and expressed in the same terms as the costs. For another, conflict plays only a minor role. As Albert Wohlstetter has pointed out,

> Somebody in the Bell Telephone System has to worry about slugs or plugged nickels in their coin boxes, but in general Bell does not have to worry about anybody jamming their microwave relay as an interruption of their normal peacetime business[5].

Today, analytic studies, conducted by military agencies, industrial contractors, or organizations, such as RAND, which were explicitly founded to do such work, have come to exert a considerable influence on many military decisions, particularly those dealing with new weapons and weapon systems for the Air Force. In fact, the character of national security problems has changed so much in the last two decades that the military decisionmaker, whatever his branch, has almost no choice but to supplement his judgment and experience with the results obtained through systems analysis. To clarify the meaning of systems analysis, it might be especially useful to move from the generality of the definition given above to what that definition implies and assumes. This can perhaps best be accomplished by contrasting systems analysis with purely scientific studies, with operations analysis, and with operations research, narrowly defined.

If science in its purest form "provides power alone, but not direction" (as Coolidge once remarked in reflecting on the lessons of World War I), it is not difficult to see that the control or manipulation of this power is at best a quasi-scientific affair—even if scientists themselves are involved. The authors of an early systems analysis, the *Report on the International Control of Atomic Energy*[6], put their task this way: "We are not dealing simply with a military or scientific problem but with a problem in statecraft and the ways of the human spirit"— an observation that, then and now, could serve adequately to separate systems analysis from science per se. Rather than merely to understand and predict, the aim is also to suggest policy or, at the very least, offer advice. Hence, systems analysis is at once compelled to "do philosophy", to consider some immediate, diverse, and complex questions of practical values.

The use of analysis to help with decisions of one kind or another in business, defense, or government has long been widespread. But even assuming that this "scientific" help is not considered complete unless it embraces some recommendations concerning policy, it still would not qualify as systems analysis. For much of it—for example, that which appears under the names

---

[5] "Strategy and the Natural Scientists", in Robert Gilpin and Christopher Wright (eds.), *Scientists and National Policy Making*, Columbia University Press, New York, 1963.

[6] Prepared for the Secretary of State's Committee on Atomic Energy by a Board of Consultants: Chester I. Barnard, J. R. Oppenheimer, Charles A. Thomas, Harry A. Winne, and David E. Lilienthal, Chairman. Department of State Publication No. 2498, U.S. Government Printing Office, Washington, D.C., March 16, 1946.

of statistical decision theory, methods engineering, or quality control—has its utility only in very narrow contexts. In broader problems of national security or military planning (and "statecraft and the ways of the human spirit"), a very different approach is required, and scientists themselves prove more useful than the methods with which they are traditionally associated.

Systems analysis has a greater complexity and scope than the operations analysis techniques of World War II, despite their common military application. In World War II, analysts were concerned with the day-to-day activities of a military organization—not with finding ways to eliminate war, or make it unlikely, or deter it, or—if these measures failed—make it possible to survive what could be a catastrophe without precedent. For example, an important problem for the earlier analysts was to discover an optimum search pattern with which our destroyers might locate enemy submarines threatening our convoys. Today's systems analyst must consider not only the threat by enemy submarines to shipping, but to the shore as well. To meet both threats, he must evaluate the utility of entirely new combinations of detection and interception devices, some not yet built or even developed, together with appropriate tactics for using them. He must not only consider the possibility that the destroyer might have only an antisubmarine role in another world war, but he must also analyze the many problems that the existence of submarines which threaten the land as well as the sea brings to the question of the preservation of peace.

Whereas the operations analysts of 1939–1945 were concerned mainly with "tactical" problems that involved the immediate future use of equipment in operation or about to be put into operation, those analysts or professional people of one kind or another who assist the military today are, to a great extent, called upon to deal with the extremely sensitive problem of the design and development of weapon systems that may become obsolete in less time than it takes to develop them. Decisions made about such weapons may not affect the capability of the armed forces for five to ten years or more. Moreover, the uncertainty of the future means that many factors which can be taken as "given" in a study of current operations become "parameters" in a study of the future. Hence, there is a vast increase in the number of questions to be investigated and explicitly treated. This applies not only to such matters as enemy reaction, technological progress, and the political and economic environment, but also to the quasi-scientific, semi-philosophical selection of over-all objectives and rules for choosing between alternatives. Technological considerations, in particular the rapid rate of change in weapons and their almost exponential increase in complexity, are now fully as important as the traditional political, economic, and military factors. Needless to say, these considerations, especially when weighed in light of the existence of an enemy whose actions are kept secret, make extremely hazardous any prediction of the environment in which the weapons or strategies are to be used, and of the effect of their introduction on that environment. In the area of long-range military planning characteristic of systems analysis, it is necessary to replace the piecemeal component optimizations that operations analysis might provide by a comprehensive treatment in which emphasis is placed on an integrated, simultaneous examination of every major relevant problem.

In a sense, the main difference between systems analysis and operations research may well lie just in emphasis. A good deal of the earlier work tended to emphasize mathematical models and optimization techniques. Honors went to practitioners who used or improved mathematical techniques like linear programming or queuing theory and found new applications for them. These people were usually associated with decisionmakers who knew what their objectives were and how to compute their costs, largely in terms of some single, clear-cut criterion. On the other hand, systems analysis—while it does make use of much of the same mathematics—is associated with that class of problems where the difficulty lies in deciding what ought to be done—not simply how to do it—and honors go to people who have the ability or good fortune simply to find out what the problem is. The total analysis is thus likely to be a more complex and less neat and tidy procedure, one seldom suitable for quantitative optimization. In fact, the process is to a large extent synthesis: The environment will have to be forecast, the alternatives designed, and the operational laws invented. Thus, with systems analysis, one associates "broad", "long-range", "high level", "choice-of-objectives" problems, and "choice of a strategy", "judgment", "qualitative", and "assistance to logical thinking". In contrast, with operations research one associates "lower level", "over-all maximization", "mensuration", "quantitative", "means-to-an-end", and "the optimal solution".

In short, the analysis of weapons or strategies for future wars presents a new kind of problem, essentially different from any treated by operations analysis in World War II, or even in the Korean War. The conditions of research are different. There is usually more time; there are large computational facilities; there is a great deal of peacetime data available, but virtually none of the desired operational information. The character of the research is different. Different sorts of questions (including, What *is* the question?) are asked; large numbers of interdependent factors must be considered simultaneously; no obvious rules exist for preferring one operation over another; and questions of value and of policy constitute an essential part of every inquiry.

As a way to bring these implications of our formal definition into focus, let us examine a relatively narrow problem in which a systems analysis approach might be helpful—that of advising on the choice of a next-generation air-defense missile from among several possibilities. How is the best choice to be made? Engineers ordinarily think of the performance of military air vehicles in terms of such qualities as range, speed, altitude, rate of climb, maneuverability, and accuracy. An excellent vehicle is sometimes said to be one in which the values of several of these performance parameters are made as high as possible. But this is clearly a meaningless statement, since these qualities are not independent. Consider, for example, guidance and control.

Without taking a "system" point of view, it might seem obvious that if the accuracy of our missile can be improved, the result will be more enemy missiles or planes shot down. It does not follow at all, however, that the most effective over-all defense system will necessarily be the one that uses the most accurate missiles, or, for that matter, will even be the one with the highest potential for killing enemy vehicles. Any numerical values that measure the kill capability of a missile-defense system must depend on at least four factors: first, the number of missile emplacements within range of which the invaders must fly; second, the number of missiles that can be launched during the time the enemy is within range; third, the probability that a given missile will be operative; and fourth, the probability that an operative missile will kill its target. An increase in the accuracy of the missile would probably increase this fourth factor. But an over-all increase of kills would occur only if the values of the other factors were not materially lowered by whatever change was necessary to bring about the increase in accuracy.

Thus, if additional guidance and control equipment were added to a missile to improve its accuracy, the resulting increase in weight might reduce the missile's range or speed. This in turn could reduce the number of missiles that might be launched in an engagement. Moreover, the greater complexity of more accurate guidance equipment might lower the missile's reliability. And there is also the possibility that the higher cost of missiles which, individually, are more accurate might actually lead to fewer launching sites and fewer missiles. A final choice of design must therefore represent a compromise of many variables. A single performance parameter, like range or accuracy, cannot be a measure of the intrinsic worth of a missile design.

The systems analyst must take a systems approach; that is, he must attempt to look at the problem as a whole. He must examine more than performance parameters to make a wise recommendation. He must consider such operational and logistic factors as mobility, data requirements, communications, supplies, maintenance, personnel, and training. Before deciding to use an unusual substance as a fuel for the missile, on the grounds that it would enhance its range, he must investigate the logistic implications of the decision. The fuel may be so toxic that it will require inordinately complex handling for supply, transport, and storage. If so, over-all system performance may once again be degraded, or the costs raised in spite of any increased range that might develop. And, indeed, in these days of deterrent weapons, the systems analyst must also consider certain less obvious factors—for example, the missile's state of readiness, its vulnerability, and its susceptibility to counter-measures—which may contribute as much to deterrence as the weapon itself, and be the items which dominate the costs of the system. Certainty that a missile can be fired after an attack may be more essential to national security than its accuracy.

Thus, in this fairly limited problem of choosing an air-defense missile, a systems approach is indicated. Despite appearances, no easy answers are possible. The context of any answer—as we have illustrated—must embrace everything pertinent to every alternative system.

The simplest category of systems analysis—illustrated by the example just given—involves a choice among essentially similar alternatives for accom-plishing a given goal. That is, possible alternative missile systems may differ widely in accuracy, range, payload, and certain other characteristics, such as alert status. However, they are likely to be similar in those fundamental aspects where the uncertainties are the greatest—for example, in the relation of their performance in combat to that on the proving ground, in enemy reactions to their development and use, and in their logistics and support problems. But these very uncertainties, taken in conjunction with a prior decision to acquire weapons of this sort, actually explain the simplicity of the analysis. Since the weapons are essentially similar means for accomplishing the same objectives and are roughly contemporaneous with each other, most of the uncertainties are likely to affect all designs in the same direction and approx-imately to the same extent. Consequently, failing to take such uncertainties adequately into account will not likely invalidate the comparison. Moreover, in analysis in which the alternatives are relatively similar, it is fairly easy to apply measures to alleviate the effect of uncertainty on the choice between them. Having once decided what we want, the analysis can proceed.

In such a case, having agreed upon the objectives and determined a way to measure the military effectiveness of the system, the analysis becomes a *cost-effectiveness* analysis. Such analysis would ordinarily take either of two equivalent forms. For a given desired level of military effectiveness, the systems analyst might attempt to determine which alternative, or combination of alternatives, would imply the least cost. Or for a specified budget level, he might try to find out which alternative, or combination of them, would maximize effectiveness. But, in either case, the total systems analysis would require numerous sub-studies of the sort we have mentioned.

On the other hand, a broader problem for systems analysis might involve the design of an entire air-defense system to protect the United States from damage. This would be difficult, but not merely because of the wider context involved. The value of an air-defense system is measured by more than its ability to prevent damage in the event of a surprise attack which begins an all-out war; thus, in peacetime it polices our borders and prevents intrusions.

Better protection results from preventing war, or, if war comes, from keeping it away from our country. Doing either of these things, however, depends at least as much on the existence of offensive power and a national policy for using it as it does on air defense—and probably a good deal more. Hence even the problem of finding a working basis for agreement on objectives and criteria is not likely to be an easy one.

But assuming that criteria and objectives have been tentatively set, considerable practical difficulties remain. Here, alternative subsystems with complementary but essentially different tasks, such as radar and antimissile missiles, would compete for resources. Moreover, even with weapons having essentially the same objectives—say, air-defense missiles for point defense and those designed for area coverage—new difficulties arise because such factors as the warning times required for their deployment, their varying usefulness under varying enemy tactics, and even their support structure may be entirely different. And again, the level of knowledge about the various systems will be different. Of course, for weapons such as aircraft there is much past experience to guide the investigator with respect to such things as maintenance requirements, reliability, and the like. But for missiles, this backlog of experience does not exist. Even more serious are the effects of uncertainties about alternatives which contribute to damage reduction in entirely different ways—say, shelters and alert missiles. Further, since (as we mentioned earlier) a better way to prevent damage is not to have a war, the analysis has to consider also how any combination of weapons will affect the likelihood of war, as well as the chances of survival if it comes.

It is clear that in the analysis of numerous parts of this broader sort of problem, some of which are of the greatest importance, no quantitative or wholly explicit guidance at all can be provided. Unfortunately, this situation is probably permanent. Hence a great deal of subjective judgment must necessarily be involved. Hence, too, a sometimes monumental frustration with systems analysis as a method is bound to arise. But regardless of the deficiencies and difficulties of an analytic approach to modern warfare, some of which may in fact eventually be eliminated, the approach as it exists today has proven itself capable, in the hands of skilled and artful practitioners, of producing results no other method can equal. Given this record, as well as an awareness of the fact that the general situation which led to the growth of operations analysis in World War II continues to exist today in industry and the military, there seem to be both a virtue and a necessity in learning something about how to "do" this sort of philosophy.

There are courses and textbooks to train analysts in the practice of operations research and systems engineering[7]. These deal mainly with mathematical

---

[7]   See Bibliography.

techniques and methods for solving problems that have been represented symbolically. But sophisticated mathematical tools are not major stumbling blocks in most systems analyses. Although one reason for this is that the simpler and more traditional mathematical tools are adequate in a great many cases, the important reason is that the real difficulties in attempting to analyze the broad problems faced by military or government decisionmakers lie elsewhere. They concern the design and definition of the problem, the selection of a rule of choice, and the interpretation of the results of the study, rather than the analyst's use of tools. There are pitfalls in the use of, or the failure to use, mathematical techniques, but the important and easily made errors in these studies are more likely to occur elsewhere.

The RAND Corporation has produced broad analyses of military problems for a number of years. Over this period, numerous suggestions have been made that RAND explain to others the methods used in these studies. We were flattered, but we found it difficult to decide just how to do more than present another discussion of mathematical techniques. Although collectively we have learned a great deal that might be useful to anyone attempting to apply analysis to military decisionmaking, we really do not feel that we know how to supply a set of steps or rules in the abstract which, if followed with exactness, would automatically guarantee a fruitful approach to problems as broad and complex as those confronting the military, let alone those of business and government as well.

In view of these difficulties, not only in the practice of analysis, but also in understanding and applying its results, we reached the decision that a set of informal lectures designed to aid military officers and civilians concerned with the evaluation and use of analytic studies might do more to promote the proper use of analysis than would any more formal effort to train analysts in established techniques. Since the emphasis would necessarily have to be on concepts and principles, we hoped that such an approach would supply information not to be found in the usual operations research text.

These lectures were therefore addressed to the "consumer" of systems analysis, rather than to the systems analyst himself, a distinction we make because the two have different responsibilities with respect to an organization. The man with responsibility for making decisions based upon analysis has to do a lot of listening to the opinions of others without being able to check on how these ideas originated. Thus, many of his decisions are based on his judgment about the competence of others and on the extent to which he is able to understand what they are trying to communicate. Yet, the civilian executive or military commander who decides he can do thus and so because some scientist or engineer tells him it will work is taking a considerable risk. At least he should question his informants and try to get some assurance that the conclusions presented either accord with common sense or fail to do so for a good reason.

This book is offered to make that process easier. It is an outgrowth of the notion that it is possible to appreciate systems analyses, and to use their results with appropriate confidence, without having to become a systems analyst. The air commander in a combat area can learn to appreciate the planning effort that went into his logistic support, so that he can confidently rely on it, without having to duplicate each step of the planning himself. And because our objective in this book is to provide this same kind of appreciation, we have included very little about such esoteric subjects as game theory, linear and dynamic programming, and Monte Carlo, which are the stock in trade of the operations researcher; such tools are covered elsewhere. Our emphasis falls almost exclusively on concepts and principles.

These lectures take a critical approach toward the role of analysis. And though differences of detail exist among them, they all agree that the solving of broad military problems requires intuition and judgment as well as analysis, and that models and the results of computations cannot, in themselves, make decisions. All of them point out how the use of analysis can provide some of the knowledge needed, how it may sometimes serve as a substitute for experience, and, most importantly, how it can work to sharpen intuition. Together, they attempt to demonstrate that systematic, reproducible analysis, developed in a framework permitting the skills of specialists in many fields to be combined, can yield results that transcend the capabilities of any individual.

Chapter 2

ANALYSIS FOR AIR FORCE DECISIONS

C. J. HITCH

The first extensive use of formal analytic methods as an aid to military decisionmaking was made by operations analysis teams in World War II.

But World War II operations analyses were very limited in character. They related to military *operations* in the immediate future—how to use existing equipment—not to decisions regarding *force composition* or the *development* of equipment, which affect the Armed Forces in the more distant future and which require an analysis of the future. Partly, in consequence, they were simple, in the sense that they considered only a small number of interdependent factors. The analyst was able, as a rule, to use some fairly obvious and straightforward objective or criterion as a basis for choosing one operation over another.

A typical example of a World War II operations analysis problem was the selection of the bomber formation in attacking targets deep in Germany. This problem had few variables and an obvious criterion: minimize losses in achieving the required target destruction.

Since the war, attempts have been made at RAND and elsewhere to use analysis as an aid to military decisions in problems of immensely greater complexity. There has been a tendency to use the term "systems analysis" to describe these more complex analyses, but there is no line of demarcation. Both operations analysis and systems analysis are attempts to apply scientific methods to important problems of military decision. Both have the same essential elements:

An *objective* or a number of objectives.

Alternative means (or *"systems"*) by which the objective may be accomplished. (These may be different weapon systems, or different strategies of using a weapon system.)

The *"costs"* or resources required by each system.

A mathematical or logical *model* or models; that is, a set of relationships among the objectives, the alternative means of achieving them, the environment, and the resources.

13

A *criterion* for choosing the preferred alternative. The criterion usually relates the objectives and the costs in some manner, for example, by maximizing the achievement of objectives for some assumed or given budget.

Important developments and extensions of operations analysis have occurred since World War II. We will discuss them in turn, considering briefly the analytic techniques involved in each.

2.1. THE USE OF ANALYSIS TO AID IN FORCE COMPOSITION AND DEVELOPMENT DECISIONS

Decisions regarding force composition and development do not necessarily require different analytic techniques from those used for operations problems. But the techniques are likely to differ because these problems are concerned with the wars of the future, and as we peer into the future the number of variables increases, uncertainties multiply, and different kinds of objectives become appropriate. It is an historical fact that the attempt to apply analysis to development problems—at RAND and elsewhere—has sparked important advances in the use of analytic techniques in all these areas.

2.2. MORE VARIABLES

The fact that we are concerned with an Air Force from three to fifteen years in the future instead of with the present Air Force vastly increases the number and kinds of variables we have to consider. All sorts of things which are given in the short run become variables in the long run. For example, in the bomber formation operations analysis of World War II the planes were B-17's, their number was given, the targets were given, the number of bombs were given, the enemy defenses were given, etc. In the longer run these are not given. They are unknown. They become variables. Some are variables subject to our control, some to the enemy's control, and others to nobody's control. But all are variables, and all are interdependent.

To illustrate how this can increase the number of systems to be compared consider a simple bomber development analysis, where the problem is to choose the preferred vehicle to develop. Suppose we ruthlessly simplify aircraft characteristics to three—speed, range, and altitude. What else do we have to consider in measuring the effectiveness of the bombers of 1965? At least the following: the formation they will use, their flight path to target, the base system, the target system, the bombs, and the enemy defenses. This may not sound like many parameters (in fact, it is far fewer than would be necessary), but if we go no higher than ten, and if we let each parameter take only two alternative values, we already have 2^{10} cases to calculate and compare ($2^{10} > 1000$). If we let each parameter take four alternative values, we have 4^{10} cases ($4^{10} > 1\,000\,000$).

In the World War II bomber formation problem, on the same assumptions, all these things were given except the formation and possibly the flight path. So just moving into the future—considering procurement and development decisions instead of operations decisions—can put us in a different ball park.

What do we do when we are confronted with a million or billion or decillion cases to compute and compare? Of course, we develop higher-speed computers every year and greater skill in using them, and I do not want to belittle the significance of this accomplishment. But even the capacities of modern high-speed computers are finite, and there are usually new confining limitations. We have to get relevant data and relations to feed into the machine on all these systems. The more parameters we deal with, the more time and people this takes—both scarce and valuable resources.

Somehow, then, for one practical reason or another, big, broad problems have to be cut down in size. We have to simplify a practical problem, that is, select those variables which are especially important for the decision with which we are concerned and "suppress" the rest. This takes good judgment; it amounts to no less than deciding in the designing of the analysis what is important and what is not.

Many systems analyses that go wrong, go wrong here. Either they include a mass of data and calculations which are just excess baggage, or they exclude some really critical factor on which a good decision depends.

2.3. EXPLICIT TREATMENT OF UNCERTAINTY

Uncertainties also multiply as we look further into the future—as we have to do because systems analysis is always concerned with the next war, not the last.

We need to distinguish several kinds of uncertainty:

First, uncertainty about *planning factors*—such as attrition rates, average bombing errors, and many other inputs of our analyses.

Second, uncertainty regarding the *enemy and his reactions*.

Third, uncertainty about the *strategic* context. Will there be war during the period covered by our analysis, and if so, when? Will it be general or local? What will be the political constraints? Who will be our enemies, who our allies? Can we rely on Britain? On Yugoslavia? On Maine? For the very short run, strategic uncertainties of this kind are sometimes trivial, for example, the typical operations analysis problem in World

War II. In the longer run they can become dominant. No force composition or development analysis can ignore them. For example, the whole composition of the Air Force may be drastically affected by our opinion about the relative likelihood of big and little wars. Who can tell us? You might say, "the President or the Joint Chiefs of Staff", but the Administration or Joint Chiefs of Staff can do no more than influence this likelihood; other factors beyond their control influence it also, and the analysis must somehow take into account all the possibilities.

A fourth kind of uncertainty that frequently dominates development problems is *technological* uncertainty. For example, until it had been tested, there was real uncertainty as to whether the H-bomb would work, and if so, when; this fact profoundly influenced all sorts of decisions and the structure of many systems analyses. There is always technological uncertainty of some degree attached to research and development.

Finally, there is *statistical* uncertainty—the kind that stems from chance elements in the real world.

What do we do in a systems analysis to take account of this proliferation of uncertainties? The most important advice is: Don't ignore them. To base our decision on some single set of "best guesses" could be disastrous. For example, suppose that there is uncertainty about ten factors (for example, will overseas bases be available and will the enemy have interceptors effective at 60 000 feet?), and we make a best guess on all ten. If the probability that each best guess is right is 60 per cent, then the probability that all ten are right is one-half of 1 per cent. If we confined ourselves to the best guesses, we would be ignoring outcomes with a 99.5 per cent probability of occurring.

The problem breaks down into two parts: First, how do we compute all the "interesting" contingencies?—essentially a technical question. But second— a more fundamental difficulty—once we have computed them (we almost always discover that one strategy is superior in some contingencies, another in others), how does the systems analyst choose the preferred strategy? What decision does he recommend?

For example, suppose analysis shows that a strategic bombing system dependent on overseas bases will be most effective for 1960–1965. Suppose further that we regard it as quite likely, but not certain, that we will have overseas bases in that time period. Suppose, finally, that if we should not have the bases the system would be very bad. What do we do in such a case?

One thing we can do is calculate and maximize the average or "expected" outcome. We all know the shortcomings of this procedure; it can lead to the choice of a reckless strategy and to possible catastrophe. A system that is not as good on the average but does fairly well in all cases in which we are interested may well be preferred. Expected outcomes, in any event, ignore the fact that we are playing against an intelligent enemy who can influence or even choose the contingency we will have to face. The theory of games suggests that in such circumstances we should "minimax"; that is, choose the system which minimizes the worst that can happen to us. But this is not perfectly satisfactory either. In many cases, minimax has the opposite fault; it is too conservative and forfeits opportunities to exploit enemy mistakes, or what we know about his predilections.

There simply is no satisfactory general answer to the problem. Different people take different views of risks—in their own lives and as decisionmakers for the nation. Some play boldly, some play for safety. What does the poor systems analyst do? He frequently calculates expected outcomes or the minimax solution or both, but in interpreting his results he is aware of their shortcomings. But he does not stop there. There are tricks of the systems analysis trade in cases where uncertainties are grossly important:

(a) He tries to *invent* a new system which is as good or almost as good if overseas bases are available, but still pretty good if they are not. We call a system which is best in any circumstances a "sure thing" or "dominant". We can seldom find a truly dominant system, but sometimes, if we are ingenious, we can come close. The systems analyst is not restricted to the systems he starts to compare. The most valuable *function of systems analysis is often the stimulus it gives to the invention of better systems*.

(b) If he fails to find a dominant solution, the analyst calculates the cost of providing insurance against the chance of catastrophe—possibly, in the above overseas bases example, by buying a mixed force with a substantial number of very long-range aircraft. Then the Air Force has to make a command decision, but at least it can do so knowing what the insurance costs.

(c) If he is concerned with development decisions, he recommends the development of aircraft and missiles only some of which depend on overseas bases. The situation may be clearer when decisions about quantity procurement have to be made several years hence. We can develop more types of equipment than we procure in quantity and, given the relatively low cost of development, we ought to. Insurance is cheaper at this stage. The analyst must guard against the implicit "either/or", when a better answer might be "both".

2.4. THE ENEMY

An unfortunate thing about military problems is that, in the real world, they invariably involve an *enemy* whose outstanding characteristic is his desire to be uncooperative. He complicates our lives, and also our analyses. In some problems, what the enemy does is obviously crucial in making the right decision, for example, in the never-ending struggle between electronic counter-measures and counter-countermeasures. But enemy behavior can also be crucial in many less obvious instances. There is thus great interest in developing models which include a malevolent enemy.

Two kinds of models are available: *game theory* models and *games* (that is, war games).

Game theory is a branch of mathematics which studies situations of conflict. The theory unfortunately is still in its infancy. Consequently, there is a strong tendency to use war games instead of game theory. Games have been developed which, unlike traditional military war games, permit many plays, so that a number of possible strategies can be tested against enemy counter-strategies. War games, like game theory, are far from completely satisfactory, but for other reasons. Different players play differently—some probably too well to be representing national governments. It is usually impossible to test which factors are responsible in determining the outcome. Results are therefore difficult to interpret.

2.5. EXPLICIT TREATMENT OF TIME PHASING

In many military problems the *sequence* of events is of critical importance. For example, should we go into production now on some particular missile defense or wait two years until a better one is developed?

To handle such problems we need "dynamic" models—models in which the parameters bear dates. We have such models, but introducing time explicitly is neither easy nor painless because

> It complicates the computation by multiplying the number of parameters—we now have a set for each date. So, if we put time in, we may have to take something else out.

> It complicates the selection of a criterion. Solution A may be better for 1960, worse for 1962; solution B, vice versa.

> It raises in acute form the question of our ability to predict; for example, will that much better missile really be ready only two years later?

2.6. BROADENING OF CRITERIA

The selection of objectives and criteria is frequently the central problem of the design of any systems analysis. What do we really want our systems to accomplish? How do we test the alternative systems to see which accomplishes our objectives the best?

We have seen that, in the typical World War II operations analysis problem, fairly simple obvious ways out of these difficulties could usually be found. So many things were fixed or given. Thus, in the bomber formation example, we can choose the formation which maximizes target destruction for given aircraft losses, or the one that minimizes aircraft losses for given target destruction. These criteria, although they sound different, are logically equivalent and so give the same answer.

Consider, by contrast, the problem of choosing bombers and missiles to include in the SAC force of the middle sixties. What *are* the relevant objectives? What do we want SAC to accomplish? Deterrence, of course. But what kind? Deterrence of a surprise attack on the United States, or deterrence of Soviet aggression in the Middle East? These may have very different implications for force composition. How do we measure deterrence in a quantitative manner? And is deterrence the only objective? Obviously not. If possible, we also want a SAC that will strengthen our alliances, that will not trigger an accidental war, and that will fight effectively if deterrence fails. But if we are to make a choice, we have to have a criterion or rule by which we can at least measure deterrence approximately.

Answering these questions is difficult. But they have to be answered and answered right if our systems analysis is to be worth anything. Here is another point at which good judgment has to penetrate the analysis. Working out a systems analysis with a bad criterion is equivalent to answering the wrong question. It is very easy to choose a criterion for a force composition or development problem that will ensure our choosing the optimal system for the wrong war at the wrong time—no matter how sophisticated the rest of the analysis is (to be fair, it is easy to make the same mistake *without* a systems analysis).

In some, indeed in most, of the hard cases, the search for *an* objective and a single criterion is too elusive. We have to apply a number of tests to our systems and feel our way toward the best or a good system, inventing as we go and making use along the way of the good judgment of the analyst and of the military customer.

One may well ask, in view of this long catalogue of difficulties and limitations, whether military systems analysis is worth supporting.

The first thing to stress in answering this question is that almost all the difficulties we have discussed are inherent in the nature of military problems. There are many variables in a systems analysis because in hard military problems lots of things just *are* important. The *real* problems are beset with uncertainties, plagued by an inscrutable enemy, and tied to elusive national objectives. You can't blame the difficulties on the analytic methods.

Before we can say anything in general about the usefulness of systems analysis we must know what we are contrasting it with. If we define systems analysis broadly to include the various techniques we mentioned earlier, what are the alternatives? Let us consider two of them.

Systems versus Nonsystems

Concentrating on the first word, "systems", the alternative to a systematic approach is an unsystematic or piecemeal consideration of problems.

This distinction is simply a question of breadth of context. In principle, one can attempt to intuit answers in a broad or narrow context or use analysis in a broad or narrow context.

It would be foolish to maintain that broad contexts are good, narrow contexts bad. It all depends on the problem. Systems contexts can be too broad, and when they are, they are wasteful. If you are a scientist trying to develop materials to withstand the heat of rocket engines, your chances of success will be reduced to the extent that you devote time and energy to pondering the relative likelihood of big and little wars. As a matter of historical fact, almost all scientific and technological progress has been achieved within very narrow contexts—by scientists wearing blinders.

Nevertheless, there are cases where the systems approach—the systematic examination of broad alternatives—throws a flood of light on important problems. The selection of a base system is such a case. Let me tell you of another that cropped up in a RAND defense study several years ago. It was at that time operational doctrine for certain interceptors to carry armament that, according to Air Defense Command estimates, gave each plane a 50 per cent probability of killing an intercepted bomber. Well, 50 per cent looked mighty good to most experienced Air Force hands. By World War II standards it was impressive.

What did we find when we examined this doctrine in a systems context? Essentially:

(a) Unlike the situation in World War II, where air strikes were continuous, we were preparing this time for defense against one (or at most a very few) massive atomic strikes.

(b) The total systems cost of procuring and operating the interceptors—to get them into position prepared to fire a rocket at an incoming bomber—was extremely high, so high that the most lavish expenditure on armament scarcely affected the total.

(c) More armament would increase the probability of kill to 75 per cent and degrade interceptor performance by a negligible amount.

(d) It was therefore obvious nonsense to economize on armament. The right answer was to load the interceptors with as much as they could carry.

Now this was an important result of looking at a problem in a broad systems context. An elaborate computation was not really necessary. It was too simple, once you thought about it in the right manner. But a systems analysis forced both the systems analyst and his military audience to think the problem through in a systems context.

Analysis versus Intuition

Let us now turn to the second word in systems analysis: the alternative to analysis is, I suppose, *intuition*.

The main point I want to make might be called the inevitability of analysis. What we call intuition is a species of logical analysis. It uses models, in our sense of simplified conceptual counterparts of reality. Not surprisingly, in military problems as in so many others, it is sometimes useful to buttress our feeble minds with some external assistance: a pencil and the back of an envelope; a few equations; a desk calculator; and in special cases, sophisticated statistical and mathematical theory or high-speed computers.

I am not selling intuition short. The unaided human mind is quite remarkably proficient at solving some kinds of problems. As an example, intuition solved the traveling salesman problem. This is a famous mathematical problem that long frustrated mathematicians. In one version, a traveling salesman starting from Washington has to visit 48 state capitals and return to Washington using the shortest route. It turns out that there are a great many possible routes—in fact, 10^{62} of them. Despite this vast number of alternatives, human beings at RAND, using pins, a piece of string, and their intuition, discovered the one that was shortest.

The human mind has some great advantages over any machine—if we think of them as rivals or alternatives. It has, by comparison, a capacious memory, which enables it to learn from experience. It has a remarkable facility for factoring out the important variables and suppressing the rest. These are the reasons human beings beat machines at chess or war games.

But, on the side of analysis: First, it is wrong to look upon intuition and analysis or minds and machines as rivals or alternatives. Properly used, they complement each other. We have seen that every systems analysis is shot through with intuition and judgment. Every decision that seems to be based on intuition is probably shot through with species of analysis.

Second, while unaided intuition is sometimes strikingly successful, as in the traveling salesman problem, it can also fall flat on its face. I shall spare the reader examples. Everyone has his own.

Third, one of the troubles with intuition is that you don't know whether it is good, at least not without an analytic check. For example, intuition was good enough to solve the traveling salesman problem, but we did not know it until we solved it analytically. Similarly, MATS didn't know its assignment of aircraft to routes was within 5 per cent of optimal until we worked out an analytic solution.

And finally, analytic and computing techniques enable us to do things we otherwise could not. They may be poor on the memory side, but they have some capabilities unaided human minds do not. This is obviously true of high-speed computers. But, let us look at a different kind of example—insights derived from theory. Take a brand-new theory—one that I have been maligning as of very limited usefulness—the theory of games.

In connection with RAND defense studies we have long been interested in the optimal deployment of limited defenses among targets, some of which are more valuable to defend than others. Unfortunately, we have found no satisfactory general rule for deploying defenses, but game theory has given us valuable insights and hints.

Here is a striking example: Suppose you have your defenses deployed as well as you can. Now you get more defenses. How do you deploy them?

Well, my intuition told me (and so did most people's) that you deploy them mainly to protect additional targets—additional cities, harbors, air bases, etc.—that you did not previously have enough stuff to defend.

Game theory says no. You use additional defenses mainly to increase the defense of targets already defended. In fact, over a wide range, the more you have, the more you concentrate it.

Informed of this startling contradiction, you think about it and begin to see the rationale. An increase in your defensive strength is equivalent to a decrease in the enemy's offensive strength. But, as his strength decreases, he has to concentrate more and more on your most valuable targets to achieve anything worth while. These are the ones on which you therefore have to concentrate your defense.

Intuition alone would not have told us this; at any rate, not unequivocally enough to lead one to act on it.

2.7. CONCLUSION

In conclusion let us ask the question, "Does analysis help more in the narrow context problems, where it has commonly been applied by scientists, or in the broad context problems, which are the special province of systems analysts?" I don't know. On the basis of results, certainly one would have to say that the case for analysis in broad context problems is comparatively unproved. However, let me suggest one reason why, when we are dealing with broad problems, explicit analysis using explicit models can be especially important.

We trust a man's intuition in a field in which he is expert. But in complex problems of military force composition or development, we are dealing with a field so broad that no one can be called expert. A typical systems analysis depends critically on numerous technological factors in several fields of technology; on military operations and logistics factors on both our side and the enemy's; on broad economic, political, and strategic factors; and on quite intricate relations among all these. No one is an expert in more than one or two of the subfields; no one is an expert in the field as a whole and the interrelations. So, no one's unsupported intuitions in such a field can be trusted.

Systems analyses should be looked upon not as the antithesis of judgment but as a framework which permits the judgment of experts in numerous subfields to be utilized—to yield results which transcend any individual judgment. This is its aim and opportunity.

Chapter 3

THE SELECTION AND USE OF STRATEGIC AIR BASES: A CASE HISTORY

E. S. QUADE

3.1. PROLOGUE

A case history should help clarify the scope and method of systems analysis. To this end, we have selected an outstanding example of an actual analysis, one that had a significant impact on United States strategic policy.

This systems analysis began in the spring of 1951 as a RAND project entitled "The Selection and Use of Strategic Air Bases". Essentially complete two years later, it was briefed to the Strategic Air Command (SAC) and to Headquarters, USAF, in mid-1953. The project leader was A. J. Wohlstetter. A full report[1] was published in April 1954. This report, originally Top Secret, has now been declassified by the Air Force.

According to *Life* (May 11, 1959, p. 101), the Air Force estimated that this analysis saved the United States a billion dollars. Such a statement calls for two comments. As analysts, we are by nature more careful than journalists with respect to questions of causation, especially within an organization as complex as the Air Force. It is difficult to say what causes what. But it is clear that not long after the first preliminary results were communicated to the Air Force, changes that looked like implementation of the study suggestions began to take place in Air Force practices. If the causation is right, however, the amount of money is far too modest, including only the savings in overseas construction costs, and ignoring the savings associated with the much larger systems costs. But more important than saving money, the changes that took place resulted in a much more secure strategic capability.

The presentation here is not modeled after the briefings given to the Air Force at the time, nor is it similar to the summary contained in the written version. Those were prepared to support conclusions, while what we want here is an illustration of methods. Rather than attempt to abstract the full

---

[1] A. J. Wohlstetter, F. S. Hoffman, R. J. Lutz, and H. S. Rowen, *Selection and Use of Strategic Air Bases,* The RAND Corporation, R-266, April 1954. The present chapter contains illustrations and extracts from the text of this report.

report, we are going to talk about the study, pointing out some of its features and sampling some of its arguments. This presentation is intended to

Show how the problem was formulated and how the analysis developed.

Point out the elements of analysis—the alternatives, the objectives, the costs, the criteria, the model—and show their relationship so that the reader may become familiar with the language and structure of systems analysis.

Illustrate some of the drastic compromises with reality that are necessary in building a model of a complex activity.

Demonstrate how, by contingency and sensitivity analysis, protection against uncertainty was attained.

In other words, this presentation gives concrete illustrations of abstract ideas introduced in the previous chapter and discussed in later chapters.

Incidentally, this example may also show where the many hours necessarily expended on the usual system study go. One might get the false impression from our emphasis on concepts in these lectures that, if certain basic principles are properly appreciated and taken into account by the analyst, the rest of the study will take care of itself. In practice, however, the work is complicated and delicate. Before the analysis itself can progress, much labor must be spent in searching out the facts of the situation. Since in most cases a systems analysis needs to be more than a guide to clear thinking, realistic quantification must be achieved. The extent of that quantification depends on the nature of the problem, but in most cases the effort required in this aspect of the analysis and the difficulties encountered in determining the facts are the great consumers of man-hours. The 426 pages of the full report, plus the numerous references to supporting papers, give testimony to the work required to carry out a large complex study.

At the time the study began, the Strategic Air Command was less than five years old and in a period of transition and growth. The strategic bombing force consisted of B-29's, B-36's, and B-50's. Although a prototype B-47 was then flying, the first wing was not to be combat ready until 1953. The B-52 was still in the design stage.

The major danger was considered to be the possibility of a Soviet attack on Western Europe. The general U.S. objective was deterrence (of such an attack) based on our unilateral atomic capability. If deterrence failed, the SAC war objective was to destroy the Soviet Union's industrial base for waging conventional war. This was expected to require a campaign of several weeks.

The Soviet Union's defense against bombers was not highly regarded by many Air Force officers, particularly in view of our own difficulties with defense. SAC was recognized as a possible target for the Soviet Air Force but was not considered sufficiently vulnerable to require special protective measures. The Soviets were known to have little long-range Air Force experience and no air-refueling capability. Even if they developed atomic weapons, these were expected to remain in short supply for a long time.

3.2. THE PROBLEM

The analysis started as the result of an Air Force request that RAND undertake a study of the selection of overseas air bases. For fiscal year 1952 some $ 3.5 billion had been authorized by Congress for air base construction, about half of which was planned for overseas construction.

Preliminary analysis soon showed, however, that the important problem was not how to acquire, construct, and maintain air bases in foreign countries but *where and how to base the strategic Air Force and how to operate this force in conjunction with the base system chosen.* It became clear that base choice could critically affect the composition, destructive power, and cost of the entire strategic force. Thus, it was not wise to consider a decision on bases merely because of economy in base cost alone. One had to take into account what a base decision means to the total cost of the entire strategic force—how, for example, it affects the costs of extending the range of bombers which cannot reach the target unrefueled, the routes they must fly through enemy territory, the consequent losses they may suffer to the defenses en route, and the difficulties the bases may have in recuperation from attack.

Base choice was also affected by the kind and number of aircraft in the force. For any study to affect force composition except marginally seemed impossible since this is largely governed by research and development, the international situation, and Congress—three areas of great uncertainty. Consequently, it seemed more useful to suboptimize—to give advice about basing a force that was very likely to come into existence rather than to work out the ideal basing system for a theoretical optimum force that had little chance of being bought. To limit the problem, therefore, a decision was made to accept as given the forces then programmed for the 1956–1961 time period.

3.3. THE RESEARCH PHILOSOPHY

The project ambition was to suggest, if possible, a close to optimum system, but, if this turned out to be too difficult, to demonstrate how significant improvements in the currently planned system could be achieved. One of the working rules of systems analysis is that ways to improve the current system and its operation can always be found. A preliminary look made it appear that this case would be no exception; for example, the implications of the possibility that the Soviet Union might have nuclear weapons in quantity had not yet been taken into account in base planning.

It was plain that, given any combination of types of bases and weapons, the level of costs to destroy a fixed number of targets or, given a fixed budget, the absolute number of targets that might be killed would vary widely, depending on how the uncertainties, particularly those in objectives and capabilities, were resolved. Consequently,

1. Throughout the inquiry the study decided to look for gross *differences* in relative cost and effectiveness of alternative base systems, and specifically for differences of the sort that have a chance of surviving *any* likely resolution of these uncertainties.

2. In analyzing relative differences, it was decided to address the question of which systems had a clear advantage rather than the question of precisely *how much* better one system was than another.

3. The comparisons were to be made with certain gross uncertainties in mind. For example, it was decided (a) to test the systems for a wide range of enemy offensive and defensive capabilities; (b) to take as one test the determination of which systems were least dependent on certain knowledge of the level of enemy capability[2]; (c) to test the systems for criteria other than the one used for the evaluations; (d) to test the systems for their performances under a variety of circumstances involving the loss of bases due to political reasons.

3.4. THE ALTERNATIVES

The point of departure for the analysis was the base-operation system programmed at the time of the study for 1956. In this system, all the medium bombers, which made up the major fraction of the force, and some heavy bombers were based in the United States in time of peace but moved overseas and operated from there in time of war. Other heavy bombers remained based in the United States after war started and used overseas areas for staging only.

The other systems compared fell into four broad groups (see Fig. 3. 1):

1. bombers based on advanced overseas operating bases in wartime,

2. bombers based on intermediate overseas operating bases in wartime,

---

[2] This is different from the preceding point, which refers to tests in which U.S. losses on the ground and in the air range from high to low figures because of different assumptions about enemy capability, but it is assumed that these capabilities are correctly anticipated. This second variety of test investigates the consequences for different strategic systems of having assumed one level of loss when in fact another is experienced.

3. U.S.-based bombers operating intercontinentally with the aid of air-refueling, and

4. U.S.-based bombers operating intercontinentally with the help of ground-refueling at overseas staging areas.

Several factors should be observed. First, all the 1956–1961 systems analyzed, not just the exclusively air-refueled intercontinental case, involved tankers as a regular part of their operation, as well as in contingencies. (In most cases, the tankers were based in the same location as the bombers, but other variants were studied.) Second, all the systems, not just the intercontinental ones, involved Zone of the Interior (zi) bases in time of peace. Third, all these systems were mixtures involving many elements.

The system using advanced overseas operating bases resembled the method formerly planned for the heavies (and later, in 1954, programmed for a larger part of the strategic force). The formerly programmed system, then, involved elements of most of these types: tankers, staging areas, and operating bases both in the United States and overseas. Increasing Russian capability compelled examination of the methods and elements used jointly in the former program in order to detect the vulnerable components and to extend

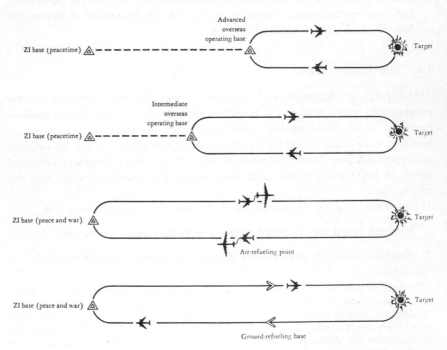

Fig. 3.1   Types of base systems

the most effective. The various systems were therefore evaluated in the context of a two-sided atomic war in which the enemy attacks SAC while it is performing its mission.

3.5. THE CRITICAL FACTORS

Gross analysis indicated that the four critical distances (see Fig. 3. 2) related to the base selection problem were from the proposed bases to (1) the targets, (2) the favorable entry points into enemy defenses, (3) the source of base supply, and (4) the points from which the enemy could attack these bases.

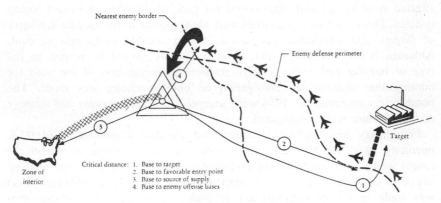

Fig. 3.2   Critical base relationships

The analysis thus was concerned with the joint effects of these respective factors on the costs of extending bomber radius; on how the enemy might deploy his defenses, and the numbers of our bombers lost to these defenses; on logistics costs; and on base vulnerability and our probable loss of bombers on the ground. The systems costs which are functions of these critical distances were called *location* costs to distinguish them from the *locality* costs inherent in a specific site, which are not functions of the critical distances, but which are traceable to local phenomena such as climate. Under this latter head may be considered variations in (1) the operations cost traceable to weather; (2) construction costs depending on climate, terrain, existence of a local construction industry and the availability of local construction materials, and the presence of existing base facilities; (3) supply costs affected by local terminal facilities for transportation and by the possibility of offshore procurement and local sources; and (4) defense costs affected by terrain and existing defenses such as the U.S. and British air defense systems.

3.6. The plan of the analysis

Although *locality cost differences* might have been substantial (the study made a thorough investigation of the added costs of basing aircraft in the Arctic), they were not amenable to presentation in functional form. In addition, the four critical base *location factors* presented a dilemma. Considerations of politics (domestic as well as international), logistics, and base vulnerability suggested pulling our bases back to extreme distances from the Soviet Union. The high cost of range extension and the contributions that a flexible flight path could make to bomber survival argued for basing close to the targets. For these reasons, the study began by attempting to analyze quantitatively the extent to which variations in the critical location distances affected systems cost and effectiveness for each of the four alternative basing systems. The results of this analysis were then applied to the specific geometry of targets and alternative base areas, taking locality costs into account. Although it was recognized that base availability should be related to the type of bomber performing a given mission, in recognition of the need for limiting the analysis no investigation of bomber choice was made. The bombers programmed for 1956 were accepted; the base systems and strategy of employment were investigated.

Preliminary investigations indicated that the last alternative listed (U.S. operating bases for the strike force with overseas refueling to extend the range) would turn out to be the preferred system. Consequently, the analysis began to take on an almost a fortiori approach. That is, a deliberate effort was made in the comparisons *not* to make assumptions or estimates that would "help" this particular system.

3.7. The distance from base to target:
the cost of increasing flight radius

Distances from farthest forward overseas bases to Russian targets ranged from 300 to 1500 n mi. From the major overseas bases programmed, the targets were anywhere from 800 to 2600 n mi away. From the zi, if routes calculated to hold down our losses to enemy defenses were followed, distances to targets were from 3300 to well over 6000 n mi.

The study first investigated by a series of generalized bomber studies how the cost to buy and operate the bombing force depended on the bomb carrier, on the radius of operation, and on the method of radius extension chosen.

The cost to buy and operate bombers big enough to reach targets *without refueling* was found to increase at an accelerated rate with distances from base to target. The exact rate of increase, in any given state of the art of aircraft design, depends on such factors as powerplant type, payload, cruise and over-target speed, altitude, etc. It is greater for turbojets than for turboprops; and greater at higher speeds and extreme (low or high) altitudes. To have built an intercontinental radius capability into a bomber of the B-47 type would have made it enormous in size, costly, and vulnerable. In fact, the heavy bombers roughly contemporary with the B-47, for example, displayed larger differences in cost than in radius capability and could not reach the whole of a Russian target system at intercontinental radius. In Fig. 3. 3, which illustrates this point, the system cost and radius of bomber types approximately similar to the B-47 in performance and design date are represented by points in the shaded region.

The costs, shown in Fig. 3. 3, of purchasing and operating bombers in peacetime are preparedness costs that do not take attrition into account. If we take into account the losses of bombers to enemy area and local defenses, the combat radius for which the bomber was designed also has a direct effect. As the design combat radius of a single-stage bomber is increased, its weight (and plan-projected area) also increases. As a consequence, its expected combat losses at a fixed speed and altitude and to a wide range of enemy defense weapons also increase[3]. This growth in vulnerability compounds the cost increases resulting directly from increases in weight and radius.

An examination of the next generation of chemical bombing systems showed that the strong influence of combat radius on system cost was not merely temporary. Supersonic and low-altitude capabilities might be sought to meet expected improvement in enemy defense. The normal advances in the state of the art would permit improvement in performance characteristics for any given weight and cost; but these, in turn, would tend to be offset by the performance demands imposed by improved defense capabilities open to a rational enemy. The resulting cost-versus-radius curves would therefore show no substantial improvement. (The curve for supersonic bombers in Fig. 3. 3

---

[3] This does not imply that a large bomber must necessarily have larger combat losses than a smaller one, but merely describes the effect of *increasing combat radius* on costs and penetration effectiveness. The study did not compare large and small bombers for a mission with a given radius. It took the speed, altitude, and payload as fixed. This included the payloads of decoys and ECM. A large bomber used at the same range as a smaller one might benefit in penetrating defenses in several ways: (a) by carrying a larger payload of countermeasures; (b) by using the extra fuel volume to alter the mission profile—for example, by flying at extreme low or extreme high altitudes; (c) by using greater penetration speeds; or (d) by using more devious routes through favorable points of entry of enemy defenses. In fact, a good deal of the study was devoted to showing the benefits that might thus be obtained. For example, the B-52A mission profile was examined, assuming pre-strike air-refueling, and was compared with the B-52A using post-strike ground-refueling and higher bomber altitudes. One of the biases deliberately introduced in favor of the air-refueled systems was the assumption, contrary to fact, that they had equal flexibility in choice of mission profile with the ground-refueled systems.

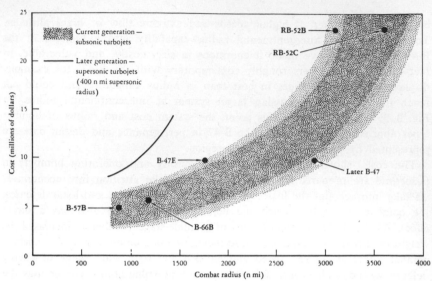

Fig. 3.3   Cost versus combat radius

illustrates this point.) If anything, combat radius would be *more* rather than *less* critical for some time to come.

Examination of nuclear-powered bombers and surface-to-surface missiles indicated that expected developments in these fields were not likely to alter this conclusion for the next decade.

As a result of this investigation, the project concluded that for the period through 1961, and possibly for some time thereafter, no bomber was likely to be capable of operating at full intercontinental radius without any refueling whatsoever. To hit a deep Russian target system we needed either to operate

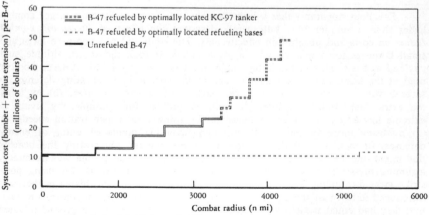

Fig. 3.4   Multistage B-47 systems versus combat radius

from overseas bases or to use the assistance of some form of refueling if we operated from the ZI.

In air-refueled multistage bombing systems, a bomber of fixed unrefueled radius is assisted to the target by tankers. This avoids the need for bigger, more easily intercepted, and more costly bombers. But the effects of radius on *system* weight or cost (including the weight or cost of the tanker as well as that of the bomber) are nonetheless very marked. Costs increase in steps (see Fig. 3. 4) corresponding to points at which additional tankers are required. As combat radius is extended, the increments obtained by the use of additional tankers become smaller and, allowing for insurance against the uncertainties of multiple refueling, the increases in cost for a given increment of radius become steeper. For a tanker-refueled B-47 system, at 3600, 4200, and 5200 n mi, costs are respectively three, five, and ten times the cost at an unrefueled radius of 1750 n mi[4].

One way to keep operating bases (and so, parked bombers—the most vulnerable and valuable system element) away from enemy striking power is to extend bomber radius by a system of refueling bases. The radius extension such a system provides costs much less than a tanker system. Aside from the costs of defense and expected damage, buying, equipping, and supporting a refueling base with modern landing, takeoff, and high-speed fueling facilities add approximately 15 per cent to the three-year cost of buying and operating a wing of B-47 aircraft in the United States.

Figure 3. 4, which shows the increase in bomber costs with extension of radius, includes support costs incurred for the peak force sortied. When the costs of radius extension are very high (for example, in the air-refueled U.S.-based B-47 system), the portion of the total system cost devoted to tanker procurement and operation can be reduced by sending fewer than the maximum number of available bombers on each strike. The smaller sortied force means slower initial rate of destruction of enemy targets. It also means more aircraft losses to area defenses per target destroyed; but the smaller operating force will, if we consider cost alone, save more than this amount in tankers for a system with high tanker requirements.

---

4 These specific figures neglect possible extra costs from bomber or tanker attrition and aborts, which were considered, at the time the study was made, likely to be associated with rendezvous problems in multiple refuelings. If such attrition were to occur, it would increase the preferences shown by the study. In fact, the multiple refuelings considered in the study offer more severe tests of air-refueling than any that have been substantiated in subsequent peacetime history. For example, they include not merely several refuelings but *post-strike* air-refuelings, where rendezvous is indeed a question, and multiple refuelings of jets by propeller-driven tankers with about half their speed, under conditions of wartime near-simultaneous scramble.

Campaign calculations were carried out using an expected-value model[5] to compare air- versus ground-refueling. The criterion used for comparison was the minimum incremental cost to bring the force up to a given capability and maintain that capability for a certain period. The capability, the period, and the type of campaign were varied.

The cost of a summer campaign[6] to destroy 80 per cent of a Russian industrial-target complex using an air-refueled system turned out to be more than three times that for a ground-refueled system (see Fig. 3. 5). These costs took into account the detailed geography of bases, identifiable air-refueling points, specific staging areas, points of entry into enemy defense, and paths to targets. For these calculations Russian area defenses were assumed to be distributed evenly over the area of their ground control intercept (GCI) network coverage, and strike paths were relatively direct to minimize the number of tankers per bomber in the striking force. (As shown later, both their defense and our offense tactics can be improved decidedly by assuming that adaptions to match our base system are made.) The bombing systems compared used identical airplanes and operating bases in the United States, but aircraft radii were extended in one case by air-refueling and in the other case by ground-refueling. The ground-refueled system used all available bombers on each strike. The air-refueled system followed the plan of with-holding bombers, which was less expensive but which also imposed some inflexibility as to rate and size of strike and proportion of the target system attacked. No allowance was made for possible bomber attrition connected with multiple refuelings. The calculations also showed that

1. The radius-extension costs for the air-refueled system were about six times those of the ground-refueled system.

2. To limit radius-extension costs even to this high level, the air-refueled system involved a considerable sacrifice in extra bombers lost (about 30 per cent of the value of bombers in the ground-refueled force).

Differences of such large magnitudes occurred in spite of the fact that

---

5   In many ways similar to the model of Appendix B.

6   The task of destroying Russian strategic targets in a summer operation was found to be much more difficult and several times more costly, in dollars and in crew losses, than in winter. A large proportion of the target systems is then in daylight adequate for the operation of day fighters. Moreover, the time of outbreak may very well be decided by the enemy, and he has a comparative advantage in choosing the summer. Strategic targets in the United States are in much more southerly latitudes, making Russian night attacks feasible in summer as well as in winter. Because the decision to attack is very likely to be the enemy's, the most unfavorable season for the campaign from our standpoint may also be the most probable. Since the force must be ready at all times, it was important to base the principal cost calculations on the worst (from the standpoint of the enemy the best) contingency. Winter campaigns were also calculated.

much of the bombing system (the bomber type and the U.S. primary bases) was fixed in the comparison.

Ten wings of penetration fighters were programmed for 1956. Whether they were used as bombers, as escort fighters, or as decoys, their strategic use appeared practicable only from an advanced primary-base system or from a more distant primary-base system with overseas ground-refueling facilities. The preference for ground-refueling over air-refueling would be greatly increased by taking these components of the programmed force into account.

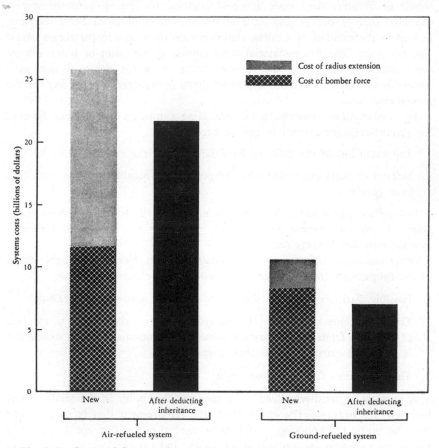

Fig. 3.5   Costs of intercontinental air- and ground-refueled B-47 campaigns

Sole consideration of the effects of increasing the flight radius to enemy targets indicated the desirability of operating from bases which were as close as possible to these targets. A decision also had to take into account the effects of distance from logistic support in the United States and of nearness to the source of enemy striking power. However, although these effects dictated operation at great distances from enemy targets, the analysis so far had suggested that it was especially expensive to store fuel far from targets and to air-transport it for transfer to the bomber.

Aside from the contrast in campaign costs, the systems exhibited differences in crew losses, fissile-material requirements, rate of destruction, and number of strikes. The air-refueled system involved a slower rate of destruction and a larger number of strikes. For this reason cumulative round-trip attrition would be greater. And since inbound attrition for the air-refueled system exceeded that of the ground-refueled system, the number of bomb carriers, as well as the number of escorts, shot down on their way to the target would also be larger. The fissile-material requirements at the point of bomb release were identical. Therefore, the fissile-material usage for the campaign as a whole, including the fissile material shot down by fighters, was greater for the air-refueled case.

The assumptions underlying the preceding campaign calculations favored the ground-refueled system in two respects:

1. The exclusion of the costs of base damage and the costs of base defense.

2. Neglect of costs associated with the political vulnerability of the refueling-base system.

In later campaign analyses, every attempt was made to remove these biases since, at this stage, there were definite indications that the ground-refueled systems were to be preferred.

Other assumptions favored the air-refueled system. For example, the effects of the following were not taken into account in computing the costs:

1. Possible attrition or aborts due to the need for a fueling-rendezvous.

2. The inflexibility of the air-refueled system's even-strike policy in the face of variance from mean attrition values or unanticipated large differences in the mean attrition values themselves.

3. The necessities for formation flight.

A number of sensitivity tests were made at this point in the study. These included, for example, the effect of (1) the requirement that repeated target visits be made; (2) imposing a high crew survival-probability constraint; (3) a ten-to-one variation in anticipated air losses; and (4) changes in the ratio of area-to-local-defense losses.

In substance, the analysis of the base-to-target factor indicated that, insofar as the effects of increasing target radius were concerned, radius-extension costs increased very sharply if all ground-base functions were removed to extreme distances from targets; and, by comparison, they increased quite moderately if only the functions associated with the storage and transfer of fuel were removed. It was also shown that, at moderate combat radii (considerably less than intercontinental combat radii), the costs of air-refueling were moderate and did not increase too sharply with small increases in distance.

These effects were reflected in campaign costs. Campaigns were examined for very wide ranges of parameters, and the results were shown to be insensitive to such variations. However, so far the study had not analyzed the costs of defending the overseas refueling function. And it had not considered the logistics costs and defense requirements of leaving all operating-base functions forward, or in some intermediate overseas position. Before considering these matters, it dealt with the question of the relation of the base systems to the choice of alternative paths through enemy defenses.

3.8. THE DISTANCE FROM BASE TO ENTRY POINTS: THE COST OF PENETRATING THE DEFENSE

The study investigated the effect of base location on the angle of approach to targets, the distance of penetration through enemy defenses, and the hours of daylight and darkness over these penetration paths. Base-location considerations were shown to affect our choice of the route to the target and the enemy's choice of defense deployment.

Preliminary investigation indicated that the distance traveled over enemy defenses, and thus the number of bombers lost to enemy fighters, would be reduced by doglegging, that is, by varying the flight path from the great circle route to avoid concentrations of the enemy defense (see Fig. 3. 6).

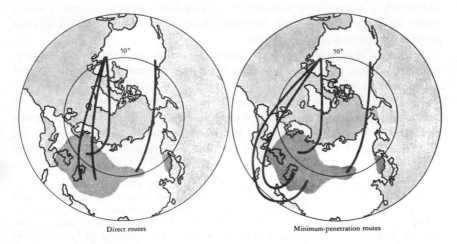

Direct routes   Minimum-penetration routes

Fig. 3.6 Routes for intercontinental air-refueled strikes

Three kinds of penetration routes were distinguished.

1. Relatively direct routes to minimize the number of tankers necessary for each bomber in a strike.

2. Routes to minimize penetration distances and thus reduce attrition inflicted by area defenses (fighters).

3. Routes to take greater advantage of darkness[7] to reduce losses to fighters.

Preliminary investigations showed that, while reduction in losses due to fighters was significantly reduced by penetration in darkness, routes chosen primarily by that criterion would not be optimal.

The study, therefore, compared systems using routes that minimized distance flown through enemy defenses with systems using direct paths that minimized tankers per bomber sortied. In both cases, strong efforts were made to utilize routes that penetrated in darkness. For air-refueled U.S.-based B-47's in a multistrike summer campaign to kill 80 per cent of the Russian industrial-target system selected, this comparison revealed a significant preference for minimum-penetration routes. The system flying minimum-penetration paths lost fewer bombers to enemy fighter defenses, therefore reducing the size of the force needed to ensure an acceptable crew-survival probability. Finally, although the system had more tankers per bomber, it had fewer tankers in total, reducing even the radius-extension costs for the campaign.

Base systems that permitted entry from the south could take advantage of the cover of darkness with little or no extra extension of radius. Since the ground-refueled U.S.-based system had many staging areas to the south, its short-route system was largely protected by darkness and was thus one that nearly minimized attrition. Bombers flying direct routes in summer would suffer no more attrition than bombers flying minimum-penetration doglegs without the advantage of darkness.

The study then turned to performing operations analysis for the enemy, a step necessary in any analysis that takes into account possible countering actions on the part of the enemy.

Analysis indicated that the enemy, in turn, might improve his defense by matching our offense capability. Against systems flying the shortest routes from the U.S. operating bases, he might concentrate fighter defenses in the north (see Fig. 3.7). Systems using peripheral operating or ground-refueling

---

[7] At the time of the study, darkness had a decided effect, since (1) even by 1956 the U.S.S.R. was expected to have a much larger number of day than night fighters; (2) only a few day fighters would be usable at night—for example, by employing the buddy system of day fighters led by night fighters; and (3) the individual effectiveness of Russian night interceptors was expected to be much less than that of their interceptors in daylight.

bases would compel a more even dispersal of enemy defenses, as shown in Fig. 3.8.

Campaign results as presented in Fig. 3.9 indicated that if the enemy could concentrate day fighters in the north, taking account of the greater density

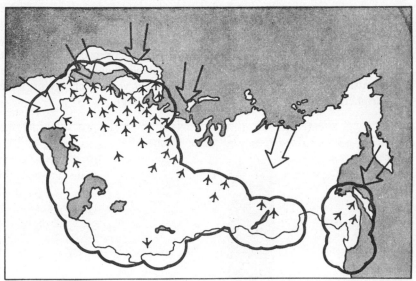

Fig. 3.7   Russian fighter deployment against direct intercontinental air strikes

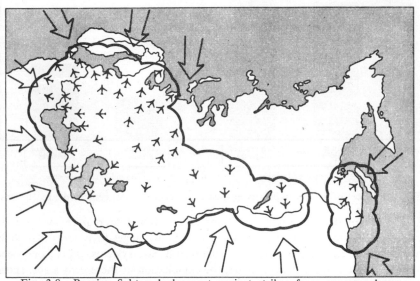

Fig. 3.8   Russian fighter deployment against strikes from overseas bases

of targets in the west, he could do better than when he distributed fighter defenses uniformly.

The Russian area defenses so reoriented were found to exact a higher attrition against all bombing systems, but in particular against "one-sided" base systems: the exclusively air-refueled intercontinental systems or a Western Hemisphere system. Russian defenses further improved by specific tailoring to meet each of our base systems could do still better, especially against a one-sided system with relatively concentrated avenues of approach to the targets. Limitation in the number of night fighters available would make it difficult for the Russians to improve their fighter deployment very much against attack from peripheral overseas bases (operating or refueling).

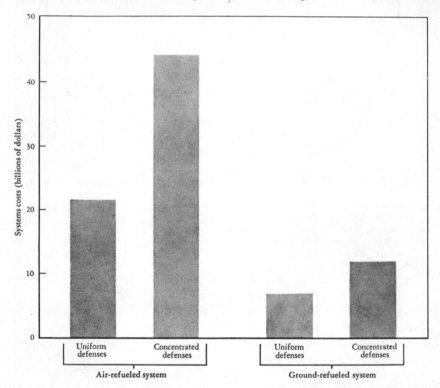

Fig. 3.9   Cost of B-47 campaigns against a uniform and concentrated area defense

The use of optimal routes and profiles was found to require increases in radius-extension capabilities, giving additional advantages to systems that could achieve them cheaply. Furthermore, peripheral base systems, unlike one-sided systems, permitted, in the short run, the exploitation of the enemy's soft spots; in the long run, they forced a dilution of his defenses.

The implications of the analysis thus far may be stated as follows. First, it was important to develop a rounded capability for many-sided attack against the enemy target system. By doing this we would force him to spread his defenses. This did not mean that on any one strike we actually needed to use a multiplicity of penetration paths starting from many sides. Having forced the dilution of his defense, we could concentrate on some portion of the target system and some few penetration paths to get the benefit of saturation. But the development of a rounded capability was a condition for concentration in its use. Second, the inferiority of the exclusively air-refueled intercontinental system, which was evidenced by the cost and effectiveness versus radius studies, was reinforced by an examination of the inflexibility this system imposed on the offense. The exclusively air-refueled system was less free than a peripheral overseas system in its choice of route, speed, and altitude of penetration. It permitted corresponding concentration on the part of the defense. On the other hand, the analysis, up to this point, while it had dissected the high costs of operating without an overseas base system, had not yet dealt explicitly with the logistics costs of operating with an overseas system. And, most important, it had not taken explicit account of the costs of defense and expected damage associated with the vulnerability of overseas bases.

3.9. THE DISTANCE FROM BASE TO ZI:
THE COST OF OPERATIONS OUTSIDE THE UNITED STATES

A detailed investigation of all the factors involved indicated that the peacetime cost of buying and maintaining a wing of bombers in the United States must be increased by over 50 per cent to cover the additional cost of operation from primary bases overseas. This extra cost was incurred for additional bases, theater support, and airlift. However, the differences among overseas base systems were not found to increase substantially with supply distances in peacetime. Transportation, travel, and stock-level costs were only moderately affected by increasing distance, even when these distances varied up to 10 000 surface miles. (*Locality* considerations, on the other hand, as distinct from location considerations, did entail substantial extra costs for peacetime resupply in the Arctic.) Except for the case of a system using refueling bases, the extra costs involved in wartime resupply and pipeline attrition were not investigated in detail. For a refueling base, the prestocking of fuel at moderate cost was shown to free the base from the problem of losses in surface transport during the early months of a war. To free an operating base overseas from such problems, a considerable quantity of air transport would have to be purchased.

While, in any case, there are extra costs for operating facilities, airlift, stocks of materiel, etc., involved in adding an overseas component to a bombing system, it was shown to be much cheaper to add refueling facilities than operating facilities, even if vulnerability considerations were neglected.

The analysis indicated that a refueling-base system overseas is distinctly cheaper than an overseas operating system as far as facilities, airlift, and stocks are concerned. The refueling base involved functions other than fuel pickup; it involved maintenance, for example. However, the purpose of maintenance in a refueling-base system was only to assist as many planes on to target as it could within a safe period of occupancy and to get the rest home. The costs of extra aborts involved in such a policy, as well as the costs of extra personnel to provide staging support, were included in the campaign analysis, as were the costs of prestocking and protecting sufficient fuel for an entire campaign.

A choice between an overseas operating base system and an intercontinental ground-refueling system was shown to have distinct consequences for the location of prestocked material. Therefore, the analysis indicated that this choice must be made long in advance of the start of any campaign.

The importance of adding bases, particularly to the south of Russia, was sustained by base-loading analyses for both the operating- and refueling-base systems.

The comparative cheapness of the refueling-base system was evidenced by campaign analyses. This system had a significant margin of advantage over overseas operating base systems, even neglecting vulnerability considerations. However, the chief motive for the use of the refueling system was the reduction of vulnerability in a period of growing Russian capabilities.

3.10.   THE DISTANCE FROM BASE TO ENEMY BORDER:
          THE COST OF BASE VULNERABILITY

Thus far the study had considered the question of bomber-base operations in the context of a largely one-sided war in which the enemy was limited to defense. Aside from the constraints imposed by defenses the enemy might employ, the study had had the option of choosing base combinations subject chiefly to aerodynamic, political, and logistics constraints. No quantitative estimate of the costs of mounting strikes in the face of enemy attack had been made. This was a critical matter, since the destruction of our strike force was clearly a matter of high priority, and it was very likely that the enemy would have the opportunity for the first attack. The damage suffered by our force on the ground, and the types and cost of base defense varied widely with differing base systems. With some defenses, only a small percentage of our bombers would survive to take part in our attacks.

The analysis next examined defenses that would be economic for alternative base-aircraft systems and the damage they might be expected to suffer in spite of these defenses. Here the "survival value" of these systems was measured in terms of the systems cost per bomber available for use after enemy attacks. The major alternative base systems were examined together with overseas refueling systems designed to have extremely low vulnerability to enemy attack.

It was shown that the vulnerability of a strategic base system and measures for its defense could be separated for the purpose of the analysis into the following five categories, which correspond approximately to the successive time phases of an attack:

1. The stockpile of aircraft and weapons possessed by the enemy, his commitments to attack SAC, and methods of employment of the force in relation to the size and location of the target system presented by SAC.

2. Expected survival of attacking bombers to the bomb-release line.

3. The value of the targets presented, as determined by patterns of base occupancy affecting the exposure of aircraft and other systems elements at the time of attack.

4. Physical vulnerability of systems elements.

5. The recuperability of the force after attack, and the effect of damage to systems elements on the accomplishment of strategic bombing missions.

Consideration of the first two critical factors (target radius and penetration routes) stressed the advantages of being close to the target and close to favorable points to enter enemy defenses. Unfortunately, when we are close, not only is our power to attack the enemy very great, but so also is his power to attack us. (The rings in Fig. 3.10 indicate the steps in which the enemy's striking power diminishes with distance from his border.) The most obvious disadvantage of an overseas base system is its increased vulnerability.

U.S. Operating Bases

The most vital and easily damaged elements of a strategic force based in the U.S. ZI were found not to be very vulnerable *if* the aircraft, personnel, and essential materiel evacuation plan of SAC were carried out. *However, a large number of U.S. bases were too close to the perimeter of our projected 1956 radar net to have even marginally adequate warning against air attack.*

Moreover, the analysis showed that, in the event of Russian use of a short-range submarine-launched A-bomb carrier, no future extension of the radar network was likely to provide adequate warning for coastal bases. Computations showed that a single, high-altitude mass Russian strike against U.S. targets,

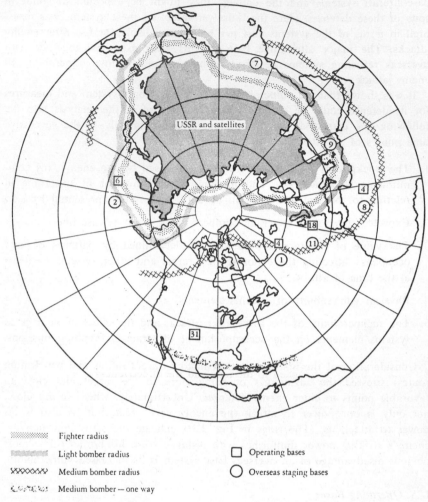

Fighter radius

Light bomber radius

✕✕✕✕✕✕✕ Medium bomber radius

Medium bomber — one way

☐ Operating bases

◯ Overseas staging bases

Fig. 3.10 Base locations relative to U.S.S.R. striking power

including SAC, with 1956 defenses could result in attrition of 75 to 85 per cent of the medium-bomber force. With adequate warning this could be reduced to an attrition level of less than 20 per cent. These estimates were based on a Russian commitment of 120 bombs to the destruction of SAC. Considerably smaller bomb commitments by the Russians could also result in high levels of destruction in the absence of adequate warning. In addition to bomb commitment, the analysis also considered varying estimates of Russian bomber stockpiles, expected operational aborts, and attrition inflicted by U.S.

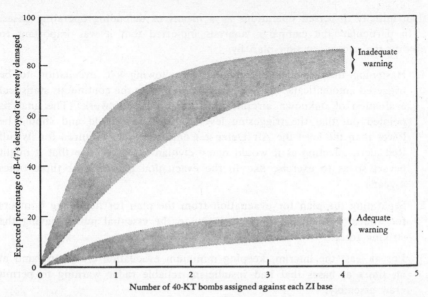

Fig. 3.11 Attrition on programmed ZI strategic bases versus enemy bomb allocation

defenses. Figure 3.11 illustrates expected ground attrition of strategic aircraft on U.S. bases in 1956 for a range of A-bombs allocated by the Soviets to the task of neutralizing this force, and for a range of probabilities of their delivering the bombs allocated. The delivery probability depends on the number of bombers assigned to the task and the effectiveness of our fighters—which, in turn, depends on the likelihood of Russian countermeasures. The lower limit of the shaded areas in Fig. 3.11 (and also in Fig. 3.12, p. 47) represents probable values of enemy bomber assignment and effectiveness of our fighters. The upper limit indicates the result of assuming a higher enemy offense capability and lower effectiveness of our own defenses.

An analysis of the reduction in U.S. bomber losses when adequate warning was received showed the benefits of evacuation. In addition, flyaway kits and operating personnel were protected by the execution of the SAC evacuation plan. Dispersed operation was considered as an alternative or an additional defense to evacuation. However, as a substitute for evacuation it turned out to be unacceptably sensitive to the number of enemy bombs directed against SAC. As a supplement to evacuation, dispersed operation tended to cost more than it saved in unattrited bombers (see Fig. 3.13, p. 48).

Wherever possible, measures (for example, addition of radar, reduction of time required for evacuation, and transfer of wings from the periphery to the interior) to provide adequate warning and to facilitate evacuation of critical elements of the striking force appeared to be more effective and less costly than initially dispersed operations as a means of defending operating bases.

In particular, the campaign analysis indicated that it was important to modify the SAC evacuation plan by

1. Hastening the decision to evacuate by allowing SAC evacuation to be triggered automatically by a warning derived from the continuous statistical evaluation of unknown aircraft within our radar network. (The analysis pointed out that the triggering level to flush SAC could and should be lower than the level the Air Defense Command (ADC) required for its full Red alert, affecting as it would many civilian activities; also that it might be set so as to exercise SAC in the evacuation plan two or three times a year.)

2. Separating the plan for evacuation from the plan for deploying bombers for attack, and giving higher priority to the essential job of saving the striking force.

3. For at least the interim, keeping minimum evacuation crews on hand at all times at bases that had insufficient reliable radar warning to permit crew assembly.

4. Providing egress taxiways, wherever possible, to permit the taxiing or towing of nonflyable aircraft off base.

Besides evacuation, other critical defense measures for bases in the ZI, described below, were discussed. (With these modifications, the probability of evacuation was high enough to make the extra insurance of operating bombers in many units of less than wing size excessively costly. However, forms of dispersal other than dispersed operation were considered quite important— for example, preparation of alternative U.S. sites for emergency use and local dispersal.)

Overseas Operating Bases

Evacuation did not appear feasible for most overseas bases (advanced or intermediate) because of the very short warning times and a high enemy capability for frequent air attacks and feints. (The inadequacy of warning time was emphasized by the threat of submarine-launched attacks.) Five-sixths of these projected overseas bases were within 100 mi of the sea. The vulnerability of units deployed to such overseas bases would be high.

Analysis of the consequences of a Russian A-bomb air attack on the whole of the projected 1956 overseas primary-based system with the projected defenses clearly showed that only small numbers of A-bombs were needed to eliminate the majority of the force surviving attack in the United States (see Fig. 3.12). (Although expected destruction of aircraft is used as a measure of vulnerability in Fig. 3.12, the combat effectiveness of the force would be further reduced by loss of personnel, bombs, base facilities, fuel, supplies, etc.) The extensive destruction indicated by rather moderate investments of Russian bombs resulted from (1) the concentration of our strategic forces on relatively few bases (a reasonable allocation of expected enemy forces provided very large attacking cells per base); (2) inadequate radar coverage and defense weapons effectiveness, especially at low altitudes (bomb carriers in attacking cells had a very high probability of reaching the bomb-release line); and (3) the high physical vulnerability of system components likely to be on the ground on overseas bases at the time of attack (the probability of destruction, given bomb release, was very high).

After the outbreak of a war, the initial vulnerability of wings deployed overseas was found to be critically dependent on the period of exposure before the mounting of the first U.S. strike. Measures could be taken to reduce the period of exposure before our first strike, but after that our B-47's scheduled to operate from overseas bases would be exposed to repeated attacks by enemy aircraft carrying high-explosive and atomic bombs. Analysis indicated that units on rotation overseas at the outbreak of hostilities must expect to suffer great damage immediately.

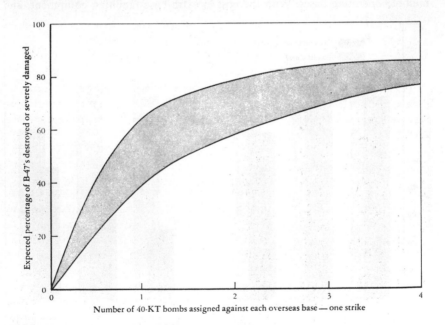

Fig. 3.12   Attrition on programmed overseas operating bases versus enemy bomb allocation (no aircraft evacuation)

The analysis indicated that the vulnerability of the formerly projected overseas operating base system to even a quite low level of enemy attack could be reduced. By allocating more of our strategic budget to the purchase of active and passive defense, rather than bombers, we could increase the total number of our bombers likely to survive all but fairly high levels of enemy bombing attack.

In the final comparison an improved overseas operating base system was considered. The three classes of passive defense measures described below were treated. They involved multiplication of bases, relocation of bases, and changes within bases (separation and toughening facilities). The first two involved large-scale changes in the base system as a whole. Of these, it was indicated that one, base relocation, might affect the warning available and the probable size of the enemy attacking force. The second would increase the number of enemy bombs required; the third—local changes—would force an increase in the size if not the number of bombs.

Passive Defense: Multiplying Operating Bases

Since evacuation is generally not feasible overseas, multiple separated bases had to be considered. Protecting the *bombers* by this means would require multiple *operating* bases. With the cost in extra base facilities, equipment, and

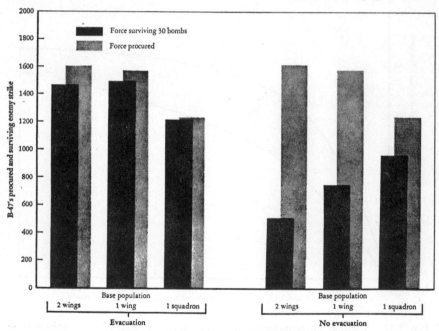

Fig. 3.13   Evacuation and dispersal

personnel held contant, the reduction in aircraft ground attrition from a single enemy strike for three degrees of operating-base dispersal is shown in Fig. 3.13. Over a considerable range of possible Russian bomb commitments against our strategic force in 1956, there would be a net gain in the number of aircraft surviving after combat, even if the extra cost of separated bases resulted in fewer aircraft being procured. However, the project could have no reliable knowledge of what Russian capabilities would be in 1956. It was noted that if the number of bombs available and allocated to this task was higher than estimated, dispersed operation would buy very little defense (see Fig. 3.14). Since the Russian capability was expected to increase rapidly as time went by, we could not rely on this method of defense.

Passive Defense: Relocation of Operating Bases

Relocation had been advocated as a measure which might counteract some threats against ZI operating bases. If applied to overseas bases, this measure would yield the intermediate overseas operating base systems previously mentioned. It would, indeed, reduce the number of sorties that the enemy

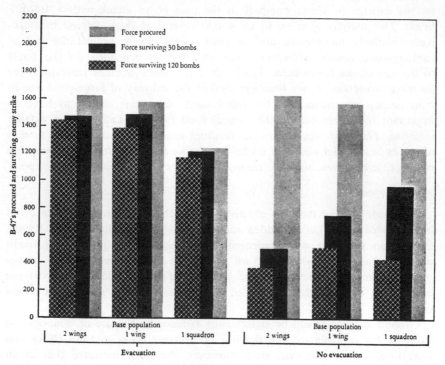

Fig. 3.14 Evacuation and dispersal: sensitivity

could mount with a fixed force. This would be a great asset against a high-explosive attack, but of little value against atomic attack. Repeated atomic sorties are not required to destroy soft targets such as bombers caught on the ground. Since intermediate base systems were not within the deep fighter-backed U.S. radar network, evacuation would be denied them as a defense. Therefore, they would be little less, or no less, vulnerable to atomic attack than advanced overseas operating base systems.

Passive Defense: Changes within a Base

No existing strategic base was specifically designed to reduce damage from atomic attack. An analysis showed that a medium-sized (40 KT) bomb dropped with a 4000-ft CEP could be expected to result in destruction and serious damage ranging from 80 per cent to almost all the aircraft, structures, supplies, and personnel exposed on ZI bases and most overseas bases. Damage to many base elements could be reduced by local dispersal and blast-protective shelters. Parking aircraft on the perimeter of our large French Moroccan bases rather than using *area* dispersal (now employed overseas for protection against high-explosive attack) would reduce expected aircraft destruction and serious damage by about one-half in the case of an attack with a 100-KT bomb. The analysis went on to show that several of these defense measures were relatively inexpensive and at least would ensure against the use of medium-sized bombs. However, their effectiveness depended on the limits to the size of the bomb used. The study found such methods inadequate for assuring protection of our bombers against the delivery of large-yield bombs with normal accuracies. On the other hand, they were shown to have an important role in protecting the critical fixed facilities and the base defense weapons. *The hardening of critical facilities against the possibility of attacks aimed at base denial would be useful, according to the results of the campaign analyses, even given sizeable enemy stockpiles of thermonuclear weapons.*

Active Defense

The study showed that the effectiveness of scheduled active defenses could be improved somewhat by added radar coverage, especially at low altitude. Over-ocean coverage was inadequate and most of the projected forward operating bases were within 100 mi of the sea, making area defenses particularly ineffective. Achieving a high level of defense by adding more defense weapons of the type then scheduled would cost about as much as it would save.

Ground attrition would be significantly reduced by the use of weapons not likely to be available for the defense of overseas bases in 1956 (Nike and Loki local-defense weapons, etc.). However, the study indicated that in all cases the effectiveness of the active defense of overseas bases was critically dependent on the performance and number of carriers, tactics, and counter-measures employed by the enemy. In view of the uncertainties about the effectiveness of various active defense measures, it appeared very risky to defend bases primarily by active means. This was particularly true of bases that could be reached by high-performance jet aircraft (IL-28, EF-150), which the Russians at the time were expected to have in large numbers.

Recuperation Plans

Another substudy dealt with recuperation. Recuperation plans were shown to drastically reduce the impact of physical damage on base operational effectiveness. In the case of an A-bomb attack on a base, a large number of the aircraft might require replacement of those parts likely to be damaged by blast (for example, control surfaces, bomb-bay doors, external plastic surfaces). As these parts normally did not require replacement in quantity, they were not stocked in quantity at bases. However, such stocks would not be expensive, and failure to stock them could mean weeks and possibly months of inactivity.

Aside from decontamination, the essential measures indicated to meet the radioactive fallout problem on home bases included (1) evacuation to emergency alternate bases and delay in using the contaminated bases (because of the rapid decay, such delay times could be short—provided the period of exposure was short), and (2) shortening the period of occupancy and exposure by staging through the contaminated home bases from the emergency alternates.

Other measures examined and found useful included duplication of vital base facilities, the training of damage-repair teams, and provision for emergency construction to replace facilities destroyed.

Combinations of active and passive defenses were found to be better than any single defense measure for the defense of an overseas operating base system. Manning and real-estate constraints acted to restrict the range of choice available. A comparison of the formerly programmed system with an overseas operating base system modified to reduce vulnerability showed an increase in the number of bombers available for combat when extra funds (out of a fixed budget) were spent for additional active and passive defense measures, including local dispersal and blast protection, augmented interceptor and local defenses, and ground and airborne early warning (AEW) radar coverage (see Fig. 3.15). Although the cost per bomber procured was found to increase by 30 per cent, the cost per bomber *surviving for combat* (along with supporting elements) decreased by 35 per cent. This combination of defense measures was not regarded as optimal, and there were wide variations in preferred measures for different overseas-base areas.

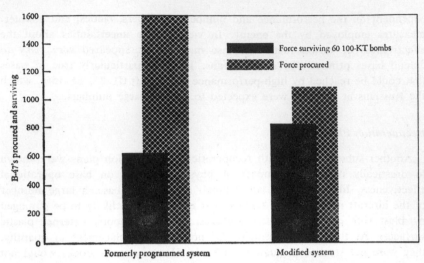

Fig. 3.15 Effect of augmented overseas-base defenses: overseas primary systems; fixed budget

Preferred Defense Measures

It appeared that the vulnerability of SAC before deployment to overseas primary bases was moderate for units stationed on bases likely to receive adequate warning of attacks, and that while many units were not scheduled to have such warning, it might be provided by the means suggested. The cost of this measure was small in comparison with the damage that it would avoid.

The campaign analyses indicated that by 1956 the vulnerability of overseas operating bases was likely to be unacceptably high. It was possible to reduce this vulnerability by applying the measures described above, but the success of such defense measures depended critically on enemy capabilities. It was also possible to reduce vulnerability by an essentially different strategic base system: one using operating bases in the United States in conjunction with overseas refueling bases. Like evacuation measures in the United States, this ground-refueling system overseas would make it improbable that our bombers would be caught on the ground. The probability of success of such measures, which reduced the chances of our being on base when enemy bombers reached the bomb-release line, was found to be comparatively unaffected by a wide range of possible increments in enemy capabilities.

Defense of Overseas Refueling Bases

The study next examined a strategic system with refueling bases as the sole overseas element. The refueling system was assumed to include all bases then scheduled for use as either refueling or operating bases.

Detailed study of overseas refueling bases showed that defense might be achieved economically by (1) having many more bases than were demanded by traffic requirements; (2) reducing the period of exposure of aircraft on bases (2 to 3 hr for a base near enemy territory; for more remote bases, safe periods were more extended) and employing a base-use pattern that would make it improbable that the enemy would find the bases occupied; (3) dispersal, multiplication, and blast-protection of minimal facilities to reduce physical vulnerability; (4) active defense even when bases were unoccupied (10 wings of interceptors, 35 battalions of Loki weapons), and, when some of the bases were occupied, concentration of fighters (and addition of 10 wings of fighter escorts) at the points of occupancy; and (5) establishing a damage repair and recuperation capability. The multiplicity of these bases, the physical toughness of the few fixed installations, and their considerable active defense would make them unprofitable targets (even assuming quite large Russian stockpiles of A-bombs and long-range bombers) so long as the bases were unoccupied by bombers.

Figure 3.16 (which shows, for one attack strategy, the percentage of the

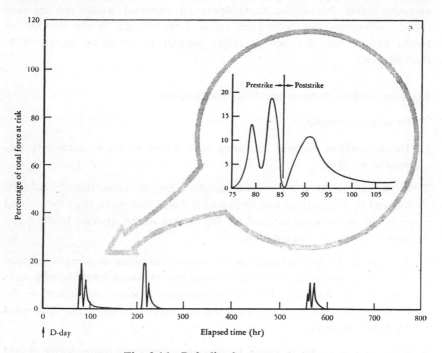

Fig. 3.16   Refueling-base occupancy

total bombing force at risk in the refueling-base system at various times during the first month after D-day) illustrates one of the most important features underlying refueling-base defense. Even if attacked at precisely the hour of maximum concentration, only a quite small percentage of our force would be risked—for some attack strategies, a percentage comparable with the unevacuable part of our force on interior U.S. bases having adequate warning. Moreover, even allowing for extensive intelligence information on the part of the enemy, we could, by using feinting tactics, random strategy, and the like, make his expectation of finding us considerably less than that indicated at the hour of maximum concentration. The feints, supplemented by such devices as B-47 dummies on the refueling bases and by the active defenses assumed, could mean a very substantial waste of enemy bombs and bombers.

A U.S.-based bomber force operating through an overseas refueling-base system so defended would suffer extremely low ground attrition compared with an overseas-based force. The projected 1956 system of operating and refueling bases would require only moderate extension and modification to adapt it to such use. A strong overseas refueling-base system would be tactically, as well as politically, feasible. Moreover, refueling bases (like U.S. operating bases, but unlike those operating overseas) would not increase sharply in vulnerability with even rather large changes in the number of bombs and carriers the Soviets might commit to an attack on the U.S. strategic force.

Summary of Base Defense and Expected Damage

The study concluded:

1. The unmodified overseas operating base system would be extremely vulnerable in 1956.

2. While SAC could not be made invulnerable, its vulnerability could be reduced by a variety of measures which would save more than they would cost. No one measure sufficed for the defense of the strategic force; many were required in combination.

3. The best of these combinations of measures involved as a major component the absence of the critical vulnerable elements when bombs were released over the base. This meant measures enabling evacuation in the United States, and measures reducing and making irregular the time spent on bases overseas.

4. With such measures it would be feasible to preserve the majority of our

strategic bombers from enemy bombing attacks, even assuming very high enemy offensive capabilities and commitment to the task of destroying sac.

5. Defense methods which left our bombers on base at the time of attack depended very much for their success on limitations in the enemy capability. This was true of the augmented defenses examined for overseas primary bases. Multiplication of operating bases could be matched by a proportional multiplication in the enemy bomb stockpile. Dispersal within a base could be matched by the increasing yield of enemy bombs and active defenses by enemy countermeasures and by the increased apparent size of enemy attacks.

6. In comparing the destructive power of the four broadly different alternative systems for basing the B-47, it was important to include both the costs of appropriate base-defense measures and also the specific effects of enemy bomb damage on each system.

Some measures that were necessary to reduce vulnerability were common to all the systems being compared. These were the measures for hardening critical facilities both in the zi and overseas, and (since all the systems involved a zi component) for protecting aircraft on the ground in the zi by itensifying the evacuation program. These measures were shown to be effective and essential. But the most critical problem was the protection of bombers overseas. The analysis made it clear that edging back, as in an intermediate base system, did not significantly reduce vulnerability to an atomic attack. From the standpoint of vulnerability, it was important to be as far back as possible. However, leaving the refueling function forward involved much smaller risks of damage than advanced operation.

The study then concluded:

> It is clear that consideration of vulnerability alone dictates operations from bases as far from the sources of enemy striking power as possible. However, vulnerability does not lessen continuously with increasing distance from enemy borders. Edging away does not help. It is only when bases of operation have been moved well within the radar network of the zi that a significant and reliable reduction in vulnerability occurs. But if any component of a bombing system is to be left forward, it has been shown that a system which leaves the refueling function forward is least vulnerable.

> Various defense measures have been tested for each of the base systems considered. Of those surviving the test of savings versus cost, some are common to all systems considered. These are the measures for hardening critical facilities, both in the zi and overseas, and for protecting aircraft on the ground in the zi. Since all systems have a zi component, at least before D-day, all have the requirement for this defense. The principal measure for the defense of aircraft in the zi was found to be evacuation.

> However, the most critical problem (except for the intercontinental air-refueled

system) is the protection of aircraft overseas. The preferred method of achieving this is the adoption of brief and irregular periods of occupancy on overseas bases. This is the method of the ground-refueled system[8].

3.11. THE JOINT EFFECTS

Up to this stage in the project, the effects of the operational distances (base to target, base to enemy border, etc.) had been examined separately. In reality, they interact. To examine the joint effects of these critical distance factors, several widely different bases and aircraft combinations were compared in the context of strategic campaigns in which, as in the previous section, after an enemy first strike, the United States launched strikes against a defended Russian target system while the U.S.-base system was concurrently under Russian attack. The systems compared were (1) an exclusively air-refueled intercontinental B-47 system, (2) a ground-refueled intercontinental B-47 system with a tanker supplement, (3) a B-47 advanced operating overseas base system (with local dispersal, more radar and active defense), and (4) an intermediate overseas operating base system (with an appropriate level of active and passive defense). In these final comparisons, a considerable number of plans with alternative force requirements were tried for each of the competing U.S. offensive systems. Each system was matched against an enemy defense and offense and deployed to take some advantage of its characteristic weaknesses. On the other hand, tanker-bomber combinations, routes of deployment and penetration, and active defenses were chosen so as to exploit advantages of each system and to reduce its force requirements and cost. Appropriate additional defenses for the overseas operating base and refueling-base systems had already been studied. In all systems the U.S. bases were well within the early-warning network. The costs, both of these defenses and of the ground damage to be expected for various Soviet bombing force and bomb assignments, were included in the total cost required by each system to destroy various Russian target systems.

Although the bombers and the U.S. operating-base locations were the same in all the systems compared, and although their methods of defense were in all respects identical except for those aspects associated with the concepts of operations, the differences in campaign costs were striking. The intercontinental exclusively air-refueled system turned out to be decidedly inferior to the intercontinental ground-refueled system. The advanced overseas operating base system studied was, assuming a low enemy commitment against SAC, intermediate in effectiveness between the two intercontinental systems. However, its cost and effectiveness were very sensitive to the assumption regarding the number and size of enemy bombs committed. Given a higher

---

8   *Selection and Use of Strategic Air Bases*, p. 336.

enemy commitment, its cost reached that of the intercontinental air-refueled system. The intermediate overseas operating base system, which combined the high radius-extension costs of the intercontinental air-refueled system and the vulnerability of the advanced overseas operating base system, made the worst showing of all. It was expensive for a low level of commitment. Figure 3.17 compares the four types of base systems for an industrial-target system[9]. (Both the relative standing of the overseas operating base systems and their

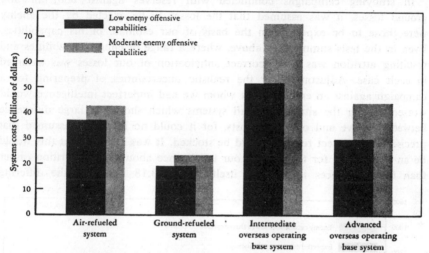

Fig. 3.17 Intercontinental and overseas operating base systems: cost to destroy an industrial-target system in the face of enemy A-bomb attack

sensitivity to differences in enemy offense would be shown to be worse if Fig. 3.17 included the indirect effects of ground attack as well as the direct damage to bombers.) These results apply to a campaign in which the air-refueled and overseas operating base systems withhold bombers to cut support and ground-loss costs, etc. If, in accordance with Air Force doctrine at that time, nearly all combat-ready bombers had been used, the inferiority of both systems would have been even more marked.

3.12. UNCERTAINTIES IN ENEMY CAPABILITY

Since all systems used the same bombing aircraft, the results were un-affected by wide alterations in the *total* enemy defense capability, but were somewhat affected by the allocation of enemy defenses between area and local defense. It was believed that the assumed local defense might be high

---

[9] Here we see what is meant by the *gross differences* in relative cost that the study set out to uncover.

relative to the assumed area defense, but a downward adjustment would worsen the relative position of the air-refueled system still further and so would not change the results. It had already been demonstrated that the effectiveness of an overseas operating base system was likely to vary markedly with the magnitude of enemy offense capability (for example, A-bomb commitments to attacks on our bases), whereas that of a ground-refueled system was relatively unaffected.

In studying campaigns conducted with reserves against both air and ground losses, it was assumed that the losses to be exacted by the enemy were those to be expected on the basis of our estimate of his capabilities. Even in the tests summarized above, where a range of enemy capabilities and resulting attrition was tried, correct anticipation of our losses was assumed in each case. Adjustment for the realistic uncertainties of preparing for a campaign against an enemy about whom we had imperfect intelligence would worsen further the situation of all systems which showed a large difference between reserve and operating costs, for it could no longer be assumed that precisely the correct reserves could be stocked. It was stressed that this would be an adjustment for the gaps in our intelligence about future attrition rather than for differences in attrition itself. Figure 3.18 illustrates the differing

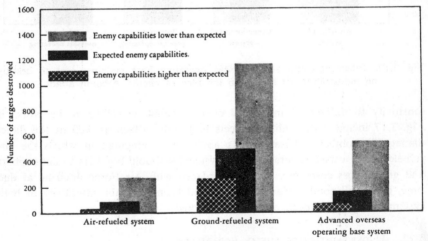

Fig. 3.18   Target destruction potential and uncertainty in enemy capability
($ 40 billion budget)

degradations in the percentage of targets destroyed by each of the systems if they all prepared for a specific enemy offensive capability (the same as the one assumed in the right half of Fig. 3.17), but if enemy capability turned out in fact to be different from our expectations.

3.13. FEASIBILITY

The preferred system—that is, the ground-refueled system—was shown to be more feasible than the air-refueled system, which, to destroy the same target system, involved more bombers, many more tankers (as high as 1700 KB-36 type), more U.S. bases, and more construction money than was programmed. The preferred system required roughly the number of bombers programmed and somewhat fewer tankers. The overseas refueling bases assumed used the sites programmed; and these were easier to obtain and to keep exclusively for refueling use than for operational use. The improved overseas operating base system required operating bases in many areas not scheduled for this purpose. It also involved a great many more bombers than the ground-refueled system.

3.14. FIXED BUDGET CAMPAIGNS

The comparisons shown thus far in this recapitulation were made in terms of the relative cost for alternative systems to do the same fixed job of target destruction. The study used the reverse criterion and compared systems, having identical budgets, with respect to the relative number of targets they could destroy. The differences shown were then drastically increased. This was due to the effect of saturation on enemy defenses: Systems that could allocate a large proportion of their budget to buying bombers in excess of the minimum needed for saturation obtained more than the proportional benefits in increased targets killed. The intercontinental air-refueled system had to spend most of its budget to procure noncombat elements, namely the tankers. The overseas operating base system had to spend much of its money on logistic support, active and passive defense, and purchase of bombers which were killed on the ground. The intermediate system spent money on all of these.

The characteristic differences in allocation of funds between combat and noncombat elements were responsible for some of the rather surprising differences in the time developments of the campaigns.

3.15. FLEXIBILITY AND CAMPAIGN TIME

Bombing aircraft operated at intercontinental distances were shown to have lower sortie rates than those operated from advanced bases. In the case of a ground-refueled system, this did not mean a longer campaign than for an overseas-based system. In both the overseas operating base and air-refueled systems, the strike rate, using a tactic of holding bombers in reserve, was limited by the operating support force (available tankers in one case, and overseas operating bases, logistic support, and active defense in the other).

To increase the support force to the point where all the available bombers could be sortied in one strike would be extremely expensive. For the ground-refueled system the extra cost of providing support for the entire force was calculated to be moderate. Inexpensive extra support would increase the potential strike rate of the ground-refueled system and permit it to finish a campaign not only at lower cost, but also in at least as short a time as any other system. In short, a ground-refueled system had a marked advantage in flexibility of strike size, rate of strike, and proportion of the target system attacked. (It also had greater flexibility in choice of route and in choice of flight profile.)

The overseas operating base systems had an advantage in shorter mission time, which, it seemed, would permit more frequent sorties per bomber. The study pointed out that several points should be observed. First, the importance of high sortie rates for a World War III atomic campaign against industrial targets would be much less than for campaigns with high explosives, of the World War II type, in which damage had to be administered cumulatively, a little at a time, and from which recuperation was relatively rapid. (This diminished significance was implicit in the Air Force's desire for an inter-continental mission capability.) Second, the proportional increase in sortie rate with decreasing mission distance was qualified by a number of difficulties, most important of which was the effect of enemy attack on our sortie capabilities. This, in fact, could reverse the apparent advantage. Finally, however, even if we assumed the sortie rates of individual bombers on over-seas operating bases to be twice those of similar bombers based in the ZI, the campaigns showed that the ZI-based ground-refueled system could achieve a higher rate of destruction for a fixed budget. The essential reason for this had been indicated: An overseas operating base system could not spend enough of its budget to buy bombers with the hypothetically high sortie rates. It had to allocate its budget to logistic support, defenses, and bombers, many of which were likely to be killed on the ground before sortieing at all.

3.16. OPERATING OVERSEAS AFTER THE COUNTERFORCE CAMPAIGN

The analysis indicated clearly how increasing Russian atomic capability made overseas operation of the strategic force unacceptably risky. What of the possibility of strategic operation after the destruction of the enemy air force? The likely difficulties in conducting a successful counterforce campaign against the Russian strategic force were suggested by the feasibility of a successful defense of our own SAC. Russian bombers might be home-based deep within their radar network, with plenty of warning to permit evacuation. Northern peripheral bases might be used for staging only, and critical facil-ities might be hardened to make a base denial campaign difficult. The enemy might use a large number of alternate bases in an emergency. Furthermore, the campaign required to make continuous occupancy of the overseas bases safe would be much more extensive than that which was generally then understood by the designation counterforce, that is, a mission to blunt the Russian attack against the ZI. Since a large fraction of these bases were within IL-28 radius and even one-way MiG range, nothing far short of the destruction of the entire Russian air force was required. Finally, we had a disadvantage not suffered by the Russians in that we would have relatively incomplete information as to the location and function of their various air bases. For such reasons, by the time the destruction of Russian atomic-delivery capability had advanced to any substantial degree, the major industrial targets, which are much softer, would have been destroyed. (This is indicated by the results of several joint industrial counterforce campaigns which were tried.) The part of our force that is unattrited at that point could be expected to be substantially less than the total force, and, most important, our principal atomic strategic job would have been done by the time it was safe to move overseas to operate.

3.17. LIMITATIONS AND FLEXIBILITY

The results presented here have been derived from campaign comparisons in which many elements were varied and some were fixed. The study analyzed, in the context of campaign, only the programmed bombers. In most of the campaign analyses, only one target system was used—a Russian industrial-target complex. It is natural to ask whether the demonstrated superiority of a ground-refueled home-based system would be confirmed by additional analyses in which these other fixed elements were also varied realistically. The composition of our potential bombing force was seen as increasingly variable when later time periods were considered. And although Russian industry would be the most familiar target postulated for our strategic force, it would not be the only objective: long-range interdiction and the destruction of the Russian long-range air force would be other prominent objectives.

Against long-range interdiction targets, the overseas operating base systems showed an advantage in coordinating the bombing schedule with rapidly changing requirements for retardation. And, even for industry bombing, the analysis indicated there were circumstances in which these systems would appear in a more favorable light. Some of the difficulties in achieving our counterair objectives had been suggested. Nonetheless, if the Soviet atomic-delivery capability could be destroyed (although it seemed doubtful that this could be done before the completion of the major part of the attack on the industrial target system), or if it should turn out to be much smaller than expected, then, once this was known with confidence, overseas operating bases could be more favorably regarded for industry bombing.

However, one of the merits of the recommended system was its adaptability. If future conditions warranted the expenditure of time and money, refueling bases could be converted to operating bases and might be combined with a certain number of overseas operating bases used in connection with retardation targets[10]. Similarly, the ground-refueled system could permit the economic use of penetration fighters. This would hardly be feasible for the air-refueled case considered. And for high-performance bombers, the ground-refueled system would provide great flexibility in the choice of routes, speeds, and altitudes of penetration, and would make possible the large payloads that might be demanded in connection with the advent of H-bombs.

The analysis indicated that a growing Russian defense had forced us to give up long-range bombers for high-performance bombers. At the same time, an increasing Russian offensive power would compel us to keep as much as we could of the vulnerable part of our strategic complex a long distance from the enemy's borders. A system for basing our bombers at home within the cover of our radar network and for extending radius to target by means of dispersed overseas refueling stations appeared to be important for a large part of our strategic task, and to be capable of combination with methods suited to accomplish the rest.

3.18 EPILOGUE

This study, originally conceived as a logistics exercise, became in the end a study of U.S. strategic deterrent policy[11]. After appraisal by and *ad hoc* Air Staff Group, the principal recommendation of the first part of the study—to reduce SAC vulnerability by cutting sharply the number of functions performed at overseas bases and thus the time during which the force was exposed on these bases—became Air Force policy in a short time. This was merely the beginning, for in addition to work on protective construction and base hardening, the study stimulated research on a bomb-alarm system, an airborne alert, and long-endurance aircraft.

A significant step in the development of RAND's approach to problems, this study did not appear as "analytical" as our previous systems analyses. No complicated mathematical model featuring an astronomically large number of machine computations was involved, nor was any modern operations research

---

[10] As part of the investigation, the study showed that the construction currently underway for the then programmed overseas based system could be adapted without expensive changes to a refueling-base system.

[11] See Chapter 7, Section 7.6.

technique such as linear programming used. Indeed, no attempt to determine a sharp optimum was made; rather the objective was insensitivity—finding a system that would work well in many widely divergent situations and even perform reasonably satisfactorily in a major catastrophe. Our efforts to convince the Air Force that the study recommendations should be implemented made one thing clear: In an analysis aimed at policy-making, the relevance of the many factors and contingencies affecting the problem is more important than sophisticated analytic techniques. A good new idea—technical, operational, or what have you—is worth a thousand elaborate evaluations.

As far as I know, this was the first study to raise as a *major issue* the question of the vulnerability of SAC, the world's most powerful force, indicating that in the 1955–1960 period it might be crippled by an enemy surprise attack. The study considered many ways to confront this possibility, and later discussions suggested others to the Air Force[12]. As a result, the necessary fixes were adopted to protect SAC against the joint threat of aircraft and ballistic missiles, and the role of active, air defense was re-evaluated[13].

Present-day critics believe that the results of this study should have been obvious before it started and that no elaborate analysis was required. They maintain that it is absurd not to take every reasonable measure to protect one's offensive force, particularly when one assumes that the enemy will strike the first blow; that it is equally absurd to transport jet fuel by air in wartime, when it can be inexpensively moved by water in time of peace and stored where it is likely to be needed. Nevertheless, these "absurdities" were not obvious at the time and did not become obvious until a number of years after the study.

---

[12] Some 92 briefings were given and a special Top Secret report prepared.
[13] For an opinion of the effect of this study on national security policy, see B. L. R. Smith, "Strategic Expertise and National Security Policy: A Case Study", *Public Policy*, XIII, Yearbook of the Graduate School of Public Administration of Harvard University, 1964.

Part Two

ELEMENTS AND METHODS

Systems analysis is an approach, a way of looking at a problem. Mathematical techniques or computing machinery may or may not be necessary, or even useful, and no formal analysis need appear on paper; straight hard thinking may suffice. But, in common with all analyses of choice under uncertainty, whether elaborate or not, certain elements are present. These elements—the *objective* or *objectives,* the *alternatives* or means of accomplishing these objectives, the *costs* or things that must be given up in order to obtain each of the alternatives, the *model* or description of the relationships between the alternatives and what they accomplish and cost, and *criteria* by which to choose the preferred alternative—are present in every analysis designed to influence policy. They are frequently difficult to choose or to formulate explicitly.

Models, criteria, and *costs* are the subjects of Chapters 4, 5, and 6, respectively. *Alternatives* and *objectives* are treated in Chapter 7, which emphasizes that the discovery and isolation of feasible alternatives and the determination of objectives are fundamental to the solution of any problem of choice. Although this book is written for those who use systems analyses and not for those who produce such analyses, the former may profit by an explanation of the methods and procedures of the latter, as described in Chapter 8.

Chapter 4

THE WHY AND HOW OF MODEL BUILDING

R. D. SPECHT

The United States periodically holds an exercise in which the capabilities of the United States and the Soviet Union, projected a few years into the future, are compared by means of an elaborate war game. In one of these exercises, an operations analyst for one of the services was briefing the exercise staff of his service when the senior officer asked how some matter had been evaluated. Now the question was a physical one, and a sensible one. The analyst satisfied his questioner by replying, "Sir, we have a model".

Let us examine this business of models and try to find out two things: what the analyst meant by his answer, and why he should have been thrown out for making it.

Before we try to find a definition of a model, let us first look at an example. Here is the model with which systems costs were computed in a missile comparison[1]:

$$C = C_L m + R C_M N m + C_M (1 - R)\, m,$$

$$N = \frac{\alpha T}{R r m p k},$$

$$p = \begin{cases} 1 - \dfrac{A}{R r m} & \text{if this expression is non-negative,} \\ 0 & \text{otherwise.} \end{cases}$$

This model happens to consist of a few mathematical equations, but this is not the feature that we shall find most important. Let us rather consider the quantities whose interrelations are spelled out by these equations. These fall into three groups. First, we have the output of the model, C, which is the systems cost (the dollar cost of the strategic system used to destroy a prescribed fraction of the enemy target system). Next we have the inputs, the numbers that describe the strategic system (the missiles and basing, in this case) and the environment in which the system will live:

---

[1] The model used in the example presented in Appendix B.

R ground reliability, the fraction of ready missiles which actually fire,

r air reliability, the fraction of missiles actually fired that do not have to be destroyed,

C_M, C_L cost coefficients (roughly speaking, the cost per missile fired and the cost of maintaining a missile in a ready state, respectively),

A a measure of the enemy defense strength and of the offense vulnerability,

T the total number of targets in the target system[2],

α the expected number of hits per target needed to give the required confidence that the desired fraction of these targets has been destroyed [3].

In some cases these simple symbols each represent a complex set of related variables—for example, C_L depends, among other things, on the time required to repeat a salvo, and C_M depends upon the kind and yield of the warhead.

Third, we have the operational variables, those elements which do not represent the design characteristics of the offense system but rather the way in which the system is operated in the campaign. We have

m the number of missiles made-ready for firing on each salvo,

k the probability that a delivered warhead will destroy the target. This includes the target characteristics, the weapon yield, and the guidance accuracy (through another model!).

Finally, and somewhat incidentally, there are two quantities in the model above that are superfluous, in the sense that they could be replaced by equivalent expressions involving the inputs and operational variables. Nevertheless, it is convenient to exhibit them explicitly, and we have

N the number of salvos in the campaign,

p the probability that a missile survives to the target.

In the real world the values of these operational variables are decisions that, in large part, need not be made now while we are deciding questions of missile selection (or, in some other study, questions of development and procurement, say). These decisions will, instead, be postponed until the system is actually used in anger. The model must take into account the operational variables, for the

---

[2] In Appendix B, $T = 100$.
[3] In Appendix B, $\alpha = 2$.

different systems may require different operational patterns in order for each to display its best performance. That is, we must compare the performance of various systems when each is operated in its optimum manner.

We shall consider a model to be a black box into which we feed inputs (reliabilities, defense strengths, etc.) and out of which we get outputs—the systems cost in our missile selection example. The model is a deliberately simplified picture of a piece of the real world; from its output we seek guidance for some decision problem in the real world.

In the example above, the model consisted of a set of equations. This is not always the case. In other instances the model exists in the form of a collection of flow charts and computer codes. There are still other possibilities, but before looking at them let us consider some things that characterize the process of building a model of any sort.

When we say that an analyst builds a model of a part of the real world, we mean that

1. He decides which factors are relevant to the questions his study is attempting to answer.

2. From these he picks the quantifiable factors—those that can be described numerically.

3. This list is cut down to size by aggregation.

4. The relations between the elements are spelled out quantitatively.

This activity is, in part, what anyone does who thinks about a problem. (We have been speaking prose all our lives without realizing it.) The model builder merely does these things explicitly and quantitatively—his assumptions laid out on the table for any man to inspect and criticize.

Let us look at each of the four parts of our definition of model building.

4.1.   DECIDING WHICH FACTORS ARE RELEVANT

Take a missile selection study as an example. We might begin by trying to draw up a list of all the elements in the situation that might be relevant to our problem. Later we may discard some of these on the grounds that they do not really matter after all. But at the beginning we can try to be fairly inclusive.

Our list will probably begin as a chaotic mish-mash: the guidance for Soviet antimissile missiles; new base construction and manning for some of the offense systems; future weapon technology; the geographic distribution of the target system; physical vulnerability, the likely strength of defense, and pre-strike reconnaissance requirements of the targets; and so on. Each of these items can in turn be expanded into many subitems. Our list is long and probably contains some irrelevant items that will not influence our choice of weapon system. We look for these irrelevant items and weed them out—if we can recognize them at this stage. Unfortunately, neither decisionmaker nor analyst may know which factors are the critical ones until the analysis is finished. In fact, one important function of the analysis may be exactly this: to show which factors are important and which have little effect.

As a small example of this, consider one detail which appears frequently in missile-aircraft comparisons[4]. To estimate the systems cost to destroy some fraction of the total number of targets, the targets are often assumed to be of equal value. Targets in the real world, of course, are not of equal value. However, assigning to the targets nonuniform values, as measured, say, by the capital investment represented by each, may be shown in the particular model being used not to affect the systems cost or the cost comparison significantly.

4.2. SELECTING QUANTIFIABLE FACTORS

For many of the factors on our list we can find numbers; for some of them we can even find good numbers. But for some aspects of the problem, numbers will just not exist. In the study of deterrence, for example, what effects will the location of missile systems at various overseas bases have on the stability of our political alliances? Or vice versa, how do political considerations bear upon the feasibility of various base locations? What is the probability of the loss of some or all of our overseas base rights through a change in political alignment or through atomic blackmail? The analyst may say that these are aspects of the problem that he will not be able to quantify.

We began by saying that we would throw out of our considerations all the irrelevant factors—all (or almost all) the things that would not affect our decisions. Now we see that we must also leave out of the model some elements that may be relevant, that may be essential for our problem. These factors are omitted for either one of two reasons:

the nature of the beast—they are just not suited to numerical measures, or

the limited knowledge and ability of the analyst—who is not, after all, as omniscient as his final report may suggest.

We have mentioned that it may be difficult to tie numbers to the politics of base location. The enemy's reaction and his shift in defense weapons and tactics as we change our offense vehicles may be quantifiable in principle, but a formidable problem in practice—one that is often passed over in silence. Mixed forces and time phasing may be left out of the model because of the computational difficulties they introduce.

The analyst who omits some elements from his model on the argument that

---

[4] See Appendix B.

they do not lend themselves to numerical study must be very sure that he is not merely shirking the hard problems. Many things that seem obviously un-measurable are in fact amenable to counting and numbering. Even if we cannot estimate numerically the political stability of our overseas base system, we may still be able to measure the cost of depending on that stability. In an actual missile selection study, for example, strategic campaigns should be studied under a variety of assumptions about the loss of overseas bases.

Those elements omitted from the model are not really discarded; they are merely filed away in a different pigeonhole—one marked "For Later Considera-tion". When later in the study we examine the results derived from our model and try to draw conclusions and recommendations, or when we assemble and relate the results from the several models that may describe various pieces of our problem, then we shall have to do some hard thinking and relate these results to the elements that were omitted from quantitative analysis. Do the politics of base location support our conclusions or do they argue against them? The important thing here is to recognize explicitly those absentee elements, those facets of the problem that have been omitted from the model because they are difficult to quantify.

4.3. CONDENSING QUANTIFIABLE, RELEVANT FACTORS BY AGGREGATION

Let us illustrate this process by one part of the example with which we began the costing of the strategic systems. The initial list of all possible items to be costed is an embarrassingly long one. We have costs for maintenance equipment, teleprinters, switchboards, personnel pay and allowances, spares, base real estate, fuel, trucks, cranes, training facilities, housing, medical facilities, the pro rata share of the operating costs of the Strategic Air Command Headquarters, of the Air Materiel Command, of RAND even. And many others.

This list can be chopped down to size by neglecting some of the items that will not vary over our several strategic missile systems and by aggregating the rest under a few categories. Trucks, cranes, power units, weapon dollies, handling slings, teletype equipment, switchboards—these and other items can all be lumped into the organization equipment of the squadron. Training costs, pay and allowances, and travel are all included in personnel costs. The costs of the installation's maintenance supplies, personnel supplies, organizational equip-ment supplies, POL[5], etc., are grouped under the term "Initial Stock Level". This item, in turn, becomes part of the larger category, "Stocks".

How far we go in this process of lumping together diverse items into a few categories depends on the particular study we are making and hence on the amount of detail we require. In one study we may arrive at a list of cost elements

---

[5]   Petroleum, oil, and lubricants.

comprising installations, major equipment, minor equipment, stocks, transportation, personnel, maintenance, POL, service and miscellaneous, and overhead.

We now take a long jump forward. We ask: How far can we go in our process of aggregation, of lumping? What are the really relevant costs? Probably not installation, equipment, stocks, and so on. But what, then?

There is no single solution to this problem of determining the relevant costs— or, more generally, the relevant variables of any sort—for the solution depends on the use to which the model is to be put, on the questions to be asked of the systems analysis.

In the example we are considering, you will recall that all costs were reduced to just two coefficients, C_L and C_M. The cost coefficient C_M is just the cost per missile used during the campaign. We might have two campaigns, in each of which the same number of missiles were fired, but in which one campaign used a Sunday punch tactic—all targets attacked on the first salvo—while the other campaign stretched out over some period of time. (Remember that in this idealization the enemy does not damage our bases between salvos.) Clearly, the first campaign requires more bases, more maintenance facilities, and quite different costs. That is, in addition to costs that are proportional to the total number of missiles fired during a campaign, there are costs that depend on the number of missiles made ready for each salvo; this cost per missile made ready for a salvo is denoted in the model above by C_L.

And, finally, there are "overhead" costs that depend neither on the total number of missiles used nor on the number mounted on a single salvo. These costs would include, for example, a pro rata share of the operating costs of the various supporting organizations in a command, such as major command headquarters, personnel processing squadrons, radar calibration squadrons, and so on. This overhead cost was not represented in the model above because the assumption was implicitly made that it would be essentially the same for the competing systems.

Notice where we are. We have replaced the real world—or at least that tremendously important and equally thorny part of it dealing with costs—by an idealized system involving just three numbers: the total systems cost and the two cost coefficients C_L and C_M. We have found, we hope, the relevant factors, and we have built a model for the costing of our systems.

Of course, I have made the process of building the costing model [6] look much simpler than it really is. To determine the cost coefficients for each system studied takes all the experience, judgment, intuition, and guesswork that can be provided by RAND's Cost Analysis Department working together with the Engineering departments. This is particularly true when we are attempting to estimate costs for a system projected into the future. To cost the operations of

---

[6] See Chapter 15.

a system that has not yet operated is not a job for either the uninformed or for the timid. In fact, the costing expert lives a more hazardous life than does, say, the missiles expert who has merely to estimate, with the aid of a very cloudy crystal ball, the reliability, accuracy, and other characteristics of his missiles. Both men must go out on a limb, but the costing expert knows that life may well prove his estimates in error long before it confronts his missiles colleague (if ever it does) with the evidence of his fallibility.

4.4. QUANTIFYING RELATIONS BETWEEN ELEMENTS

Having come to some tentative conclusions as to what the relevant factors are, we must now do some thinking about the way in which these various elements interact. In some cases the effect of a factor upon our conclusions is fairly evident, but in many cases the interrelations between factors are not simple and the effects are not obvious. This does not mean that analysis makes intuition unnecessary. On the contrary, we must intuit our way through the problem using analysis to make our results precise, to sharpen our intuition, and, occasionally, to show us that our intuition is fallible.

If we relax the accuracy required of a missile, that is, increase the allowed Circular Probable Error, one effect is to increase the total cost of doing a given job. This increased cost may be paid in dollars or in fissile material or both. We could send decoys along to increase the probability that the bombing missile reaches the target and thus make up for the lower probability that a delivered warhead destroys the target (remember that we are now dealing with a less accurate missile guidance system). Alternatively, we could attack the target again on a later salvo if the guidance errors result in a miss on the first salvo. Or, we could increase the yield of the warhead.

We cannot say how important the direct effect of lower accuracy on increased cost is until we have estimated its magnitude. Suppose we accept a missile with 10 000 ft as its expected miss distance instead of demanding 5000 ft. Which of the three ways just mentioned of making up for the lower accuracy is cheapest? How much does each cost in dollars, in fissile material? And, what sort of trade between fissile material and dollars is implied here?

If the direct effect of a less accurate missile guidance system is to increase costs, there is an indirect effect that may work in just the opposite direction. A less accurate guidance system may mean a simpler system, and a simpler system is very likely to be a more reliable one. A moment ago we were trading guidance error for fissile material or dollars. Now we see that guidance error and reliability may also be objects of barter. Increased reliability means lower costs, again either in dollars or fissile material or both. An increase in reliability plays much the same role as a decrease in enemy defenses. The reliability increase may be even a bit more desirable, for the missile that goes astray and attacks the North Pole has not even exercised the defenses. A second effect of simplicity is that development time may be decreased; the simpler and more reliable but less accurate system may be available some years before its more complex counterpart. We find ourselves trading not only dollars and fissile material, but time as well. What are the rates of exchange and are they favorable? These are questions that will be difficult indeed to answer, even with analysis, and almost impossible if we rely only on intuition and unbuttoned judgment.

Let us examine a second example of the difficulties we get into in trying to see how our various factors are related. Consider a strategic campaign consisting of a series of identical salvos, in each of which the same number of targets is attacked, say 20. To be explicit, let us assume that four missiles are sent against each target to allow for reliability failures, attrition due to enemy defenses, and guidance error. If, now, we increase the number of targets attacked on each salvo, then several things happen. The total number of salvos, and thus the length of the campaign, decreases. The number of missiles engaging the defenses on a salvo increases, these defenses are more nearly saturated, and thus the probability that a missile survives to reach the target is now greater. We may, in fact, be able to economize on our four missiles per target. The total number of missiles used in the campaign to destroy a given target system may decrease, and we have then a corresponding decrease in the total cost as measured in dollars and fissile material.

But, on the other hand, to launch a greater number of missiles on each salvo calls for more launchers and thus for increased support and logistic costs. Whether or not these overbalance the decreased cost of missiles and warheads used is not obvious. We started by considering a change in only one variable, targets per salvo, and we find ourselves in a situation in which all is flux— number of missiles per salvo, length of campaign, best number of missiles sent to each target, missile cost, support cost. All of these elements are interconnected, and the man who can intuit his way through this situation is rare indeed.

4.5. MODEL BUILDING AND THE REAL WORLD

The analyst can help the decisionmaker in other ways besides building a model and using it to help analyze a problem. The analyst can furnish a collection of empirical data, or he can write a "think piece"; but even in these, some aspects of the model building process appear. For there is unlimited empirical data and the very process of choosing some for presentation and discarding others involves implicit assumptions as to what is important, what considerations are relevant, what variables may be interrelated. Again, in a "think piece" the decision process may be broken down into stages. It may be pointed out to the decisionmaker what decisions must be made at each stage, what are the relevant factors, and what are the likely outcomes. However, we will use the term model to refer to the explicit, quantitative variety.

The model we invent will, of course, depend on the thing being modeled— the part of the real world in which we are interested. But this is not all. There is not a *single* model for strategic missiles, another for the tactical air war, and so on. What model we design depends also on what questions are to be asked of the model and what decisions are to be given some guidance by the use of the model. There is no universal model of which we can ask help on all questions. Rather, we have to tailor the model to fit the questions.

Let us illustrate this point by considering a study made by the Martian counterpart of RAND concerning Flying Saucer Systems. This study is about flying saucers made on Mars and dispatched on pioneer reconnaissance flights to the United States.

While the saucer is being built, it may represent to the costing expert only a pair of numbers—its serial number in the production of this model and the number of man-hours (or Martian *augenblicks*) required to produce it. These numbers are the essential ones in determining the learning curve with which future costs may be estimated.

After production the saucer is shipped to the depot by boat—canal boat, naturally. Here the saucer can be replaced by a different set of numbers—linear dimensions and weight, together with the freight classification (3B in the case of saucers). The machinery of the model, in this case, consists merely of the set of tables that give freight rates in terms of weight, cubage, classification, and route.

After the saucer has been launched and is in free flight in the gravitational fields of Mars, Earth, and Sun, not to mention Phobos, Deimos, and Luna, a discussion of trajectory necessitates a different model. The saucer can now be idealized as a point-mass having position and velocity. Any practical man could object that we are being quite unrealistic; that we are neglecting size, shape, material; that the saucer has a span of 100 ft, is colored bright red, and carries a crew of three. But these things have little effect on the answers to the questions we ask of this model. The interrelations between the factors of the model—that is to say, the inner machinery or structure of the model—may be given by a computing schedule expressing Newtonian gravitation. Into this schedule we enter positions and velocities and from it we calculate future path.

The saucer now enters the earth's atmosphere and becomes an object of interest to the aerodynamicist rather than to the astronomer. Where our last model was that of a point-mass, we now have to deal with shape and drag coefficient as well as velocity.

If the Air Control and Warning network of the Air Defense Command picks up the saucer on its Early Warning radar, then the saucer is merely a radar echoing area as determined by material, size, form, and aspect.

If the saucer proves to be hostile and an interceptor makes a firing pass, then a different model comes into play. For vulnerability calculations we are interested in the two-dimensional profile, fuel storage, and other vulnerable components.

And so on. The same part of the real world may be modeled in many ways. Factors relevant to one model may be completely immaterial to another.

Let us consider another example. As man begins to fly outside the atmosphere —at altitudes above 50 000 ft, say—problems of aviation medicine become important that were not as pressing at lower altitudes. Imagine a group of experts in aviation medicine, each studying a different set of problems. To one expert the pilot is an analog computer. He has inputs through the senses of hearing, sight, touch, and balance. The outputs of this computer, the responses to the inputs, are the motions by which the pilot controls the aircraft. Inputs and outputs are related through the pilot's transfer function. In one model, highly simplified, the relation between input and output is taken to be the same as the relation between input and output voltages of an electrical circuit containing a resistor, inductor, and capacitor, together with a time-lag device.

Another medical expert is concerned with the fact that the center of this pilot-computer, the brain, must be kept in a sheltered environment, protected from external stresses. While the temperature outside the body may vary from 40° to 120° F, the temperature of the brain-computer is held constant within $\pm 1°$ F by sweating, radiation from the skin, other reactions, and fat insulation, together with a servo-control mechanism within the body. The model used to describe and analyze this system will be quite different from the preceding one. Still a different model will be used by the cardiovascular specialist to study the constant blood flow to the brain. And, finally, consider the problem of protecting the pilot's brain from mechanical shock. The brain is suspended in the cerebrospinal fluid, encased in the thick cranial vault, mounted on a curved spine with its springy intervertebral discs, all resting on a padded posterior. A simple model—and an adequate one for some purposes—is that of a mass connected by a spring to a movable platform. This same model happens also to be used sometimes to discuss the motion of a building during an earthquake.

And so we see that many different models may be used to represent the same physical system. One model's relevant is another's immaterial.

Note, by the way, that this last model—the mass connected by a spring to a movable platform—bears little resemblance to the missile-selection model we first discussed, a model which consists of a few mathematical equations. These two models do, however, have some important features in common: Both are idealized representations of some aspects of the real world; both are imitations of systems in the real world, imitations that can be manipulated either analytically or mechanically; and both neglect many features of the situations they represent. This neglect does not rule out the usefulness of the models when shaken well and taken according to directions; it merely limits their fields of usefulness. Both models tie together a number of quantities whose interrelations are too complex to be readily intuited—in the one case, quantities such as defense strengths, cost coefficients, and reliabilities; in the other, forces, displacements, and elastic coefficients. Expressed otherwise, each model allows us to specify the value of inputs and then to compute or measure the value of outputs (systems cost in one case, motion of a mass in the other, say). Both models yield these output values with impressive accuracy and assurance. This, however, must not mislead us into supposing that we know the corresponding quantities in the real world with comparable accuracy and assurance. What relevance the results from the model have for the real world depends upon the wisdom, judgment, and skill which the model-builder exercises in choosing the assumptions, the variables, the relationships, and the numerical values employed in the model.

You may recall that the missile-selection model, the one used in Appendix B, involved what we called operational variables—such things as the number of targets attacked on each salvo and the number of missiles assigned to each target. Now this particular model is sufficiently simple and designed with sufficient cunning that the optimum values of these operational variables may be determined analytically, in the same way that a calculus student determines the highest point on a curve. In other models we might determine such optimum values by calculating many cases with the help of computing machines, digital or analogue. In still other cases, human judgment is used to arrive at what are hoped to be good values of some variables.

That is to say, we can have a model in which a human is an integral part of the machinery of the model. We can make the man part of the model, for example, by giving him potentiometer knobs to twist and dials from which to read the values of variables in an analogue computer. The man continually interacts with the other elements of the model: when he turns the potentiometer knobs he affects the rest of the machinery by changing the values of some of the variables in the model; in turn, the rest of the machinery affects the man as he reads from the dials the values of variables of the model.

If our model includes two or more of these human decisionmakers engaged in a competitive struggle, then we say that we have a war game. In one such example at RAND, if you were one of the humans used you would find yourself cast in the role of a theater air commander deciding how to allocate your forces of fighters, fighter-bombers, bombers, tactical missiles, and atomic weapons to enemy targets of airfields, supply lines, and troops. Your opponent has similar decisions to make, and the two of you sit twisting potentiometer knobs to allocate the desired percentages of your forces to the several targets.

This model is one in which the Red and Blue players are integral parts together with the mechanical elements. The players use judgment and intuition throughout the game to make decisions about the operation of their forces.

But if the humans are indispensable to this model, so also is the machinery. The man plays a limited role. He is not free but rather is bound by all the constraints of the model; constraints that have been built into the machine to represent the results of component studies on various pieces of the problem and the pooling of experience and judgment concerning portions of the problem.

4.6. HUMAN JUDGMENT

It is possible to use the spirit of war gaming without the formal paraphernalia. For example, in analyzing the problem of defense of the United States against attack, a RAND analyst thought through the problem from the defense standpoint. He then changed hats, mentally, and did his best as the Red commander to beat the defense system. Then he put the defense commander's hat on once more and tried to counter the best offense threat. And so on. This use of the spirit of war gaming—of free competition—may often be the most valuable contribution that gaming has to make to a given problem. If a staff is planning the possible deployment of a mobile tactical force to use in a peripheral war, then the staff's best man should be given the thankless job of fighting the plan, of acting as obnoxious opponent and obstreperous umpire. And, just as it is possible to have competition without a formal game, it is also possible to go through the motions of a game without really having free competition. For example, there is often a tendency to avoid making the Red attack too ungentlemanly.

We have been talking about the use of human judgment as an explicit and integral part of a model. In the more usual situation, human judgment and intuition also enter in but not in so explicit a fashion. In the first place, man designs the model, that is, he decides what factors are relevant to the problems and what the interrelations between these factors are to be in the model. In the second place, the user of the model decides the numerical values of the input variables fed into the model. And, finally, man inspects, analyzes, and interprets the results, the outputs of the model.

This fact—that any model is imbedded in judgment and intuition and guess-work—should be remembered when we examine the results that come, with high precision, from a model. It is important, too, for us to remember that there is nothing magic about a computing machine—whether the machine is a slide rule or a digital computer. In any case, the machine merely serves to speed up the process by which we discover the implications of our assumptions, our estimates, our planning factors. Regardless of the machinery used, it is to the assumptions that we must turn when we ask for an explanation of the results of the model.

4.7. A COMPUTER MODEL

The model with which we began this talk was a very simple one involving no more hardware, perhaps, than slide rule, pencil, and paper. Now let us go to the other extreme in this matter of hardware and look at a model in which a high-speed electronic computer is the central element.

As described in one of the study reports[7]:

> The Strategic Operations Model is one in a series of developments at RAND concerned with creating computer models as strategic planning aids. It is an attempt to simulate, using a high-speed computer, most of the major elements of a two-sided strategic air war. It plays through, in time, the detailed activities of base operation, dispatching planes, flying them along their routes, refueling, attacks by fighters and local defenses, bomb damage to military installations, and restriction of operation by fallout—all within the concrete limitations of geography, forces in being, aircraft characteristics, defense effectiveness, base capacities, and weapon effects.

> The model is of the type that has become known as Monte Carlo[8]; that is, there are many events represented which are dependent on chance—about thirty different kinds of events in the present routine. Whenever such an event arises in the course of a simulated war, the machine computes a random number and compares it with a probability to determine the outcome.

> To play through one run of the first two and one-half days of a full-scale central air war—that is, one involving most of the air forces of both the Soviet Union and the United States and their allies—requires about six hours on the IBM 704 computer.

> The model deals with the war in a straightforward fashion—about the way anyone might think through the course of a two-sided conflict if he could keep track of all the details. It starts with a list of initial conditions for each side, namely, aircraft (bombers, tankers, transports), bomber bases, defense installations (radar sites, local defense sites, and fighter bases), including the status of all these. In addition there must be a set of plans for each side. Plans are more like strategies than control schedules of takeoffs and check points. They must take into account contingencies that arise during the course of the war and allow for alternative actions. This is because the model is completely automatic. Once the inputs are set up, the machine fights the war without interruption.

> To define a full-scale conflict requires a very large set of numbers. The inputs for our present runs, for example, consist of some 150 000 separate numbers.

> The basic output of the model is a set of cell histories. Every significant event occurring to each cell of aircraft in the course of the war is recorded on

---

[7] N. C. Dalkey and L. H. Wegner, *The Strategic Operations Model: A Summary Report* (U), The RAND Corporation, RM-2221 (DDC No. AD 304988), July 28, 1958 (Confidential).

[8] See Chapter 13 for an explanation of Monte Carlo.

magnetic tape and can be printed out as a surprisingly readable story. In
addition to cell histories, a number of significant indices are kept track of: the
count of planes killed on base, planes killed by the two types of defenses,
number of ground zeros, bases and defense installations destroyed or inoperable
due to radiation, and so on. These can be printed out as tables showing the
variation with time, or, often more usefully, as graphs photographed from a
cathode ray tube[9].

A model—whether a large scale one using a high-speed computer or one
using slide rule, pencil, and paper—can be a useful tool in assisting the analyst
to arrive at solutions to difficult problems in the real world. The model must be
used within the restricted area in which it is applicable. It must be used by
analysts who understand its capabilities and limitations. To attempt to use a
model as a modern, electronic version of the Delphic oracle from which one
may request answers to large and difficult decision problems invites nonsensical results.

4.8. CONCLUDING COMMENTS

The past ten years have seen marked changes in RAND's approach to systems
analysis—that is, to analytic studies that deal with complex problems of choice
in the face of uncertainty. Let me put the difference inaccurately but graphically: In our youth we looked more scientific. That is to say, we attached more
importance, years ago, to the business of representing that part of the real
world with which we were dealing by a single analytical model. With the context
chosen, the assumptions determined, the criterion selected, we could turn our
attention to the more intriguing questions of how best to apply modern
mathematical techniques and high-speed computers to produce a neat solution
from which conclusions and recommendations could be drawn.

There are many problems in the world for which this is a sensible, even a
recommended approach. There are problems impossible to solve without the
use of the most powerful tools of mathematics and of computers. The optimal
distribution of weight and thrust between the several stages of a lunar probe,
the determination of its initial trajectory—these are well-defined questions and
yield to neat and orderly solution. On the other hand, the stability of the
thermonuclear balance or the composition of a strategic deterrent force or the
character of the next generation of tactical weapons—these are not questions
that may be attacked usefully in this manner, although essential fragments of
these problems may be solved analytically. A trivial reason for this is that even

---

[9] This model has been amplified by the Air Battle Analysis Division of DCS/
Plans and Programs, Headquarters USAF, in versions known as the Air Battle
Model and STAGE. For some studies, these more extensive routines require
considerably longer running times (for example, up to 30 hours on an IBM 709).

modern techniques of analysis are not sufficiently powerful to treat these problems without brutal simplification and idealization. The major reason, however, for the inadequacy of simple optimization procedures is the central role that uncertainty plays in this sinful but fascinating world. No longer are we analyzing a problem with a given and definite context and with specific equipment. We may not have clearly defined objectives. Instead, we must try to design—not analyze—a system that will operate satisfactorily, in some sense, under a variety of contingencies that may arise in a future seen only dimly.

We have learned that new tools—high-speed computers, war gaming, game theory, linear and dynamic programming, Monte Carlo, and others—often find important application, that they are often powerful aids to intuition and understanding. Nevertheless, we have learned to be more interested in the real world than in the idealized model we prepare for analysis—more interested in the practical problem that demands solution than in the intellectual and mechanical gadgets we use in the solution.

The statement that we now put less faith in the neat analytical approach to complex problems is not to be taken as an argument for nonscientific studies, for illogical arguments, for seat-of-the-pants speculation. Detailed quantitative work of high quality is as important—in its place—as ever. The project leader must be able to defend his thesis, not by assertion but by logical analysis, against the questions of a hostile, but rational audience.

Let me close by reminding you that, as former RAND staff member Herman Kahn says,

> Today, systems analysts are getting to be both more modest about their claims and better at their work. If the trend continues, we may well come out with a match between claims and product[10].

---

[10]   H. Kahn and I. Mann, *Techniques of Systems Analysis,* The RAND Corporation, RM-1829-1 (DDC No. AD-123512), December 3, 1956, p. 37.

Chapter 5

CRITERIA

R. N. McKEAN

Systems analysis is intended to help pick out from a list of alternatives the preferred weapons system or course of action. The criterion problem is one of devising the *test of preferredness*. For instance, the test of a strategic deterrent system might be the lowest cost of maintaining a designated capability, taking into account both the enemy's offense and his defense. The nature of this criterion is of great importance to the evaluation of the rival systems. Note how results change with the use of other possible tests. As an extreme example, maximum damage per vehicle lost would favor aircraft, while maximum damage per crew lost would favor missiles, if one were comparing aircraft and missile systems.

It should be recognized that analysis may simply trace out some of the consequences of alternative weapons or actions and exhibit these consequences to decisionmakers after the fashion of consumers' research. By this term I mean the kind of research that is often done to help consumers choose an item such as an automobile or a refrigerator. Usually the results do not take the form, "Automobile A is the best one", but simply state, "Here are the costs of alternative automobiles, and here are some of the important characteristics and indicators of performance". This can be a highly useful function of analysis. Insofar as analyses are merely supposed to do this, there is no criterion proper that points a finger at the preferred weapon or action, and no problem of deciding on a definitive test of preferredness. There is nonetheless a closely related problem of deciding *which* are the consequences and indicators, knowledge of which would help most in choosing among alternatives. This discussion will deal chiefly with the devising of formal tests of preferredness as though systems analyses were always supposed to indicate definitively the best course of action. A good deal of what is said, however, applies to the related problem of devising consumers' research indicators that would be most helpful to decisionmakers.

As pointed out in other parts of this book, criteria involve *both* costs and the achievement of objectives. To say, on the one hand, that we want the lowest-cost system is no test. What would this mean? The lowest cost to do what? To say, on the other hand, that we want the system that can destroy at least 80 out of 100 targets is not sufficient. There are several ways to go about this task if it is feasible at all, and the criterion is supposed to sort out the *preferred* course of action.

Let us see how both cost and the objective could enter into the criterion. The objective might be "fixed" at the ability to do a particular amount of damage, and we could then seek the lowest-cost way to achieve this ability. Or, the objective and cost might enter into the criterion in a different way: The objective could be defined as the ability to do a certain type of damage, without the damage level being fixed; instead, cost could be fixed, and the way to achieve the greatest amount of this objective at the specified cost could be sought. Note that the term "objectives" is used to mean tasks or missions. Unless this is kept in mind, the term may cause confusion because in an ultimate sense the objective and the criterion may appear to be the same thing. That is, our ultimate objective might be described as the maximization of military worth with given constraints, and of course a very fine criterion (if it could be used) would be the maximization of military worth with the given constraints. Hence, it is necessary to remember that by objectives we mean positive values or desirable achievements that ordinarily entail some negative values or costs. And the criterion must take both of them into account.

Unless restrained, the criterion problem can embrace the spelling out of objectives and cost in full detail, swallowing up most of the problem of analyzing systems. If the measure of damage is shifted, if the manner of measuring costs is altered, or if different constraints are imposed, all *can* be regarded as changes in the criterion. In other words, it is hard to draw the line between problems of criteria and problems of measurement. In this discussion, however, we shall confine ourselves to *general* questions about criteria, excluding questions about detailed measurements.

5.1. The inevitability of proximate criteria

Perhaps ideally we should choose that weapons system or course of action which maximizes military worth (gains minus costs). But this is no more helpful than saying that we want the best. For nobody knows precisely how military worth is related to the outcomes of various courses of action. Military achievements and costs can rarely be expressed in the same units (for example, in dollars), and we cannot compute gains *minus* costs for each of the alternative systems. For these reasons, workable proximate criteria, rather than perfect ultimate ones, must be used. But we do not have to use perfect criteria in order for analysis to be valuable. To use a homely aphorism, "Shoes don't fit perfectly very often, but a lot of ground can be covered just the same".

The minimum cost of having a designated capability is not an ultimate or perfect criterion; if we specified a different time period or capability, or looked at consequences outside the ability to destroy targets, the outcomes under various systems might look different. Nonetheless, to the extent that this is the sort of capability we desire, this criterion points to the best system. In any event, it is pertinent to see how various striking forces rank in terms of this test, for it is important to have at least this much information about the outcomes under various systems.

5.2. SUBOPTIMIZATION AND CRITERIA

The selection of good criteria is made difficult in part by the fact that problems of choice must be broken down into component pieces or sub-problems. It is inevitable that decisionmaking be broken into component parts, some decisions being made by "high level" officials or groups, and some being delegated to "lower levels". All decisions cannot be made by one official or group. Similarly, the process of analysis must be broken into parts; alternatives at all levels cannot be analyzed simultaneously. (No connotation of greater or lesser significance should be associated with these terms "higher" and "lower levels".)

Either analysts or decisionmakers, then, always compare alternative courses of action that pertain to a *part* of the military problem. Other choices are temporarily shelved, possible decisions about some things being neglected, specific decisions about others being taken for granted. The resulting analyses are intended to help find optimal solutions, or rather policies that are improvements over proposed solutions, to subproblems. In the language of systems analysis, these are "suboptimizations".

Figure 5.1 may help to show exactly what is meant by suboptimization and what its advantages and disadvantages are. When trying to solve each of the problems indicated in Fig. 5.1, we simply have to put many of the others aside temporarily. In comparing courses of action at each level, only a few of the things open to decision can be allowed to vary simultaneously. Otherwise, the models would become impossibly cumbersome, and, as pointed out earlier, the number of calculations to consider would mount into the thousands. Thus, if we compared alternative oxygen suppliers, we would take for granted most decisions at higher levels. In comparing weapon systems for strategic air warfare, we might not simultaneously seek the optimal allocation of the Air Force budget to the Air Defense Command, the Tactical Air Command, and all other missions; and we would not simultaneously search for the best oxygen mask or pre-flight procedure. To be sure, where other choices (for example, the use of electronic countermeasures or dogleg courses) were crucial to the performance of alternative vehicles, we would vary these factors

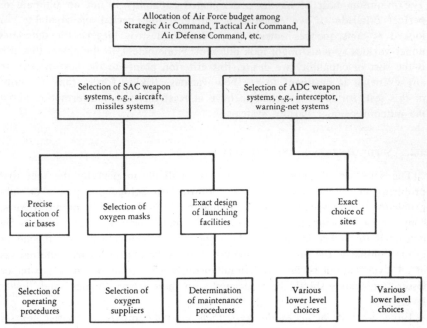

Fig. 5.1 Suboptimization illustrated

and try to choose optimal ways of employing each vehicle. Nonetheless, we
would "slice off" a subproblem in each case and fix or ignore numerous
choices at other levels.

Suboptimization brings with it, on the one hand, certain advantages. One
is that more detail can be taken into account by analysis in the small than
by broader analyses. Models can be less aggregative, and they may for that
reason yield more accurate predictions. On the other hand, suboptimization
brings great difficulties in the selection of criteria, because lower level tests
can so easily be inconsistent with higher level criteria. Let us consider the
procurement of a bombsight and take an extreme illustration: If the test we
use is the minimum cost of achieving some specified laboratory performance,
the bombsight might be too big to put inside any feasible bomber. It is
hazardous to "factor out" this decision from the larger problem, the selection
of the bombing system. A good decision about the sight depends upon the
rest of the bombing system. The criterion of the best bombsight should be
consistent with the criterion of the best bombing system. Consider another
extreme illustration: Suppose that we compare alternative machine guns and
adopt as our test the lowest-cost gun that will fire a number of rounds
equivalent to three years' steady combat operation. Experience may indicate,

however, that such durability is superfluous, since guns are usually lost after, say, the equivalent of three months' combat. The criterion of the best machine gun should be related to the test of an effective ground force. Hence, it is always urgent at least to ponder higher level criteria in order to avoid serious inconsistencies.

In summary, then, plausible tests in lower level choices can easily be inconsistent with higher level criteria. This is not to say that we should always carry out analysis only for the highest level problems of choice. On the contrary, systems analysis *must* attack subproblems. Many such problems *can* be factored out and sensible criteria selected. To help choose SAC missiles, an analysis need not simultaneously seek the optimal helicopter for the Navy or the optimal defense budget. The effects of different budgets (within a reasonable range) or of different helicopters on the performance of missile systems may be slight, and to ignore them in making the comparison may do no great harm. All this is to say, however, that we must keep the advantages and disadvantages in mind, and make the scope of each analysis a reasonable compromise that will avoid impossibly aggregative models, on the one hand, and excessively narrow criteria, on the other.

5.3. SOME COMMON CRITERION ERRORS

Because proximate criteria and piecemeal analysis must be employed, there is always danger of adopting wrong criteria. Some of the errors that occur most often can be put into categories and should be given particular emphasis.

Ignoring Absolute Scale of Objective or Cost

One common test is the ratio of effectiveness to cost, that is, the ratio of achievement-of-objective to cost. For instance, in the selection of bombing systems, the test might be the maximum ratio of targets destroyed to cost, that is, maximum targets destroyed per dollar cost. This sounds like a reasonable criterion, yet it could let the scale of the system wander freely from a $ 500 billion system to cheap weapons of low effectiveness. As a matter of fact, it would probably favor existing weapons of early vintage. Suppose, for instance, that one bombing system, already on hand and relatively simple to maintain, would destroy 10 targets and cost $ 1billion (a ratio of 10 to 1), while another system would destroy 200 targets and cost $ 50 billion (a ratio of 4 to 1). Should we choose the former—a weapons system which might merely invite and lose a war inexpensively? The answer is no, we cannot afford to ignore the scale of the activity — the absolute amount of damage the system could do, or the absolute amount of its cost. To bring this point home, let us suppose that we are comparing two dwellings, and we accept floorspace as a suitable measure of what we want.

How does the ratio of effectiveness to cost perform as a criterion? Dwelling A has 1500 sq ft and costs $ 18 000 (a ratio of 1 to 12); B has 2800 sq ft and costs $ 28 000 (a ratio of 1 to 10). Is B an obvious choice? Clearly we must be concerned about the scale—about the absolute amount of space the house will provide or the absolute amount of money the house will cost. The real question, concealed by the ratio, is the following: Is the extra 1300 sq ft worth an extra $ 10 000?

Without constraints on the budget or the scale of effectiveness, then, ratios may point to extreme solutions and may not be consistent at all with higher level criteria. Now, suppose that we impose a constraint confining our consideration to a sensible budget range. Indeed, the example above might be considered as a case in point. In that case, the ratio is prevented from carrying us outside the constraint, but its significance is not clear until the range is narrowed to a fixed budget or objective.

Setting the Wrong Objective or Scale of Objective

It appears that the most suitable criterion form in most problems is to maximize the achievement of the objective for a given cost, or to minimize the cost of achieving a specified objective. These two are equivalent criterion forms if the scale of either the objective or the cost is the same in the two tests. That is, if the test of maximum target capability for a budget of $ 1 billion points to the policy that destroys 10 targets, then the test of minimum cost to achieve a fixed target capability of 10 will point to the same policy. The two tests also yield equivalent information if calculations are carried out at numerous different scales of cost and achievement. The choice between the two criterion forms depends largely upon whether it is cost or objective which can be fixed with the greater degree of correctness.

This leads us to the next type of criterion error: fixing the objective, or alternatively the cost, incorrectly. The difficulties apply to fixing either cost or objective, but let us focus attention on the latter. In the example just discussed, if the objective is fixed as the ability to destroy 10 targets, one system is best; if it is fixed as the ability to destroy 200 targets, another system is best. The preferred system may also be sensitive to the severity of damage that is counted as destroying a target. Thus, to set the objective uncritically may be to choose a bad criterion.

Ignoring Uncertainty

Another type of criterion error is to ignore uncertainty. For example, the specified objective, say the capability of destroying 200 targets, may ignore uncertainty about the kind of war, and hence the kind of target, that should be considered. There is a chance that the appropriate targets will turn out to be solely the enemy's military installations, or solely his industrial-population centers, or various mixtures of the two. If the criterion is in terms of one particular objective, ignores the possible relevance of other objectives, and diverts us from the aim of hedging against contingencies, the criterion may be misleading.

The criterion may ignore uncertainty about the kind of war and the strategic situation. Also easily neglected is the uncertainty surrounding technology or the occurrence of chance events. Suppose that one system would *"on the average"* destroy a given target complex for the least cost, or destroy the most targets for a given cost. However, suppose this system fails miserably one time out of five. Clearly, outcomes other than the "average" or expected result are important to the choice.

Some of the things that can be done to deal with uncertainty are indicated in the final section of this chapter. Some fairly subtle criterion problems arise under conditions of uncertainty. Here I wish to discuss only the simpler and more general issues and to emphasize that devising criteria in such a way as to conceal uncertainty can lead to grievous error.

Ignoring Effects on Other Operations

Another type of error is to choose criteria that neglect the impact of alternative courses of action on costs or achievements in *other* operations. Suppose fighter-aircraft designs are being compared, and the test is the minimum cost of getting a .9 probability of destroying enemy fighters in duels of one against one. Here, the scale of effectiveness is pinned down, and no ratio is going to pick out the old P-39 as the best of the lot. But we still have trouble. A fighter with this effectiveness in a duel of one against one may be fine individually, yet comparatively ineffective in a group's mission. The test ignores the impact on group effectiveness in combat, reliability and aborts, range and frequency of contact with the enemy, and so on. With this test, the plane might cost so much that we could buy only a few. Thus, it is difficult to factor out this subproblem in this fashion; one almost has to fit the fighters into a larger operation in order to select a sensible test.

Even effectiveness in a broad fighter operation (or other mission) may decrease the achievement of tasks elsewhere (or increase the cost of achieving those other objectives). As a simple example, a weapon may be sufficiently effective that the enemy shifts some of his counterforces to another mission. The apparent effectiveness of the weapon must be partly offset by the new difficulties encountered in other missions[1].

---

[1] See Charles Hitch, "Sub-Optimization in Operations Problems", *Journal of the Operations Research Society of America,* vol. 1, no. 3, May 1953, p. 92.

Adopting Wrong Concepts of Cost

Suppose the test is maximum targets destroyed for a given fissile-material stock. This test would point to a system which used planes and crews wastefully; in effect, the analysis would treat inputs other than fissile material as if they were free and had no value. Maximum targets destroyed for a given set of *specific* inputs would also be wrong if in fact the purchase of various sets of inputs is feasible. As these types of errors are discussed elsewhere in this book, I shall do no more than mention them here.

Ignoring the Time Dimension

In choosing policies for deterrence, time is an important factor in the statement of the objective and hence of the criterion. Note how the recommendations might differ if different time periods were considered. If the criterion is minimum cost of maintaining the designated capability in 1965–1967, a modification of existing systems might be preferred; when the test pertains to a longer period after 1965, other systems would probably be superior.

Consider a lower level problem of choice. Suppose the test in comparing alternative means of storing aircraft fuel is the minimum cost of keeping fuel up to certain specifications, for example, gum content not to exceed x milligrams per gallon. In this comparison, time is of the essence. If the results are to be at all useful, one must ask: storage as of what date and for how long? In some problems, time may be the most important part of the criterion. Resources may be considered as fixed, and the task too may be specified in every detail except date of achievement. If such constraints make sense, the test would be to accomplish the given task at the earliest possible date. In any event, we cannot afford to be careless with respect to the time dimension of the objective (or of costs) in choosing the criterion.

Trying To Use an "Overdetermined" Test

It is often said that through systems analysis we can get "the most striking power for the least money". Consider the criterion implicit in the following statement: "The Germans' triumphant campaign . . . was inspired by the idea of . . . achieving the unexpected in direction, time, and method, preceded by the fullest possible distraction and followed by the quickest possible exploitation along the line of least resistance to the deepest possible range[2]." Such tests are "overdetermined" in the sense that all these things cannot possibly

---

[2] B. H. Liddell Hart, *Strategy,* Frederick A. Praeger, Inc., New York, 1954, p. 240.

be done at one time. It is like maximizing the amount of aspirin you buy while simultaneously minimizing the amount of money spent for them. This type of error may not seem serious, since analysts cannot actually use such criteria when they prepare quantitative estimates. Nonetheless, this misconception should not be taken too lightly, for from such confusion some rather wild compromise criteria may emerge.

Applying "Good" Criteria to the Wrong Problems

A good criterion in the comparison of one set of alternative actions may not be a satisfactory test in the evaluation of a different set of policies. Consequently, the criterion used in analyzing one problem of choice should not be applied *mechanically* to a different problem. For instance, suppose we compare the capabilities and costs of procuring and using alternative strategic deterrent systems. The payoffs and costs are quite properly the estimated costs and performances that would result from operating those weapon systems, and the criterion can be minimum cost of achieving a designated performance. Suppose the alternatives to be considered are not the *purchase-and-use* of the alternative systems but rather the *development-to-the-next-stage* of such weapons. In other words, suppose the question is not "Which weapons should be procured and operated?" Instead it is "Which weapons should be developed further?" In answering the latter question, we cannot mechanically apply the test used to compare procurement policies. The reason is that the payoffs and costs of procuring and operating the weapons are not the same as the payoffs and costs of deciding to develop them. The performance and costs of buying and operating the alternative systems indicate the *potential* payoffs from the successful development of each one. These estimates provide information about the potential worth of alternative weapons, *if* successfully developed. On the cost side, the estimates directly pertinent to the development decision are the costs of developing each weapon to the next stage, that is, excluding procurement and operating costs.

Note too that the test used in comparing alternative procurement policies says nothing about the best path to the development of any weapon system. The alternative paths include (a) trying to develop a weapon *as a system*, with detailed specifications drawn up at the outset, or (b) proceeding toward these weapon systems by one of many step-by-step possibilities, with preliminary tests of components, experimental configurations, and series of "breadboard models". Choosing the sequence of developmental steps is a different problem from either selecting the general type of weapons to develop or choosing the ones to be procured.

To repeat, determining the lowest-cost system to maintain a stated capability is pertinent to development as well as to procurement decisions, but the significance of the analysis is different in the two cases. A good criterion for comparing procurement policies cannot be a definitive test in comparing development policies.

5.4. WHAT CAN BE DONE?

What can be done to keep bad criteria from leading us astray? The prescription in general terms is to "be careful", but perhaps one can be at least a little more specific. First, we can guard against nonsense tests and the more obvious errors discussed above. Second, we can make a careful inquiry into possible criteria for each analysis—that is, inquire into the relationship between proximate tests and higher level criteria. This calls for analytical effort. We cannot just put our heads in our hands and come up with correct criteria by means of introspection or intuition. We have to keep asking whether the criterion is consistent with higher level tests and whether the test takes into account major effects on other operations. Such inquiry has to be on an *ad hoc* basis. We cannot analyze alternative criteria in general and come up with a permanent shelf of acceptable ones. The "appropriate" test is peculiar to each problem.

Third, we can compare the systems in terms of more than one test, and look for dominance with respect to these tests. In comparing policies for deterrence, suppose several tests are used: minimum cost of achieving a specified capability with two different target objectives or two different enemy strategies. If the same system is best for all these tests, that system is dominant. Fourth, we can try to use a fortiori reasoning wherever possible, that is, to reason that if a system is best in one set of circumstances, it is, with still stronger force, best in some other set of circumstances. Thus, if an aircraft system turned out to be better than a missile system against soft targets, one could argue that the aircraft system (because of its greater accuracy) would show up all the more favorably against hard targets.

Fifth, we can sometimes allow for shortcomings of the criterion when interpreting the analysis, drawing conclusions, and drafting recommendations. One study of offensive systems showed that a particular system would probably do a given job at minimum cost—yet concluded that this system, on account of uncertainty, might well be the worst rather than the best choice. Finally, we may in some instances perform "consumers' research" explicitly, giving up the use of any neat criterion. In other words, we can simply spell out, for sensible alternatives, certain relevant consequences called costs and others called the achievement of objectives. The analyst or the customer may then use the information in making recommendations. This would mean using judgment in drawing the conclusions rather than in devising a definitive criterion.

Some or all of these things have been done, or these precautions taken, in various studies. The difficulties stressed here do not pull the rug out from under analytical effort. While the criterion problem is tough, its recognition hurts only the *misuse* of systems studies, and surely enhances the fundamental usefulness of analysis.

Chapter 6

THE RELEVANCE OF COSTS [1]

MALCOLM W. HOAG

There is a very general sense in which cost considerations are relevant to many—probably to most—of the diverse studies that fall under the heading of systems analysis. Whenever, for the attainment of a fixed level of any objective in a particular operation, we seek to minimize the drain upon the inputs because they are valuable to the attainment of objectives elsewhere, we are concerned with the minimization of real cost. By real cost we mean the value of the alternative objectives that are sacrificed. Once we proceed beyond this generality, however, cost considerations are relevant in different ways for different groups of operations research studies. Sometimes real costs are pertinent, sometimes not; and where real costs are pertinent, they may or may not be acceptably approximated by money costs. To apply cost considerations properly, it is important to discriminate among different groups of problems.

6.1. FIXED INPUTS, ONE OBJECTIVE

When the operations analyst is concerned with securing maximum output from inputs that are both fixed in total amount and specific to the one use, we can identify a first category of problems in which no cost considerations enter. If the inputs are really specific to the one use, they are of no value elsewhere. The real cost of their employment is zero. Consequently, the only advice about cost considerations that is relevant is that the operations analyst should proceed with a straightforward maximization uninhibited by any historical information on costs that he may happen to have. There is no point in economizing in the use of a particular input merely because it was once expensive: "Bygones are forever bygones".

To say that cost considerations are not involved in this first category of problems does not in the least mean that such problems are easy or unimportant. Many challenging problems for operations research probably approximate the conditions that define this category, although it is probable that

---

[1] This chapter was published in *Operations Research,* vol. 4, no. 4, August 1956, pp. 448–459.

very few would meet those conditions strictly. Suppose an analyst for the Air Force were given the problem of recommending tactics to maximize damage to a particular kind of target, subject to specific constraints of current weapon and airplane availabilities. Clearly this is a formidable problem. There are many interrelated variables of interest, and many difficult problems of estimation are bound to be involved in his analysis. In order to provide a convenient hypothetical example for present purposes, however, I assume that this hard problem can be and is solved.

6.2. FIXED INPUTS, MULTIPLE OBJECTIVES

We can identify a second category of problems encountered in operations research when two or more objectives compete for the employment of inputs whose total current supplies are fixed. Let us see how and why real cost considerations enter in this category of problems, although production costs are not involved. Suppose we have two Air Force combat units, each assigned a different kind of target, and each eager to maximize its combat capability. Suppose further that the available inputs can be conveniently aggregated into just two items, units of fissile material and numbers of airplanes of a particular type. I assume that the initial allocations are 8 units of fissile material and 32 airplanes to Type I targets, and the exact reverse, 32 units of fissile material and 8 airplanes, to Type II targets.

We can now pose a different, or, if you like, higher level problem for operations analysis. Can a better allocation of these two aggregate inputs between these two target objectives be recommended even if we are unable to relate the military worth of one kind of target objective to the worth of the other? A better allocation can clearly be recommended if we find that more of one objective can be attained without loss to the other, that is, if the real cost of the one objective had not been minimized. Now the problem of the operations analyst is to establish the conditions for allocations of these inputs that will minimize real cost.

For this different problem an operations analyst would have to estimate for each kind of target the probable results from alternative combinations of the inputs in question when, for each combination considered, the maximum possible result is sought. Here I simply assume that the hard work of this analysis is done, and that the probable relations between different combinations of inputs and outputs have been established. Moreover, given the great convenience of a hypothetical example, it is assumed that these relations can be approximated in a tolerable way by very simple functions. I assume that one result of the study of Type I operations is the curve drawn in Fig. 6.1. That curve describes the alternative combinations of these two inputs that would be consistent with retention of the target capability that was the

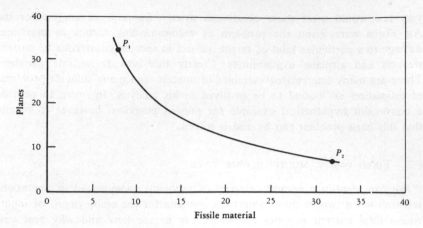

Fig. 6.1 Constant-output combinations

maximum possible with the initial allocation of inputs, and every point on the curve reflects the optimal tactics for the given combination of inputs.

The slope of the curve reflects possibilities of substituting one of these inputs for another. Greater supplies of fissile material would make it possible to have more bombs or bigger bombs. That, in turn, would make it possible to fly fewer sorties, for a greater number of bombs or more powerful bombs would raise the probability of target destruction on any particular sortie, a diminution in the requirements for pre- and post-strike reconnaissance might be possible, and so forth. But the possibilities of substitution are limited. In the nature of the case, one would expect that substitution would become increasingly difficult the more one attempted to substitute fissile material for airplanes. That phenomenon is illustrated, very conveniently if very unrealistically, by making the incremental rate of substitution between inputs at any point equal to the input proportions at that point. At the initial allocation to Type I targets—32 planes and 8 units of fissile material, or P_1 in Fig. 6.1—the incremental rate of substitution is 4 planes for 1 unit of fissile material. Should the allocation of inputs be reversed to 32 units of fissile material and 8 planes at P_2, however, the incremental rate of substitution would be 1 plane for 4 units of fissile material. Between P_1 and P_2 the incremental rate of substitution changes sixteenfold.

One would certainly expect to find a somewhat different functional relation for the second and different kind of target. But let us assume, again for simplicity, that the same relation prevails for both. Consequently, the initial situation for Type II targets is described by P_2 on Fig. 6.1. The diversity in proportions of inputs provided for the two uses is striking when the functional relation between inputs and outputs is the same. But that can happen in practice. The initial allocations of inputs to the two uses might have been derived quite independently, and an occasion for inquiring about any consistency in allocations between the two uses might never have arisen. It is even possible that the difference in initial input proportions arose because the allocations were decided by different operations analyses. Perhaps the initial allocation to Type I targets was decided upon in the light of an operation analysis whose criterion was that of maximizing likely target output per unit of fissile material, because that input was held to be in particularly scarce supply. On the other hand, an operations analysis for Type II targets may have used a criterion of maximizing likely target output per airplane because of a natural concern with operational losses. Either criterion is obviously incomplete because it concentrates upon one input as if the real cost of employment of the other input in question were zero.

To show that this sort of incomplete criterion is treacherous, we need only look at our two allocations simultaneously. It is convenient to do so by turning the diagram that applies to Type II targets by 180° in order to super-impose it on the diagram that applies to Type I targets. That generates Fig. 6.2, in which allocations to Type I targets are measured by the lower set of axes and allocations to Type II by the upper axes. The initial allocations to the two commands are now represented by a common point. Figure 6.2 is a box diagram in which any point represents a feasible allocation between the two uses of the given total supply of inputs that exhaust the available supplies. But while all points are feasible, some are clearly better than others.

What is wrong with the initial allocation is best demonstrated by showing the results of changing it. The general direction of a rewarding change is easily perceived. For Type I targets, fissile material is so scarce that the sub-stitution value of one unit of it is worth four planes. In great contrast, fissile material for Type II targets is so plentiful that one unit of it is valued in substitution terms at only one-fourth of a plane. Because of the great in-consistency between the substitution values of an identical unit in two different uses, there is room for mutual gain by trading inputs between these two uses. Suppose, for example, that inputs are traded between the two commands involved on the basis that each gives up one unit of its less valued kind of input in order to get one unit of the kind of input it values more, so that they are trading at terms of 1 : 1. Each command gains markedly by such a transaction. Initially what each receives is worth four times as much as that which is given. Since trade is so mutually profitable, each will desire to expand it. A limit to mutual gain from such trade is imposed, of course, because the substitution value of one input for the other can be expected to change in an offsetting way as trade proceeds. One point at which the limit would be reached, for example, is P_3 in Fig. 6.2. At P_3 the allocation would be 20 units of fissile material and 20 planes to each command, and the rate

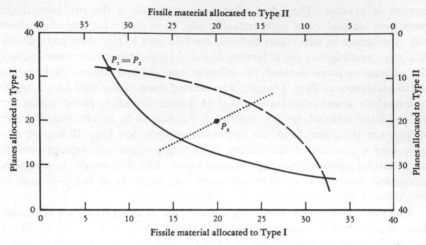

Fig. 6.2   Joint allocations

of substitution between the two inputs for either target type would have fallen to $1:1$ in correspondence with the trading rate between them. There would no longer be a possibility of trading a less valued for a more valued input. But in moving from P_1 to P_3, the combat capability of both commands would be markedly enhanced[2].

There are other points in Fig. 6.2 that satisfy this condition of a rate of substitution between the two inputs of $1:1$ in each use, a rate that makes the use value conform with the ratio of total input availabilities. These points define the set of efficient allocations for this problem, shown as a dotted line in Fig. 6.2. This set has the property that more of one kind of target capability cannot be achieved except at the cost of the other capability. Such is not the case with inefficient allocations like the assumed initial ones. Consequently, it is important that allocations of shared inputs between competing uses be at one of these efficient points, and it should be the objective of the operations analyst to establish where the efficient points lie. When he has done so, he will have established the necessary conditions for minimizing

---

[2]   The simple relation assumed was complicated just enough to be realistic in (1) showing increasing lack of substitutability of one input for the other as substitution proceeded, and (2) exhibiting constant returns to scale, that is, doubling both inputs doubles output. The relation is

Accordingly, at P_1 or P_2
$$\text{Targets} = 16 \ \sqrt{FM} \ \sqrt{P}.$$

and at P_3
$$\text{Targets} = 16 \ \sqrt{32} \ \sqrt{8} \ = 256,$$
$$\text{Targets} = 16 \ \sqrt{20} \ \sqrt{20} \ = 320.$$

the real costs of obtaining stipulated amounts of one objective in terms of the other objective foregone.

The analyst who works on Type II problems must derive measures of the scarcity value in the use of one input in terms of another, which may, but probably will not, accord with the past record of the prices at which one input was secured relative to another. The measures would only be in accord if past planning had been optimal, or, if you prefer, lucky. Incidentally, the derived measures of scarcity value are by-products of a linear programming optimization when that technique is employed, and may be familiar to some as "shadow prices". The analyst will be concerned with the achievement of consistency in the scarcity values of inputs in different uses. The "operation" at issue then involves more than one objective competing for the same inputs, and that operation must be looked at as a whole if appropriate measures of efficiency are to be derived from considerations that are internal to the analysis.

6.3. VARIABLE INPUT SUPPLIES

The problem of an operations analyst may be longer in range than the example I have used, and there may be more time to adjust the operations in question. Where this is the case, we have a third category of problems to which the rest of our discussion applies. Under these circumstances it is no longer appropriate to solve allocation problems as if the aggregate supplies of inputs were fixed in amount and specific in form. To do so would be to ignore possible great improvements in efficiency due to changing the form and amounts of the inputs to be supplied. The same argument for consistency in the substitution value of different inputs among alternative uses still applies, but an extended application is required. Procurement costs, and therefore ultimately production costs, become relevant. We must now ask, "At what rate can one input be substituted for another, not only in use, but also in prospective availability?" If the rate at which one input can be made available in terms of the other diverges from the rate at which the one input can be expected to substitute for the other in the particular use in question, there are opportunities for futher improvement. The inputs to the one operation are outputs elsewhere in the economy, and more of one can be obtained at the cost of less of the other by shifting resources from the production of one to that of the other. Should resources be shifted?

The application of this extended test of efficiency is simple only if it is clear that the appropriate general constraint is a budgetary one and if unlimited quantities of all the inputs in question can be bought and sold at known prices. Or, if they can be bought on these terms but not sold, the test is simple only if the inputs are similar in vital respects, namely, in our military example, if they can be expected to have a similar service life. For our military example, we should have a simple solution only if we could buy and sell fissile material or airplanes at a rate of, say, two units of fissile material for the same price as one airplane. If that is possible, we can enhance our target capabilities or reduce our total costs still further by buying fewer airplanes and more fissile material. A new set of efficient allocations would be defined. In terms of the constant output curve in Fig. 6.1, it would now pay to move to a point on the curve at which the rate of substitution of fissile material for airplanes would be expected to be $2:1$ rather than $1:1$.

But our military example was chosen to raise some hard problems: What costs are pertinent to whom, and how are they to be measured? "To whom?" is an especially pertinent question because at least two governmental organizations are involved—the Air Force and the Atomic Energy Commission. If an operations analyst works on a purely Air Force optimization, clearly he will get an answer that military capability will be maximized for given Air Force budgets by using fissile material so liberally that further units of fissile material could not be put to any use at all (that is, to a point where fissile material no longer had any scarcity value). From the point of view of the United States this is undoubtedly a bad solution because the excessively liberal supplies of fissile material can only be provided at real cost. To get any sort of a sensible answer from the point of view of the government as a whole, a joint optimization must be tackled involving the operations of the Atomic Energy Commission and its current and prospective customers. Needless to say, such a joint optimization is a staggering problem[3].

The problem of whose costs ought to be considered in the analysis comes up often in operations research. The analyst must confine his attention to a workably small segment of a problem, but he must beware that no great costs or benefits that "spill over" between the operation in question and other operations are improperly left out of account. For example, in the design of a car parking operation for an airport, one size of lot and pricing policy may be derived from a criterion of maximizing net parking revenues, and another size of lot and pricing policy from the criterion of maximizing net revenues for the air operations as a whole[4]. Given the first criterion, the revenue lost because a few people will not be able to park, and thereby will miss their planes, might seem a small consideration. But it may be a major consideration to the airlines to whom the major loss "spills over".

---

[3] For a suggestive unclassified discussion, see S. Enke, *Some Economic Aspects of Fissionable Material,* The RAND Corporation, P-462, November 25, 1953; also published in *The Quarterly Journal of Economics,* vol. 68, no. 2, May 1954, pp. 217–232.

[4] S. Waldron and J. Steinhardt, "Comments on 'Evaluating the Adequacy of Airport Parking Lots'", *Operations Research,* vol. 4, no. 1, February 1956, pp. 122–123.

The problem of what costs are to be considered is an allied question. I assume here that the operations analyst has some latitude in choosing or advising what costs ought to be considered, rather than simply being told the ones to consider. To revert to our fissile-material illustration, an analyst tackling the ambitious joint optimization would like to estimate explicitly the increase in aircraft production that would be made possible by a given release of resources from fissile-material production. Such an estimate would give him a real measure of available supplies of the one in terms of the other, and that measure could be compared to his estimate of prospective substitutability in use. But, as we all know, adjustments in the economy to altered patterns of production typically take place indirectly rather than directly, and with many subtle ramifications. The highly qualified chemical engineer released at Hanford does not move directly to a job as an aeronautic specialist at Seattle. If, for a particular Type III problem, the indirect adjustments involved in resource shifts can be traced explicitly by an operations analyst, and satisfactory measures of comparative real resource cost derived, all power to him.

If comparative real costs cannot be derived explicitly, which is likely, the operations analyst is left with a choice between two broad alternatives. He can use a measure of efficiency derived from considerations internal to his analysis that do not involve production costs, or he can assume that a dollar's command over resources involves the same real costs in one place as in another in the economy, and substitute estimated money costs for real costs in his analysis. Neither alternative is perfectly satisfactory, for each is likely to involve some arbitrary elements. The elements of arbitrariness are likely to be gross, however, if the analyst resorts to the first alternative. What is his measure of efficiency to be? One possibility is to use the same sort of measures that are appropriate for Type II problems, and be content to seek consistency in scarcity values within the operations at issue on the assumption that specific constraints similar to those that govern current operations will govern future operations. In this case, the treatment of cost considerations stops short of production costs. But clearly this is no answer, for it ignores Type III problems rather than solves them.

Another possibility is to substitute efficiency measures that do not involve costs at all in the general sense that I have been using the term, but involve physical measures internal to the analysis. The man-hours required directly in certain future operations may be minimized, to use one obviously bad example. But if such a partial measure is used, inputs left out of the measure are illicitly assumed to be free. What of the cost of the capital equipment required to lower direct man-hours? Moreover, the inputs included in the measure may not be weighted appropriately. What of the value of a highly skilled engineer man-hour relative to a common labor man-hour? The inclusion of all the inputs in the measure in an appropriately weighted way is required, and that means we are back at the starting point in search of measures of comparative real cost to supply the needed weights for the measure.

The second alternative of using expected money costs as measures of real costs assumes that relative prices in the market place are appropriate measures of the rates at which one item can be substituted for another in production. The analyst has only one argument in support of that assumption in general. Suppose the expected relative prices of items diverge from their potential rates of substitution in production. That will make some lines of production more profitable than others. In a competitive economy the more profitable lines of production will tend to expand at the expense of the less profitable, and the resultant altered flows of products to the market will tend to bring relative product prices into conformity with their rates of substitution in production. Ideally, a tendency toward perfect conformity will exist. The strength of that tendency, and hence the validity of the general assumption that the operations analyst makes when he uses dollar measures of costs, depends critically upon general policy measures that are likely to lie outside the purview of any particular operations analysis. One can only mention here, for example, that governmental antimonopoly measures vitally affect the strength of that tendency in the economy.

6.4. SOME SPECIAL ASPECTS

One of the general functions of government regulatory measures, incidentally, is to convert what would otherwise be "spill-over" costs and benefits between different operations in the economy into costs and benefits that are internal to the decisionmaking unit and will appropriately constrain its actions. Thus we want to tax smog creating activities enough to transfer the costs of smog back to its creators and give them an inducement to alleviate it. That general function of regulatory measures is especially relevant to operations researchers. As this function is better performed, the validity of using money costs in various operations analyses is strengthened. And to perform this function better, many good operations analyses are needed. There are many situations, particularly but not exclusively in government, where rigorous demonstrations of the existence and magnitude of "spill-over" costs and benefits are required to define truly efficient operations, but those demonstrations are lacking.

My general argument is that an operations analyst is unlikely to be able to estimate comparative production costs explicitly in real terms, and that the substitution of estimated money costs is the least unsatisfactory of the alternatives left him. This does not imply that he should use conventional money estimates uncritically. For a particular problem, an analyst may find good reason to alter some cost estimates because he discovers divergences between conventional dollar figures and the real resource costs that are pertinent to his problem.

Consider an analyst concerned with the planning of government investment projects, say the building of dams. Suppose the use of a conventional market interest rate in his calculations as one cost parameter leads to a recommended list of three dams, each of an ambitious size. But suppose a congressionally imposed budget constraint makes it impossible to build all the dams that big. One feasible solution may be to leave the plans of two dams unaffected, and drop the third. A better solution may be to build all three at reduced sizes. The way to test whether it is a better solution is to calculate what the scarcity value of capital funds really is for this government operation at various budget levels. That is, at what percentage rate must future opposed streams-over-time of costs and receipts from various alternative investment plans be discounted to make those streams equal? At a particular budget level the investment plan with the highest rate is the one to adopt. Capital funds that have a productivity of 20 per cent in an operation should not be diverted wastefully to 5 per cent uses just because that market rate of interest irrelevantly prevails elsewhere. The market rate is relevant to the private firm because it can hedge a probable pattern of future monetary returns and disbursements by investing or disinvesting in the market at about that rate. Consequently, one aspect of an analysis of the investment plans of a firm may be easier than for a government agency. But that alternative of hedging is not open to a government agency, the congressionally imposed budget constraint is especially determining, and the special features of the budget constraint must be taken into account. Different situations, of course, call for different solutions.

The treatment of time series of costs is an acute issue in our earlier military illustration. If the costs of fissile material and airplanes that would be incurred by particular choices in various future years are estimated, how are they to be summed into one measure for any effectiveness-cost comparison of alternatives? That issue is acute because fissile material is longer lived than airplanes, and may well have an appreciable salvage value in future years, while the desired military capabilities cannot be sought for only one particular contingency at one particular time. For our inherently imprecise military problem, no one neat solution is possible.

But we can improve upon the arbitrariness of a typical summation of costs over n years when one dollar in year n is valued equally with one dollar now, while one dollar in year $n + 1$ is valued at zero, a procedure especially likely to make our choices sensitive to the number chosen for n. We can apply various discount rates without such an abrupt discontinuity, experimenting with higher rates of discount than those conventionally employed because of the special uncertainty attached to future disbursements, and test the sensitivity of our results to such variation. In short, we can and should apply sensitivity tests for this rate as for other critical parameters in our analyses of whose magnitude we cannot be certain.

One general disclaimer is in order. Throughout these remarks only the efficiency aspect of choice problems has been considered. Obviously all objectives cannot be reduced to that of efficiency alone, which is one reason for using from the outset an example where important issues of efficiency can be handled despite the incommensurability of different objectives. Even in the case of a business firm, it may be very difficult to value one objective in terms of others. The managers of a business firm may desire not only high money profits, but a "quiet life". More generally, we may be interested not only in efficient allocations of inputs among différent uses in the economy as a whole, but also in "fair shares" in the distribution of wealth and income. We are not able to reduce efficiency to a common denominator with equity in any general sense.

My concern has been to identify some conceptual problems raised by cost considerations in operations research, and to stress the need to discriminate among groups of problems. In practice, of course, the entire problem will probably not fall neatly into one of the three categories that have been identified. A typical problem will have to be handled subject to a judicious blend of a general constraint and some specific constraints. An analyst probing for inefficiency in a particular operation, for example, may become convinced of manifest inefficiency before he knows whether, in our terms, it was occasioned by a neglect of proper cost considerations at a Type I, II, or III level.

I am fond of the story of the military commander who was sharply reprimanded for using coffee as a sweeping compound in his command. Presumably coffee is so valuable in its use as a beverage that it should not be diverted to sweeping, even if technically efficient in that use. But perhaps the commander was allocated so much coffee that his men could not possibly drink it all. Forbidden to sell it, his only alternative to using it as a sweeping compound was to throw it out. If that was the case, the commander was criticized for honoring the very precepts of minimizing real costs that I have been talking about.

Chapter 7

ANALYSIS AND DESIGN
OF CONFLICT SYSTEMS[1]

ALBERT WOHLSTETTER

The subject of this chapter—the design and formulation of system studies—is among the most important and at the same time among the most difficult to say anything very formal, precise, and positive about. It is easy to say a lot of negative things on the subject. But it must be clear at the outset that no rules will guarantee an effective system design. For systems analysis, or what I shall call conflict system design, is not the same thing as model construction or game building. I would like to say a bit about the distinction between them.

7.1. SYSTEMS ANALYSIS VERSUS MODELS, AND THE PROBLEMS MOTIVATING ANALYSIS

A systems analysis is an attempt to discern and answer questions of importance in choice of policy. A mathematical model, as R. D. Specht has made clear[2], is frequently a most useful device in obtaining answers to these questions. Sometimes two or three mathematical models are even more helpful. However, as he suggested, the construction and manipulation of such models is by no means the whole of the job. In fact, asking fruitful questions, ingeniously designing alternative systems to be compared, and skillfully interpreting the results of the calculations performed in the comparison, relating them to the problems that motivated the inquiry, are much more critical phases than the manipulation itself. Analysts are sometimes prone to forget this because most of their time is spent in manipulation, and because the manipulatory techniques are most easily explained and transferred—cookbook fashion.

---

[1] I want to thank J. F. Digby, Daniel Ellsberg, F. S. Hoffman, H. J. Kahn, and E. S. Quade for stimulation in connection with this chapter. An abstract of it was presented at the Second International Conference on Operational Research, Aix-en-Provence, France, September 1960.
[2] See Chapter 4.

A careful study of the Palmer method of penmanship is no foolproof formula for writing a good novel, though a clear hand, speed in at least one-finger typing, knowledge of grammar, and ability to spell all help. For a systems study, skill in quantitative model building is useful and, where the problem is complex, even essential (unlike the case of penmanship and the novel). But it is not enough. A systems study would be much easier if it were *merely* model construction.

C. J. Hitch has made it clear that systems analyses are anything but easy[3]. You will recall that he illustrated how the intrepid analyst, interested in comparing alternative systems for development, might be attempting to pick one out of a million or more alternatives. I would like to stress in this connection that the difficulties Mr. Hitch recounted arise largely because of the necessity to relate the results of calculation to the defense problems motivating the inquiry. They are, in fact, the Defense Department's difficulties. The four-to-the-tenth-power alternatives that explicitly beset the analyst are present in equal multiplicity, if not equal explicitness, whenever the Department of Defense makes a decision to develop a specific type of bomber or missile. The analyst's problem is the same, in this respect, as that of the decisionmaker.

I have talked of military decisions. My point applies at least equally to analysis for decisions and agreements to reduce or to restrict the operation of military forces, that is, arms control. The perplexities involved in arms control decisions are at least as great as those plaguing the more familiar military decisions. For one thing, an analysis for arms control needs to *include* an evaluation of the effects on the military stance of both sides and their adequacy for the political and military objectives of both sides.

It is fashionable to suggest that arms control conferences could settle issues easily if only the participants were sincere. Sincerity undoubtedly has something to do with it, but is hardly the whole of the story. Decisions on arms control, even more than decisions on arms, are extraordinarily complicated.

By pointing to the complexity of the decisionmaker's problem, I do not mean to suggest that sensible decisions are impossible without systems analysis. It is quite clear, in fact, that several have been made. Some of the million alternatives can, with impunity, be dismissed by a sensible fellow, whether an analyst or a decisionmaker. On the other hand, it is also plain that frequently in the past very important alternatives have been ignored. And while systems analysis is no guarantee that we will consider all the relevant important alternatives (systems analysis is no substitute for sense), it does force much greater explicitness and it does make the alternatives examined—and the omissions—a little more open to scrutiny.

Much debate in recent times has centered on the problems of government

---

3   See Chapter 2.

choice among the "cardinal" alternatives confronting our society, that is, the life and death issues: the decision to develop the H-bomb or to go all out on the ballistic missile program, and so on. These choices involve advanced technology, the disposition and operation of military forces, and a great many political, military, economic, and technical estimates which are intrinsically uncertain. Some of these estimates must be concealed because of the possibility of hostile use of the information. Such decisions are all too fallible, yet the exigencies of time, and the need for many sorts of specialized knowledge, as well as the requirements of secrecy, unfortunately limit the opportunities for criticism. In what follows we shall have occasion to talk about strategies for dealing with these intricate and intimately associated problems of complexity, uncertainty, and secrecy. In fact there is no final "solution" to such problems. They can only be reduced or made somewhat more manageable. However, it is worth mentioning at this point that the systematic and explicit character of a systems study does widen the possibilities of criticizing it, and so reduces to this extent the possibility of error.

The complaints not infrequently heard about the Assumptions Made in Systems Analyses do not, I think, mean that by comparison staff studies and staff decisions by military men are innocent of arbitrary or unrealistic assumptions. Much less, as I heard suggested once, that they are innocent of assumption altogether. The comparative frequency of such complaints, which are, sad to say, sometimes quite well founded, is a tribute to the relative explicitness of the assumptions and reasoning in a systems study. Intuitive judgments based on informal experience are conditioned, of course, by assumptions that are less easily penetrated. And when the judgments of experts conflict it is often hard to explain and reconcile the differences. The *ad hoc* committees that sprang up during and after the war usually have reached conclusions by pooling and compromising such expert judgments, and sometimes the assumptions underlying the conclusions are even more obscure than in the case of individual experts. Yet if the decisionmaker is not to take advice on faith, he may want to review the assumptions and evidence and the formal process of reasoning. In such a case especially, systems analysis can assist decision.

At its best, operations research or systems studies in national defense should be conceived as the quantitative method of science applied to the refractory problems described. So far in the application of such a method to decisions for unilateral national defense, the record is, I believe, rather spotty. And it has hardly been applied at all to the design and serious evaluation of bilateral arrangements for arms control.

However, there have been some signal successes. These have, I think, been greatest when the systems studies have concentrated, not on the elaboration of large-scale models, but on the difficult problems of decision described earlier, on the framing of questions which are both answerable and relevant to these problems and on the work of actually designing new and better systems. Mathematical models figure then as necessary but quite subordinate tools.

Like intuition and experience, the more elaborate models are useful primarily in much more stable situations. For example, linear programming has been useful in the petroleum and transportation industries, where the technology and markets are rather well understood and where experienced decisionmakers have arrived at fairly good solutions and find it hard to advance further. Then even small percentage gains, arrived at by securing the exact optimum allocation, more than reward the effort involved in locating this optimum. The situation is quite different where technology and objectives both change very swiftly. The problem here is not to locate the exact peak of a rather flat curve, but generally to get on some entirely different curve. I have seen studies that try to determine the exact best way to perform an operation which shouldn't be performed at all.

Unfortunately, operational researchers are sometimes infected by the disease diagnosed as "new toolism" by the mathematical statistician L. J. Savage. They come possessed of and by new tools (various forms of mathematical programming, vast air-battle simulation machine models, queuing models, and the like), and they look earnestly for a problem to which one of these tools might conceivably apply. But, if one is interested in defense decisions, it is best to begin the other way around, with the problem itself, to analyze the quantitative consequences of impending technological and political change for the systems that are currently programmed, and to devise significantly better alternatives. The tools that turn out to be useful for analysis here are likely to be more homely, but more productive.

Finally, the above suggests that a systems analysis is likely to be most helpful if the analyst has taken care to examine closely the character and source of the problem confronting the decisionmaker, the objectives he wants to achieve, the obstacles he must surmount to achieve them, and what achieving them does for him.

7.2 AN AIR FORCE EXAMPLE: GENESIS OF THE INTERCONTINENTAL MISSION

Let me illustrate three points—the complexity of the decisionmaker's problem, its substantial identity with the problem tackled by the analyst, and the usefulness to the analyst of examining the way the decisionmaker's problem arises—by recalling the history of the B-36 and the genesis of the Air Force requirement for an intercontinental bombing capability.

The B-36 was conceived in April 1941, after the fall of France and a succession of defeats isolated the United Kingdom and consolidated the German position in Western Europe. It was thought of as a hedge against the possible loss of England: an insurance that in the event of this loss, we would be able to fly over the bodies of our fallen friends to administer some damage to Germany. Major Vandenberg and a small study group in the Air Plans Section called for a bomber of 10 000-statute-mile range, capable of delivering 10 000 pounds of high explosive. By the fall of 1941, after a design contest, two prototypes were ordered.

In the B-36, it is clear that the Air Force successively confronted development, procurement, and operations problems with all of the difficulties that Mr. Hitch listed—and a few he did not mention in totting up his four-to-the-tenth-power possibilities. Questions that were explicitly considered at various times concerned alternative bases, target systems, cruise and maximum speeds, cruise and bombing altitudes, bomb loads and yields, enemy defense performance, enemy offense, feasible production schedules for the B-36 and its alternatives, distinct methods for accomplishing intercontinental bombing without an unrefueled intercontinental bomber, and a variety of others. And under each head, in general, many more than four alternatives (four values each for the development parameters) actually were considered or were forced upon us. For example, what bases might be lost or won by our forces during the war? After the war, what bases could be made available by negotiation? Would we use the B-36 against Germany? Japan? Russia? The B-36 was designed before the development in the United States of jet engines. It ended up with four jets added to reinforce its six props. And it ended up with the prospect of facing jet fighters of a performance quality its own designers could hardly have foreseen. Most striking of all perhaps, as revealed by the testimony of General Frederick Smith[4], none of the people who had been concerned with the development of the B-36 were aware of the parallel development of the A-bomb, dropped on Hiroshima, until they read the news in the daily papers.

While the two prototypes were being readied, the situation changed drastically. The prototypes had not been delivered by the summer of 1943, and by then it was clear that the United Kingdom would not be lost. We were, however, now at war with Japan. Although we had won Guadalcanal, the outcome of the stepping-stone campaign remained uncertain. The B-36 was then conceived of as a hedge against failure there. To shorten the slow development-procurement-operation cycle, we ordered 100 B-36's in advance of delivery of the prototypes. Also, at some point in this process there was trouble with the B-29, and the B-36 then assumed the role of insurance against trouble with the B-29.

---

4 *Hearings on the B-36,* Armed Services Committee, House of Representatives, *The National Defense Program—Unification and Strategy,* 81st Congress. 1st Session, Washington, D.C., October 1949.

But the stepping-stone campaign succeeded. The B-29's began to look very good, and, since there was an aluminum shortage, the B-36 program was stretched out. After VE day it was clear that the B-36 would not play a role in World War II. The Air Force, however, recognized that the possibility of World War III had to be considered, and there was a serious problem as to the base-target radii that might be then forced on us. What bases could we obtain for use in a next war, and how long would it take us to get them in time of peace or war? As we know, now that we have secured military rights in a great many countries, such negotiations are long drawn out and uncertain. The former Major (by then General) Vandenberg recommended buying the B-36 to hedge against the uncertainties of peacetime negotiation and as an alternative to seizure after the outbreak of war.

This brings us to the post-war period. Up to this time the B-36 had been conceived entirely in terms of the delivery of high explosives, with all of the limitations this imposes on effectiveness at extended distances. Hiroshima changed the aspect of strategic bombing in general and improved in particular the prospects of intercontinental delivery, which up to then could have had only a marginal value even as a measure of desperation. Now it appeared that if we could get the B-36 into production, we might have a real hedge for assuring a devastating bombing of Russia if this became necessary. The succession of war scares (beginning with the Berlin airlift) before we had developed an extensive overseas base system suggested that it might indeed be necessary.

Meanwhile, early in this period, more troubles had beset the B-36. There were performance problems, for example, in achieving military missions with the range originally called for; there were various modifications incorporating some of the advances in the state of the art not originally anticipated. By the end of 1947 other instruments for accomplishing very long-range missions were being given favorable consideration. In particular, air-refueling was recommended by the Heavy Bombardment Committee of the Air Staff. This would permit an extended radius for a system consisting of both bombers and tankers. In the state of the art as it was then, even short-radius bombers and short-radius tankers would have greater speeds and other desirable performance characteristics. The need for high performance in the penetration segment of the mission was emphasized by the perfection of jet fighters.

About this time the well-known interservice disagreements on the subject occurred, and there were also a good many differences of opinion in the Air Force. These tense disagreements centered on the relative importance of range, altitude, speed, and weight. Within the Air Force there were advocates of the B-29 as well as advocates of the B-36. The former stressed the B-29's speed superiority, the latter emphasized the B-36's longer legs. The controversy among the services flared over the bomber losses likely to be imposed by enemy active defenses and the proper targets for bombing and the effects of such bombing on the conduct of the war in Europe.

The role of strategic bombing at this time was conceived rather differently from the way we understand it today. But it was a natural extension of the problems and functions of strategic bombers during World War II. The main problems of strategic bombing in World War II were (1) to penetrate enemy defenses, reach and find the target, and (2) to destroy it. The rate of casualties that could reasonably be sustained in (1) getting to the targets and back depended on (2) the rate at which the targets could be destroyed[5]. After the war, favorable advances in bomber navigation—but, even more, the increasing deadliness of defense technology typified by the jet interceptor and surface-to-air missiles—transformed the first problem for the bombers. The net effect was to make it harder to get to the target and back. On the other hand, fission weapons greatly increased the rate of destruction possible, and thus completely transformed problem (2). We had, and assumed we would continue to have for some time, only a very limited supply of A-bombs. We assumed the enemy had none and could wage only a high-explosive campaign against the United States and our bases. The B-36 atomic attack against the enemy's vital industrial and administrative centers appeared then not merely as a retaliation to an attack on our major allies and a deterrent, but, by interrupting the slow process of attrition—which was all the enemy could hope for in a high-explosive campaign on air, ground, and sea—it appeared also as a wartime defense of our own and allied military potential. Nuclear weapons

---

[5] See the excellent *History of the Strategic Air Offensive Against Germany* by Sir Charles Webster and Noble Frankland (4 vols., Her Majesty's Stationery Office, London, 1961). The authors group the problems somewhat differently, but make essentially the same point (see vol. 1, *Preparation*, pp. 17–18).

> The operational requirements of a strategic bombing force are easy to express and difficult to attain. First, the force must have the ability to reach the designated targets, which is a question of range, penetration and navigation. Secondly, it must be able to strike effectively at those targets, which is a question of bombs adequate both in quality and in quantity and of the accuracy with which they can be aimed. Thirdly, the force must be able to return to base without suffering more than the bearable casualty rate.

The authors go on to explain that the casualty rate that's bearable depends on the rate of target destruction. The casualties that were thought of as having to be sustained were either the natural hazards of terrain and weather, *et al.*, or man-made. These latter were conceived of as enemy defenses.

> The man-made hazards consist of the enemy defenses—the fighters, anti-aircraft guns, searchlights and other countermeasures such as radio-jamming, bogus radio or visual navigational or bomb aiming signals, dummy targets and so on. (Vol. 1, p. 18.)

technology, as we shall discuss, was destined to raise quite new problems for ·
strategic bombing which did not fit neatly into the framework of bombing
before and during World War II. But these problems were much more obscure
precisely for this reason. They were not prominent in the issues agitated at
the start of the post-war period.

Throughout the discussion one thing was evident: Speed and range were
both desirable performance characteristics, as were also altitude, military load,
and a good many others; but, in general, if you obtained a maximum of one
in any given state of the arts, you sacrificed one or several of the other
performance features of the plane. Unfortunately, it is not possible to get
the best of everything; you have to trade something of one for something of
another. But, at what rate should we trade? How do speed and altitude affect
our anticipated attrition in the air? How does range affect our dependence on
our allies? Or, to take a question whose central importance emerged only
rather slowly in the course of the last decade, how might range and other
operating characteristics of the aircraft affect location, readiness, and the
prospects for destruction of these aircraft on the ground? If in the long
history of the B-36, which was part of the strategic force until 1956, no very
clear-cut answers to these questions were given, this is hardly a derogation
of the disputants. These essays in systems analysis, I am afraid, will make
evident that there are at least a few aspects of such questions that are not
exactly settled now. In fact, it is not easy to describe exactly how you go
about answering them.

The Morals

One question I do not intend to raise is whether the decisionmakers were
always right or sometimes wrong in the extended sequence of decisions they
had to make in the press of this fascinating history. Such a question I feel is
useful only to counter extreme claims. It is, of course, much easier to be
wise at this stage. (Many of the decisions, I think, were correct in context,
even if improvable with hindsight; others were questionable.)

There are, however, several morals. The first is that the military decisionmaker's lot is not an easy one. The history of the B-36 development, procurement, and operation illustrates vividly the process of selection among a huge
multiplicity of uncertain alternatives. Bases, targets, range, speed, altitude,
bombs, enemy defense and offense all assumed in prospect and in actuality
at least as many values as Mr. Hitch has suggested are present in a systems
analysis. These were not trivial variations. Just think of the change in our
bomb load from high-explosive bombs to the Hiroshima A-bomb and then
to the multimegaton H-bomb; and the change in the enemy's defenses from
props to jets and surface-to-air missiles.

Second, the objective of an Air Force decision may itself be far from simple. In the case of the B-36, the Air Force had not one but many objectives, and these were altered radically by swift changes in the political, strategic, and technical situation.

The third point also concerns objectives. It appears that differing vehicle types, like the B-29 and the B-36, might serve partially different (as well as partially identical) objectives. But how then do we compare them?

The fourth point this history illustrates is that while choice among nice or, at any rate, desired things is difficult, it is also necessary. Objectives conflict. It is not possible to move ahead simultaneously in range, speed, altitude, and everything else. How do we choose a particular combination when we make up, say, a general operating requirement for the Strategic Air Command? And how do we design our systems studies so as to answer rather than beg such questions?

The fifth point the story illuminates is the function of hedging, or insurance objectives, and the role of intercontinental bombing. The B-36 was conceived as a hedge, and the problem of hedging against analogous uncertainties is always with us. Such a problem should generate plans for contingencies which might not eventuate, in fact may be unlikely. But most military staff studies and systems analyses have overlooked this problem. How do we design studies which tackle it? And how can we best design a force that includes an insurance capability?

I have stressed that serious systems studies of military problems are no more difficult than responsible military decisions. In a sense, they are no less difficult either. They should start and end with the military objectives or, better, with the political objectives that the military means serve and with the obstacles to obtaining these goals. In the process of analysis, however, such objectives are almost certain to be refined and are very likely to be drastically altered. I would like to examine the way in which objectives enter into the process of development and to use once more some Air Force examples.

7.3. Objectives and Constraints in the Design of Systems Studies

The Air Force used to get out—in the course of planning development for an interceptor, for example, or for a bomber—various documents called Development Planning Objectives and others called General Operating Requirements. These and related documents have since been replaced by another set that perform many of the same functions but partition them somewhat differently. A hypothetical General Operating Requirement for a chemically fueled bomber might have stated as an objective that the plane be able to travel 4500 n mi and return without refueling; that it be able to go Mach 2.5 for 1200 of these 4500 n mi; that it be able to carry bombs of a certain size and weight and deliver them with an average error of less than, say, 1500 ft; and that the altitude of penetration and bombing be greater than a certain minimum. Another General Operating Requirement, say for a nuclear-powered bomber, might have stated (in addition to a certain combination of the familiar performance parameters) that the radiation dose absorbed by the crew must be no greater than .2 roentgens per hour. In a similar way, the Air Force sets certain goals in the field of base installations. For example, in the past, it has asked builders planning air bases in the continental United States to concentrate the elements on a base and so reduce to a minimum the cost of utilities, such as roads, water, and drainage pipes[6].

So far as the defense contractor is concerned, these goals are taken as constraints within which he does his work. The aircraft designer might then consider, in the light of his knowledge of the state of the arts, such questions as the best system for controlling armament on a platform moving in the way required of the given aircraft, and the optimal configuration for wing and fuselage in order to house the required military load at minimum weight or cost. If the contract concerns bases, the contractor will consider the best configuration of runways, parking areas, housing, etc., given a certain site, to keep costs to a minimum for the desired operation. If we call the objectives which the Air Force specifies "O_i", and the means which the contractor uses to obtain these objectives "M_i", we might describe this situation as follows:

$$M_i \rightarrow O_i . \tag{1}$$

Now, within the contractor's organization, in perfecting the detailed design of M_i it will be usual for M_i itself to appear in the form of a constraint or objective toward which some smaller section of his organization is working, clearly a lower-order objective than O_i. We might call it "O_{i-1}", and rewrite formula (1) as

$$O_{i-1} \rightarrow O_i . \tag{2}$$

Just as little fleas were once supposed to have smaller fleas to bite 'em, and so on ad infinitum, this process of division of labor might be continued with profit, so that we could write formula (3) as follows:

$$\ldots \rightarrow O_{i-2} \rightarrow O_{i-1} \rightarrow O_i . \tag{3}$$

For example, to achieve one component objective in the development of an interceptor there might be a very large group working on the fire control system. This group might have separate teams working on the airborne radar

---

6 See A. J. Wohlstetter, F. S. Hoffman, R. J. Lutz, and H. S. Rowen, *Selection and Use of Strategic Air Bases,* The RAND Corporation, R-266, April 1954, p. 7. See also Chapter 3 of the present book.

system, the analogue computer, and the armament systems, all of which are components of the fire control system.

The team might take as an objective the design of the airborne radar with, among other things, a scan angle 70° each side of dead ahead, and work within this constraint. The point to recognize is that just as we have extended our horizon to the left of O_i, describing the way "means" to the Air Force objective might appear in the form of narrower goals, we might also, and on occasion must, extend it to the right, looking to see what further ends are served by the Air Force requirement:

$$\ldots \to O_{i-2} \to O_{i-1} \to O_i \to O_{i+1} \to O_{i+2} \to \ldots . \tag{4}$$

Or, take our example of the fire control system for the interceptor. We might have a sequence of increasingly comprehensive systems: airborne radar, fire control system, interceptor, interceptor wing plus ground radar, a defended offensive wing consisting of an interceptor wing plus a ground radar plus a bomber wing, and so on. Figures 7.1 and 7.2 illustrate these systems.

While the narrowest systems can be treated, and, in fact, most frequently must be treated, in comparative isolation, this isolation is only comparative and never final. It is always possible that there is some important interaction affecting design on other levels. For example, it might be that it is difficult to design the radar to have a scan angle of 70° either side of on course, but by designing the interceptor to have a tighter turning radius this scan angle could be narrowed. Or one might have to move further up the echelon of systems: it might be best to relax both of these constraints and increase the accuracy of the ground data-handling process in order to achieve a better solution, thus increasing the kill probability of the interceptor plus ground radar system.

A still wider analysis of the problem of defending a strategic wing might indicate solutions in which interceptors were not involved at all. Local defense missiles, for example, might be a better way to do it. Or some form or forms of passive defense, such as dispersal or shelter or an alert permitting flyaway on receipt of warning. Or, to take an example to which we will recur, a method of operating that minimizes the presence of aircraft on the base as a regular matter in peace, as well as immediately after the outbreak of war. This last example is illustrated overseas by the practice of limiting the use of foreign bases essentially to refueling and, in the continental United States, by the air alert for heavy bombers or for a fraction of the heavy bomber force. Some specific constraints are necessary at every point in such an analysis, but none of them can be regarded as final, and on occasion relaxing the constraints will alter the problem totally.

The history of the B-36 illustrates that no set of specifications for combat radius, Mach number and the like, can be accepted as ultimate. The development of the B-36 represented a choice among alternative combinations of speed, altitude, radius, etc., and inevitably compromised some performance in order to improve others. Whether or not such a choice is a good one depends on a variety of uncertain variables whose interaction is bound to be understood better during the process of design and development, and whose aspect may change over time.

The requirement that a base design concentrate elements in order to keep utilities to a minimum is sensible so long as these bases are not seriously subject to enemy bombing attack. Up to the end of the 1950's overseas bases were designed for protection against high-explosive attack only, and those in the continental United States were designed with no protection against enemy attack whatsoever. Even in the case of intercontinental missiles, which did not enter our strategic force until the start of the 1960's, their first installations were "soft"—that is, offered very little resistance to blast and other effects of nuclear weapons. But given the past and, in particular, the prospective growth in enemy capability, it had slowly become clear that we must choose a different combination of operational convenience, cost of utilities, and resistance to attack[7]. The objectives of base design had therefore been re-evaluated. "Hard" Atlas and then Titan and Minuteman bases became operational early in the 1960's.

It is not merely that changing circumstances alter cases, that what was a correct choice at one time is outmoded by events; at any instant of time such choice is a very complicated act. The crew dosage limits for nuclear-powered aircraft, mentioned above, will illustrate this point. The question of dosage limits was central in that program. To reduce the dose rate meant increasing the shield. But, when we add such dead weight to a plane, we have to increase the gross weight by a very much larger amount. Implicit in the limits first set was the assumption that nuclear-powered bombers would be used frequently for training in time of peace, the way we use chemically fueled bombers. But, if the crew was to fly frequently for training purposes during peacetime, each man had to be limited to a very small hourly dose in order to keep lifetime doses within tolerable bounds. Small dose rates and large shields mean large sacrifices in other tightly connected performance parameters: for example, reactor size and energy output, turbine inlet temperatures, and the maximum speed attainable for the dash through enemy defenses. Frequent nuclear operation in time of peace involves large costs, not only in aircraft design to protect the air crew but also in base design and in base operation to protect the ground crews against radiation. The peacetime training requirement, then, which had an obvious utility, also had a large cost.

Later in the program two other possibilities appeared, one affecting the

---

7   *Selection and Use of Strategic Air Bases,* pp. 45 and 48.

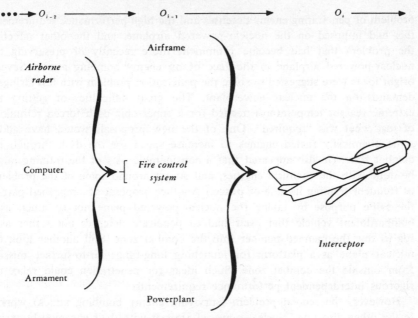

Fig. 7.1   Contractor's objectives

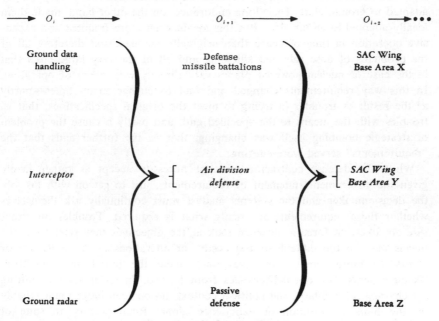

Fig. 7.2   Air force objectives

problem of penetrating enemy defenses and the high performance requirements this had imposed on the nuclear-powered airplane, and the other affecting the problem that had become prominent more recently of preserving the nuclear-powered airplane in the face of an enemy bombing attack. Several bright ideas were suggested to solve the penetration problem with less stringent demands on the nuclear powerplant. The great difficulties of getting the extreme reactor temperatures needed for a supersonic dash forced rethinking of just what was "required". One of the new proposals would have added some chemically fueled engines to increase speed for the dash through the combat zone. (It also appeared that a considerable part of the training might be done with the chemical engines, and so get around some of the problems of frequent training in time of peace.) Another proposal accomplished part of the same purpose by taking the nuclear-powered plane not so much as a bombardment vehicle that itself had to penetrate defenses but rather as a tug to tow the manned bomber into the combat zone. Still another took the nuclear plane as a platform for launching long-range air-to-surface missiles from outside the combat zone. Such ideas for penetration could relax the rigorous interdependent performance requirements.

However, the second problem (surviving enemy bombing attack) worked in the other direction. Nuclear-powered aircraft with their enormously expensive and cumbersome, remotely controlled maintenance were very poorly adapted to ground alert. Their long endurance, on the other hand, made them ideally adapted to an air alert. But this meant even more frequent and expensive operation in time of peace than originally planned, and therefore all of the problems of dose rate and shielding and all of the very large costs that in the case of nuclear-powered planes vary directly with hours of operation. In this way requirements changed and had to change many times—partly as the result of troubles in trying to meet the original specifications, that is, troubles with the means to the specified end, and partly because the problem of strategic bombing itself was changing, that is, the further ends that the "requirements" served were altering.

While the defense contractor must of necessity accept as rather firmly given the government statement of requirements, just to get on with his job, the decisionmaker and the systems analyst must continually ask themselves whether these requirements are really what is required. Troubles on either side are likely to force a quizzical look at the objectives they start with: the means may be too difficult or too costly, or alterations in the substance or clarity of more remote objectives may make the initial aims doubtful. "Requirements" are not deliverances from heaven. In so drastically shifting a technological, military, and political context, no one can judge them reliably on the basis of intuition or experience alone. Requirements, in spite of suggestions to the contrary that might be gleaned from public statements at congressional hearings, come down to the procurement officer from higher up, but not from On High. The scrutiny of constraints is one of the most fruitful aspects of a thoughtful systems study. To conclude then, goals set down in the course of policy decision are never final. Ends are means to further ends and on occasion must themselves be evaluated. One man's means is another man's objective.

7.4. BROADER OBJECTIVES: PARALLEL AND FURTHER ENDS

If we are to evaluate the fairly narrow or specific objectives we have referred to so far in terms of broader ones, what are some of these broader objectives? Are they final? I wrote formula (4) in a way that suggests that they are not. I ended up with some dots — " $O_{i+2} \rightarrow \dots$ " — suggesting "and so on". The aim of defending a strategic wing touches collateral aims such as the defense of our cities, and is a means to the further end of enemy target destruction. But what enemy targets? His war industry? Cities? Strategic forces? His ground and tactical air forces? Both the targets the enemy might attack and those that might be attacked by us are connected. And their ties are multiple and fiercely knotted.

Some of the interdependences are favorable: For example, an active area defense might jointly defend a region containing both air bases and neighboring cities. A radar warning system which serves to warn and vector the active defenses in cities might help not only in the active defense of a strategic base, but also might warn bombardment vehicles at that base in time for them to be launched, and so permit a passive defense exceeding in importance the active defense. On the other hand, some of these connections, when examined quantitatively, are less favorable. For example, looking at the continental United States in the large as well as in the small, we see that cities and strategic bases have quite different geographical distributions: aside from local separations, our urban and industrial heartland is in the northeast, and most active defense is concentrated there; strategic bases are mostly elsewhere. Or to take the example of warning, the requirements for warning a strategic force differ from the needs for active or passive defense for cities: a strategic force can be on high alert and respond quickly to warning of approaching aircraft. Still other connections might be distinctly unfavorable. For instance, aircraft evacuated in emergencies might move to airports closer to cities; very hard shelters for aircraft might require very large attacks by the enemy, and this might appear to increase by-product damage to cities.

It should be stressed that just because there are many connections, some favorable and some unfavorable, merely ticking them off on a list is barely the beginning of an analysis useful in decision. For any given set of measures many connected effects have to be evaluated numerically, and with some sophistication. This has not been well understood.

Take the by-product effects of sheltering strategic missiles. It is true that the destruction of sheltered missiles is likely to have a larger effect on neighboring cities than the destruction of unsheltered missiles. This has led some defense analysts to enunciate as a general principle: "Hardening Attracts Fire". However, in sheltering our missiles we do not donate resources for their destruction to an aggressor. In an attack directed at the destruction of these missiles and at cities an enemy would have to devote much greater resources to the attack on the missiles, if they are hard. And the distance separating missile sites from population centers is enough to make such an attack much less damaging to cities than if the brunt of the attack had directly to be borne by the cities. In short, a closer, more quantitative scrutiny would suggest a favorable interaction.

An analogous though somewhat more sophisticated point could be made for a defense of strategic missiles by keeping them moving. If this strategy does not directly divert the enemy's bombers and missiles, it may nonetheless divert enemy resources aimed at tracking our missiles, at finding them on or below the surface or in the air, or at shooting them down in the space over the enemy's own territory. The intricate knot of connections between such collateral aims requires careful quantitative analysis to disentangle.

Relating the aim and method of protecting a strategic force to further ends—the purposes for which it will be used—is quite as demanding as connecting these ends with collateral aims; and at times has to be dealt with in a systems study. Bombers of short air endurance, when placed on ground or air alert, may be useful for a first quick strike against enemy targets of high urgency, as, for example, some military targets which may call for early destruction. But if it is important to pose a *continuing* threat, after the outbreak, against enemy targets, as a means of discouraging attacks on our own cities and as a way to help bring the war to as favorable an end as possible, then we shall not want to destroy all the targets we can in a quick response. We would want to preserve both enemy targets and the means to continue threatening them. Here mobile or hard systems are likely to have the advantage of greater endurance in a wartime environment.

The aim and method of protecting a strategic force then depend among other things on the targets to be hit by the force protected. Previous examples suggest that these targets, as well as the schedule for attacking them, have altered many times and drastically: Russia's war-supporting industries, its ground forces when launched against Europe, its strategic forces, cities, and various combinations of these, and many others.

But what do we get out of threatening or attacking any of the various target systems? There is a thicket of interdependences here too, and, like it or not, under some conditions we are forced to try to penetrate it for a still broader look.

Still Broader?

There *is* something to look at. We have wanted the ability to threaten or to destroy targets inside an enemy's territory not—as some of the more lurid advocates of unilateral disarmament have imagined—out of simple blood-thirstiness; but for reasons beyond such threats or acts of destruction. As the cold war got under way, near the end of the 1940's, we started the elaborate process of building a strategic force because we needed to restrain forcible expansion by the Communists. We were concerned then especially with the problem of deterring a land war on the continent of Europe; and, if this could not be done, we wanted to bring the war to as favorable a conclusion as possible to limit the damage done. In particular, we wanted to prevent the Russians from occupying or destroying our allies. But, of course, we wanted to use means of fighting the war which would not defeat the purpose. Appropriate means would not themselves destroy our allies.

Our aims here were not simply altruism. The occupation or destruction of Europe would vastly increase the dangers to the United States. And with the growth of Russian nuclear capability, a threat to the United States itself became increasingly direct and immediate. We wanted then to deter direct attack on ourselves, and, if we did not succeed, to come out as well as we could.

In the postwar period then, it is apparent that we have pursued a number of apparently distinct, but evidently related, broad aims in developing our strategic force; to deter or to fight; and to have both these capabilities for the case of either a continental or an intercontinental aggression.

Moreover, these aims of our strategic threat have had many complex connections with other broad goals. They link directly with the possible uses of our own and allied ground, sea, and tactical air forces in local or continental wars. (Smaller wars can grow into more violent and bigger ones, through the familiar mechanism of escalation. The occurrence of local wars and the need to discourage them are associated with the probabilities of larger ones. Yet it is not always clear whether the possibility of escalation will encourage or discourage local aggression. The belief has been widespread, for example, that a near certainty of mutual destruction in a big war invites quite high levels of local violence on the assurance that both sides will keep it local. On the other hand, the great powers have moved in a gingerly way in Lebanon, Southeast Asia, and the Caribbean.)

Aside from the numerous and uncertain connections among the aims of deterring or fighting local, continental, and intercontinental wars, all of these objectives ramify further, affecting still wider and less clearly defined things that matter to us and to our friends. We discourage or combat aggressions because yielding to them would badly affect how we and our friends would live and govern ourselves. On the other hand, the way we prepare to defend ourselves affects these matters too. These ramifications get discussed when we talk of relationships of military aid to the political and economic development of less developed countries. They clearly dominate in guerrilla wars. But they also affect life in the industrialized and democratic societies of our principal allies. The "Garrison State" and "Life Underground" figure then in polemics if not in analysis. The actual proposals for national defense, and civil defense in particular, that are seriously entertained today show a vast disparity in scale between these polemical nightmares and the proposed realities. Moreover, the possible utility of analysis rather than polemics is suggested by the fact that the polemicists have reversed themselves several times; for example, on the subject of civil defense. (Not long ago, they proclaimed its benefits for urban planning, solutions to the traffic problem and the growth of greenbelts.) Nonetheless, while both the scale and direction of the effect of military choice raise essential questions, there should be no doubt as to the relevance of the effects of fulfilling our broad military aims on our even wider concerns for the amenities of life in a plural society.

Aims such as reducing the probability of attack or limiting its effects can be more or less ambitious. (1) We are likely to want highly reliable methods for keeping the probability of nuclear war low. So long as that probability is significant we might want (2) to limit its effects drastically in all circumstances of attack if it were feasible and if it could be done at reasonable cost; or, if not, we'd like (3) to soften somewhat the catastrophe in at least some plausible circumstances.

In brief, the things we want or that might be affected by military choice are extremely varied. They range from things that might be nice to have through some we might willingly settle for, to others we would take as the minimum necessary for the life of our society; and they include alliance goals, as well as interests extending beyond our allies to friendly neutral powers. In a limited sense, they extend even to our enemies since we have limited interests in common with them.

7.5. Deriving or modifying objectives

How do such broad objectives as to deter attack or to contain its effects figure in an analysis as distinct from a polemic? Systems analysts and operational researchers, as well as staff officers, in general feel rather uneasy dealing with broad aims. They are more comfortable when examining or elaborating comparatively low-level means; or with techniques for *analyzing* alternative means to a *given* end. That sort of thing seems, if one doesn't look at it too closely, much firmer ground. The larger goals, we may prefer to think, are not themselves the subject of analysis. They affect it, but—it seems—are not affected by it.

How then are they derived? Two sources that suggest themselves are (1) authority, that is, higher authority, and (2) intuition, that is, the intuition of the analyst. In fact, staff papers and systems analyses frequently start by listing some rather grand national objectives—even The National Purpose— before they pass quickly to the body of the work itself. This procedure permits concentration on the professional functions about which we all feel more comfortable.

However, though we may start with objectives derived from authority or intuition or, happily, both, regarding either of these methods as conferring validity or finality on our goals can prove troublesome. First, the author- itatively received objectives, at these higher reaches, are likely to be not merely broad, but extremely thin and rarefied; too vague to have any clear operational sense. Second, the authorities, so far as they say anything definite, and even where they don't, are likely to conflict. Among others, there will be national differences within an alliance and, within the nation, interagency, interservice, and intraservice differences and so on down to rather minute institutional subdivisions. Third, even shared or common objectives (like deterring a general war) conflict with other common objectives (like living as well as possible in the immediate future). Or they overlap with other shared objectives in obscure ways that offer quite as much trouble for the analysis. A favorable interdependence forces us into a welter of considerations as to the incremental cost to do a certain job with a defense weapon that serves a double purpose by comparison with a defense weapon serving only a single purpose. And the interdependence may be unfavorable. We may not want to kill both of two birds with one stone. Fourth, the attractiveness of an objective depends on its cost. The game may not be worth the candle. In the limiting case it may not be feasible at all.

We cannot in general settle the question as to whether there is a net divergence of several plausible complex objectives or whether they support each other without a hard and specific quantitative look. To determine costs and feasibility and effects on other ends requires close analysis and empirical investigation and is more likely to bear fruit if our investigation is not simply passive, but goes with a search for new ways of making several goals compat- ible which under existing circumstances are not. Whether aims support or detract from each other would vary with the means used; and therefore they frequently can be made to converge, that is, be made compatible by the invention of new means. Just as a poor design unnecessarily and sometimes thoughtlessly sacrifices one vital objective for another, an inventive systems design frequently can get a useful compromise of both. Earlier we spoke of the need to break through constraints, to look up sometimes from our focus on lower level needs to higher level ends. The present comment suggests the necessity of looking back down again from ends to means, to evaluate ends.

In fact, we are always in the process of choosing and modifying both means and ends. We appraise the end in terms of the means required, as well as the reverse. In short, we look at them together.

All of this may seem to conflict with familiar sayings about "values" being "ultimate", unaffected by "facts", unarguable. *De gustibus,* we all know, *non est disputandum.* Such aphorisms suggest that intuition will do, or at any rate is all that we have available.

Yet they are not totally compelling. First there is a conflict of authority even here. There have been some quite respectable sages holding the very opposite: tastes are the only things worth arguing about. Whether or not we go along with this counter-statement, it is quite clear that, where "tastes" are interpreted to include such complex preferences as we have described in defense and arms control, they are unclear, uncertain, alterable, frequently altered and *actually* argued about all the time.

Second, these matters are much too complicated for any analogy with simple sensuous preferences—like chocolate tasting better than vanilla— though such an analogy is suggested by the word "taste". Preference orderings among alternative combinations of such large aims as to deter or to fight local, continental, and intercontinental wars cannot be safely established by the touch of a tongue or its vivid recollection; or by any other unreflective impression.

Third, we can do rather better than simply to debate differences about goals. In a plural society, objectives do get changed, and not always by out-shouting or simple pressure. A systems analysis can extend areas of agreement by increasing information about uncertain events, exploring what it takes to achieve a given goal and its compatibility with other ends, and by working out systems that are good for more than one purpose.

Fourth, even where a systems analysis doesn't set out primarily to affect objectives, it is likely to.

Some of these points can be illustrated by elaborating a bit on the objective of deterring continental or intercontinental attacks and of limiting damage in case deterrence fails. I shall draw again on the history of the intercontinental mission and on the role of systems studies during the 1950's.

7.6. DETERRENCE: THE INTERCONTINENTAL MISSION AGAIN

The objective of deterrence has assumed increasing importance throughout the postwar period. The harshness of the possible outcomes of a nuclear war leads naturally to a stress on making such a war less likely. Deterrence itself, of course, is nothing new, nor is the possibility of winning hollow victories. But the classic model of Pyrrhus and Pyrrhic victories are more relevant than ever before. There may be, as the slogan says, no substitute for victory; but victory is not a substitute for everything else.

The powers differ in their willingness to take risks, and perhaps even more in their understanding of what the risks may be. Nonetheless, the wary behavior of the great powers—and of many of the minor ones—testifies that they are conscious of the risks that local contests of limited and non-nuclear violence may spread or become nuclear.

But even if deterrence is more important now than ever, it still may be asked whether this has much pragmatic significance for military decisions. Isn't the best deterrent also the force best able to execute the threat, to fight, and to come out favorably? And doesn't the reverse hold true?

This is not the sort of question that can be answered in the abstract. Nor do I think the answer is a simple yes or no. Capabilities designed with only one of these objectives contemplated might differ from capabilities developed with another primarily in mind. This is an important point that has become increasingly obvious in the last decade. On the other hand, there is a very large overlap, and this is vital too. To illustrate the possibilities of divergence, let me use an example, which is, alas, familiar to all of us: the activities of the traffic cop.

The city fathers would like to reduce the number of violations of the law. They would also like to fine or put in the clink as many violators as they can. There are two well-known alternative techniques for accomplishing these ends: one is the familiar ambush technique; the other is sometimes called the visible patrol technique. The first increases the probability of interception and arrest. The second discourages culpability. Now if our goal is to maximize the number or proportion of speeders punished, or the total of municipal revenue through fines, probably the best way to do the job is by ambush, however uneasy such a sneaky tactic makes us. If our goal, on the other hand, is a reduction in the total number of traffic accidents, say, or in the number of attempts to violate the law (even if on the whole such attempts at evasion as do take place are more likely to be successful, since the culprit is aware of the cop's presence), it may very well be that the most frequent, obvious presence of policemen capable of instantaneous retaliation against speeders would encourage caution, and so achieve such goals best. (It might also avoid some of the undesirable side effects of the ambush technique, such as the occasional, faintly ludicrous vision of a burly grownup on a motorcycle trying to look invisible behind a palm tree, with its possibly dissolving effect on our respect for municipal authority.)

Another simple example from my own experience concerns the inter-continental mission. In the early 1950's when the crucial problem of the vulnerability of strategic forces was beginning to be understood, a great many alternative methods of protecting the force were being considered. One of a great many methods that I heard suggested then for protecting SAC would have ingeniously reduced the chances of SAC's actually being hit by deceiving the enemy into thinking SAC was very vulnerable some place where in fact it was not. The enemy, the argument ran, tempted by our seeming weakness, might attack our strategic force at the apparent soft spot, expend its bombs fruitlessly, and so gain us a crucial advantage toward winning the war. The particular line of deception suggested in this argument involved costs of over a billion dollars, and it seemed clear that the deception might not work even then. Fortunately, there were alternative strategies which were both cheaper and more deceptive. But the essential weakness of the argument was that it ignored the fact that if the enemy answered this invitation to clobber a supposedly soft SAC with a joint attack against our cities and our strategic force, he might very well miss SAC but, unfortunately for us, hit Washington, D. C., New York, Los Angeles, and the rest of our major cities. He would then open a war he might not have dared to start unless he had been deluded into thinking he could destroy our retaliatory force. Deceiving the enemy into thinking SAC is vulnerable some place where it is not ignores the fact that SAC's deterrent effect depends on a reputation for invulnerability everywhere.

This one clear-cut example of how it is possible to neglect deterrence in choosing preparations to fight is an unimportant though lucid example of the possibility of divergence. At the start of the 1950's there were more obscure but more important cases, programs which would have given us a strike force powerful under some circumstances of outbreak, but dangerously weak under other quite likely conditions; and therefore of questionable reliability as a deterrent when the going got rough. However, these weaknesses were not clear. Their disclosure and their implications for the objective of deterrence took systematic and very detailed analysis of actual and projected operations. And the base study, described in Chapter 3, which undertook such a laborious analysis, held its preliminary findings quite tentatively for many months.

In fact, at the start of the 1950's the problem of protecting bombers on the ground from enemy bomber attacks did not figure prominently in our aims. Part of the explanation for this is implicit in my earlier description of strategic bombing and the growth of the intercontinental mission. First of all, the major purpose of our intercontinental force was to deter a continental threat, the threat of land invasion in Europe. We expected to strike with a strategic force substantially undamaged, since essentially unattacked. In short, we didn't have the problem of "striking second" in the sense in which it is used today, namely, striking back with a force that is under attack. Not, of course, because we contemplated aggression but because we planned to respond to an aggression directed primarily against our allies. Moreover, we planned to fight a long war in Europe after expending our strategic nuclear capability to destroy as much as we could of the economic war potential of Russia, at that time the principal strategic target system. In time of peace, we expected to base our bombers in the continental United States with a fraction of them on rotation overseas. After the outbreak we expected to move overseas and to prepare to operate back and forth with our medium bombers between targets and the overseas bases without returning to the United States. Even neglecting the possibility of enemy bombing attack, there were enormous difficulties in assembling an adequate number of bombers, tankers, trained crews, storage, logistics, and base capacity. Given the maintenance problems of the heavy and medium bombers, the short range of most of the force, and the problem of bringing together all of the disparate elements (fast bombers, slow tankers, stocks of rather primitive, unready bombs stored on a few separate bases, etc.) needed for a strike, the strategic bombardment war would have taken days before it began. Enemy bombing attack on our strategic forces then would have been leveled against an extremely time-consuming, complex, cumbersome operation.

Second, as we explained in sketching the history of the B-36, the problem of strategic bombing was conceived quite differently from the way in which it is thought of today, although it was based on a body of doctrine and predisposition, evolved between the wars and during World War II, as to what was useful for a strategic force on each side to attack (mainly the industrial sources of enemy power and his will) and what were the principal obstacles to reaching these objectives (mainly, the enemy's active defenses)[8]. It was natural that nuclear weapons were first absorbed into our thinking in terms of how they helped achieve the established objectives against the established obstacles. This focus and this definition of the problem are visible for example in the interservice controversies, such as the B-36 investigation, where key issues concerned the ability of the B-36 to penetrate modern defenses, the effectiveness of nuclear weapons, and the morality of bombing nonmilitary targets. And they are visible also in systems analyses of this period. Systems analyses to assist bomber choice looked at speed, altitude, bomb load, small versus large aircraft in their performance through enemy defenses and over targets, and the like. And, as the bombing systems analyses matched our bombers essentially against his defenses, our defense systems analyses with minor exceptions matched our active defenses against enemy bombers. In none of these was the problem of protecting bombers against enemy attack in the center of attention as it is today.

The vital difference between an objective of getting a first-strike capability and the objective of getting a second-strike capability did emerge, but only in the course of extended empirical work. The base study, as described by E. S. Quade in Chapter 3, proceeded by a method of successive approximations. It compared forces for their efficiency in carrying a payload between the

---

[8] See quotations from Webster and Frankland cited on page 109.

bases and targets without opposition either by enemy interceptors or enemy bombers. Then, it introduced obstacles successively: first, enemy defenses; then enemy bombardment of our bombers and other elements needed to retaliate. In essence, then, the alternative systems were tested for their first-strike capability and then they were compared for their second-strike capacity. And the programmed system performed in a drastically different way, depending on the order in which the opposing side struck. In the course of analyzing counter-measures and counter-countermeasures, the enemy bombardment turned out to be a dominant problem. This was true even for a very much improved overseas operating base system. The refueling base system was very much less sensitive to strike order. It is only the fact that strike order made such a difference among systems contemplated that gave the first-strike, second-strike distinction an interest. And it was not known in advance of the analysis that few of the programmed bombers would have survived to encounter the problem of penetrating enemy defenses which had previously been taken as the main obstacle. The analysis then not only was affected by the objectives considered, it affected them.

The first-strike, second-strike distinction continues to have an interest in the on-going design and redesign of the strategic forces of the major powers, but even more in evaluating the objectives and likely accomplishments of the so-called "nth country", or independent nuclear powers. Its application to their cases should remind us that deterring a great power does not follow automatically from possession of nuclear weapons; it is an empirical question, a question of fact. And, in the case of a smaller nuclear power's attempt reliably to deter a great power, there are feasibility issues, which are always relevant in choosing objectives. Smaller powers may have to choose between very risky low confidence deterrence and alliance.

Finally, the base study illustrates how a systems analysis may affect objectives without intending to. It was mainly concerned with choosing among alternative basing systems. In fact, while it analyzed some of the interplay between target objectives, bases and bomber performance, it deliberately attempted to evolve a basing system that would perform well, not simply against the rather arbitrary 100-point industry system with which it started, but against a variety of other target objectives (a 1000-point complex, urban complexes, and various military target systems); and it examined the systems it compared for their sensitivity to changes in the geography and time requirements likely to be imposed by alternative goals. Nonetheless, in spite of this explicit and quite successful attempt at developing a method of basing comparatively *indifferent* to substantial changes in objectives, a principal outcome of the base study for its authors was to clarify the aim of deterrence and to display the possibility of divergence between a capacity for destroying an enemy's strategic force under some circumstances and the ability to deter attack.

The base study illustrated the possibility of this divergence. It did not show its necessity. In 1955 when the lectures on which this volume is based were first presented, one had to argue for the importance of studying deterrence and for distinguishing it from the capacity to fight a war. Today it is hardly necessary to argue for deterrence. The tendency has been to go to the opposite extreme: to consider deterrence only. It is popular to assume now that there is almost no connection between deterrence and fighting, in particular that it is bad for a nation to be able to fight and limit damage to itself in the event of war since an enemy might then expect an attack and pre-empt it.

This brings us to the second objective.

7.7 FIGHTING A WAR

The objective of fighting and coming out as favorably as possible if deterrence fails sounds innocent enough, yet it does run counter to the currently popular notion that the ability to limit damage is incompatible with the even more innocent and praiseworthy objective of deterring attack and avoiding war altogether. A serious analysis of the overlap and divergence of these objectives requires a great deal of concrete information and rigorous reasoning. Possibilities of conflict or mutual support between these two objectives are a suitable subject for systems analysis, not dogmas to be taken as unquestioned in such an analysis.

Nonetheless, presumptions of an identity between deterrence and war fighting, or of an inevitable conflict between them, have motivated some fragmentary analyses, but have themselves not been the results of analysis or tested by it. Such dogmas have been intensively held and then lightly and forgetfully reversed. There are, in any case, some prior questions for the objective of limiting damage and coming out favorably during a war.

The first of these concerns feasibility. It seems clear offhand that it might be nice to have steadily during a long period of peace a highly reliable capability to come out nearly unscathed in a nuclear war with a major opponent, no matter who started it. It is doubtful that this is feasible for either of the great powers vis-à-vis the other so long as the opposing power exercises intelligent care. On the other hand, for a great power the ability to moderate the catastrophe somewhat in *some* reasonably likely cases raises much less stringent problems of feasibility. Here is a region in which there are interesting empirical and analytical questions requiring close examination of utilities, costs, and the possibilities of conflict or mutual support between damage limiting and deterrence objectives.

Deterrence is directed against continental and local aggressions as well as intercontinental ones. And it is in connection with deterring these especially that there has developed a body of opinion on the subject of whether deterrence and limiting damage conflict or support each other. The theory of massive retaliation, like the theory that we should aim at deterrence only in connection with intercontinental war, rests on the premise that the more horrible the threat the better the deterrent. Moreover, the horrors we must avoid limiting, it is said, are those presented the victim as well as the aggressor. But it may be doubted that the effectiveness of the deterrent is a function simply of the damage likely to be done. Critics of massive retaliation have for a long time suggested that it depends also on the plausibility that the threat will be executed. And this in turn may depend on how things look at the moment of decision: How does the potential aggressor see his own alternatives? And how does he expect the alternatives to look to the victim of his aggression during the crisis when the victim must decide on backing down or getting ready to strike back?

Sometimes the scale of a threat may crucially lessen the likelihood of its execution. It seems that in Korea, and a little later in Indochina, the probability that the United States would actually exploit its near monopoly in nuclear weapons was diminished by the fact that the extreme violence of such weapons seemed inappropriate both to key U.S. decisionmakers and to many of our allies. Our traffic example can serve to illustrate something of the same. It might seem that if the visible patrol of speeding traffic were linked to a most dire punishment of the speeder when caught, we would have a nearly ideal deterrent to traffic violations; and the worse the punishment, the closer to the ideal. On this theory, the best way to discourage traffic offenses might be to make them capital crimes, punishable by death. While such a punishment appears ferocious enough to discourage anyone's going faster than a crawl, it is not clear that this is so. Some relevant historical experience even suggests that it might lead to an increase in speeding and general disregard for the laws of traffic. Doubts are suggested by the familiar principle that such punishment would be "cruel and unusual". Picture the problem presented in a society like our own by a group of teenagers caught exceeding the speed limit. It is doubtful that they would be arrested; if they were arrested it is unlikely they would be convicted; and if convicted the execution of sentence would be extremely uncertain. We would need most hard-hearted police, juries and judges, and a society that would accept them. Moreover, if the chain of events leading to punishment broke down as a regular matter, and it became clear that in fact speeding went unpunished, speeding might increase.

Such an example is by no means purely hypothetical. The development of the English common law provides a body of historical experience illustrating how excessive penalties may increase the probability of crime. In the eighteenth century when Blackstone wrote his famous *Commentaries on the Laws of*

England, Parliament had declared no fewer than 160 offenses to be punishable by death. "So dreadful a list", Blackstone wrote, "instead of diminishing, increases the number of offenders, because the injured party, through compassion, sometimes forbears to prosecute; or juries for the same reason acquit the accused or mitigate the nature of the offence; or judges likewise recommend mercy".

Now picture what might happen to deterrence if the horrors visited fell not only on the criminal but also on those concerned to execute the law. The likelihood of punishment for speeding, in our example, would be even smaller if in all such cases the group of teenagers included the daugthers of the judge, the jury, or the police; that is, if the penalty directly affected those making judgment rather than simply their feeling as to what was just or appropriate.

The analogy in the field of international security is apparent. Once the nuclear monopoly was lost, a threat of massive nuclear retaliation to a local and minor non-nuclear incursion was likely to become less convincing since the threatener might be badly damaged in executing the threat. This applies to a great power, but even more to the lesser nuclear powers who adopt a policy of massive retaliation; they are likely to be more vulnerable.

But the possibilities for overlap or divergence in objectives for deterring or limiting damage in local, continental, or intercontinental wars need examination in terms of the specifics of the threats and conflicts envisaged.

7.8. THE ENEMY'S OBJECTIONS AND AGREEMENTS

In discussing the objectives which a military systems analysis might help to further I listed a hierarchy of desires ranging from nice to desperate minima. I said nothing of the enemy's objectives and the objections he might have to our fulfilling our own desires. But, of course, it is part of the essence of the problems we are considering that they must always be looked at symmetrically. The enemy has a variety of goals which are counterparts of ours and sometimes in direct conflict with them[9]. (He also, fortunately, has some goals in common with us, but not enough to make our problem a simple one.) Clear as this is in principle, it is frequently forgotten both by

---

[9] For such reasons and related ones I prefer to distinguish systems studies for conflict problems from what is ordinarily called systems engineering, for example, in the field of public utilities, by calling the former "conflict systems design". For a contrast between these two types of study, see my "Strategy and the Natural Scientists" in Robert Gilpin and Christopher Wright (eds.), *Scientists and National Policy Making,* Columbia University Press, New York, 1963, and my forthcoming book, *Scientists, Seers, and Strategy.*

analysts and decisionmakers. It is not easy to introduce the enemy into our calculations in a way that assigns him the degree of freedom, which he in reality has, to frustrate our simple desire to maximize our safety at his expense. In considering the enemy's active defense through which our offensive systems must penetrate, do we take into account the devices available to exploit the peculiar weaknesses of each of these systems? In most of the analyses I have seen, *either formal systems analyses or staff papers,* I think not.

For example, in the early 1950's, studies deficient in this respect did not permit the enemy to adjust his defense budget so as to spend more money on local defense to combat systems primarily vulnerable to local and not area defense. This was bad. But many studies used to leave the enemy *offense* out of account altogether. While differential air attrition has been looked at, differential ground attrition for a long time was not allowed to figure at all. This deficiency was, of course, by no means trivial. The effects of ground attrition in a strategic bombing analysis frequently dominated the air attrition effects. Some analytic empirical method of dealing with ground attrition, however grossly, is, in general, essential. I stress empirical method because there have been some studies of strategic bombing systems in which the outcome of the comparison was determined almost entirely by costs of defending SAC bases on the ground. The whole very considerable margin of superiority of the preferred system over the rejected system was attributable to these defense costs. But unfortunately these costs were wholly arbitrary and not themselves the results of analysis. While this arbitrary assumption was embedded in a fairly elaborate model, it hardly fulfilled the requirement that I am describing, namely, taking enemy offense into analytic and empirical account. Finally, even now when a study of ground attrition is likely to use at least hypothetical numerical estimates, it is still somewhat rare to find empirical analysis of the interaction of ground attack and penetration, much less of the interplay between the entire sequence of operations, including command and control on both sides. The simple models of missile duels which abound in the public literature on strategy seldom have any empirical content at all.

Mr. Hitch mentioned games and game theory as devices for taking enemy reactions explicitly into account. Like Mr. Hitch, I take a temperate view of the present uses of both game theory and operational gaming[10]. Game theory, as he stressed, is helpful conceptually, but as far as its theorems are concerned,

---

10 Many popular articles—some friendly, some hostile, but all uninformed—have been written suggesting the central role of games and game theory in systems analyses and strategy. I have written of this phenomenon in "Sin and Games in America", an essay in Martin Shubik (ed.), *Game Theory and Related Approaches to Social Behavior,* John Wiley & Sons, Inc., New York, 1964, pp. 209–225.

it is still a long way from direct application to any complex problem of policy. Games can be a useful component of a systems study. I would like to stress here that it is essential to take enemy reactions into account, and that this need not be done in the framework of a formal game, with its apparatus of explicit rules covering permissible moves and determining the payoffs for each play. For example, RAND analysts, in conducting map exercises to determine the performance of alternative defenses, typically try some defense tactic and then attempt to figure the best means the enemy has available for countering this tactic; then they try another tactic, examine the possible countermoves again, and so on. In this way each strike calculated is actually the result of a rather extensive canvass not only of our tactics but also of enemy reactions. Matching best enemy countermoves to our own choices was also an important part of RAND's work on air base choice. This sort of matching is one kind of "minimax" analysis. Precisely the same sort of matching of move and countermove is relevant in designing and evaluating bilateral arms control arrangements which should not be taken as a matter of simple faith. Such attempts to introduce the enemy by letting him, in his best interest, do his worst to our forces and then seeing which of our forces accomplishes the job most effectively in the face of this best enemy attempt, usually tell us more than a formal game. In the latter, too frequently the real questions in doubt concern the rules of the game, but the players of a game are likely to be concentrating all their ingenuity on how to exploit the rules[11].

It is sometimes said that strategists and systems analysts must (or, at any rate, do) assume that preparations for wars and wars themselves are conducted in a perfectly rational way on both sides. This sounds rather foolish and, in fact, would be. Heads of state and military commanders, like other humans, are not always intelligently purposeful. They are not purely rational beings, and even if they were, their purposes would almost surely be blurred in transmission through the vast noisy channels of the bureaucracies informing them and executing their decisions. And, of course, there is nothing in the nature of a conflict system design which forces the analyst to assume that the opposing parties are perfectly intelligent. A candid appraisal of our own history and that of our allies, to say nothing of what we know of enemy institutions and history, quickly establishes the likelihood of irrationalities.

Nonetheless, the possibilities of rational behavior have a large if not an exclusive role in a systems analysis. If men are not always rational beings, they are the only beings who are *sometimes* rational.

Enemies frequently do roughly hew their own decisions to their purposes and in so doing, frustrate our own. At the time of Pearl Harbor, for example, we left the northern approach to Hawaii uncovered by ship or aerial recon-

---

11 When they can so exploit the rules, of course the rules should be changed.

naissance. The Japanese had it open to them to make a somewhat round-about route precisely through this approach; and they did[12]. Again, we assumed that the range of the Japanese Zeroes was too short for an attack on our Philippine bases from Formosa. We were right. But we also assumed that this would not change, and in this we were wrong. The Japanese had made the calculation too, and, through a combination of minor equipment changes and pilot training, extended the range of the Zeroes to do the job[13]. A very large number of similar examples could be cited in which one side in a war wishfully assumed its adversaries would not adapt their behavior to exploit its weakness.

Another example from World War II concerns an incident in which assuming rationality on the part of the Germans helped the British design a countermeasure. During the Battle of Britain the British discovered that German bombers were navigating with a radio beam system known as Knickabein. The British were able to intercept this beam by anticipating where the attack would be made. They did this by simply reasoning that the Rolls Royce works at Derby, which were making substantially all the engines for the Battle of Britain, would be the best target from the standpoint of the Germans, and that they therefore would attack it. The Germans did and were intercepted. In short, opponents sometimes do behave in a roughly rational way. To ignore this possibility is sometimes disastrous; to acknowledge it sometimes can be very fruitful.

On the other hand, in a sprawling and complicated mechanism like a Department or Ministry of Defense in the highly uncertain situation of military technology today, there are bound to be plenty of irrationalities. Doctrine and understanding are likely to change slowly, and even when they change they do not affect the forces in being either immediately or totally, particularly with the long periods of gestation necessary in research and development of complex equipment. The history of the B-36 illustrates both the long period between the conception and the reality and the many hazards that attend pregnancy and birth. The forces in being at any time are likely to be composed largely of weapon systems chosen under quite different circumstances from those that eventuated, and, very likely, on the basis of a hazy and erroneous surmise as to what was coming. We may expect lags, then, but it is hard to tell just what they will be. Some adaptations are likely to be swifter than others. Specifically, a change in a method of operation can be effected more

---

[12] Radar stations covering this approach were operating only from 4 a.m. to 7 a.m., and the warning of approaching Japanese aircraft, picked up a few minutes after 7 a.m. by two radar operators in training, was misinterpreted as a flight of our own B-17's.

[13] For these examples, see R. M. Wohlstetter, *Pearl Harbor: Warning and Decision,* Stanford University Press, Stanford, Calif., 1962.

quickly than a change in equipment. Therefore it may be more hazardous to count in the immediate future on the persistence of irrational behavior in enemy operations or strategy than to depend on stability or slow change in enemy force composition.

How should a systems study deal with uncertainties as to the enemy's capabilities and intentions? We have seen that one way of avoiding the problem, where the enemy is considered at all, is to limit consideration only to some fixed composition of offense or defense which is not allowed to shift in response to aspects of our strategy certain to be known to him. This makes a comparison of alternative systems subject to at least an unconscious bias in favor of systems that deviate from the norms that this fixed force might have been invented to counter. And it makes the problem of meeting the enemy too easy. We assume some fixed combat ceilings for his fighters and then devise a bombing force capable of flying slightly higher. Or, we assume some specific limit to the range of his local defenses and then work out a device for sending off bombs from just outside this boundary.

What is the alternative to this? To assume no resource performance constraints on his part at all? This also would simplify analysis by making the problem insoluble. If our resources are limited and his are not, not much calculation is required to obtain the result. We hardly benefit by merely assuming that we have an absolute defense against his hypothetical absolute offense. There is a germ of wisdom contained in such attempts to release the enemy of any constraints whatsoever. It suggests that in addition to trying various reasonably estimated constraints, it is good to find the enemy capability at which our strategy breaks down. This, of course, will always occur at some finite point of enemy capability.

In general, then, it is important to make bracketing estimates of at least the *general* resource limitations in order to keep the subject short of the realm of science fiction. On the other hand, we must give the devil his due and permit the enemy freedom of allocation within those resource constraints applicable for the time period under consideration. This means that for development problems there are very few *specific* resource constraints, that is, inflexibilities, which we can safely assume for the indefinite future (although there may be some we can prepare to exploit).

The trouble with most air attrition models that have been used to answer development questions is that they treat such questions as if they concerned procurement or operations. Each of a few offense vehicles, for example, will be represented by a specific combination of numbers designating speed, altitude, payload, accuracy, etc. Each is matched against the same fixed area and local defense force deployed in the same way. But even if such a model covered only procurement and operational alternatives, it is clear that this procedure omits significant possibilities open to the enemy—and to us. For even when we are buying an item already developed, we invariably find it open for some growth and adaptation with changes in the state of the arts during its period of use. So the B-36 acquired jets. Such models omit much of the real freedom of choice available to both sides.

For development problems in particular we cannot take performance parameters as fixed. We need some technique for picking good performance requirements—useful goals for the designer. How might we go about this? I have suggested that one method would be to test each system which fulfills a given set of performance goals against an enemy counter strategy that—within only general resource constraints and using information reasonably likely to be available to him — is devised precisely to exploit the weaknesses of the system we are testing. It is clear, of course, that the problem of choosing optimal or even good matching strategies for the enemy and our-selves increases in difficulty as we consider strategies more distant in time. We will have to consider not just a few air battles involving specific bombers versus specific fighters, but very large families of battles with offensive vehicles of various types opposing various combinations of local and area de-fenses, and a variety of circumstances involving differing resource allocations, by both ourselves and the enemy, among active and passive defense and offense.

One way to deal with uncertainties as to the enemy's capabilities and intentions, then, is to assume that, within limits set by his resources and the time and information available to him, he will do what is from his standpoint the best, and, frequently, from yours the worst. I do not think that this is the only kind of opposing strategy to consider. Some nonoptimal strategies demand analysis. In a way, dealing with nonoptimal strategies is even more difficult in analysis than dealing with optimal ones. If the analyst is lucky there may be only one optimal strategy; but it is clear that there are always many bad ones. Which of these are worth looking at?

There is at least one worthy of careful attention. This is the sort of strategy we may call an "inert strategy", that is to say, one in which the enemy continues to behave as your intelligence tells you he is presently doing, even though circumstances, and in particular your own strategy, have changed. Bureaucracies have a great deal of inertia and it would be a great mistake to ignore this fact. Both the great powers, for example, had extremely inadequate basing policies in the 1950's. I have already indicated that I think it would be very unwise to depend exclusively on the assumption that an opponent is going to be stupid or grossly inefficient. But it would be a great mistake to ignore this possibility and so find yourself unable to exploit error. When you work on such problems as the job of limiting urban damage in case of attack, which can be very difficult if he behaves intelligently, you may want to combine such moderate success as you are able to assure in the face of a well designed and substantial enemy effort, with a capability for drastic success just in case he is "inert". Inert strategies are important as benchmarks, but they also are useful in developing low-confidence measures. For high confidence one must assume a well designed opposing strategy and try minimax.

The above example displays the enemy in his familiar role of being precisely in conflict with us. The next subject concerns some items in which his interest coincides with ours; that is, an interest in not starting something in which both sides may sustain as many as fifty million or more casualties. It is only because the enemy has such points of agreement with us that deterrence can work. This brings us once again to the subject of deterrent measures.

7.9. THE MODEST VALUE OF MUTUALLY UNSATISFACTORY STRATEGIES

Measures that give us a high confidence of destroying the enemy's cities or military potential are a powerful deterrent. To have such measures fulfills our fondest desires, precisely because they decrease the likelihood of war and at the same time provide powerful assurance just in case war does break out. While it is possible to obtain some such high-confidence measures in critically important areas, this is not always the case. And therefore it is useful to consider some measures that fall short of providing us with such high-confidence wartime capabilities.

You will recall that we listed earlier several high-confidence objectives in describing a hierarchy of possible goals. The second goal mentioned there was the aim to have a high degree of confidence that substantially all of our cities could survive an enemy surprise attack under all circumstances. Let us say we mean by high degree of confidence at least 90 chances out of 100. Another high-confidence objective, which is more realizable, is the goal of maintaining a SAC of which a large and powerful portion will remain undestroyed by an enemy surprise attack.

The enemy also has some fond desires which are symmetrical to these. He might hesitate to go into a war if he could not be fairly sure of destroying enough of our urban areas to reduce our military potential seriously. Even more obviously, he would hesitate before undertaking a surprise attack that left our strategic striking force in a position to return a devastating blow. Let us say, then, that we would like to preserve our striking force with very high confidence (at least 90 chances out of 100). He would like to have a high confidence (at least 90 chances out of 100) of destroying all of our SAC not certain to be handled by his defenses. Now, suppose we have such a high-confidence measure for a certain fraction of SAC, and then think up another measure which gives us a 50–50 chance of preserving a considerable additional fraction. It is clear that this additional measure does not fulfill our fondest desires. On the other hand, it should be observed that it does prevent the enemy from having a better than 50–50 chance of realizing his fondest desires. It makes a surprise attack a gamble and therefore acts as a deterrent. (If at Pearl Harbor we had operated our inadequate air reconnaissance force so as to leave not one fixed approach uncovered but intermittent random unpredictable holes in all approaches, both we and the Japanese would have had to gamble.) Particularly where we don't have high-confidence measures, the value of such low-confidence measures is clear.

How basic is the distinction between high- and low-confidence measures? Do two or three low-confidence measures add up to a high-confidence measure? Not necessarily. What we are trying to do with low-confidence measures is to decrease the enemy's confidence rather than raise ours. One of the ways we might decrease his confidence with respect to the success of some particular attack strategy might be to increase the variability of his result, even if we do not affect the average outcome. This would increase the risks for him, and might help the deterrent function. But it also means that since we have increased the variability, we have also reduced our own confidence.

Therefore our fondest desires are not satisfied. That is one reason why we continue to seek high-confidence measures for crucial goals where we do not already have them. They cannot be replaced by low-confidence measures. However, it is important to study systematically this less ambitious class of measures, especially where we are not able to find means of satisfying our more ambitious goals.

7.10.   UNCERTAINTY AND THE FRAMING OF WORKABLE OBJECTIVES

Low-confidence measures offer an example of how we might exploit uncertainty. I have said enough to indicate that whether it is useful or merely annoying, uncertainty is a central problem in the design of systems studies. (Most contributors to the volume are forced to engage this dragon.)

We are uncertain, then, even about what we want to do (and clearly unsure about what we can do), about what the enemy can and will do, and about the physical and political environment of both our actions. How do we deal with any of these uncertainties in designing a systems study? I have said a little about the treatment of enemy intentions and capabilities. How about the first of these uncertainties, the uncertainty as to our objectives? This should be somewhat easier to handle than the other dragons.

There are several ways to deal with the problem of framing an objective for our analysis that is both workable and of some policy interest. Some appealing methods merely avoid the problem. For example, we might make the objective narrow enough to measure, thus making it workable but also too narrow for validity or interest. Some of the issues raised in the course of the B-36 history illustrate this. We are clearly being too narrow if we select one performance characteristic and simply maximize it, or maximize it subject to a few constraints; for example, if we attempt merely to pick the fastest plane, or that having the longest radius. In the 1950's, the plane having the longest radius possible within the state of the art of powerplant and airframe design, neglecting any considerations of payload, speed, etc., might have travelled some 7500 n mi and returned. Such a plane would hardly do a militarily useful job, however. We might therefore specify certain minimum performance in speed, altitude, and payload, etc., and then call for the maximum radius plane subject to these conditions. Alternatively we might maximize speed, subject to certain minimum requirements placed on radius and the other performance parameters. Both these courses are simple but leave us no method of choosing between them, nor do they suggest precisely what minimum constraints to place on the performance parameters we are not maximizing. For this reason, the selection of general operating requirements for SAC bombers cannot be solved so simply. Such a procedure merely evades the problem.

A second way of evading the problem might be to take the opposite course, formulate the objective with perfect breadth but fatal hollowness. We do this, for example, when we merely formulate criteria that appear to test for a variety of contingencies but, in fact, do not because of the presence of a variable which cannot be determined in the degree of specificity needed for decision. It is easy to write out criteria for choosing the best system considering the maximum expected performance under a variety of contingencies, each of which is supposed to have a specific probability associated with it. The contingencies in one case might be outbreak of war next year, and the year following, and the year following that, and so on. In another case they might be defection of England, defection of Libya, defection of Canada, defection of one of the original 48 states, and a series of similar catastrophes. But if our choice depends on our being able to assign *exact numbers* to the probabilities of each of these contingencies, such a formulation does not advance us very far, since nobody knows how to do this. (The case, I shall argue, takes on a different aspect if we can find or construct systems among which the choice depends only on very gross inequalities in some such probabilities.)

In going about the job of framing workable and useful objectives, it is not inconsistent with our cautions about narrow criteria to use narrow criteria as an intermediate step. In fact, in a systems study this is one of the most useful ways to frame workable and useful objectives. "Ideal kill potential" is sometimes used in this way in RAND analyses of air defense. Intermediate criteria enable us to compare large subsets of alternative weapons and to sift out grossly inefficient ones. The comparisons must be made carefully and only between devices essentially similar in the way they enter broader optimizations. For example, an analysis of air defense may make such direct comparisons among defense weapons with ranges of, say, 15 to 25 mi, and it may make direct comparisons among weapons of 200- to 300-mi radii. But it must not use the kill potential concept to compare the 20-mi radius weapon with the 200-mi radius weapon. Similarly, the RAND study of air base choice used as one of several intermediate criteria "maximum number of enemy targets killed in the face of enemy defense (but neglecting enemy attack)"; and as another, "maximum number of bombers surviving enemy attack on the ground". In some cases, systems could be compared usefully here, even though they were expected to enter broader optimizations with contrasting success, because the difference between the systems was likely to be *emphasized* by taking a broader criterion and including certain additional variables. For some of the comparisons, in other words, the intermediate criteria provided an a fortiori argument—that is, a system best in one set of circumstances loaded against it could, with greater certainty, be presumed best in some other set of more favorable circumstances. Such intermediate criteria fall short of complete trustworthiness. For example, let us take the criterion of maximum number of bombers surviving an enemy attack on the ground. This criterion neglects the offensive function of SAC (just as the other intermediate criterion cited neglected defense). Therefore, it is not hard to construct a system on this criterion that would look very good but that would fail in performing the essential strategic function. We might envisage a system that kept the parts of SAC bombers unassembled and buried each under concrete some place in the Antarctic far beyond the reach of Soviet bombing attack. Our bombers would in this case be quite safe. But so would the enemy.

This is an extreme example, but it is only an extreme form of systems suggested frequently. Some less extreme forms of long-range operation would have sacrificed more bombers to purchase tankers than the number of bombers that could have been saved from being killed on base by these remote operations. There are analogous difficulties with some extreme forms of dispersal and shelter. We must, then, use a broader criterion that takes into account the fact that in defending SAC we are defending an offensive force, and therefore the measure of success of any defense must reflect the performance of the offensive job. One such broader criterion is "least cost to destroy any given enemy target system (or maximum enemy targets killed for a fixed budget) in the face of enemy attacks as well as enemy defense". Our Antarctic SAC would not measure up to such a criterion. And neither would several less extreme proposals.

This spreading hierarchy of working criteria can be related to our example used earlier. You will recall that Figs. 7.1 and 7.2 represented the corresponding sequence of formally labelled but unspecified contractor and Air Force objectives and an unlimited sequence of increasingly comprehensive systems. Similarly, a hierarchy of criteria, each useful at the level of the corresponding phases of the work, might be:

1. minimum cost for airborne radar with a given performance,

2. maximum kill probability per pass for given interceptor investment,

3. maximum area kill potential,

4. maximum number of our bombers surviving an enemy attack,

5. maximum enemy targets killed considering enemy attack and defense.

We need not stop here. As I have stressed, if we are to take into account the problems that motivate the Air Force desire for long-range operation, we must broaden our criteria still further. We should consider the performance of various systems in a variety of contingencies. We must consider not only the expected case, but also the eventualities against which the Air Force must ensure itself, even though—like the events against which the B-36 hedged—they may not occur. I will have more to say about contingency planning in the final section of this paper.

Besides the uncertainties as to our objectives and criteria for evaluation, the design of our studies must take into account a number of other uncertainties. Some of these, such as the weather, are not likely to be resolved (neither small-scale nor large-scale weather is likely in the near future to be controlled in a way that would discriminate between allies and enemies).

There are some uncertainties which might be resolved by tests within our control. For example, the behavior and loading of structures under very extreme overpressures was not well understood a few years ago. The results of systems analysis suggested that highly resistant structures might have a number of important military uses. The policy implication of that analysis was to undertake design and tests to learn more about the feasibility and costs of resisting extreme overpressures. In this case, the analysis resulted in a program for clearing up an important item of uncertainty.

Although some uncertainties can be resolved, others cannot, and the problem of uncertainty remains central in any systems study.

7.11. SYSTEMS DESIGN VERSUS SYSTEMS ANALYSIS

Do the multiple uncertainties we have outlined make analysis impossible or, at any rate, fruitless? Are we optimists if we hope to find the one alternative which is the optimum of all the millions? It would appear that dominance is a miracle.

Let me recall that these uncertainties are not merely a problem for the analyst, but one of fact. The factual indeterminacy of the political and physical environment, the variety and instability of our objectives, and the multiplicity and uncertainty of the obstacles the enemy can interpose suggest that we must design systems that are good or viable in a variety of circumstances. That is to say, the problem is one of devising flexible, strong systems, not merely one of taking systems that have so far been suggested and comparing them. Inventiveness in systems design has a double function. The primary function is that of helping solve the decisionmaker's problem of being ready for many contingencies. The second function, dear to the heart of the analyst, is that of simplifying the analysis.

Let me offer one example of how this happens in the daily business of the analyst. In the course of a broad study of bomber systems one has to worry about the vulnerability of their various components to enemy bombing attack. Ground facilities, including the runways, are one such component. It happens that runways can be made one of the least vulnerable elements. Getting a model for the vulnerability of a runway is considerably complicated if we have to worry not only about such questions as the maximum continuous length of runway surviving, but also about whether there is a continuous clear path along enough taxiways to provide access to this surviving length of runway. In a so-called Monte Carlo random bomb drop to be programmed for the machine, the number of such possible paths of access we might have to ask the machine to examine is very large and might make the computation prohibitively expensive, if we were trying thousands of repetitions of bomb drops as one small component of a much larger investigation.

One way to go about this is to multiply the number of access taxiways so as to make it very unlikely that there will be any length of runway long enough to be usable without access. Multiplying access taxiways is quite inexpensive, not only by comparison with total systems costs but also by comparison with base installation costs. If we do this we might have a stronger taxiway-runway system. We can have a higher confidence in its survival. At the same time, the small excursion necessary to approximate the required number of access taxiways makes it unnecessary to complicate the analysis by considering the problem of access. (An even more powerful short excursion might be the use of rocket assists for short- and even zero-length takeoff. This might dispose of the runway analysis problem completely.)

Analysis is easier for strong systems. It is also easy for very bad ones. The really bad ones do not hold us very long because, for example, we need not worry about the interdependence of a destroyed plane and a destroyed fuel system. If the facility has many critical vulnerable elements, the capability undestroyed by bombing will be very, very low, and shown so by a simple measure of the percentage killed of one critical, badly damaged element. A subtle analysis could measure more closely the extent to which even the small surviving elements are rendered useless by the destruction of complementary items. Why bother? We have already seen that the system is very bad.

Similarly, if we so design a system of elements that the chances are very small that any critical element will be destroyed for reasonable ranges of bombing attack, the interdependence questions are quite relaxed. In some cases a quite inexpensive amount of overdesign furnishes an a fortiori argument.

Hundreds of such problems occur in the course of a systems analysis. It is always important not to take the systems as they come, but to modify them in the light of inefficiencies revealed in the course of analysis. The aspect that I am stressing here is that strong systems permit a fortiori arguments.

Are there any principles for designing strong systems? There are no prescriptions for ingenuity, and the design of military systems must proceed on the basis of the empirical characteristics of the military problems. Some of these are pervasive enough to suggest certain guidelines. I will mention two. One is to exploit the great difference between the war and peacetime requirements imposed on the system. We might call this "The Thermonuclear-War-Is-Not-Peace Principle". Another is to exploit, in devising strategic systems, the very different requirements for the approach and penetration segments of the mission. This is the "It's-Hotter-in-the-Combat-Zone Principle". Let me offer an example of a system that ingeniously exploits this second difference.

With a fixed state of the arts and an airplane of given size, higher speed can be obtained only at the cost of shorter range. Supersonic speed is very useful in reducing attrition while within the range of enemy fighters, but not so important for the long leg of the mission between our bomber bases and the edge of the enemy defended area. The B-58 design represents an ingenious compromise between our desire for great over-all range and high speed by including a "supersonic dash" capability, through the addition of afterburners on the engines, for use only when penetrating enemy defenses. In this way it is possible to attain virtually all the benefits of supersonic speed and subsonic range.

There are a number of examples of weapons systems that exploit the difference between peace and atomic war to advantage. Consider the case of shelters for missiles or aircraft against atomic attack. Over an indefinitely extended period of peace, shelters will be subject to the same forces as normal civilian structures in the same locality. In a short atomic campaign, however, they will receive very much more severe loads but only once or twice. Intelligent design practice takes advantage of this difference. Wartime design loads are allowed to exceed the elastic limits of materials in the structure and cause distortions which could be unacceptable in civilian use, or in military use if they were to occur very frequently. They do no harm, however, to the wartime function of these shelters. Other examples could be cited of systems that exploit the great difference between peacetime and atomic wartime requirements. Earlier I suggested, in connection with nuclear-powered aircraft, that the shielding problem of both the air and ground crews might be attacked in a way that could exploit this difference. The ground-refueling method of operating bombers is another example of a system which exploits this difference much more completely than do air-refueling systems. Air-refueling systems haul POL (petroleum, oil, lubricants), the cheapest and bulkiest element in the weapon system, over long distances by air in time of war. The ground-refueling systems haul it the long distances overseas by slow freighter in time of peace and, for the most part only in time of war or on maneuvers, pick it up in aircraft. Some of the contrasting forms of dispersal make a good deal of this difference by avoiding the high logistic and operational costs of operating separately in time of peace, limiting the time of dispersal essentially to the wartime emergency. Some systems using assisted takeoffs as an *emergency* device also exploit this difference.

How about the possibility of devising systems that are good because they can meet a variety of contingencies? The B-36 example illustrates the Air Force's desire to have a hedge against political and military bad luck. The uncertainties we have outlined suggest that this is a good idea.

Mr. Hitch presented an example of the problem in dealing with uncertainty that relates to the specific uncertainty against which the B-36 was a hedge. I would like to use his example and to expand on some of the considerations he made. Table 7.1 shows two systems, more or less related to the bombers available in the 1950's; one is dependent on overseas bases, and one is made up of very long-range bombers, operating from the ZI. It shows these two systems operating under two conditions: (a) with overseas bases available, and (b) without them. I would like to expand both the list of alternative systems and the list of alternative contingencies. Figure 7.3 does this and also shows in a few of the cases how the system might fare in the various contingencies.

TABLE 7.1

Targets destroyed by hypothetical bomber forces

System	If overseas bases available (a)	If overseas bases not available (b)	Expected outcome if probability of (a) = 90%	Worst
System dependent on overseas bases	100	20	92	20
Very long-range bombers from ZI	50	50	50	50 "Minimax"

Aside from the state of the weather, the six contingencies shown in Fig. 7.3 relate to distances from enemy territory: loss of all bases within 250 n mi

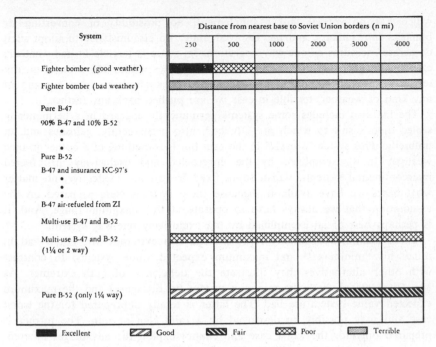

Fig. 7.3   Some bombing systems and base loss situations

of Russian boundaries, loss of all bases within 500 n mi, and so on in several discrete lumps. We might, of course, lose bases in different types of lumps, say all bases in certain politically connected areas, but this illustration will suffice. You will observe first that the contingencies listed, while only a small subset of those possible, are rather more extensive than those presented in the table. Having all our overseas bases or none are extreme cases. We have a very large number of bases in a couple of dozen different countries. While the behavior of these countries is not by any means completely independent, there is nevertheless a considerable amount of independence. The probability that we would lose all such bases, including, say, Canada and Maine, is positive but quite small. I have included Maine as a possible defection to indicate that anything is possible: We cannot even be sure of our base at Limestone. (The last contingency shown in Fig. 7.3, the loss of all bases within 4000 n mi of the Russian border, includes this disaster as well as the loss of Canada.)

You will observe that the list of alternatives for operation under these varying circumstances is also longer, though by no means exhaustive. It includes some systems which can only operate in "lovely" weather. This, for example, is literally true of the pure fighter-bomber limited-radius system which has no special tanker supplement, no possibility of converting its bombers into tankers, and has resolved under no circumstance to adopt such desperate measures as one-way operation. Its score is terrible in bad weather; excellent in good weather, provided we have bases within 250 n mi of enemy territory; even then, poor if we get pushed back another 250 n mi; and in any kind of weather, terrible in case we are pushed back any farther.

The list also includes some systems permanently encased in a hermetically sealed diver's suit to which are attached, also permanently, galoshes and an umbrella. This system is useful in the rain but is something of a bother in nice weather. It is exemplified by the unrefueled and exclusively air-refueled intercontinental systems, which for a fixed budget are ineffective, no matter what bases we have available, because these systems were prepared on the assumption that we always have to operate at the maximum range. And, it is perhaps best of all exemplified by the exclusively one-way system.

These examples essentially represent the two extremes Mr. Hitch had in mind: his "minimax"[14] and maximum expected value systems. In contrast with other alternatives they illustrate the deficiency of both extremes. As Mr. Hitch stated, both the minimax system (in his sense) and the maximum expected value system are bad. The latter is totally unprepared for the worst case and may possibly be destroyed by a faint sign of rain. The former is prepared only for the worst case and cannot exploit the advantages inherent in any of the much more likely, more favorable circumstances. Moreover, as I have already suggested, I have not defined the worst case or the system that would minimize our cost to do the job in the event of this catastrophe. I have assumed that Maine would not defect and that we would have Limestone. But just what other disasters might we consider? Can we even be absolutely sure of Omaha? There is a real problem in defining the maximum disaster we want to minimize, but we should recognize in moments of calm that some of the contingencies we are talking about in this connection—the political defection of Maine among others—are not very likely and also are not entirely subject to the enemy's control.

I would distinguish here several types of disaster. One, for example, an enemy attack aimed at denying our bases, is subject to enemy decision. If our bases are extremely weak, the attack may be both likely to take place and likely to be successful. This sort of disaster is not just bad luck. We can measure enemy capabilities and our susceptibility to attack and introduce the results of attack as an integral part of our systems analysis. Such disasters might be called systemic. We have discussed ways to deal with this problem.

Another sort of disaster is the kind of thing that we are ordinarily thinking

---

14 Observe that this kind of "minimaxing" differs from that treated earlier. Earlier we were concerned with techniques for minimizing the maximum damage likely to be administered *by an intelligent enemy.*

of when we talk of contingency planning. It is typified by extremely bad weather which denies us the possibility of operating from various bases. This is subject for some time to come neither to our control nor the enemy's and is a case of bad luck; an extra-systemic factor. It must be prepared for, but we must recall that here we are countering nature, so to speak, and not the enemy. When you are faced with an intelligent opponent it is sensible to suppose that he may choose the best of a number of alternatives likely to be known and available to him for exploiting soft spots. Nature, however, in spite of some evidence to the contrary presented in Thurber's short stories, is not malignant.

From the standpoint of contingency planning, political disasters lie somewhere between brute nature and a bombing attack, and rather closer to brute nature. The consequences of diplomatic moves are not as subject to systemic prediction as the result of a bomb exploding on a concrete runway. But, like the weather, they must be taken into account. To take them grossly into account in contingency planning we need not assign exact numbers to the probability of defection by one of our allies. We do have to be able to place some rough limits on the likelihoods involved and to make some judgments, such as (1) it is more likely than not that in the next ten years or so we will lose at least a few of our hundred-odd bases; (2) it is not nearly so likely that we will lose all of them; (3) New England is politically reliable as a base area.

It is important, however, to be prepared for some of the less likely contingencies and not just the most probable ones. This is the subject of insurance. A large variety of systems indicated in the list of alternatives in Fig. 7.3 provide various degrees of insurance in contingencies. It seems unlikely that a pure force will be optimal in the complex and uncertain circumstances for which the United States must prepare. In making development choices we are wise to hedge and develop more than we will procure. Mr. Hitch made this point and so have others. This means that we are putting off the procurement choice until later. Such a tactic of delaying decisions occurs not only in development hedging but also in choosing any flexible system at any stage of the development-procurement-operation cycle. Figure 7.3 shows several systems which can be *operated* in a multiplicity of ways in appropriate contingencies. When we *procure* such a system we leave open the choice of which way we will operate until the contingency arises.

The alternative systems shown in Fig. 7.3 exploit a third principle we might call "The Multiple-Use Principle". Preserving flexibility then means delaying decisions. You may get the impression that we conceive the task of systems analysis not so much as that of assisting decision as of teaching the military man to resist it. Is Hamlet then our model of a modern major general? Hamlet did, in the end, decide; and so must we. The point made about preserving flexibility is best phrased not in terms of postponing decision, but in terms of not rushing it. Decision implies choosing one course of action rather than others. It means cutting out some alternatives.

How is the necessity of decision consistent with the need to develop flexible systems viable under a wide variety of alternative circumstances? The answer is that a flexible system is not defined as one that incorporates all weapons alternatives by simple addition. This is the simplest sort of mixture. Because we are constrained by a budget, even if we choose one weapons system type for each alternative contingency we are sacrificing some quantity of weapons of other types merely by introducing a new type into the mixture. A system that will perform well in alternative contexts is good precisely insofar as it enables us to meet one contingency without sacrificing capability excessively in others. It is good, for example, if it enables us to preserve capability in contingencies and yet to eliminate some special systems as redundant. In this list the systems that involve multiple uses for the same item are of this character.

Figure 7.3 lists a variety of forces of strategic bombers, some pure, some involving a mixture of bomber types each of which is largely convertible, and some involving various convertible systems. In making our choice among these forces it is essential to consider their performance in all the interesting contingencies and not just in one. This means we must look not only at the expected case but also at the insurance contingency. It also means that it is not enough to look at the insurance contingency alone—even when we are talking of a weapon system which is primarily thought of as a hedge—because there may be alternative hedges. It is always good to ask whether some of these hedges also may be useful in other fairly likely circumstances. There is an interplay, then, between our insurance and our other objectives. If we have two systems operating from the Continental United States that are equally good, but on the premise that at least Canada is still with us, one is a great deal better, then clearly this second system is preferable, unless we are dead certain that we will lose every one of our allies. Our choice is even clearer if the two systems compared have the performance of the last two shown in Fig. 7.3.

Let me refer to another pair of contingencies mentioned earlier: the case in which we get the first strike in a war against the Soviets and one in which this least undesirable order is reversed. There are many who think the most unsatisfactory order more likely; there are some who are more optimistic. In any case it is clear that we are far from sure. We saw earlier that systems which look just fine when we get the first strike (say an enemy attack on our allies) can look very bad indeed when we do not. Designing a system that does well in both of these contingencies, then, is of great importance. Such a system might, for example, limit significantly the damage to our civil society if we respond with an undamaged strategic force to enemy aggression against our allies. And in any event it could make clear to the enemy that even if he should strike directly at our strategic force, his own military and civil society could be devastated. Such a system would be a reliable deterrent to attack on the United States. It could offer some insurance in case deterrence failed. On the other hand, as suggested earlier, this insurance capability should not make it more likely that deterrence would fail.

It is correct that the system just described would dominate the other systems listed in Fig. 7.3 and described earlier. We are not likely to stumble upon this sort of dominance. It is more frequently the work of design.

The work of designing such comprehensive systems involves ingenious construction of detailed systems components, of the force as a whole, and of its operation strategy. Such invention is fruitful, even if concerned only with smaller systems which we are in the habit of thinking of as "components".

The familiar mathematical theory of utility postulates a complete ordering of preferences. I doubt very much whether this postulate is realistic or even meaningful as applied to individuals; still less as applied to nations. It is doubtful in particular that we have the means for comparing every pair chosen at random among such complex policies as confront us in making national defense decisions. In some cases we simply don't know whether we prefer one to the other or whether we are indifferent. On the other hand, there are partial orderings that are possible, and in the course of a systems study we can expand such partial orderings as we increase our knowledge about the systems that have been proposed, as we develop more inclusive criteria, and, above all, as we design policies that dominate ones currently contemplated. Preference schemes are perpetually and necessarily incomplete, always in the process of construction, as we find out more about what alternatives are open and more about what we want.

Given the tremendous range of uncertainties and the other difficulties described earlier in this chapter, it may be asked: Is it possible, except as an extraordinary stroke of luck, to invent any system in the small or in the large that dominates its many million alternatives? If this question concerns whether we can find the optimum in the sense of the best possible, I am inclined to think that it is beside the point.

The point is to get something better. And here the difficulties of the problems we are attacking offer a kind of inverted comfort. The solutions currently accepted for many problems of importance may be quite inadequate. This would hardly be surprising in the light of our review of the difficulties brought about by the swift and continual changes in modern weapon technology. The implications of such changes are complex, far reaching, not easily understood, and still less easily faced in practice. The organs for making decisions in this area and carrying them out have to be big in order to handle the immense detail of administering programs. But big institutions, as we remarked earlier when we noted the possibility that one's opponent might use a less than optimal strategy, exhibit considerable inertia. The same is true for both sides. Actual programs may lag. Strategies may be inert. Thus there is an opportunity for the inventive systems designer, detached sufficiently from the detail of everyday operation, to examine the wider implications of impending technical and political change.

Even if a systems analysis cannot determine an ideal "best" (and defining "best possible" has difficulties related to those that beset the definition of "worst possible"), it is helpful if it can find and prove some system that is distinctly better than those likely to be accepted otherwise. That it can do this much, systems analysis has already demonstrated.

Chapter 8

METHODS AND PROCEDURES

E. S. QUADE

8.1. INTRODUCTION

It is not easy to tell someone how to carry out a systems analysis. We lack an adequate theory to guide us. This must be expected, for systems analysis, even more than operations research, is a new discipline. History teaches us that good theory usually comes late in the development of any field and after many false starts.

The attention of the practitioners, when it has turned to methods, has been focused mainly on the development of mathematical techniques for handling certain specialized problems, common in operations research, rather than on an attempt to build a basic theory for the treatment of broad context questions such as occur in defense planning. This attention to technique has met with great success. Models have become easier to manipulate, even with many more variables represented, and the computational obstacles in operations research now cause comparatively little difficulty. The more philosophical problems, however, such as occur in providing assurance that the model is meaningful, in devising schemes to compensate for uncertainty, or in choosing appropriate criteria, are most troublesome. Therefore, the many important and useful mathematical techniques of operations research are treated very cursorily in this book, although Chapter 13 tries to give some indication of their nature and limitations. Concepts and understanding—areas where the analyst as well as the user is more likely to err—are emphasized instead.

When the possibility of preparing a lecture on the procedures of analysis was first considered, the proper approach seemed obvious: Examine all available studies carried out to help military decisionmaking and extract the principles and methods common to the successful studies. In other words, isolate the ideas that make an analysis a good one. This effort did not turn out to be very productive. Either the sample was too small or we were not sufficiently perceptive, or (what now seems more likely) no universally accepted set of ideas existed. It was even difficult to decide which studies should be called good or successful.

One hope for guidance is to turn to science. In fact, it is frequently argued that operations research should be considered a science. But the goals are different. Science is concerned primarily with the pursuit of truth and a better understanding of the world we live in. Operations research, almost without exception, is concerned with policy, that is, with more effective manipulation of the real world—even if this may have to be accomplished without full understanding of the underlying phenomena. Its purpose is seldom merely to understand or to predict.

There is little difference in method:

> ... Both the exact scientist and the operations analyst tend to make use of what is sometimes called a mathematical model of the subject matter; in the case of the scientist such a model is apt to be part of the well-confirmed body of our scientific knowledge, whereas an operations research model is of a more tentative, *ad hoc,* character. In other words, even if the current status of science provides no well-established theory for the phenomena to be dealt with by the operations analyst, the latter must nevertheless construct a model as best he can, where both the structure of the model and its numerical inputs may be based merely on intuitive insight and limited practical experience by the analyst himself or by whatever expert advisers on the subject matter may be available to him. As further insights accrue and more experimental data become available, the operations analyst has to be ready to discard his first model and replace it with an improved one. This tentative procedure, dictated by pragmatic considerations, is thus essentially one of successive approximation. In this regard, operations research has a status similar to that of the so-called inexact sciences, of which medicine, engineering, and most of the social sciences are examples.

> Therefore, in comparing operations research with an exact science, it is with regard to exactness that operations research falls short, but not necessarily with regard to the scientific character of its methods. . . .[1]

Operations research attempts to use the methods of science. This means in essence that it strives for the same traditions. Scientific tradition holds that (1) results are obtained by processes that another scientist can duplicate to attain the same results; (2) all calculations, assumptions, data, and judgments are made explicit and thus subject to checking, criticism, and disagreement; (3) the scientific method is objective; its propositions do not depend on personalities, reputations, or vested interests; where possible it is quantitative and experimental. For operations research and systems analysis, however, these are still unachieved goals.

---

[1] Olaf Helmer, *The Systematic Use of Expert Judgment in Operations Research,* The RAND Corporation, P-2795, September 1963.

8.2. ENGINEERING AND SYSTEMS ANALYSIS

Operations research and, to an even greater degree, systems analysis seem to be more nearly engineering than science. For the purpose of making a distinction here, one might say that science finds things out, while engineering uses the results of science to do things cheaply and well.

While there are similarities between the typical engineering problem and the typical military systems analysis or operations research problem, there are important distinctions. Most of these are of a quantitative rather than of a qualitative nature. In military systems analyses

1.   There are relatively many more factors that can only be estimated rather than measured or experimented with. Consider as an example the design of a "flyaway" kit, that is, a package of spare parts, tools, and equipment to be airlifted into the field to support a tactical bomber. Among a host of factors, the design depends upon the character of the war in which the bomber is to be used. But the pattern of future wars in which a tactical bomber might be used is a real uncertainty—not something that can be experimented with.

2.   Even when measurements can be made, the results of field tests or of experiments made on the proving ground are likely to differ radically from results obtained under combat conditions.

Again refer to the flyaway kit problem; the peacetime demand for spare parts does not necessarily reflect the wartime demand the kit should be designed to meet.

3.   The time period after which the answers become worthless is almost always extremely brief.

In these days weapons become obsolete rapidly. If we spend enough time in testing even to establish the peacetime demand for spares for our flyaway kit, we may have our answer too late to be of any help.

The time limit is important to the engineer also, but ordinarily not to the same extent. To the academic scientist, time may not be of particular consequence. He is after a high degree of confidence in his results, and whatever time it takes to get the degree of confidence he is after, he can usually take. The military analyst, on the other hand, must frequently reach his best possible conclusion in a limited time.

4.   There is frequently no way to verify the conclusions of the study.

If we are lucky, before there is a war our flyaway kit will be replaced by another to complement a more modern aircraft, and we will never find out whether the original kit would have been satisfactory.

5.   The value concepts are much more troublesome. Like engineering, the military analyses seek to help someone take action; unlike most engineering,

however, the determination of objectives, costs, and criteria represents a difficult problem.

6. In military analysis, as opposed to its civilian counterparts, the interaction of the enemy's alternatives, objectives, and costs with our own is usually the major problem, and the interaction between our own alternatives, objectives, and costs is relatively minor. While the need to treat *conflict* aspects of the problem does not necessarily make the analysis more difficult, it does introduce an additional set of uncertainties and complexities.

There are also some more subtle differences.

For one thing, systems analysis is engineering at a high level in the sense suggested by the following example. A glass engineer successfully plans the production of certain kinds of optical glass on the basis of chemical knowledge; a lens-designing engineer designs camera lenses on the basis of a knowledge of optics, the techniques of lens manufacture, and the general capabilities of the glass engineer; a camera engineer designs a camera on the basis of his knowledge of many things, including what the lens designer can do; the aeronautical engineer designs a reconnaissance plane, using, among other things, his knowledge of what he can expect from the camera designer; the systems analyst designs a reconnaissance system knowing what he can expect from the plane designer. Of course, there is communication up and down the list.

Military systems analysis may differ from ordinary engineering in its enormous responsibility, in its relatively poor data, and in the unusual difficulty of appraising the value system applicable to its problems, but these differences are not violent; they are quantitative, not qualitative. All the difficulties referred to occur in some measure in the humblest engineering problem such as designing a simple dog kennel [2].

Perhaps no set of lectures has ever been directed toward those who employ civil, mechanical, or chemical engineers, and while it would not be impossible to imagine such a course being useful, it is significant that it is nonexistent or rare.

If a city hires an engineer to design a bridge, it may perhaps have his work checked by another engineer, but the city fathers will not presume to study his report with a view to seeing for themselves whether the proposed bridge is likely to collapse. They believe, with more or less reason, that the field of civil engineering is sufficiently well developed and a licensed engineer so likely to be firm in his science that his judgment in this matter

---

[2] Unpublished communication from L. J. Savage commenting on an earlier version of this chapter.

is overwhelmingly better than their own. Similarly, they will trust the authority of their engineer that the clearance, carrying capacity, safety, and durability of the proposed bridge cannot all be increased without an increase in cost. The trade-offs among these values might in principle concern the city fathers, and in special cases they will. But, by and large, there will be none among them capable of or feeling the responsibility for going deeply into these matters. Where, however, a defense system for the nation is concerned, tradition cannot be relied upon; for there is too little of it. The trade-offs between the various values involved are properly felt to be high concerns of the nation and the immediate responsibility of high government officers. Of course, even in the case of the bridge, there are some trade-off considerations that the city fathers cannot dodge. They must make some decisions that depend on their estimates of the political temper of the city and of its probable future growth—decisions for which the civil engineer has no particular competence[3].

8.3. THE PHILOSOPHICAL ASPECTS OF ANALYSIS

Systems analysis, particularly of the type required for military decisions, is still largely a form of art. An art can be taught in part, but not by means of fixed rules which need only be followed with exactness. Thus, in these analyses, we have to do some things that we think are right but that are not verifiable, that we cannot really justify, and that are never checked in the output of the work. Also we must accept as inputs many relatively intangible factors derived from human judgment, and we must present answers to be used as a basis for other judgments. Whenever possible, this judgment is supplemented by inductive and numerical reasoning, but it is only judgment nonetheless.

In fact, to a large extent, systems analysis and operations research are successful aids to policy determination in areas such as national security, where there is no accepted theoretical foundation, precisely because they are designed to make systematic and efficient rather than haphazard and unguided use of judgment by specialists or experts in the fields of interest. The essence of their method is to construct a "model" appropriate to the problem; such a model— which may be a game, a computer program, or a politico-military scenario— introduces a precise structure and terminology that serves primarily as an effective means of communication, and, through feedback—the countermoves in a war game, for instance—helps the experts to arrive at a clearer understanding of the subject matter and the problem.

There is a distinction here between operations research and what we term systems analysis. To be more explicit, consider what might be called a "typical"

---

[3]   *Ibid.*

operations research problem by many of its practitioners. Although there may be several resource variables which are subject to choice, the problem usually can (by making enough assumptions) be put in a form where there is only one dependent variable—termed the criterion or measure of merit (frequently cost); this is to be optimized subject to some set of constraints. The relationship between this dependent variable and the resource variables is formulated mathematically. This allows trade-offs between resources to be investigated. On the other hand, the "typical" systems analysis problem is often first: What is the problem? It is frequently difficult to formulate a criterion because the objectives may be multiple and conflicting. Trade-off may have to be investigated between objectives as well as between resources. Moreover, it may be impossible to describe the relationship between objectives and resources in terms of known mathematical functions or even to describe it numerically or graphically. Without a means for expressing the relationships between these classes of variables, the only recourse for investigation of trade-offs lies in the judgments and intuitions of experts. Such judgments in systems analysis are, of course, in addition to those which are inherent in even the simplest operations research problem—for example, judgments about the scope of the problem.

To emphasize further this distinction between operations research and systems analysis, we quote (in essence) from one military report.

> The participants were asked to project their experience and thinking into an uncharted future where formal doctrine offered little or no guidance and where concepts of future war would not necessarily be limited by practical considerations of current organization, weapons, and budgets. *The work of the group, therefore, was not operations research.* Concepts and hypotheses were presented and discussed that could not be supported immediately by facts and figures or be analyzed in terms of experience or experimental data, simply because the necessary data did not exist [4].

Again, from another source.

> The formulation of objectives and the action on the recommendations are not properly included in the activity of the operations analyst, being literally boundary conditions imposed on the freedom of his operation[5].

While such activities may not be operations research, they are part and parcel of the activities which go on under the name of systems analysis.

This suggests that analysis in support of defense decisionmakers at the national policy level is different from operations research as traditionally viewed.

---

[4] Italics supplied.
[5] Thomas L. Saaty, *Mathematical Methods of Operations Research,* McGraw-Hill Book Company, Inc., New York, 1959, p. 4.

As one participant puts it:

> ... The traditional formulation of operations research problems in terms of ends and means—how can I maximize the achievement of an objective or a set of objectives for a given cost, or alternatively, how can I minimize the cost of achieving a certain set of objectives?—is proper, but limited. At the national policy level, the major part of systems analysis is the exploration of the interaction of ends and means. By that interaction is meant that what are objectives from one point of view are means from another; that what is worth trying to do depends on what is possible to do, or on how effective the means for doing it are; and that any given objective is likely to be one of a number of alternative ways of achieving a still broader objective[6].

Decisions pertaining to choices of alternative weapon systems or force structures and the strategies for their employment, made five to ten years in advance, are essentially matters of economic choice. Certain elements are common to such problems, although these elements may not always be explicitly identified by the analyst. These were stated earlier by C. J. Hitch in Chapter 2 and have been discussed separately in the last four chapters.

1. *The objective* (or objectives).　Systems analysis is undertaken primarily to suggest or, at the very least, to help choose a course of action. This action must have an aim or objective. Policies or strategies, forces or equipment are examined, compared, and preferred on the basis of how well and how cheaply they can accomplish the aim or objective.

2. *The alternatives.*　The alternatives are the means by which it is hoped the objectives can be attained. They need not be obvious substitutes or perform the same specific function.

3. *The costs.*　Each alternative means of accomplishing the objectives implies the use of specific resources which cannot then be used for other purposes.

4. *A model* (or models).　The model is a representation of the situation under study designed to predict the cost and performance of each alternative. It abstracts the relevant features of the situation by means which may vary from a set of mathematical equations or a computer program to an idealized description of the situation in which judgment alone is used to assess the consequences of various choices.

5. *A criterion.*　A criterion is a rule or test by which one alternative can be chosen in preference to another. It provides a means for using cost and effectiveness to order the alternatives.

---

[6] Alain C. Enthoven, "Operations Research and the Design of the Defense Program", *Proceedings of the Third International Conference on Operational Research,* Dunod, Paris, 1964, pp. 531–538.

It is easy to find statements in the literature of operations research which imply that analysis to aid any decisionmaker is really nothing more than the "scientific method" extended to problems outside the realm of pure science. Even though it is by no means clear that there is any unique method which might be termed the "scientific method", what is usually meant is that the analysis advances through something like the following stages:

Formulation — Defining the issues of concern, clarifying the objectives, and limiting the problem.

Search — Determining the relevant data, looking for alternative programs·of action to resolve the issues.

Explanation — Building a model and using it to explore the consequences of the alternative programs, ordinarily by obtaining estimates of their cost and performance.

Interpretation — Deriving the conclusions and indicating a preferred alternative or course of action. This may be a combination of features from previously considered alternatives or their modification to reflect factors not taken into account earlier.

Verification — Testing the conclusion by experiment.

A systems analysis always involves the first four of these stages but frequently must omit the last. For military problems, experiment, other than a pseudo experiment by simulation, may simply not be available.

The discussion of methods is divided into four sections, corresponding to the first four stages listed above. Much methodology is discussed elsewhere, however. For instance, model building in Chapter 4, gaming in Chapter 10, and taking account of the enemy in Chapter 12. This chapter repeats some of the material of the earlier chapters, not only for emphasis but also for perspective.

Formulation

Formulation implies an attempt to isolate the questions or issues involved, to fix the context within which these issues are to be resolved, to define the meaning of the variables or factors that are operative, and to state relationships among these factors. The relationships may be extremely hypothetical because empirical knowledge may be in short supply, but they will help make the logical structure of the analysis clear. In a sense, this is the most important stage, for the time spent restating the problem in different ways, redefining it, or expressing its limits brings to light whether it is spurious or trivial and points the way to its solution. The tendency all too frequently is to accept the original statement of what is wanted exactly as proposed, and then to set about building a model and gathering information, scarcely giving a thought to how the answer will contribute to the decisions which it is trying to assist. In fact, because the concern is with the future, the major job may be to decide what the policymaker should want to do. Since systems studies have resulted in some rather important changes, not only in how the policymaker carries out his activity but in the objectives themselves, it would be self-defeating to accept without inquiry the customers' or sponsors' view of what the problem is.

An analogy with medical practice may be drawn. No doctor ignores a patient's description of his symptoms, but he cannot allow the patient's self-diagnosis to override his own professional judgment. The medical analogy is not entirely applicable, however; the businessman or military commander ordinarily knows more than anyone else about his actual operations and what, if anything, might be wrong with them.

How then is the analyst to know his formulation of the problem is superior? *His only possible advantage lies in analysis.* That is, the process of problem formulation itself has to be the subject of analysis. The systems analyst always has some idea as to the possible solutions of the problem; otherwise, he probably should not be working on it, for his analysis will prove to be too formal and abstract. At this early stage the analyst essentially makes an attempt to solve the problem before the facts are known. It is this attempt which gives him a basis for better formulation.

Let us take an example of how an analyst might go about problem formulation. Take the choice of a criterion. It may be hopelessly impossible to think out a good one in advance. The practical way may be to take a rather crude value scale, see what solution its use leads to, and then, if the solution is not in accordance with common sense, revise it. For instance, consider the analyst who needed to lose weight and set out to use a linear programming model to evolve an optimal reducing diet. He decided that an ideal criterion would be to get the most volume within the constraints of the necessary nutrients and calories. Well, he put his model on the machine, ground away, and came up with watermelon. That showed him he had better consider dried weight to exclude water. When this was done he came up with bouillon cubes, which consist largely of salt. Since this would not be very palatable and might be injurious to health, he made still another choice, and continuing in this way, he finally evolved a satisfactory rule of choice.

The problem itself does not remain static. Interplay between a growing understanding of the problem and of possible developments will redefine the problem itself. Primarily, as the result of discussion, the original effort to state the problem should suggest one or more possible solutions or hypotheses. As the study progresses, these original ideas are enriched and elaborated upon. Each hypothesis serves as a guide to later results—it tells us what we are looking for while we are looking. The final statement of the conclusions and recommendations usually rests on a knowledge of facts about the problem which are not

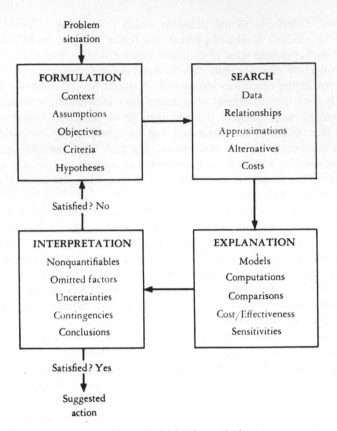

Fig. 8.1   Activities in analysis

known to the analyst at the start. Frequently, a hypothesis must be discarded and an entirely new one considered. In the early stages it is not a mistake to hold an idea as to the solution; the pitfall is to refuse to abandon such an idea in the face of mounting evidence.

The process of analysis is thus an *iterative* one—a cycle of problem formulation, selection of objectives, design of alternative systems, data collection, model building, a weighing of costs against effectiveness, the questioning of assumptions and objectives, the opening of new alternatives, reformulation, etc. Figure 8.1 attempts to indicate the iterative character of systems analysis. The various stages are ordered only with respect to a single cycle; the approximate solution we obtain at the end of the first cycle helps us to better prepare a second formulation. Thus, in a sense, it is impossible to formulate a problem completely before it is solved, or, in other words, the final problem statement may have to be written simultaneously with the final answer.

In the problem of choosing objectives, the iterative character of systems analysis stands out. It is impossible to select satisfactory objectives without some idea of the cost and difficulty of attaining them. Such information can only come as part of the analysis itself.

It is a common error to believe that goals should, and can, be set independently of the plans to attain them. Yet there is overwhelming evidence that ultimate objectives are, more often than not, the result of opportunities that possible alternatives offer rather than a source of such alternatives. The point is that only part of the consequences of different goals can be anticipated without analysis.

Military analysis must frequently be undertaken with only partial information about the objectives, criteria, and preferences at higher levels. At the highest level, official statements of national objectives are likely to be either nonexistent or so vague that they are not very helpful. This is a situation that gives rise to "suboptimization"—that is, the selection of intermediate objectives and criteria for the problem that are consistent with and that approximate in some sense or other those at the higher level. Given limitations on time and manpower, a suboptimization may be the only feasible approach. For example, a recommendation to choose a particular defense weapon system may be made on the basis of its capability to intercept and destroy enemy missiles; this may be a substitute for the broader objective of minimizing the number of nuclear weapons detonating on our territory. Whether or not this is a good way to ensure that the analysis pursues the higher objective of limiting damage to population and property if war should come must itself be the subject of analysis.

Although many of the most valuable systems analyses have been suboptimizations, suboptimization may not be good enough and may not be the best that can be done. Analysis can sometimes eliminate, uncover, and reconcile objectives.

There is frequently more than one objective for a system; for example, "to make war unlikely and, in the event war does break out, to limit the damage to ourselves and to achieve a favorable military outcome and political settlement". To choose a system one needs to find some method of weighing competing objectives. How can we decide on a single objective? For one thing, we can examine each objective to see if it is important only as a means to another objective; if it is, then we can eliminate it. For another, we can examine each alternative to see if the attainment of any of the objectives would be unaffected by a choice among the alternatives. Again, if it is, we can eliminate it.

One technique to uncover objectives may be to confront the man who must act on the basis of the analysis with a list of alternatives and ask him if he would be willing to follow the course of action implied by each of the alternatives, were the analysis to indicate it as optimal.

If objectives compete, that is, if people disagree on objectives or if an individual cannot determine what his objectives are—one can try to find still higher objectives on which there is agreement. It then may be possible either to carry out the analysis with the higher level objectives or, by examination of the original objectives for consistency with the one agreed on, to make a choice. One thing we cannot do is construct from all the individual objectives some group objective by appropriately weighing all separate ones; this is a practical absurdity and it has been theoretically demonstrated that there is no unique and satisfying way to do it. If, in the end, all attempts to reduce objectives fail, it may be helpful to carry out the analysis for each objective.

A characteristic of systems analysis is that the solutions are often found in a set of compromises which seek to balance and, where possible, to reconcile conflicting objectives and questions of value. It is more important to choose the "right" objective than it is to make the "right" choice between alternatives. The wrong objective means that the wrong problem is being solved. The choice of the wrong alternative may merely mean that something less than the "best" system is being chosen. Frequently we must be satisfied with merely a demonstration that a suggested action is "in the right direction", anyway. This may be all that is possible.

To choose among alternatives, we must do more than determine which alternatives can attain a desired objective. Some criterion or test of preferredness must be employed; say, a rule to select for us the alternative (or alternatives) that yields the objectives for the least expenditure of costs or resources[7].

Two rules for guidance in choosing a criterion, originally stated by C. J. Hitch[8], are

1. A criterion used in a lower level problem should be consistent with that appropriate to the next higher level.

2. A criterion should not have to be repeatedly hedged by constraints to prevent it from giving absurd results.

As an example to illustrate the first rule, in determining a parking lot policy for an amusement park, the policy at the level of the people running the lot might be that of maximizing net revenues from parking. But this may well be different from the policy of the people running the park whose criterion might be to maximize the net revenues from the amusement park as a whole. In considering parking lot revenues, lack of parking for a few people, who then go

7   See, in addition to Chapter 5, C. J. Hitch and R. N. McKean, *The Economics of Defense in the Nuclear Age,* Harvard University Press, Cambridge, Mass., 1960; and Hitch, "Economics and Military Operations Research", *Review of Economics and Statistics,* vol. XL, no. 3, August 1958, pp. 199–209.

8   "Comments by C. J. Hitch", *Operations Research,* vol. 4, no. 4, August 1956, p. 427. His statement is paraphrased here.

elsewhere, might lead to considerable savings in land costs for parking and in salary for attendants, and thus in greater revenue for the lot, but the loss of good will might result in considerable loss of revenue for the park as a whole. A policy more consistent with the higher level, and thus a better policy for the lot, might simply be to provide parking for all who come—or even to provide this parking free of charge.

We cannot know a priori, however, that income from a parking lot should be small relative to income from the facility it serves. Whenever there is little opportunity of visiting the facility except by private car, the possibility of disguising a significant general admission charge as a parking charge may merit serious consideration.

As an example to illustrate the second rule, we can take any "ratio" criterion where a constraint must be imposed to keep the denominator away from zero. Cost must be treated as a major element:

> Furthermore, there has long been a tendency in the Defense Department to state military requirements in absolute terms without reference to their costs. But the military effectiveness or military worth of any given weapon system cannot logically be considered in isolation. It must be considered in relation to its cost—and in a world in which resources are limited, to the alternative uses to which resources can be put. Military requirements are meaningful only in terms of benefits to be gained in relation to their cost. Thus, resource costs and military worth have to be scrutinized together[9].

The costs to be considered in choosing among alternatives, moreover, should be the "new" costs, that is, the net additional resource drain or "incremental cost" that would be incurred because of the choice of a particular alternative. Because a certain system may inherit facilities, personnel, or equipment from previous systems, its incremental costs may be much lower than what it would cost if it were to exist "in isolation". Also, in a comparison of military capabilities, costs have sometimes been computed on the basis of what the various systems would cost independent of the existence of other systems or other capabilities. In this light consider, for example, a Navy supercarrier. In a paper comparison to estimate its value in a limited-war role, if no credit were assigned to its central war capabilities, then on a cost-effectiveness basis it would be handicapped unfairly in comparison with a weapon system that had only a single role.

Great attention must be paid to initial conditions; that is, to the assumptions that limit the problem and set the background against which the initial attempt at a solution is to be made. The situation is not like that of an empirical science,

---

9 Charles J. Hitch, Assistant Secretary of Defense (Comptroller). Testimony in *Systems Development and Management (Part 2)*, Hearings before a Subcommittee of the Committee on Government Operations, House of Representatives, 87th Congress, 2nd Session, U.S. Government Printing Office, Washington, D.C., 1962, p. 515.

which starts with observed facts, but more like that of mathematics, where the results take any "validity" they might have in the real world from the initial assumptions. The difference is that for the systems analysis to give correct guidance, it is important that the assumptions be the "right" assumptions.

Even for small-scale problems, the number of factors under consideration at any one time must be reduced until what is left is manageable. In systems analysis, the complexity of the "full" problem frequently far outruns analytic competence. To consider in detail anything like the complete range of possible alternative solutions may be impossible. The vast majority will obviously be inferior, hence there is no harm in leaving them out. The danger is that some alternative better than that uncovered by the analysis will also have been left out. Constraints must be imposed on the number of alternatives to be examined, but by preliminary analysis, not by arbitrary decree. Such constraints must be regarded as flexible so that they may be weakened or removed if it appears in later cycles that their presence is a controlling factor.

Sometimes problems can be reduced by factoring out subproblems. This can be done when a group of variables having relatively little interdependence with the other variables can be treated separately.

Once the problem has been broken down into its components—which is what analyzing the problem means—some of the components can be further analyzed, using various techniques; but others may defy analytic techniques. In that case, because the problem has been broken into smaller pieces, the systems analyst may be able to find individuals who have direct, sound experience and on whose "considered" judgment he can rely.

Considered judgment differs from ordinary or intuitive judgment in that the logic behind the opinion is made explicit. Both are based on an individual's experience and background, but when the reasoning is explicit, an observer can form his own opinion from the information presented. Judgment permeates systems analysis—judgments as to which hypothesis is better than another, or which approach is more fruitful, or what facts are relevant. The ideal is to keep all judgments in plain view.

One methodological aspect of operations research, the reliance on expert judgment, has received little attention[10]. Only by replacing the surreptitious use of expertise by explicit and systematic application of it can objectivity be safeguarded.

---

[10] Except by Olaf Helmer. For additional information, see Helmer, *The Systematic Use of Expert Judgment in Operations Research,* The RAND Corporation, P-2795, September 1963; Helmer and Nicholas Rescher, "On the Epistemology of the Inexact Sciences", *Management Science,* vol. 6, no. 1, October 1959, pp. 25–52; N. Dalkey and Helmer, "An Experimental Application of the Delphi Method to the Use of Experts", *Management Science,* vol. 9, no. 3, April 1963, pp. 458–467. (The discussion on the use of experts presented in this chapter is based on Helmer's paper.)

Usually two or more experts are available. When they differ, there are several ways to try to bring them together. Using the consensus approach they can work individually and then seek methods for the best combined use of their findings; or they can work jointly in a group exercise—ranging from simple round-table discussions to reacting through a sophisticated simulation model— to obtain expert judgments from the group as a whole. Operational gaming, or simulation involving role-playing by the participating experts, is particularly promising when it is desirable to employ several experts with varying specialities in a context in which their forecasts cannot be independent but are likely to interact. Here the game structure or model furnishes the experts with an artificial, simulated environment within which they can jointly and simultaneously experiment, acquiring through feedback the insights necessary to make successful predictions within the model environment and thus indirectly about the real world.

Another method, falling somewhere between individual and group action, is the so-called Delphi technique. It needs further development and testing but is regarded by this author as very promising. It tries to improve the basis consensus method by subjecting the experts' views to each other's criticism without actual confrontation and all its psychological shortcomings (such as specious persuasion, an unwillingness to abandon publicly expressed opinions, and the bandwagon effect of the majority). The Delphi technique replaces direct debate by a carefully designed program of sequential individual interrogations (best conducted by questionnaires) interspersed with information and opinion feedback derived by computed consensus from the earlier parts of the program. Some of the questions directed to the respondents may, for instance, inquire into the "reasons" for previously expressed opinions, and a collection of such reasons may then be presented to each respondent, together with an invitation to reconsider and possibly revise his earlier estimates.

Systems analysis, as the name suggests, must be systems oriented. It is important to recognize that anything going on in one part of an activity, organization, or weapon system will likely affect what goes on in every other part. The natural inclination might be to factor out parts of the problem and analyze each separately, neglecting their interactions. However, the aim of analysis is to extend the boundaries of the system as far as required, determine which interdependences are significant, and then evaluate their combined impact.

For this reason, and because the context is naturally broad anyway, systems analysis usually calls for an interdisciplinary team consisting of persons with a variety of skills. This is not required merely because many factors and aspects are involved. Even more important is that a problem looks different to an economist, to a mathematician, and to an engineer, and different ways of looking at a problem are important in finding a solution.

Uncertainty in long-range military planning problems being as great as it is, it is well—particularly early in the study—not to attach much significance to small differences in cost and effectiveness of alternative systems. Specifically, it is important to look for differences that have a chance of surviving *any* likely resolution of the uncertainties. Rather than ask precisely how much better one alternative is than the others, the question to address is which alternatives have a clear advantage or even, initially, which will move us forward.

Search

This phase is concerned with finding the facts, or evidence, on which the analysis is based. It is necessary to look for ideas (and evidence to support them), including the invention of new alternatives, as well as to look for facts. Unless we have alternatives and ideas about them, there is nothing to analyze or to choose between. If in the end we are to designate a preferred course of action, we must have discovered earlier that such a course exists. In long-range problems, the total number of alternatives may be endless, and we must use judgment to eliminate those that are unreasonable.

Many facts are hard to come by. The actual operational performance of future weapons in combat cannot be predicted with any degree of certainty. Purely theoretical studies or operations research of weapon characteristics must be depended upon. In systems analysis, as contrasted with most other forms of engineering, a great many more inputs depend on judgment than on measurement or engineering analysis.

For many problems it is the availability of the facts which makes a solution possible. Consider, for example, the flyaway kit problem we mentioned earlier. The computation per se of the optimum kit according to some standard of performance, measured in terms of the expected loss in combat effectiveness attributable to kit shortages during the support period, is a relatively trivial problem. Surprisingly enough, the difficulty comes in getting the input data. This may involve such a seemingly easy item as getting a complete list of spare parts, as well as such an acknowledgedly difficult one as getting the data that tell how frequently particular spares are needed.

Indeed, even if the analysis is never completed, the collection of facts and their orderly presentation in tables and graphs can sometimes make the solution obvious.

It is sometimes said that when all the facts are known, the problem is solved. This may be true in a philosophical sense, but in a practical sense the real work may have only begun.

In practical problems for systems analysis, however, all the facts are never known. For example, to recommend a preferred interceptor combat radius, it is necessary to study interceptor performance characteristics, radar coverage requirements, effectiveness, and cost as functions of combat radius. This involves a study of the possible target systems the enemy might select and the pattern of enemy attacks. Such things as radar, costs, proper deployment, interceptor armament, attrition, and the effect of other weapons must then be considered.

When should an inquiry stop? It is important to remember that in this sort of a problem, inquiry is rarely exhaustive. Inquiries are partial, and the decision-maker must get along without the full advantage of all the potentiality of operations research and the scientific approach. Inquiries cost money and time; they cost in whatever values are concerned. They can cost lives; they can cost national security. It might be interesting to know what the Russians could do if we dropped an armed Atlas on Moscow. It might be an easy observation to make, but some of the costs seem to prohibit this type of investigation. One should never fall into the error of feeling that inquiry is free of cost. There are many contexts in which we can ignore the cost of inquiry; but paradoxes arise if we allow ourselves to forget that almost all inquiries must stop far, far short of completion either for lack of funds, of time, or of justification for spending further funds or time on them. It is out of the question to collect all the information that is required for exhaustive analysis, and it is out of the question to process it.

As an analogy, consider the example of a physician who uses a clinical laboratory to help him decide whether or not his patient has one of several ailments that have many similar symptoms. Even when all the reports are in, the doctor's inquiry may not be complete. He could probably do a lot more laboratory analysis or call in a specialist for consultation. If the problem is simply one of diagnosis, one of the best procedures might be to slaughter the patient and perform a thorough autopsy. The cost here is prohibitive, not only by the standards of modern society but simply by the fact that the physician's goal is to help the patient live a longer and fuller life. He would only frustrate himself if he bought knowledge at the price of the life he was trying to guard [11].

Explanation

After obtaining some idea of what the facts and alternatives are, it is necessary to build up some way to explain them and to determine their implications.

In order to make much progress with real-world problems, we must ignore a great many of the actual features of a question under study and abstract from the real situation certain aspects—hopefully, the relevant ones—and their interaction, which together make up an idealized version of the real situation. This idealization we call a "model".

---

[11] This is not to say he might not risk life in trying to guard it; he might order such tests as a spinal puncture or a liver puncture, or other inherently dangerous procedures. Many diagnostic procedures are dangerous and are used when the danger is justified, but a doctor will not make a complete sacrifice of what he is trying to protect.

In the general process of formulating a problem and gathering data about it, the analyst will have developed some ideas of what the major influencing factors are, that is, the factors which provide discrimination with respect to the possible courses of action. To produce quantitative results, it is necessary to assign a scale of measurement to each factor and to show its dependence on certain parameters. Next, the interaction of the factors must be described. Then we have a model. In other words, isolating those factors pertinent to the problem or the decision at hand, abstracting them, assigning a scale of measurement, and then describing their interactions build the model.

The difficulty in model building is that we do not know at the start what is superfluous and what is relevant. We must proceed on the basis of experience and trial with preliminary models, conducting pencil and paper experiments to illuminate our preliminary judgments. Analysis, being iterative, is self-correcting; as the study goes on, the original model is refined and replaced so that behavior of the relationships being investigated is represented with greater accuracy.

For most phenomena, there are many possible representations; the appropriate model depends as much *on the question being asked* as on the phenomena about which it is asked. R. D. Specht made this important point in Chapter 4. A town can be modeled by a map if the question being asked is how to walk from A to B; but if the question is how to speed up the flow of traffic between the same two points, a much more elaborate model may be needed. There are thus no "universal" models—that is, say, no one model that can handle all questions about a given activity.

Sometimes representation by the model is mathematical, by means of a series of equations. At other times, particularly where detailed specification of the relationships between factors is extremely difficult—for example, in studying the behavior of human organizations—the representation may be by simulation or by a war game.

In operations research parlance, the term simulation is applied to the process of representing, without using formal analytic techniques, the essential features of a system or organization and analyzing its behavior by operating with the representation. Simulation is a broadly inclusive word used to describe various physical or analogue devices, such as a Link trainer, or a computer program which traces a strategic campaign through Monte Carlo operations, or a group of people or machines acting as if they were an air defense control center.

If working with the representation or model has some of the aspects of playing a game, particularly if human players are involved, the simulation is called a game. A gaming model cannot be expected to tell us what an optimal response to an uncertain state of affairs might be, but it can do much to make the players aware of such uncertainties and of the necessity of formulating their plans in such a way as to cope with all foreseeable contingencies. Indeed, an important asset to all systems analysis is the spirit of gaming. This consists in explicitly looking at possible moves and countermoves, in examining and designing a wide range of alternatives, and in looking for substitution possibilities—all against a hostile opponent.

Simulation, although relatively new in wide-scale applications, is an established operations research technique, which uses quasi-experimentation in an artificial environment for actual experiment in the real world. Its outstanding virtue is that it can be used to tackle seemingly unmanageable or previously untouched problems where a traditional analytic formulation appears infeasible. It is ordinarily an inefficient technique, however, to use in determining a sharp result, and it yields only a quasi-empirical form of knowledge, inferior to the functional relationships built up through the more traditional approach of using an analytic model. Simulation is a device appropriate to use before one has an adequate theory, for it provides a means to use the intuition and advice of experts in a systematic fashion and a way to go about building an analytic model by approximating the behavior of the random numbers, or physical counters, or human players with mathematical expressions.

The primary function of a model is "explanatory" rather than descriptive. Frequently it is not used to guide computation but solely to organize our thinking.

It should be emphasized that, in many important systems analyses, no need arises to build formal models explicitly. When such cases occur, the analysis may be extraordinarily effective since it can be completely understood by the policymaker. The essence of systems analysis is not mathematical techniques or procedures. A computing machine or a technique such as linear programming may or may not be useful, depending on the problem and the extent of our information. The essential thing is a listing of the alternatives and an examination of their implications and costs so that they can be compared. What we say about models thus does not have much significance for analyses that require no more than a listing of alternatives and their implications, but is included because many difficult problems do require the use of well-defined models to guide computation.

The widely useful operations research techniques for optimization, when they are used at all in systems analysis, are used much more extensively in component studies than they are at the heart of the over-all problem. Before any mathematical technique can be applied to a real-world problem, we must construct a quantitative model of the processes involved. This model expresses the effectiveness of the alternatives under examination as a function of a set of variables, some of which are under control. Once this is done, a solution can be determined mathematically, since formal statements of relationships between the variables exist. The solution obtained from such a model will be a usable solution to the real-world problem if and only if the model is a reasonably accurate representation of the real-world situation with respect to the question at issue. In situations of great complexity, such as those associated with major military decisions, only pieces of the problem can be represented with confidence. The submodels for these pieces or components can frequently be put into a form in which they can be handled by such techniques as dynamic programming or queuing theory. But even here, the new and more advanced techniques, while they are useful and promise to become more so, are seldom necessary since—except in relatively few instances—more elementary tools are usually adequate.

The design of models to assist in the decision process is in large measure an art. Wide experiences and the collaboration of many people are helpful, but it requires selection or composition, plus instinct and a sense of form, to achieve a desired effect.

Rules for model building are few in number and not very helpful. For example, it is sometimes suggested that the analyst should try to find models which explain more and more things within the same context. In operations research this leads to the construction of overly big models and attention to the model and not to the problem.

In building a model, assumptions are frequently made in order to handle something that is too difficult to investigate. For example, in the missile comparison of Appendix B, the model was built up step-by-step by a process of "simplification by assumption". Each target, for instance, was taken to be like every other target. This meant that in the model the targets (1) were of equal value to the offense, (2) required the same bomb yield to destroy, (3) were at the same range, (4) were protected by the same defense, and (5) were isolated so that destruction of one did not imply destruction of another. In essence, we made use of the assumption, fundamental to working with models but seldom stated, that by studying a simplified hypothetical situation we will get approximately the same answer we would get by studying the most realistic situation imaginable.

All of the assumptions of a model must be made explicit. If they are not, this is a defect. A mark of a good systems analyst (or any wise person communicating with others) is that he state the basis on which he operates. This does not imply necessarily that he makes better assumptions, but only that his errors will be more evident.

The contrast between the relative amount of time usually spent on designing a model and that spent in computing its consequences can give bias in judging what is important. The design of the model and the faithfulness with which it represents those aspects of the phenomena being modeled are significant for the question under consideration, not how far we push the computation.

The military analyst does not have, and cannot be expected to have, the precise and flexible means available to the physical scientist for testing his models experimentally. He cannot, for example, experiment with an actual war. The best he can do is to test his models by their workability. For example, he can try to determine answers to the following questions.

1. Can the model describe correctly and clearly the known facts and situations?
2. When the principal parameters involved are varied, do the results remain consistent and plausible?
3. Can it handle special cases in which there is some indication as to what the outcome should be?
4. Can it assign causes to known effects?

Whether or not one model is better than another does not depend on its complexity, realism, or computability but solely on whether it gives better predictions.

"Working" the model, trying out various strategies and concepts of operation, is the closest systems analysis comes to scientific experimentation. Deductions based on operating with the model frequently suggest new directions of effort. That is to say, starting with the relatively few parameters that characterize a system in terms of the model, it is sometimes possible to show that changes in these would improve the performance of the system as measured by the model, and then to suggest corresponding changes that could be made in the real system which would lead to improved performance in the real world. In this way, working the model contributes to system design.

It is also important to go outside the model: to contemplate changes that violate its assumptions and, in so doing, achieve a better model.

Two aspects of model building are particularly troublesome: quantification and the treatment of uncertainty.

Some variables are difficult to quantify, either because they are not calculable, like the probability of war, or because no scale of measurement has been set up like the effect on NATO solidarity of some unilateral U.S. action. This leads either to their neglect, for they tend to be ignored, or to their recognition only through a qualitative modification of a solution reached by manipulation of quantified variables. Thus, when the problem of what action to recommend on the basis of the solution from the model arises, effect of the quantitative variables is built in, while the nonquantitative ones may be easily lost in the welter of qualitative considerations that must be weighed.

One argument for the omission of a particular variable is that the solution of the problem is virtually insensitive to it. The fact that many variables fall into this category makes analysis possible. If the results were *not* insensitive to all but a relatively small number of variables, analysis would have to yield completely to guesses and intuition. Insensitivity can occur either because a factor is irrelevant or trivial in its quantitative effects or because it has roughly the same effect on all the alternatives under consideration. *The point is that*

this insensitivity must be discovered. Sometimes logical reconnoitering is sufficient, but usually analysis is required, possibly with arbitrary values assigned
to factors we are unable to calculate.

If nonquantitative variables are not to be neglected without mention or
dismissed with some spurious argument, such as the one that they act in
opposite direction and hence cancel out [12], then how are they to be treated?
The usual method is to attempt to take them into account through modification
of the solution rather than to incorporate them into the model. But this in
itself represents a particular method of quantification, for, by altering the
solution to take account of the previously omitted variables, the analyst is
implicitly valuing them. Since we always have some insight into the range of
values that a factor might take, we can, even in the worst cases, assign the
factors an arbitrary value and observe the effect on the solution. It seems to be
an empirical fact that actions taken on policy questions are based on the
available numbers, no matter how relevant or sound they may be; consequently,
every effort should be made to quantify.

Most aspects of problems of choice in national security require numbers;
others do not. But the real issue is one of clarity of understanding and expression. Numbers are part of our language. When a quantitative matter is being
discussed, the greatest clarity of thought is achieved by using numbers instead
of by avoiding them, even when uncertainties are present. Only in rare cases
is it possible to make a convincing comparison of alternatives without a
quantitative analysis of the relevant numbers.

Systems analysis is concerned with problems in which the essence is
uncertainty about the future; not only uncertainties about technical and
operational parameters and the actions of the enemy, but also conceptual
uncertainties. Such analysis, as well as any other attempt to answer the same
questions, must necessarily face this uncertainty squarely, treat it as an important element in the problem, and take it into account in formulating recommendations. The treatment of uncertainty is not merely a difficulty in principle,
but is a considerable practical problem. Somehow the number of cases made
necessary by the presence of uncertainty must be limited and the total effort
kept within reasonable bounds.

There are different degrees of uncertainty, but for discussion here we will
recognize two categories: We will call them, for want of better terms, statistical
uncertainties and "real" uncertainties.

Statistical uncertainties—those having a more or less objective or calculable
probability of occurrence—can be handled in the model by Monte Carlo or
other methods. For instance, our knowledge of the situation may be complete
and accurate, but a quantity may be stochastic or "noisy". An example might

---

[12]   It is not enough to know that two variables act in opposite directions; their
quantitative impact must also be estimated.

be the accuracy of a missile system. Alternatively, the quantity involved may have a unique value, but the determinate factors may not be measurable. Then again the quantity involved may be related to measurable factors in such a complex way that it is beyond our mathematical or engineering power to describe, and we must approximate the real situation by a simple description. For example, take the "lethal radius" concept of a nuclear bomb. Such uncertainties, like those in cost or missile accuracy, lead to risks that can be estimated and accepted. They can be annoying but not devastating, like, say, the uncertainties due to ignorance or to competition associated with the prediction of what the environment may turn out to be or the enemy may do during the lifetime of the systems under consideration.

Uncertainties about human factors, which have no necessarily logical construction, or about the future behavior of things, which is beyond the practical ability of analysts to predict, belong to the class of real uncertainties. Under real uncertainty, we consider events—like the probability of war—to which individuals may attach subjective probabilities, but which we cannot calculate. With regard to air defense, for example, real uncertainty involves such questions as "Will we have warning? If we get it, will we believe it? What surprises does the enemy have?" For such uncertainties, there is frequently widespread disagreement about the pertinent probabilities, and even confusion and vagueness within any one individual.

As a simple example, my son when he had just turned sixteen wanted to drive the car. Since he could not walk through a room without bumping into the furniture, the problem I faced was whether to let him drive or not. Here I had uncertainties as to how not driving would affect his personality and character during the next year or so, as well as those about his capability to survive in freeway traffic. This was uncertainty about empirical facts that were not and would not be available and that could not be made available to me by a realistic or thinkable course of inquiry. Therefore, my solution to this problem had to involve guesses and judgments which would never be confirmed, and even now I do not know whether I chose a good solution or not.

There is no foolproof recipe for handling uncertainty, but there are almost always measures that can be taken to make the consequences of possible mistaken prediction less devastating.

With regard to my son's driving, for instance, there were various ways in which I might have sought a good solution. For example, I might have (1) deferred granting the driving privilege for a while to see his reaction, or (2) set up a policy in which a near accident as well as an accident would result in revocation of his privileges, or (3) required him for a period to drive only in specified areas or at specified times. The last, incidentally, would have been not so much a way of getting data as a way of keeping him out of dangerous traffic while he acquired proficiency. I chose still a fourth way, requiring him to pass a course in a driving school reputed to have high standards (rather than teaching him myself and passing my own possibly bad driving practices on to him), and then taking the recommendation of the instructor that if he passed the test for a license, he be permitted to drive without restrictions.

In the analysis, as a prelude to finding ways to compensate for uncertainty, an effort can be made to *forecast* or map the many possible futures, rather than to *predict* a future environment in the sense of specifying a *single* sequence of events. Since the future is inherently unpredictable, it is too hazardous to proceed solely on the basis of a "best estimate" about the future military-technological-political environment. Instead, the analysis must reckon with the wide scope of possible developments and serious uncertainties that the future holds.

To do this, as far as the technical and operational parameters are concerned, one way is first to explore their limits and then make the calculations in terms of the range of uncertainty, using an upper and lower estimate in addition to a best guess. Although initially it is usually necessary to design the system or strategy primarily on the basis of best estimates, this type of investigation, through feedback, helps to modify them so that their performance will not be sensitive functions of parameters whose values are essentially unknown. And it must be kept in mind that alternatives are to be evaluated also by their flexibility to meet the unforeseen, rather than solely by their optimality in meeting expectations. In cases of doubt, to overestimate one's opponent and to under-estimate our own capabilities is not necessarily the safe thing to do. Over-estimates do not necessarily lead to safety and insurance. They are just as likely to lead to despair and loss of morale, to the feeling that the attainment of certain policy objectives is hopeless, and thus to "strategies of desperation".

Of course, the best way to compensate for uncertainty would be to "invent" a better system or policy which would provide insurance against the whole range of possible catastrophes; the difficulty is to discover how to do this.

In view of the uncertainties present in any operations research model, how can one obtain useful information? This fundamental question confronts every scientist and requires *sensitivity* and *contingency* analysis. In addition to calculating initially with a range of values, it is necessary to find out how changes in the information put into the problem and the assumptions made affect the results.

In "sensitivity analysis" an attempt is made to determine how sensitive the results are to variations in key parameters and assumptions. The hope is to obtain a dominant solution in which the ranking of the preferred alternative is essentially insensitive to reasonable variations in values of the parameters or assumptions in question. "Contingency analysis" investigates how a system chosen with one assumption about the environment measures up to the performance of its alternatives when radical changes in the environment occur.

Thus, sensitivity analysis might test the alternatives for a wide range of enemy capabilities or for the consequences of having planned for one level of capability when another is experienced. Contingency analysis might test the alternatives under a change in criteria or compare them in an environment in which France, say, had become part of the Communist Bloc.

Since a systems analysis is a study which attempts to influence policy, it must in the end present a convincing comparison of the relevant alternatives. Although it may be clear to the analyst that a certain course of action A is better than alternative possible courses of action B, C, D . . ., it may not be clear to someone who has not "lived" with the problem. One way to show that under any reasonable assumption the system or policy designed or selected by the analyst is indeed to be preferred is to use either an a fortiori or a "break-even" analysis.

To make an analysis a fortiori, we bend over backward in making the comparisons to "hurt" the system we think is best and to "help" the alternative systems. If it then turns out that after we have done this we can still say we prefer the handicapped system, we are in a strengthened position to make recommendations. Sometimes we cannot do this—say, if we concede the exaggerated performance claims for rival systems and the pessimistic estimates about the systems we like. In this case, we might try a *break-even* analysis: We decide what assumptions must be made about important values in order to make the performance of the two systems essentially the same. Then we can simply ask people to judge whether these assumptions are optimistic or pessimistic. As Kahn and Mann put it:

> *More than any other single thing, the skilled use of a fortiori and break-even analyses separate the professionals* from the *amateurs*. Most analyses should (conceptually) be done in two stages: a first stage to find out what one wants to recommend, and a second stage that generates the kind of information that makes the recommendations convincing even to a hostile and disbelieving, but intelligent audience[13].

Interpretation

After a solution has been obtained from a model, this solution must be interpreted in the light of considerations which may not have been adequately treated by the model, since the model was but a single representation of the real world chosen by the analyst. For example, the systems analyst (or for that matter the designers of the strategic offensive force) may have established the requirement that a force assure the destruction of, say, 95 per cent of the targets at a minimum cost under a certain range of contingencies. But many questions

---

[13]   H. Kahn and I. Mann, *Techniques of Systems Analysis,* The RAND Corporation, RM-1829 (DDC No. AD 123512), December 3, 1956.

occur. Perhaps the minimum cost is too high; maybe the tasks of deterrence and limiting damage could be better done by spending less on strategic forces and more on air defense. The 95 per cent may be too high, or too low. Someone must translate the percentage of target destruction into its implications in terms of more meaningful criteria, such as the balance of military forces, the will to continue fighting, and the effect on our diplomacy. The analyst may be able to help here, but the responsibility is someone else's.

The solution that has been simplified and possibly reduced to mathematical form by drastic idealization and aggregation is not necessarily a good solution of the original problem. A different model might be called for. At this stage, not only does the analyst attempt to interpret his work, but the sponsor or the real world gets into the iterative cycle again, to counteract the analyst's ignorance and thus produce better answers.

To form a basis for recommendations, any military systems analysis must at the very least give adequate consideration to

1. The objectives both of the nation as a whole and of the forces that are to implement these national objectives.
2. The military capabilities required to attain these objectives.
3. The enemy capabilities and objectives.
4. The technological possibilities.
5. The effectiveness of each posture, system, or plan considered.
6. The costs or resource implications of the choices.
7. The uncertainties in the above.

These things, of course, cannot be specified absolutely. They depend on each other, on the degree of security deemed adequate, and on the enemy's interpretation of our objectives and the actions we take to implement them; and they vary over time. Moreover, the entire structure is based on a set of assumptions, hopefully not arbitrary but objective. If action is to be taken on the basis of the analysis, it is important that the assumptions, as well as the goals, be the right ones.

There are special problems associated with military questions. Many factors used in the computations are not and cannot be measured. Sometimes this is because of time limitations; other times it is because factors such as the enemy defense strength, or degradation in combat of complicated man-machine combinations, are not accessible to measurement but have to be assessed on the basis of experience or pooled judgment. The results of computations must be examined to see if they depend critically upon estimations such as these.

In military problems, there are always considerations not subject to any sort of quantitative analysis. To achieve efficiency in a military context, factors other than cost-effectiveness are important—discipline, morale, esprit de corps, tradition, and organizational behavior. Such problems involve more than purely military questions. The size, composition, location, and state of readiness of forces influence our foreign policy and the freedom of action we have there. They also have a major impact on our domestic economy and public morale. The men who must somehow integrate these factors with the study are really doing systems analysis, but at a level so high it is hard to consider it as such.

It is important for the user of analysis to distinguish between what the study shows and the recommendations for action the analyst makes on the basis of what he thinks the study implies. Frequently, when new minds—management, for example—review the problem, they bring new information. Even though the solution obtained from the model is not changed, recommendations for action based on it may be. A model is only an indicator, not a final judge. In our expository example (Chapter 3), while comparisons of basing systems were made under a great many different assumptions, using various models, no one would expect the decision to be made solely on the basis of those comparisons alone—and the same would have held even if an immensely more complicated version of such a study had been carried out.

There are numerous reasons why an interpretation is necessary. Mainly it is because major decisions, in the field of economic or military policy, are part of a political as well as part of an intellectual process. Consider, for instance, the following.

The relationship between "cost" and "effectiveness" of a weapon system for some given objective typically plots as in Fig. 8.2.

If a weapon system plots at A, then clearly the objective is too ambitious for the budget and someone must decide to look for a less ambitious objective or to abandon the system, or, as another possibility, to decide to spend a lot more money to get it to B. If at C and we still have money to spend, clearly we've put

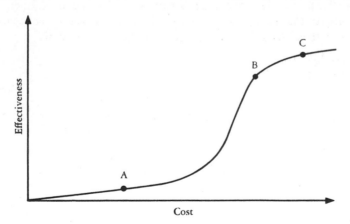

Fig. 8.2   A typical cost-effectiveness curve

more money into the system than was economic and should look for another system and more ambitious objectives.

If, in the judgment of the analyst and those who use his analysis, the alternative ranked highest by the model is good enough, the process is over; if not, more and better alternatives must be designed or the objectives must be lowered. Analysis is sufficient to reach a policy conclusion only when the objectives are agreed upon by the policymakers. In defense policy in particular, and in many other cases as well, objectives are not, in fact, agreed upon. The choice, while ostensibly between alternatives, is really between objectives or ends, and nonanalytical methods must be used for a final reconciliation of views. Although the consequences computed from the model may provide guidance in deciding which objectives to compromise, such decisions are not easily made, and judgment must again be applied.

In the end, military decisionmaking, like systems analysis itself, is an art. After a certain stage, calculation may no longer be helpful. There are always considerations that cannot be measured—say, the importance of military gains against political losses, or public reaction to a temporary setback against the enhanced chances of a long term gain. Moreover, there are always considerations that have been measured or determined by judgment but not to the decisionmaker's satisfaction.

By definition, no judgment is known to be correct. Because systems analysis ordinarily goes beyond objective analysis, it relies heavily on considered judgment. No matter what may be the hopes of professional analysts, the judgment applied by the decisionmaker in the last phase of a study limits the influence of the previous analyses. At its best, analysis can only embrace a part of a broad-scope problem; it gets no foothold at all on many subjective elements, and before it organizes an understanding of all objective elements it becomes too complex to handle. Thus analysis can go so far and no further. But the restrictions on the use of analyses imposed by the refusal of policymakers to use it when they should can be pushed back by better analysis.

Part Three

SPECIAL ASPECTS

In addition to the "elements" of analysis, there are a great many other important aspects, and we have selected some of these for more detailed discussion. This selection was somewhat influenced by the willingness of lecturers to talk about a particular subject, but, regardless of the topics selected as headings, an attempt was made to cover all the significant ideas about systems analysis. Indeed, one of the real problems in the original course was to keep the lecturers somewhat near their subject; the tendency was for each one to try to give under his topic everything he thought important about analysis.

In many military analyses, technological considerations are major factors in determining the availability of alternatives. The discovery of how trade-offs may be arranged between various performance parameters and how these affect the relationship between costs, effectiveness, and risks is an important facet of analysis. Chapter 9 deals with a number of technological considerations that are important in any analysis for development decisions.

In military analyses, enemy behavior and its treatment occupy a central role. It is not enough to say that we must design our systems against the enemy himself and not against a specific enemy tactic. To achieve such a design, the analysis itself must reflect the enemy ability to change his objectives and forces in response to changes in our own. Chapter 10 raises some of the problems of taking enemy capabilities and intentions into account in analysis.

For problems of military decision, and, in fact, for some problems of business and industry, behavior in conflict situations is extremely critical but hard to analyze. Although such behavior has long been observed and recorded, it is difficult to abstract. Recently, game theory has made great progress in that direction. Its advocates hold that many of the difficulties described in Chapter 10 might be resolved by using the formalism and results of the theory of games. For example, they feel that the notion of "strategy" bypasses the information and "who moves first" difficulties, while the notions of "mixed strategy" and "solution" overcome the guessing problem.

Yet game theory, although its concepts are universally applied, has not yet begun to handle really complicated problems of the business and military world. But there is a practical approach—one long known and used by the military— that of war gaming. Chapter 11 discusses gaming and its companion, simulation, with particular emphasis on their use as research tools.

A number of years ago, RAND carried out systems analyses in which the objective was to determine the best combination of such parameters as speed and range for a coming generation of strategic weapons—to the nearest ten knots and hundred miles. Today, the uncertainties in development being what they are, we realize that such efforts are not likely to meet with great success and do not help very much with the central problem in development—that of making the world more stable with respect to its uncertainties. Chapter 12 indicates how systems analysis is as applicable to questions of research and development as it is to other problems of choice.

Military analysis ranges from scientific decisionmaking of the commercial and industrial type—housekeeping applications—to decisions involving capital issues for or against essentially unique actions that may determine whether we live or die. The housekeeping role has been the most fruitful one for analysis. In this context, mathematics and the mathematical techniques of operations research have played a most important part. Chapter 13 discusses the relation of mathematics to systems analysis and indicates where it is likely to be most useful.

Although a discussion of specific techniques and tools is largely omitted from this work, we have singled out the computer and its use for a special word. One of the reasons mathematics has been able to tackle certain large problems such as the command and control of modern weapons systems has been the phenomenal growth in the digital computer. In principle, we can now build a machine, or teach an existing one, to do any intellectual task we can do, provided we can describe what is to be done in enough detail. But many people expect even more; Chapter 14 tries to set some limits.

While Chapter 5 establishes the case for the relevance of cost in systems analyses and in all problems of decision, it does not discuss how to assign numerical values to the cost of items that cannot be purchased in the market-place. Chapter 15 describes relevant costing factors and methods.

Finally, because systems analysis deals with difficult problems and uses largely undeveloped techniques, errors occur frequently. Chapter 16 attempts to point out some of the pitfalls for which the analyst and his clients must watch.

Chapter 9

TECHNOLOGICAL CONSIDERATIONS

R. SCHAMBERG

9.1. Introduction

In Chapter 2, military decisions were divided into three groups: operations decisions, force composition decisions, and development decisions. In this chapter we take a more detailed look at a number of matters that are pertinent to development decisions. In particular, we consider a number of technological considerations that make a significant contribution to analysis for development decisions. Since it is clearly impossible to present in a few pages a condensed background course in physics and engineering, the approach will consist of pointing out certain concepts and ideas that should prove useful to either a consumer of technical studies or a generator of such studies who is not a specialist in technical matters. Several such concepts expressed in terms of "O.K. words" or phrases frequently used by analysts, scientists, and engineers are performance parameter, trade-off, state of the art, constraint, relativity, scaling law, optimum, reliability, and complexity.

As we shall see, many of these concepts are interrelated and no particular significance is attached to the order in which they have been listed. We discuss these concepts in terms of a number of illustrations drawn from a variety of technical fields, including rocket-powered missiles, airplanes, communications, and nuclear weapon effects. While these illustrations are, it is hoped, interesting and informative in their own right, the reader should not be distracted from the much broader issues they are intended to point up.

9.2. Performance parameter

A performance parameter may be defined simply as the description of a physical property or capability of a hardware item, such as a vehicle or an airplane. A performance parameter is decidedly *not* a measure of the military or economic worth of such a hardware device. This can be readily illustrated by considering the most popular of all performance parameters—speed.

179

Speed is simply the ratio of distance covered to the time required to do so, that is,

$$\text{Speed} = \frac{\text{Distance}}{\text{Time}}.$$

Under some conditions one desires high speed, whereas under other conditions low speed is preferred. Consider, for example, the case where one wants to cover a large distance in a specified length of time, such as a space trip to a distant planet, which is to be accomplished in a short number of years. In this instance the large distance poses the requirement for high speed. Conversely, if for a business trip one wants to cover a specified distance, say from Los Angeles to London, in as short a time as possible, this short-time requirement also makes high speed desirable. Similarly, high speed is an objective in the case of a bomber or a ballistic missile that must cover a specified distance from base to target in as short a response time as possible.

On the other hand, there are other situations (or missions, in military jargon) where one desires to cover only a small distance, or sometimes no distance at all, and to remain in a confined space for a long period of time. Thus certain reconnaissance, surveillance, or patrol missions emphasize longer endurance in a relatively stationary attitude, so that low speed rather than high speed will be desirable. It follows that the knowledge of an aircraft's speed capability, be it high or low, does not enable one to decide whether it is good or bad without knowing the purpose for which the craft is to be employed.

Having thus defined the performance parameter speed, one may wonder next what the physical limitations on speed are. The lower limit on speed is obviously zero. Yet for this statement to be meaningful, we must define speed relative to something; hence let us say zero speed relative to the earth. In fact, the reader himself is at this moment probably at zero speed relative to the earth and experiences no difficulty in maintaining this state for a long period of time. However, one experiences some difficulty trying to maintain zero speed in the atmosphere at some height above the earth. This might be achieved theoretically with a balloon or other lighter-than-air devices, all of which are subject to wind drift as well as limitations in payload carrying ability, so that it is not always easy to maintain zero speed. In fact, sometimes it is impossible. Another way to obtain zero speed above the earth's surface is to ascend in a more maneuverable machine, such as a helicopter or a vertical-takeoff airplane. However, such heavier-than-air machines must exert a continued propulsive effort to overcome gravity, and the consequent continuous consumption of fuel limits their endurance.

Another type of device able to maintain zero speed relative to the earth is subject to neither the wind drift of the balloon nor the limited endurance drawback of the helicopter; this is the so-called 24-hour satellite which, when injected into an equatorial orbit about the earth, can maintain zero speed relative to some point on the earth's surface. Yet this illustration is in a sense deceptive because of the very relative nature of speed. Thus, although the 24-hour satellite has zero speed once in orbit, a relatively high rocket speed of some 25 000 ft/sec is required to transport this satellite from the surface of the earth into its equatorial orbit at an altitude of about 23 000 miles. In other words, such a satellite is at once a high-speed device from a technical (propulsion) point of view and a low-speed device from an operational (mission) point of view.

Within the confines of our present knowledge of the universe, the upper limit on speed is the speed of light, that is, the speed at which electromagnetic radiation is propagated through empty space. The familiar value of the speed of light, 186 000 mi/sec, implies that a signal could be sent once around the earth in one-eighth of one second. The next question of interest is "Can this upper limit, the speed of light, be obtained?" The answer is certainly "yes", so far as radiation in a vacuum is concerned, that is, for the propagation of a signal. For a material body, however, such as a space probe or a rocket ship, the theory of relativity tells us that it is not possible to reach the speed of light because an infinite amount of energy would be required to accelerate the body to the speed of light. Our interest shifts, therefore, to determining how closely the speed of light can be approached by such a rocket ship. As shown in Fig. 9.1, the maximum speed which can be attained is determined primarily by how much energy can be packed into and released from a rocket ship.

The vertical axis of Fig. 9.1 represents the performance parameter we are examining at the moment, the burnout speed of the rocket. The scale on the left is a logarithmic scale of this burnout speed divided by the speed of light. The highest value, 1.0, represents the speed of light, and the lowest value shown, 10^{-5}, is equivalent to a burnout speed of about 10 000 ft/sec. The vertical scale on the right shows the absolute values of burnout speed expressed in thousands of ft/sec. Also shown at the right are some specific earth and space missions which can be achieved by rockets having the specified burnout speed. For example, typical intermediate-range ballistic missiles (1500-mi range) require a burnout velocity of 15 000 ft/sec; earth satellites approximately 25 000 ft/sec; vehicles designed to escape from the earth, somewhat in excess of 35 000 ft/sec; and a one-way space mission to the most distant planet, Pluto, requires approximately 50 000 ft/sec burnout velocity. A slightly higher burnout speed is required to escape from the solar system entirely. Speeds required for space travel to solar systems other than our own depend primarily on how much time our hypothetical space traveller wants to spend. As an example the uppermost arrow on the right shows that about 0.2 times the speed of light would be required if one desired to reach the nearest star, Alpha Centauri, in 30 years or about the useful half-life of a man.

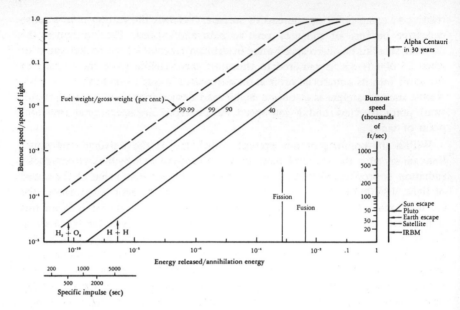

Fig. 9.1   Speed-energy spectrum for rockets

The curves shown in Fig. 9.1 represent four families of space rockets which differ from one another in the amount of fuel contained in these rockets at take-off. Current rockets are generally bracketed by the curves labeled 90 and 99 per cent fuel weight relative to gross weight. The upper dashed curve has been added to show that even a tremendously advanced rocket, whose fuel content exceeds even the purity of Ivory soap, is limited to burnout speeds far less than the speed of light unless extremely high energy releases are hypothesized.

The horizontal scale of Fig. 9.1 represents the amount of energy which can be released from whatever fuel is carried by the rocket. The maximum energy release theoretically conceivable is termed the annihilation energy; this is precisely the amount of energy which hypothetically would be released if the entire matter composing the fuel were converted into energy, according to Einstein's equation $E = MC^2$. It is convenient to plot the energy which can actually be released by various processes as a fraction of this annihilation energy, and the horizontal logarithmic scale of Fig. 9.1 serves this purpose. Note that even the most powerful reaction presently known to science, the nuclear fusion reaction, is capable of converting less than 1 per cent of matter into energy. The uranium fission nuclear reaction is somewhat less energetic and is equivalent to slightly less than 1/1000 of the annihilation energy. Nevertheless, these nuclear reactions have an energy release which is roughly a million times greater than that released by ordinary chemical reactions, such as the relatively potent hydrogen-oxygen reaction shown near the left end of the horizontal scale of Fig. 9.1. The vertical arrow labeled "H + H" represents the theoretical energy release from a class of "super-chemical" reactions between unstable reagents, such as atomic hydrogen (H) [1]. Unfortunately, no practical technique is known for lightweight storage of these unstable reagents, so that the potential of these fuels cannot be exploited, at least not for a long time to come.

In this connection, it should also be mentioned that the energy releases shown for fission and fusion reactions are theoretical values in the sense that the burnout speeds indicated by the curves are obtainable only by 100 per cent efficient conversion of the nuclear energy to kinetic energy of the thrust-producing jet. Nuclear reactors now being considered for rocket application require heat transfer to a working fluid and have relatively low efficiency of energy conversion, so that the usable energy from the fission reaction exceeds that of the ordinary chemical reaction by a factor of 100 rather than the theoretical factor of one million indicated on Fig. 9.1.

Several rather broad conclusions concerning technological capabilities can be deduced from a generalized study such as that shown in Fig. 9.1.

1. Even if it were possible to utilize the most potent reaction known (fusion) with 100 per cent efficiency, rocket speeds achievable would be lower than one-third the speed of light, using reasonable mass ratios.

2. It will probably be possible to escape from the solar system with rockets of reasonable size when moderately efficient means for conversion of nuclear energy have been developed. However, distances to heavenly bodies outside our solar system are so immense that the requirement for rockets with extremely high fuel-weight to gross-weight ratios would probably render it infeasible to make a round trip to even the nearest star in a man's lifetime.

3. Chemical reactions are sufficiently energetic for space missions within our own solar system but not beyond.

More important, from our present point of view, Fig. 9.1 shows how a performance parameter, namely the burnout speed, is uniquely determined by two other parameters which we might call state-of-the-art parameters. These are the fuel-weight to gross-weight ratio and the energy release divided by annihilation energy ratio. At any one time period—past, present, or future—the technology is capable of providing certain values for these parameters; that is, a particular maximum practical energy release and some minimum value of

---

[1]   These reagents are usually called free radicals.

structural-weight to fuel-weight ratio, corresponding to a maximum of fuel-weight to gross-weight ratio. As shown by Fig. 9.1, the performance parameter plots very beautifully as a smooth function of the two state-of-the-art parameters. It does *not* follow, however, that one could plot with equal facility the burnout speed versus either the calendar time at which it might be achieved or the dollar cost required to develop the necessary technology. The estimation of time and cost required for research and development must be based on a detailed examination of the fundamental knowledge of such limiting factors as high-temperature materials, methods of producing fuels, as well as the facilities and manpower required to produce necessary research information, fabrication techniques, etc. As is pointed out in Chapter 12, such estimates are difficult to make and, when looked at in retrospect, have generally turned out to be inaccurate.

9.3. STATE-OF-THE-ART ·PARAMETERS

In the lower left corner of Fig. 9.1 is an auxiliary scale labeled "specific impulse". Specific impulse, measured in seconds, is defined as the number of seconds for which one pound of propellant can produce one pound of thrust. As shown, there exists a one-to-one relationship between the energy-release parameter and specific impulse, which is the conventional way of expressing the state of the art of rocket performance. We will confine our attention to what can be achieved with chemical propellants and will examine in more detail the

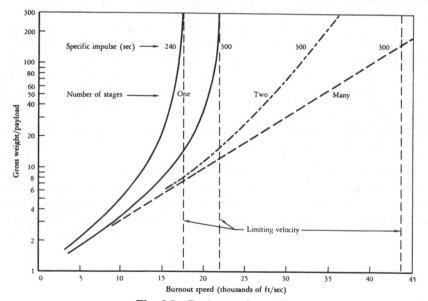

Fig. 9.2 Rocket performance

lower left portion of Fig. 9.1. For this purpose, let us consider Fig. 9.2 in which our sample performance parameter, burnout speed of the rocket, is shown on a horizontal linear scale.

The ordinate of Fig. 9.2 represents the ratio of gross weight to payload of a rocket. Consider first the left-most solid curve which represents a family of single-stage rockets, all of which are designed to the same state of the art, and are characterized by a specific impulse of 240 sec. This specific impulse is representative of current liquid rockets using hydrocarbon fuels and liquid oxygen as oxidizer. This curve represents the trade-off or exchange ratio that is inherent in a fixed state of the art. Thus, if the burnout speed is to be increased, a bigger rocket is required to accelerate a given payload to the specified burnout speed. Conversely, if the rocket gross weight is held fixed, the payload which can be accelerated to the burnout speed decreases as the burnout speed is increased. Note also the limiting maximum burnout speed of roughly 18 000 ft/sec, denoted by the dashed vertical line. This represents the maximum speed which can be reached by any single-stage rocket of this state of the art, that is, a specific impulse of 240 sec no matter how large the rocket or how small the payload [2]. The second curve shows the effect on rocket performance of increasing the specific impulse of the rocket from 240 to 300 sec. This value of the propellant state of the art is typical of high-energy liquid propellant combinations, such as hydrazine fuel and fluorine oxidizer. The general nature of the 300-sec curve is the same as that of the 240-sec curve; however, the advance in the state of the art permits a higher limiting speed to be reached, or a reduction in gross weight for the same payload and burnout speed.

It is interesting to note that there are some design tricks which can be as effective in improving performance as advances in the basic state of the art of rocket propellants. A particular design trick illustrated in Fig. 9.2 is the familiar concept of staging. The staging principle simply recognizes that it is advantageous to jettison any piece of hardware which has served its purpose—such as an empty fuel tank or a rocket motor whose thrust is no longer needed—in order to accelerate as small a weight as possible to the final burnout speed. The broken curve in Fig. 9.2 shows the benefits obtainable by changing from a one-stage to a two-stage design. It will be noted that the closer the single-stage design is pushed to its limiting speed, the greater are the benefits obtainable by shifting to a two-stage design. The two-stage design also has a limiting maximum burnout speed which, in this example, is about 42 000 ft/sec. As indicated in Fig. 9.1, this would suffice for escape from the earth's gravitational field.

---

[2] This limiting speed also depends on the value of another state-of-the-art parameter, the ratio of propellant weight to propulsive system weight (rocket motor, propellant tanks, and propellant). For the sake of simplicity, this ratio is held fixed at a value of 0.90 for all cases shown in Fig. 9.2.

Similarly, one can add more and more stages; but by doing so, the complexity of the rocket will be increased considerably. The lowest curve in Fig. 9.2, labeled "many stages", represents the limiting performance which can be achieved by exploiting the staging principle when the propellant state of the art has a fixed value for the specific impulse of 300 sec.

One additional feature of Fig. 9.2 is worthy of note. This is the fact that the ordinate is the ratio of gross weight to payload, so that the particular set of curves shown can be used directly to determine the gross weight of rockets designed to carry various payloads. This situation, in which gross weight is scaled in direct proportion to the payload, is quite typical of many transportation systems. The magnitude of the scale factor depends on the values of specified performance and state of the art available; in this example, on burnout speed and specific impulse. The same principle applies, for example, to airplanes flying through the atmosphere, to trucks on highways, freight trains, submarines, and surface ships. For these transportation systems, a plot of gross weight versus the payload is approximately a straight line whose slope depends on the performance and state of the art. Consequently, the term "linear scaling" is frequently used to describe the relationship between two quantities which are directly proportional to one another. The general usefulness of this concept of scaling, other scaling laws, and their applications are considered below.

9.4. SCALING LAWS

Scaling laws, such as the linear scaling law pointed out on Fig. 9.2, are useful in engineering, systems, or military analysis principally for three reasons.

1. They facilitate an understanding of the principal interactions either in a physical system or in an analysis, particularly in complicated situations where the analyst must consider many variables. In cases where analysis shows that the outcome of the study is determined primarily by the dominant effects of a small number of variables, the results can generally be represented by relatively simple scaling laws.

2. Where scaling laws apply, much effort and expense in calculation can obviously be saved, since, as in the case of Fig. 9.2, one calculation will suffice for and represent an infinite number of situations.

3. Scaling laws are also useful in transferring information from one skill to another or from one problem to another. A corollary of this is that it makes possible model testing of aircraft in wind tunnels, or the testing of nuclear weapons of reduced yield, with obvious economic benefits.

We shall now use a communications problem to illustrate the rather simple derivation of a nonlinear scaling law. Consider the problem of communicating from one space ship to another, as shown schematically in Fig. 9.3a. This figure

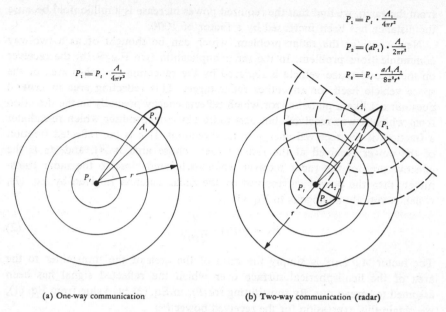

(a) One-way communication   (b) Two-way communication (radar)

Fig. 9.3   Communication scaling laws

shows a transmitter which radiates a power P_t in all directions. This energy is radiated along spherical wave fronts into space and a part of this energy is intercepted by the receiver of another space vehicle which is at a distance r from the transmitting space vehicle. If the antenna on the receiving vehicle has an effective area A_1, the strength of the signal received is just equal to the transmitted power times the fraction of the spherical area of the wave front which is intercepted by the receiver, that is,

$$P_1 = P_t \cdot \frac{A_1}{4\pi r^2}. \tag{1}$$

This equation is equivalent to $P_t \sim P_1 \cdot r^2$, which means that if the received signal is to have a specified strength P_1 then the transmitted power must be directly proportional to P_1 and to the square of the distance. Here we have both a linear and a quadratic scaling law, since the power which must be transmitted scales linearly with the power to be received and also with the square of the distance separating receiver and transmitter. Note also that there is no limit to the distance over which a signal can be transmitted through a vacuum, since, in principle at least, the power can always be increased to compensate for the increase in distance. For example, if we compare the power required to communicate from the earth to a satellite whose orbital altitude is 240 mi with the power required to communicate to a moon probe at 240 000 mi from the earth, we find that the required power increase is a millionfold because the distance has been increased by a factor of 1000.

Next consider the radar problem, which can be thought of as a two-way communications problem. In the radar application (see Fig. 9.3b) the receiver on the second space vehicle is replaced by the reflecting (or echo) area of the space vehicle itself, or any other radar target. This reflecting area in general does *not* act like a plane mirror which reflects energy precisely in the direction from which it was received, but acts more like a transmitter which re-radiates a fraction of the received energy in all directions. If a is the reflected fraction of the power received at the radar target, whose area is A_1, and A_2 is the effective area of the radar receiver which is located close to the radar transmitter, then the power P_2 received by the radar antenna is given by Eq. (2), which is entirely analogous to Eq. (1):

$$P_2 = (aP_1) \cdot \frac{A_2}{2\pi r^2} . \qquad (2)$$

The factor $A_2/2\pi r^2$ is simply the ratio of the area of the transmitter to the area of the hemispherical surface over which the reflected signal has been assumed to spread out. By substituting for P_1, in Eq. (2), its value from Eq. (1), we obtain this expression for the received power P_2:

$$P_2 = P_t \cdot \frac{aA_1A_2}{8\pi^2 r^4} . \qquad (3)$$

Equation (3) is a form of the familiar radar equation which states that for a fixed transmitter power, target echo area, and receiver antenna area the received signal is inversely proportional to the fourth power of the distance between the radar target and the transmitter. Conversely, to receive a radar echo of specified strength P_2 the transmitter power must be made directly proportional to the fourth power of the separation distance r. Extending now our previous example from one-way to two-way communication, we find that the power required to track the moon rocket would be 10^{12}, or one thousand billion times that for tracking with the same size antenna the earth satellite in its 240-mi orbit. It is not surprising, therefore, that it turns out to be advantageous to supply space ships with batteries or some other power source so that they can have a beacon which can be used for tracking. When this provision is made, the quadratic scaling law of one-way communication applies and the tracking problem is facilitated enormously.

Another field of technology in which scaling laws are usefully employed concerns the effects of nuclear or chemical explosions. Here again the energy release by the explosion is propagated away from the point of detonation along spherical wave fronts; hence in Fig. 9.3a the transmitter can be replaced by the exploding bomb at the center of the spheres. If, to be specific, we consider the blast effects produced by such spherical shock waves, then it turns out that the yield of the explosion required to produce a specified overpressure at some distance r from the center of the explosion is proportional to the volume of air contained within the spherical shell passing through that point. This is equivalent to stating that the required yield is proportional to the cube of the radius. Conversely, if we think of this radial separation distance as representing the lethal radius against some type of structure for which the specified overpressure produces destructive damage, then it will be seen that the lethal radius is directly proportional to the one-third power, or cube root, of yield.

A number of other properties characteristic of airburst nuclear weapons also scale with the one-third power of the yield. These include the time of arrival of the shock, the duration of the positive pressure pulse of the shock wave, and the total impulse imparted by the shock wave to a structure. The one-third power scaling law also applies to some of the effects of surface bursts. For instance, the diameter of the crater dug by a surface explosion also is proportional to the one-third power of the yield of the explosion. However, not all properties of nuclear explosions scale with the one-third power of the yield. For example, the depth of the crater of a surface burst scales more nearly with the one-fourth power of the yield. Furthermore, certain aspects of the thermal effects of nuclear explosions scale more nearly with the one-half power or square root of the yield. These include the maximum thermal power emitted by the explosion and the time at which it occurs.

Scaling laws such as those mentioned above are particularly useful in nuclear weapon testing and the associated reduction of test data, which are both complex and expensive operations. Use of these scaling laws permits the application of weapon effects data taken from the test of a weapon of a particular yield to predict the results that would have been obtained from the explosion of a weapon of similar nature but a different yield. Furthermore, these scaling laws can be used to predict the effects of explosion at distances from ground zero other than those at which the measurements were taken. It is evident that such scaling laws permit considerable savings in both experimental and analytical efforts in those fields of technology where they are applicable. There are, of course, limitations to the usefulness and accuracy of such scaling laws. Some of these are illustrated in the following discussion.

9.5. Optima and Constraints

To illustrate certain limitations of scaling laws, as well as to point out some features of suboptimization which frequently arise in arriving at "optimal designs" of aircraft, let us turn to an example drawn from a design and cost study of subsonic, turbojet-powered cargo aircraft. The results of interest to us, for illustrative purposes, are contained in Fig. 9.4. Consider, for the present,

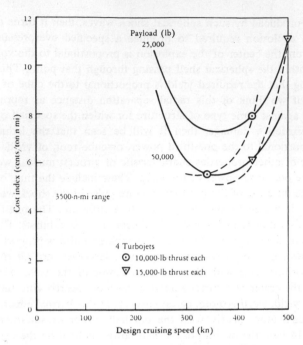

Fig. 9.4   Optima and discrete constraints

only data shown by the solid curves of this figure. Each point on the upper curve represents a different airplane which is designed to carry 25 000 lb of payload for a total range of 3500 n mi at the design cruising speed indicated by the horizontal scale. The lower curve represents similar but larger airplanes which are designed to carry a payload of 50 000 lb for various design cruising speeds, but for the same range of 3500 n mi. The vertical scale, labeled "cost index", and expressed in cents per ton nautical mile, is a measure of the direct operating cost of these aircraft. The general shape of these curves, which display some minimum cost at some "optimum design" cruising speed, is the result of the interaction of two opposing factors. First, an increase in cruising speed reduces the contribution to cost per mile flown of those elements of cost that tend to be constant per hour, such as the pay of the crew or amortization charges of the airplane. The second factor represents the effect of increasing cruising speed beyond a certain level, which results in reducing the aerodynamic and structural efficiency of subsonic aircraft.

The fact that aircraft designed for 25 000-lb payloads and those designed for 50 000-lb payloads have different curves for cost index versus cruising speed is an indication that here the previously discussed linear scaling law for transportation systems does not apply. Since the cost index is the cost of transporting one ton of payload for one mile, one might expect this cost to be the same whether that ton of payload is carried in an airplane designed to carry 25 000 lb of payload or in one designed for 50 000 lb. The reason this is not so is evident from the data in Table 9.1.

TABLE 9.1

Characteristics of airplanes with design cruising speed equal to 350 kn

Design payload (1000 lb)	Gross weight (1000 lb)	Gross weight/ Design payload	Cost index (cents/ton n mi)
25	150	6.0	7.1
50	250	5.0	5.4
100	500	5.0	5.1

This table gives characteristics of three aircraft, which have design payloads of 25 000, 50 000, and 100 000 lb. The third column of figures indicates that the ratio of airplane gross weight to payload is six to one for the smallest aircraft, and five to one for the two larger ones. The reason for this effect is that all airplanes have certain common elements, such as crew compartments, radio equipment, etc., which constitute a larger fraction of the weight and volume of the smaller airplanes than of the larger ones. In our example, this effect becomes negligible for airplanes larger than 250 000 lb; so that for airplanes larger than this, the linear scaling law between gross weight and payload applies quite accurately. The last column in Table 9.1 shows that a similar effect is taking place with respect to the unit cost (cents/ton n mi) of these aircraft. The explanation is also similar since certain "fixed" cost items—such as crew pay and allowances, basing costs, and some maintenance cost items—constitute a larger fraction of total cost for the smaller aircraft than for the larger ones.

The observed effect of reduction in unit costs with increasing payload of the transport vehicle occurs very frequently in the analysis of transport systems, at least at this particular level of "suboptimization". It must be kept in mind that when aircraft characteristics such as these are combined with the characteristics of the cargo route structure, or the cargo job to be done, then the smaller fleet size associated with the larger airplane may lead to greater difficulties of scheduling, or an operation wherein the aircraft is carrying, on the average, considerably less than its design cargo. It should be noted that the cost data shown in Fig. 9.4 does not account for this since it is based on the implicit assumption that all airplanes are carrying their full design payload.

The reason for the appearance of a minimum cost for a particular payload class of aircraft has been pointed out before. In addition, it should be observed that this minimum on the curve is quite "flat" in the sense that all airplanes designed for a cruising speed between 300 and 430 kn have cost indexes which lie within 10 per cent of the minimum value. Thus, on the basis of those factors considered explicitly in the construction of Fig. 9.4, a variation in design and cruising speed by as much as one-third from the theoretical optimum value produces such small changes on the calculated cost index that the choice of a design cruising speed would probably be made on the basis of factors beyond the scope of this particular analysis, since extraneous factors generally exert a greater influence on a cost index than the speed variations shown here.

The flatness of these curves in the region of their minimum is by no means unusual. In fact, experience at RAND has led to the belief that the flatness of such curves, which define an optimum in a technical or economical application, is the general rule. Thus, whenever a very sharp maximum or minimum appears in a curve of this sort the analyst should regard it with considerable suspicion. The appearance of a sharp optimum generally implies that some artificial constraint has been introduced somewhere in the analysis, frequently inadvertently, so that not all significant factors in the design of a hardware system or its operation have been properly optimized. Frequently, of course, such artificial constraints must be introduced intentionally because they are part of the real world which the analysis tries to approximate. We shall illustrate the implications of such constraints by the broken curves shown in Fig. 9.4.

Each point along the solid curves represents an airplane which differs from its neighbor both with respect to cruising speed and gross weight. This implies that the size and/or number of engines required also change along either of these solid curves. In particular, the dotted circles denote those airplanes which could be powered by four turbojet engines of 10 000-lb rated thrust each. The dotted triangles denote larger and/or faster airplanes which could be powered by four turbojets having 15 000-lb thrust each. The broken curves indicate various possible airplanes which could be powered by each of the engine types indicated. Along either of these curves, the total engine thrust remains constant and consequently the design payload decreases, as does the gross weight, when the cruising speed is increased. Note that these broken curves are considerably steeper than the solid ones because of the more severe requirement that engine thrust be kept constant as the speed is increased. Let us examine what the consequences of this situation might be.

To illustrate an extreme case, consider the hypothetical situation where a design requirement has been issued for a four-engine aircraft which is to have a design range of 3500 n mi and a design payload of 25 000 lb. Suppose, furthermore, that only one type of engine will be available in the time period for which it is required, and that this happens to be an engine of 15 000-lb thrust. Under these unfortunate circumstances, the designer has little choice but to design the airplane represented by the triangle in the upper right corner of Fig. 9.4. This airplane has the high cost index of eleven cents per ton n mi, because the use of this relatively large engine with the relatively small airplane results in a design speed which is much higher than necessary for economical operation. If, however, the payload specification had been stated more flexibly, such as "the design payload is to be on the order of 20 000 to 50 000 lb", the designer would be able to come up with an aircraft more nearly like the lower triangle, which has a cost index nearly half that of the upper triangle, and at a reduction in design cruising speed of less than 20 per cent. The moral of this illustration is that wherever possible, design requirements should be stated in as flexible a fashion as possible so that a hardware designer can exploit the number of trade-offs available to him to the best ultimate advantage of the customer; particularly in common situations where unavoidable practical constraints, like engine availability, severely curtail the number of trade-offs which are possible.

9.6. Reliability considerations

Earlier we defined a performance parameter as a quantity which describes the capability of a particular hardware item. Perhaps it would be wise to modify the last phrase to read "the capability of the item if all its components function properly". If one or more components of an aircraft or a missile, for example, do not perform properly or fail altogether, then performance may be degraded considerably below the values we discussed earlier. Disastrous consequences may even ensue. Reliability analysis concerns itself principally with two aspects of this problem: (1) trying to estimate the probability of failures of this sort, and (2) trying to influence hardware design and operation so as to reduce the probability of component or system failure, or at least to reduce the severity of the consequences should failure occur. Here we illustrate some of the problems encountered and principles involved in such analysis by considering the hazards of vertical ascent and transition to horizontal flight of a multiengine vertical takeoff aircraft.

Figure 9.5 shows schematically the situation to be analyzed. This VTO aircraft rises vertically by means of the thrust exerted by several vertically mounted jet engines, their number being arbitrary at this point. After the aircraft ascends to a height sufficient for terrain clearance, noise considerations, etc., the thrust vector is inclined toward the horizontal and the airplane makes a gradual transition to normal forward flight. Consider now the consequences of the failure of one jet engine, as a function of the altitude at which loss of thrust occurs. If an engine should fail during the run-up period while the airplane is still on the ground, the remaining engines can, of course, be turned off without damage to the airplane or harm to its crew. If this is a combat airplane employed during wartime, an aborted mission may, of course, be a very undesirable event. If engine failure occurs after the aircraft has lifted just a few feet off the ground, the airplane strikes the ground more or less hard, but

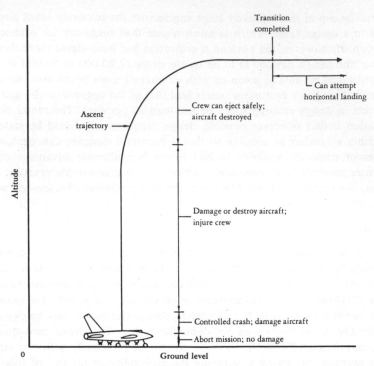

Fig. 9.5   Schematic representation of hazards in VTO ascent with engine failure

the shock-absorbing system in the landing gear prevents damage to the aircraft or injury to the crew. If the engine should fail at a somewhat higher altitude, the pilot may be able to negotiate a "controlled crash landing" in which the airplane may be damaged more or less severely but the crew escapes injury. In this instance, not only is the mission aborted but the aircraft may be out of commission for a considerable period of time. If engine failure occurs at still higher altitudes, the resulting crash, even if controllable, may result in injury to the crew as well as in damage or destruction to the aircraft. If engine failure were delayed to somewhat higher altitudes, say on the order of 200 ft [3], it might be possible for the crew to eject and to make a safe parachute landing, although the aircraft would undoubtedly be destroyed. If engine failure were to occur after transition to horizontal flight is substantially completed, then it may be possible to perform a more or less conventional horizontal landing, which again results in an aborted mission, though hopefully without damage to the aircraft or injury to the crew. Finally, it is hoped that in the overwhelming majority of

---

[3]   For the purposes of the present example. It is recognized that ejection seats can be built for safe ejection from ground level.

cases no engine failures at all will occur and that the aircraft makes a successful transition and carries out its mission as planned.

The probability with which each of these possible outcomes will occur depends, of course, on a number of factors. These include the inherent reliability of each engine, that is, the probability that any one engine will fail during the ascent maneuver; the number of engines installed in the airplane; and the nature of the trajectory used for ascent and transition. Figure 9.6 shows quantitatively, for illustrative purposes, the outcome of such a calculation. The horizontal scale indicates the number of engines installed in the aircraft. The vertical logarithmic scale indicates the probability with which various events depicted by the curves are expected to occur. All of the data shown in this figure are based on the arbitrary assumption that the probability that any one engine will fail at some time during the ascent and transition maneuver is 1 per cent ($p_1 = 0.01$)[4].

As shown by the upper curve, the probability of aborting the mission increases with the number of engines from 1 per cent upward because the more engines there are the greater the probability that at least one will fail. Hence, if the avoidance of aborted missions were the chief and sole requirement, a single-engined aircraft would be preferred.

In a similar manner the probability of damaging the airplane during the ascent and transition maneuver depends on the number of engines. However, for any number of installed engines this probability is always slightly less than the probability of aborting the mission because engine failure may occur while the aircraft is still on the ground or at a few feet of altitude. However, when the number of engines gets large, say on the order of 12 or more, the loss of one engine will not be serious since its thrust is such a small fraction of the total that the aircraft can negotiate a landing with a very low sinking speed. However, even for large numbers of engines the probability of damaging the aircraft does not drop to zero, but to some low finite level which represents the probability that two engines may fail under circumstances which will result in damage to the airplane. As shown by the lower right portion of the middle curve, this probability of damaging the airplane due to failure of two engines also increases, though slowly, with further increase in the number of engines.

The lowest curve in Fig. 9.6, defining the probability of injuring the crew, is similar in nature to that for damage of the airplane, as just discussed. However, the probability of injuring the crew is always less than that of damaging the airplane because of the assumed ability of the crew to escape uninjured

---

[4] The ordinates calculated in Fig. 9.6 approximately follow a linear scaling law. This means that the scale shown on the left side actually represents a ratio of the probability of the occurrence of one of the compound events (i.e., aborting the mission or damaging the airplane, etc.) to the probability of failure of any one engine.

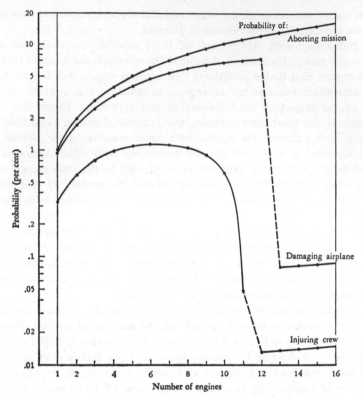

Fig. 9.6   Reliability aspects of multiengine VTO airplane

from a "controlled crash landing", as well as its ability to eject safely should engine failure occur above some critical altitude.

Figure 9.6 is presented not for the quantitative information which it contains but rather to impress upon the reader two important points. The first of these is that the term "reliability" in a quantitative sense is nearly meaningless by itself because the number that one calculates for the reliability of the hardware device depends very strongly on the criterion that is adapted for measuring this reliability. Thus, to cite an extreme case in this particular example, the probability of aborting a mission with a 12-engine airplane is roughly one thousand times at great as the probability of injuring the crew. Of course, the question as to which criterion is the appropriate one to use cannot be answered on the basis of the limited calculation presented here for discussion. The choice of an appropriate reliability criterion, whether it is one of those illustrated here or some other one, must of necessity come from a much broader consideration of the function and operation of the particular vertical-takeoff aircraft under consideration in a complete military or commercial system. A second point worthy of note is that reliability is by no means necessarily a smooth or monotonic function of the number of components, such as the number of engines in our example here. For example, if one desired to minimize the probability of injuring the crew, and an aircraft with 12 or more engines was considered to be impractical from a logistic point of view, say, then it might be preferable to decide on a single-engine aircraft (provided a large enough engine is available) rather than on one designed with some intermediate number of engines, such as six.

Unfortunately, Fig. 9.6 contains a most unrealistic simplifying assumption. This is, as previously mentioned, that the probability of having any one engine fail is the same, namely 1 per cent, for all sizes of engines. Since in the real world engines of different size are generally produced by different manufacturers, have different detailed arrangement and functioning of their components, as well as different histories and service life, their individual probabilities of failure in a specified operating time can also be expected to vary. The consequence of such variation in unit failure probability of engines is illustrated in Table 9.2.

TABLE 9.2

Effect of variation in unit failure probability of engines

Number of engines (N)	Probability that any one engine fails (P_1)	Probability of injuring crew/ P_1 (From Fig. 9.6)	Resulting probability of injuring crew
10	0.01	0.6	$0.6 \times 0.01 = 0.0060$
6	0.001	1.1	$1.1 \times 0.001 = 0.0011$

The first line of the table represents a 10-engine airplane design using engines having a 1 per cent probability of failure (as assumed in Fig. 9.6). As shown by the lower curve of Fig. 9.6, the associated probability of injuring the crew is 0.006. The second case considered is that of a 6-engine airplane wherein each of the larger engines is more reliable than those considered before, having a unit probability of failure of only 0.001. The resulting probability of injuring the crew is 0.0011, which is less by a factor of five than the probability of injuring the crew with the 10-engine airplane, despite the impression given by Fig. 9.6.

9.7. SUMMARY

The purpose of this chapter has been to present some technological considerations pertinent and vital to analysis for military decisions. These considerations have been presented by means of a number of illustrative examples drawn from a variety of technical fields. While these examples are of considerable interest in themselves, they have been used chiefly to illustrate the following principal points.

1. A performance parameter (like speed or altitude) is a description of a capability of a piece of hardware and *not* a measure of its intrinsic worth (military or economic).

2. The performance capability of a vehicle, or other hardware item, can readily be extrapolated in terms of specified changes in state-of-the-art parameters (like specific impulse) but not directly in terms of calendar time or dollar cost.

3. Use of design tricks, like rocket staging, can be important supplements to basic state-of-the-art advances for increasing hardware capabilities.

4. Physical scaling laws are very useful in understanding the principal physical interactions in a system or analysis as well as for economy in calculation and experimentation. Their limits of application, particularly where economic factors are concerned, should be recognized.

5. Physical and economic optima curves are generally "flat" when artificial constraints are avoided.

6. Where practical constraints limit the number of choices available to the hardware designer, it is important to specify design requirements in a flexible fashion so that beneficial trade-offs can be exploited.

7. The criterion or criteria by which reliability is to be measured should be clearly defined.

Chapter 10

ASSUMPTIONS ABOUT ENEMY BEHAVIOR

T. C. SCHELLING

10.1. INTRODUCTION

In any analysis that leads to a choice of a particular strategy or weapon system from among several alternatives, there is typically some assumption about the behavior of the enemy. If it is not explicitly stated, it is embedded somewhere in the analysis. The weapon system or strategy that appears best for us usually depends on what weapon system or strategy the enemy is expected to have.

It might seem that we could always be on the safe side by assuming that the enemy will just do his worst to us. But the worst that he can do to us is not necessarily the best that he can do for himself. The idea of *deterrence*, for example, rests on the possibility of making the worst for us (being struck by surprise) coincide with something pretty bad for the enemy (retaliation). To assume that he would simply do his worst, therefore, would be to assume the inevitability of a war to the finish.

But even in the cases where our interests and those of the enemy are strictly opposed, we still cannot pin down the enemy's behavior by just assuming that he will do his worst. The reason is that he is in much the same position as we. While the best choice for us depends on what he is going to do, his best choice depends on what we are going to do. We want to know what air defense he is going to have when we design our bombing system; he wants to know what bombing system we are going to have when he designs his air defense. While we are trying to exploit the weaknesses of his system, he is trying to exploit the weaknesses of ours. The only safe assumption that we can make is that the enemy will be *adaptive*: to the best of his ability he will adapt his system to what he knows or can predict about ours.

This means that we have to do systems research for the enemy as well as for ourselves. To anticipate his strategy and choice of weapons we have to look at the problem from his point of view. And while there are naturally differences in the detail with which we study his problem and our own, the logic of systems research requires us to play both sides of the game.

We can place this problem in the broader context of planning with uncertainty. In almost any analysis of alternative weapon systems we face uncertainty. One of the many sources of uncertainty is the enemy himself; we do not know as much as we would like to know about how he would perform in a war, how good his technology is, how rapidly his research and development are progressing, how cohesive the Soviet bloc will be, and so forth. Among these uncertainties about the enemy there are some that are particularly intriguing because they involve the *decisions* that he is going to make. They involve what *he* knows or guesses about what *we* can do and about the decisions that *we* are going to make. There are, in other words, certain decisions that we and the enemy make in which we are trying to outguess each other and to avoid being outguessed, and trying to adapt to the decisions and choices that each of us has already made and to forecast the choices or decisions that each of us is going to be led to. That is the particular kind of uncertainty discussed in this chapter.

I warn the reader in advance that in trying to come to grips with this particular kind of uncertainty we are necessarily dealing with intangibles. We are dealing with the enemy's expectations rather than his capabilities. It is worse than that. We are not just dealing with the enemy's expectations about future *events*, but with *his* expectations about what *we* are expecting of *him*. This may be an uncomfortable kind of analysis to get engaged in, but there is no comfortable alternative. If we make the optimistic assumption that we can guess what the enemy is actually going to do, or that whatever we do he will be caught doing exactly what we want him to do, we shall be resting our whole strategy on the precarious assumption that our enemy is foolish. If we go to the other extreme and make the conservative assumption that whatever we choose to do the enemy will always have outguessed us in advance, we are not only being pessimistic and perhaps missing some opportunities, but we are supposing that the enemy knows what decisions we are going to reach before we have reached them. Either of these two extremes is so unsatisfactory that, whether we enjoy it or not, we have to devise some means for coping with the intangibles.

10.2. AN ILLUSTRATIVE PROBLEM OF CHOICE AMONG ALTERNATIVE WEAPON SYSTEMS

I want to organize my discussion around a specific example. But I am confronted with a dilemma. If I pick an actual example of a problem that RAND has worked on, it will be too large to handle in a short presentation and too complicated to make my points stand out clearly. At the other extreme I can deal with A, B, and C, and X, Y, and Z, which have the virtue of being honest about their hypothetical nature but are not vivid enough to keep in mind. I am going to compromise. I shall talk about the problem of choosing a weapon system for bombing the Soviet Union from among three hypothetical alternatives, A, B, and C; but to enrich the illustration I shall give the strategies descriptive names. To keep the example manageable I am going to do violence to the facts and give these attacks attributes that provide a versatile illustration rather than a set of valid estimates.

Attack strategy A will involve short-range aircraft based overseas at several points near the Soviet Union. B is an intercontinental strike along dogleg routes that minimize penetration distances within Soviet territory. C is an intercontinental strike along routes that minimize fuel consumption. We shall suppose that overseas-based bombers, because they are vulnerable to counterattack on their bases, have little likelihood of carrying out more than one strike, while the intercontinental systems involve a safer system of basing. Attacks B and C, therefore, involve a smaller number of more expensive bombers capable of repeated strikes; they differ from each other in that B enjoys less exposure over enemy territory, while C enjoys superior performance due to shorter flying time and less dependence on refueling in flight, plus some economy in the use of tankers that can finance a somewhat larger number of bombers. In summary:

Attack A =   overseas-based strike,

Attack B =   intercontinental strike, minimum penetration,

Attack C =   intercontinental strike, minimum range.

Against any one of these three bombing systems the Russians could devise a "best" defense. By "best" I mean best against the particular American attack that the defense is designed to meet. The alternative Russian defense strategies, we shall assume, differ according to two main factors. The first is location: against Attack C they would base their interception equipment in the general direction of the United States, while against either the overseas-based or the dogleg attack they would distribute their interception equipment more widely. Secondly, their equipment depends on whether they expect one large attack from a nearby and highly vulnerable American base system, or repeated attacks by a smaller number of longer-range bombers. (The importance, for example, of intercepting American bombers on the way home from target depends on which system the Americans use.) In summary:

Defense A′ =   best against Attack A,

Defense B′ =   best against Attack B,

Defense C′ =   best against Attack C.

What makes the problem interesting is that the Russian defense that is best against a particular one of our three attacks may not be the best against all three of our attacks. So the Russians may not be able to choose their weapon system for defending against our attacks unless they can make a guess at what decision we will reach in deciding among our three attacks. But, in the same way, our choice among the three available attack strategies depends on a guess of what defense strategy our attack must penetrate. I am going to assume, in other words, that we do not enjoy the luxury of a "dominant" strategy—one that is *superior* to the alternatives no matter what defense the Russians choose. In my example, furthermore, no one of the three is definitely *inferior* to the other two, either; each of our three attack strategies can boast of being the best one against at least one type of Russian defense.

Approaching the Problem of Choice

How do we decide which one to choose? The first point to notice is that we and the Russians have comparable problems; our situations are symmetrical so long as neither one of us tips his hand prematurely. In effect, we have to try to guess what they will guess that we will do. To put it differently, we have to play both sides of this game if we want to figure out what it is reasonable for us to do if the Russians succeed in doing what it is reasonable for them to do.

As a first step, we might rank our three possible strategies as "best", "medium", and "worst" against each of the three Russian defenses separately. If we do we may get a table something like Table 10.1. (Note that the three attacks are being compared *in each column* with the particular defense listed at the head of the column.)

TABLE 10.1

Evaluation of attack strategies

Attack	Defense		
	A′	B′	C′
A	worst	best	best
B	medium	worst	medium
C	best	medium	worst

There are three points to make in connection with Table 10.1. First, it is drawn up on the basis of what we might call "objective" estimates. That is, it depends on what we estimate to be the outcomes of a set of specified clashes. *The judgments expressed in this table make no assumptions about the enemy's choice.* They simply consider all possible courses of enemy behavior and all possible courses for us. To decide whether A or B is the better strategy, all things considered, would depend on what we expect the enemy to do; but to decide whether A or B is best against Defense A′ we need only to estimate what happens if A meets A′, what happens if B meets A′, and which of the two looks better to us.

Second, there is no way to choose among A, B, and C unless we have some way of thinking about the relative likelihoods of A′, B′, and C′.

Third, when the enemy looks at *his* problem of choice he presumably gets the same comparisons in reverse. If the outcome of A against A′ looks worse to us than does B against A′, it must look better to the enemy.

We could pursue this problem in either of two directions. One is to ask how to go about getting estimates of the relative likelihood of A′, B′, and C′. Here the problem gets circular. The choice that the enemy will make depends on which choice he thinks we are going to make; and if that is an open question, there is no way to deduce from it what he will do and therefore what we ought to do.

Refinement of the Evaluations

The other direction is to compare the alternatives in greater detail. Instead of comparing in each column (that is, for each of his defenses) our three attacks with each other, let us compare all nine possible outcomes to see which is best, which is next best, and so forth, all the way down to ninth best outcome. Let us estimate, that is, the consequences of Attack A against Defense A′, Attack A against Defense B′, Attack B against Defense B′, and so forth for all the nine combinations. We estimate such things as how many targets destroyed, how many aircraft we lose, what this does to the outcome of the war, and so on. For simplicity let us rank the nine possible outcomes just in order of targets destroyed, and suppose that this gives the result shown in Table 10.2, where rank 1 corresponds to the most targets destroyed. This table, in effect, summarizes in relative terms an elaborate computation of target damage carried out for each of nine different cases. Notice that, with this table, we again have reason to suppose that the enemy's feelings about the relative desirability of these outcomes are opposite to ours. If our object is to maximize damage, his is to minimize it; if our first choice is that one among the nine cases that yields the largest number of targets destroyed, that case is his ninth choice.

TABLE 10.2

U.S. order of preference among outcomes

	Defense		
Attack	A′	B′	C′
A	9	2	1
B	4	7	6
C	3	5	8

We can now rephrase the problem as follows. We have a choice among three strategies, he has a choice among three strategies. There are nine possible outcomes; we have estimated enough to know our order of preference among those nine outcomes, and simultaneously we know his order of preference which is just the reverse of ours. The enemy and we are both contemplating this table, each trying to make a choice that is reasonable in the sense of being consistent with the other's best effort to make his own reasonable choice.

Here is our chess game; but before we break our heads trying to wrestle with it, let us see whether it simplifies itself in special cases.

Timing and Intelligence Information

First, let us think about *who moves first*. Suppose we had to pick A, B, or C before the enemy committed himself to a choice among A', B', and C'. (This would be the case if our attack had a longer lead time than his defense, in terms of aircraft procurement, airbase construction, and so forth.) Knowing that he gets the last move, what is it prudent for us to do? We certainly cannot pick our "favorite" outcome, our first choice in the upper right-hand corner, which is Attack A directed against Defense C'. This would be splendid if he had already committed himself to Defense C'. But he hasn't; he is waiting to see what we do. And if we pick A, he can exploit the advantage of second move by confronting us with Defense A', which gives us the worst of all nine possible outcomes. If we pick B, he can hold us to our seventh choice by picking B'. And if we pick C, he can pick C' and we get our eighth choice. If he is at all sensible these will be his responses to our choice of A, B, or C. So we know in advance that we get ninth, seventh, or eighth on our order of preferences, according as we pick A, B, or C. The best we can do is seventh place, so we pick B. We have not done very well, but at least we have made an intelligent choice in the face of his having the advantage of second move.

If *we* had the advantage of second move—if his defensive equipment and structures had the longer lead time—he would have to look at his first choice as we just looked at ours. If we see him choose A' we can pick C and enjoy our third favorite outcome. If he picks B', or C', we can pick A and enjoy our second or first choice. Knowing we can do this, he has to pick A'. We are a good deal better off in this case than when we had to move first. (A classic illustration of this kind of play and counterplay in the game of weapons development was the successive shift in armament, armor, and speed of "dreadnoughts" from the turn of the century to the Second World War.)

Notice that *intelligence information* plays a role here. If he has to move first, locating his air bases or producing particular types of interceptors with a lead time long enough to allow us to pick our best bombing system in the light of the choice that the enemy has already made, we get the advantage of second move only if we can find out what choice it is that he has made. An intelligence disadvantage can cancel out a lead-time advantage.

Timing, then, and intelligence information are two factors affecting the relation of the enemy's behavior to ours. In terms of these two factors the problem may decompose itself into some smaller subproblems. In our illustrative problem a choice of A requires a firm commitment now on the bases we develop and the aircraft we produce, while if we choose system B or C we can leave open till much later the question of whether it is B or C that we shall finally decide on. If B and C differ mainly in the attack routes involved, and not so much in the location of bases or types of aircraft, we may manage to keep the enemy guessing up to the time of his choice if we pick B or C, rather than A, at the time of our lead-time commitment.

Choosing in Favor of Flexibility

Notice that it could be worth some extra expense to keep this added flexibility. Suppose that B and C do involve some difference in the ratio of tankers to bombers, or in the decoys that would go with the attack. B involves longer dogleg routes, and more tankers; C might involve more ground-launched decoys to overcome the disadvantage of longer penetration times. Because of the advantage in being free to choose either B or C at the last moment and to keep the enemy guessing or to make him commit himself first, it might be wise to spend some extra money (even at the expense of bombers) in order to have both the tankers required for Attack B and the decoys required for Attack C, even though one of these will eventually be somewhat superfluous or of low priority depending on which attack is finally chosen. The enemy may also keep *us* guessing. It may be that we have better intelligence about the type of equipment he possesses than about the location of his air defense bases. In that case, we could tell early whether his equipment was suitable to a Defense A' or to the kind of defense involved in B' and C'. If it is the latter, we have to know something about the location of his air defense bases to tell whether B' or C' is, in fact, the defense he has chosen. If we lack that information, we may end up with a choice problem that involves uncertainty on our side between his B' and C', uncertainty on his side between our B and C, with the four possible outcomes contained in the lower right-hand corner of Table 10.2.

Again, the enemy might build bases sufficient for both B' and C', but have to deploy his interceptor aircraft in a way that is either concentrated to meet our Attack C or dispersed to meet our Attack B. If he does not know which way we are coming, he does not know where to keep his aircraft deployed. If he thinks we know how his aircraft are stationed so that we can pick B or C accordingly, he may prefer to rotate his aircraft between the spread-out posture and the concentrated posture so that we have no way of guessing whether we will find B' or C' waiting for us when we arrive. If he rotates them so that approximately half the time he is in posture B' and half the time in posture C', we are confronted with some statistical uncertainty. If we pick B, we have a 50/50 chance of getting our fifth or eighth best choice. If we pick C, we have a 50/50 chance between sixth and seventh best choice. Which should we prefer?

Data Required for Dealing with Probabilities

Let us pause at this point, and restate the problem. Suppose that we knew that we had a 50/50 chance of finding B′ or C′ waiting for us. In this case there is no question of trying to outguess the enemy or to avoid being outguessed; we know his mode of behavior. It is as though the weatherman said there is a 50/50 chance of cold weather, and we had to decide whether or not to take a coat. Have we enough information in Table 10.2 to cope with this problem?

We are now dealing with four possible outcomes, of which our favorite is the combination C-B′, our second best is the combination B-C′, with B-B′ third and C-C′ fourth. To sharpen the point, let us look at Table 10.3 in which we have these four outcomes denoted by our order of preferences for them.

TABLE 10.3

Preference among four possible outcomes

	Defense	
Attack	B′	C′
B	3	2
C	1	4

Is this a soluble problem? The answer is no. We have not yet done enough work to provide our table with information. We cannot place our bets intelligently unless we know the payoffs better. Our table shows only our *relative* estimates of the outcomes—our order of preference toward the outcomes—but to take a calculated risk, or to place an intelligent bet, we have to take account of the *absolute strengths* of our preferences. It is not enough to know that some outcomes are better than others; we have to consider how much better they are. If our table referred not to target destruction but to money prizes, we would feel very differently about the two prize schedules in Table 10.4 below, assuming a 50/50 chance of B′ or C′ occurring. C looks good in Schedule I, B looks good in Schedule II; but both these schedules contain money rewards that are identical when we express them just as first, second, third, and fourth, in order of size, as in Table 10.3.

TABLE 10.4

Absolute strengths of four possible outcomes—two examples

	Defense			
	Schedule I		Schedule II	
Attack	B′	C′	B′	C′
B	3	5	7	9
C	10	2	10	2

Let us take this idea back to Table 10.1. Recall that first we started with just an indication of best, medium, and worst in each column. That proved insufficient for certain problems and we replaced the three-way comparisons with a nine-way comparison, comparing the outcomes in all nine cases, expressing them in order of damage to the enemy. Now we have come to the conclusion that we need some kind of numerical scale that will indicate not only which outcome is better than which other outcome, but *how much better*. How can we get such a numerical measure?

We might just take some measure of damage done—percentage of targets destroyed, for example. This might not be bad as a crude first approximation; but it seems likely that it will not be a very good approximation. Just how much it is worth to destroy another 10 per cent of the targets may depend on whether we were already counting on destroying 90 per cent, 50 per cent, or 20 per cent. It could be, for example, that the difference between 60 per cent and 70 per cent destruction is significant in terms of what the enemy can do with what he has left over, while the difference between 90 per cent and 100 per cent is a little like shooting a dead horse.

Furthermore, our feeling about the relative merits of different outcomes would probably reflect more than one single component of the outcome. We may have to weigh the advantage of more targets destroyed against the greater cost to us in planes lost; and since these may not vary in the same proportions as we move from one outcome to another, we have to find some way of weighing together, in the balance, several different components of the outcome.

Without in any way implying that this is an easy thing to do, but just insisting that it has to be done, let us get on with our decision problem by putting some numbers in the table. We have to pick some scale of measure; let us arbitrarily give a value of 100 to our first choice among the nine outcomes, and 0 to our last choice. Now we try to give numerical values to the other outcomes that in some way express how much difference there is between them in our evaluation of them. I have put some numbers in Table 10.5, which are perfectly arbitrary but do have the virtue that they correlate properly with our earlier evaluation of the outcomes. What was our best possible outcome, A against C′, is valued at 100; the worst possible outcome, A against A′, is valued at 0, and the values in the other seven boxes are in the same order as the numbers in Table 10.2.

TABLE 10.5

Numerical evaluations of outcomes

Attack	Defense		
	A′	B′	C′
A	0	80	100
B	60	40	50
C	70	55	30

I should remark that I am simultaneously making our table both harder and easier to deal with. As far as the decision problem is concerned, I am making it easier. By assuming more and more research into the relative merits of these various outcomes, I am assuming that we have more and more data to deal with. And the more data we have in our table, the less intractable our problem will be. At the same time, it is getting harder and harder to handle it within the scope of a single chapter. We are probably now at about the extent of what we can handle in a limited discussion. This does not mean, I should stress, that our problem has become hopelessly complex from the point of view of solving it. If we were actually engaged in the research, instead of just trying to describe and illustrate a type of research, we could stay with it for hours, days, or weeks, until we thought we had it pretty well thrashed out.

We can do more with these new numbers than we could do before. Let us look again at the problem that the Russians pose for us when they rotate their planes between a B' and a C' posture. Suppose that we earlier had to decide between A on the one hand or B and C on the other, and chose a dual capacity for either B or C, and that we must now decide which of those two to pick. If we pick B, we have a 50/50 chance between 40 and 50; if we pick C we have a 50/50 chance between 55 and 30. B looks somewhat better; if these were money bets we should almost certainly pick it. These are not money bets, but at least we have already tried to make an allowance for any disproportionate differences among the different outcomes so that the numbers approximately represent their "worth" to us, and the difference between two outcomes like B-B' and B-C' is supposed to measure how important that difference is to us. So although we may not be quite ready to say that we will look at these numbers as a gambler or an investor or an insurance company does, computing expected values from known odds, at least it is not wholly senseless to look at the problem that way; but it was when all we had to go on was the first, second, third, fourth preference designations. We have at least now tried to get the numbers in a form that permits us to make use of their numerical values.

Notice in this case that the Russians, if they are rotating their planes half the time in a B' stance and half the time in a C', can guess what we will do. We are likely to pick B. Knowing this, they might like to pick B'. The reason they cannot is that if they pick B' and stay with it, we shall pick C; they have to keep rotating in order to keep us from adapting to them.

Redesigning the Strategies

With these numbers, we can now talk about another important possibility. Not only may it be possible to mix two strategies like B' and C' by random rotation, it may be possible to mix them physically by designing a compromise strategy. The Russians, instead of rotating their planes between a concentrated configuration and a dispersed configuration, might leave them permanently in a compromise stance—more dispersed than they would be for a C type of attack, more concentrated than they would be for a B type of attack. Such a defense posture would not be as good against B as B′ is, and would not be as good against C as C′ is, but it might have the compensating advantage of being not nearly so bad for the Russians as if we came in with the particular kind of attack that they were not prepared for. Also, it avoids the need for rotation among a fully duplicate base system.

Similarly, *we* might design a compromise attack that is somewhere between B and C. The compromise attack is less able to exploit the enemy's mistake if he chooses the wrong defense, but it is better than B or C if he were waiting with the right one. The question arises, do we gain as much as we lost? The point I want to make is that our table (Table 10.5) now has the *kind* of numbers in it that are needed if we are to give an answer. Let us add the compromise strategy, and call it BC. Suppose we evaluate it just as we did the others, and we find that it results in outcomes as shown in the third row of Table 10.6. It looks fairly good. In the case of B′ it is nearly as good as C; in the case of C′ it is nearly as good as B. And, viewed conservatively, it achieves *at its worst* a score that is much better than C at C's worst and appreciably better than B at B's worst. On the other hand, if it were evaluated as shown by the numbers in parentheses, the numbers would probably help us to reject it. It is only slightly better than B where B is the wrong strategy, and substantially inferior when the enemy chooses C′.

TABLE 10.6

Numerical evaluations—compromise strategy

Attack	Defense	
	B′	C′
B	40	50
C	55	30
BC	50	45
(BC)	(45)	(35)

Tentative Summary

I am going to put some more numbers in the table. Before we take that plunge let us stand off a minute, get away from the numbers, and see if we can sum up. We started out with the idea that in many important cases we cannot really evaluate our own choices and decisions unless we make a guess at what the enemy is going to do. But the enemy's basic mode of behavior, if we are going to concede him any intelligence, is to adapt to what we do, exploiting our weaknesses just as we are trying to exploit his. Whenever we have to commit ourselves first, he will do what he can to get around the strategy we have chosen. To minimize his ability to adapt his strategy to ours, we try to design weapon systems that are good in a variety of contingencies, even though they may not be as good in the best possible case as a more specialized but less versatile system. We can try to make adaptation difficult for the enemy by keeping him guessing about our strategy, cultivating versatile capabilities instead of highly specialized capabilities, postponing decisions where we can, so that he has to choose in ignorance of ours or—better still for us—to commit himself in a way that we can see before we have to make our final choice.

Making the Enemy Adapt

There is another way to look at this problem of enemy adaptation. In those cases where we have to choose first, and must assume that he will intelligently pick a response to our system that exploits the weaknesses of ours, we need not think of his adaptations as nullifying our actions. We can think of his adaptation as an *objective* of our actions. To illustrate, suppose we build a distant early warning (DEW) line in the north and supplement it with other warning arrangements in the south. There are three ways of evaluating what the warning system does. The optimist will say that as the enemy flies in with his large fleets of bombers we shall see him several hours before he reaches us, certainly get off an enormous retaliatory strike, and even have our defenses alerted to meet his bombers when they come in. The pessimist will say that the enemy will redesign his attack so that he relies on a much smaller number of planes that can sneak in through the weakest parts of our warning net; the DEW line will never catch them coming at us, because either he will not fly over the DEW line or, if he does, he will do it with numbers and flight patterns that give us little likelihood of recognizing him. In between is the view of the moderate who takes enemy adaptation for granted and builds his systems analysis around it. According to this view, the purpose of a DEW line is not necessarily to spot an enemy attack when it comes; it is to force the enemy to go to the trouble, the expense, and the risk involved in designing an attack that does not alert the DEW line. The DEW line closes a loop hole, and makes the enemy shift to a second-best strategy. This kind of evaluation may or may not make a DEW line a good investment; but it does imply that the worth of a particular warning system is not settled by the question of whether it will ever spot his attack coming in. Instead, one wants to ask what it *costs the enemy* when we deny him the possibility of an undetected mass attack over the Arctic region, and what it *costs us* to build the warning system.

In the same way, we might consider dispersing some of our attack forces at bases on the far side of the Soviet Union. Whether or not this is a good idea is not settled by whether the enemy can design his air defense in such a way that those particular bombers that we send in from those distant bases never reach target. The pertinent question is whether it is difficult and costly to the enemy in terms of the military resources that he has to divert to be prepared to meet this particular attack. If at little cost we can force him into a costly diversion of air defense resources it may look like a good idea. But, if at great cost we force him to divert a small amount of resources, it does not look good.

In other words, granted that the enemy will adapt to the decisions we make, whenever the timing of our choices and his intelligence information permit him to, we want to evaluate proposals in terms of the *adaptation that they force the enemy to undertake*. And this means looking at the relative costs of what he has to do compared with what we do.

This point can be illustrated with the table we already have. Looking at Table 10.6 suppose we have already committed ourselves to strategy C, and the enemy is ready for us with Defense C'. It is proposed to buy more tankers so that we can mount an attack of the type B. An optimistic view, imputing foolishness to the enemy, is that we will raise our score by 20. A pessimistic view is that the enemy will redesign his defense against us so that we gain only 10 points. The analyst, however, should try to calculate what it costs the enemy in diverted resources if he adapts to our new strategy, what this does to his over-all defense, and how we come out on balance. He looks at the more modest increment that we get as we shift from C versus C' to B versus B'. In the particular table we are using this is a good idea. It can mean either that the enemy's adaptation is incomplete, or that he completely adapts to the wider dispersion of our forces but at a cost in the number and quality of his own weapons, so that the net balance is in our favor and the outcome is better for us.

10.3. BROADER INTERPRETATION—A COMPREHENSIVE STRATEGY

I want to consider a broader interpretation of my illustrative problem of choice among alternative weapon systems. Up to this point I have discussed that problem as though it related to a tactical choice rather than to a comprehensive strategy. I have left at least two important things out of account. One is *casualties*—as distinct from immediate military damage—and the other is the possibility that our choice among strategies for fighting a war may affect the *likelihood* of war itself.

It may not be immediately apparent that I have necessarily left casualties out of account. Table 10.6 now contains numbers that are supposed to represent, in a quantitative way, our evaluation of the different possible outcomes. We talked a little about what might lie behind those numbers, such as the damage to enemy targets, our own losses of aircraft and crews, and similar factors. Might we not—for the purpose of this illustrative example—just give our numbers a more sophisticated interpretation, and say that we weighed civilian casualties, economic damage, political prestige, and other elements all in the balance. This would mean more research, more statistics, more soul-searching, and more argument over intangibles; but assuming that we spend the necessary time and ingenuity on it, we should be able to reach a more comprehensive evaluation of the relative merits of the different outcomes. We would undoubtedly reach different numbers depending on what we take into account; but we still should end up with a table in the general form of the one we have.

The reason we cannot simply reinterpret our numbers—for the purpose of this discussion—to include casualties is that up to this point we have assumed that what is better for us is worse for the enemy, and vice versa. We have supposed that we like to damage his targets but he does not like us to, so that we have exactly opposite preferences for different levels of damage. (Alternatively, if we interpret our numbers as denoting the odds of "winning" the war, any pair of attacks and defenses that gives us relatively high odds of winning gives the Russians relatively low odds, and vice versa.) But when we come to take casualties into account, it is no longer true that of the various possible outcomes we and the Russians have exactly inverse evaluations. As between a pair of attack and defense strategies that gives us three-to-one odds of winning, with moderate casualties on both sides, and another that gives us the same three-to-one odds of winning, but with much greater casualties on both sides, we and the Russians may both prefer the same one of these two alternative outcomes. And aside from civilian casualties and economic damage, there are such questions as the survival of the regime in Russia, the cohesion of the Communist bloc, the balance of power among pressure groups in the Soviet Union, and so on, as well as comparable factors on our side, which the Russians may appraise quite differently from the way we would appraise them.

For that reason, in appraising all the consequences of the different attacks and defenses, as distinct from their immediate military consequences, we can probably *not* make a *single* set of numbers serve as an index of *our* evaluation and of the *enemy* evaluation at the same time. We need *two sets of numbers* to represent our two different appreciations of the consequences.

If I have made it clear that this is true in principle, it remains to be asked whether our decision is affected by the Russian evaluation of such things as their own civilian, economic, and political losses. The answer is that it is.

Revised Illustration: A "Poor" Strategy

To show this in an extreme case, and to avoid increasing the size of our table, let us change the character of our Attack C and replace the numbers in Table 10.6. Ignoring for the moment what kind of an attack C is now, but supposing that our comprehensive evaluation of the outcome is as shown in Table 10.7, what conclusions can we reach about the choice among A, B, and C?

TABLE 10.7

Numerical evaluations—"poor" strategy

Attack	Defense		
	A'	B'	C'
A	0	80	100
B	60	40	50
C	-20	10	25

Our earlier analysis would undoubtedly have led us to reject Attack C altogether. No matter what defense the Russians use, as among A', B', and C', our
Attack C is invariably worse for us than A or B. There is no case in which we
would not prefer B to C, and no case in which we would not prefer A to C. We
cannot even profitably fool the Russians by using C, thinking that they would
expect us to reject it; we do so badly that they are delighted at our choice of C,
even if they expected A or B.

The Enemy's Evaluation

But now let us introduce into Table 10.7 some illustrative numbers that
might represent our estimate of the Russian evaluation of these nine different
possible outcomes. In Table 10.8 I have put numbers for us and numbers for
the Russians (that is, for our guess at a Russian evaluation) in each of the nine
cells of the table, ours to the lower left, theirs to the upper right.

TABLE 10.8

Numerical evaluations—possible Russian evaluations

Attack	Defense		
	A'	B'	C'
A	0 | 100	80 | 20	100 | 50
B	60 | 20	40 | 40	50 | 30
C	-20 | 0	10 | 10	25 | 0

In doing this let us distinguish broadly between two kinds of elements in their
evaluation: first, their estimate of the odds based on winning or losing the war,
or on the bilateral power position between us once the war is over—matters on
which their evaluation ought to run directly contrary to ours; and second, the
various factors that I have broadly termed "casualties", on which there is no
strong reason to suppose that the kind of war that they like least is the kind of
war we like best, and vice versa. Just to make the illustration concrete: if we

suppose their evaluation of the outcome when Attack A meets Defense B′ is 20, a comparatively low number, it reflects the fact that our number is comparatively high. Looking at the intersection of Attack A with Defense C′, we see that it is not necessarily true that because our number goes up, their number goes down; there is no logical inconsistency in giving their appreciation of this case a value of 50. To put the matter crudely, A against B′ and A against C′ may be roughly similar in terms of who wins the war, but one may just be a good deal bloodier on both sides than the other, so that the differential in the estimates goes in the same direction for the Russians as for us.

We need not look at the numbers in Table 10.8 in great detail, since I want only to illustrate a rather simple point: that there is no necessarily logical inconsistency in the way I have supposed the Russian figures relate to ours. Let us look at our Attack C. C is a strategy that we might have rejected out of hand on the basis of the figures representing the U.S. evaluation of the outcomes. But the numbers I put in for the possible Russian evaluation may give us reason to keep C in the running.

According to these numbers, the Russians dislike the outcome when C is used just about as much as we do. Attack C seems to be a bloody attack of the kind that is popularly referred to as "mutual suicide" or something of the sort. We dislike it because of what it does to our own country. We may not take particular satisfaction in the fact that the Russians would be desolated too. So, if we were sure that once we had adopted the strategy we would have to fight the war (or if we thought the probability of having to fight the war was independent of which attack strategy we chose), we would avoid C. But, if we are interested in *deterrence* as well as in the outcome of any war that comes, Attack C may have some attraction. If our problem is to confront the Russians with a potential attack that is as unattractive to them as we can choose, C has some virtue compared with A and B.

Secrecy and Flexibility Reconsidered

There are some interesting observations to make about the adoption of a strategy like Attack C. We earlier put a premium on secrecy, because it seemed to our advantage to keep the enemy uncertain about which of our attacks he should prepare for. But a strategy as purely deterrent as C would only make sense if we advertised it to the enemy. We also, in our earlier analysis, put a high premium on flexibility, on having the freedom to make a final choice at a last moment, again to keep the enemy guessing or to adapt to the posture that the enemy might have adopted by then. But Attack C is a pretty unconvincing kind of deterrence if we have any flexibility for switching to A or B at the last moment. At the moment that war starts, we have no more interest in pursuing strategy C than the Russians have in being hit by it, and the Russians know that we have every incentive to switch to A or B if it is physically possible. The only way that they could be fully persuaded that they would be hit by Attack C would be for them to be persuaded that we could not choose anything but Attack C even if we wanted to.

The essential difference here is that earlier we were trying to accommodate ourselves to the fact that we and our enemy had opposite interests, while in the situation represented by strategy C we are trying to structure the Russians' incentives so that they have a common interest with us—a common interest in choosing still another strategy, namely the strategy of behaving in a way that makes the war unnecessary! We are now trying to manipulate their incentives, not just to adapt to them. We are trying to present them a choice that we have designed in such a way that if they choose what is best for them, they are choosing the course that we want them to take.

A Strategy That Looks "Too Good"

At another extreme, we might put in a new strategy—or new numbers for our still unspecified Attack C—that makes it look very good by comparison with A and B on the basis of our own numerical evaluation. It could look too good. To keep my illustration simple and hypothetical I have not discussed the question of who strikes first in this war. But if we made our table big enough and complicated enough we could give each of the two sides an attack and defense posture together with the option of waiting or trying to go first. We might in that case find a strategy that looked very good when we struck second, and even better when we struck first. But if *in fact* we do *not* intend to strike first, it is possible that the very effectiveness of that posture as a springboard for striking first is an embarrassment. It may look too good to us. Rather, it may look to the Russians as though it looks too good to us, so that while the strike-second capability of our posture is a potential deterrent, its strike-first capability may provoke a countervailing urge to pre-empt.

I raise this possibility not in order to discuss it in any detail but only to show how far we may have to compound some of the intangibles that go into our analysis. We not only have to evaluate the outcomes from our own point of view, and then estimate how the Russians would evaluate the outcomes from their point of view, but to deal with this last case we also have to estimate how the Russians estimate our evaluation of the various outcomes. If we could by striking first destroy Russian power at the cost of X million American lives, it is important for us to have the best possible understanding of what the Russians think our feelings are about X million casualties.

10.4.   CONCLUDING SUMMARY

In summary, I would like to make two points. First, the only sensible assumptions we can make about enemy behavior in dealing with problems where his interest is strictly opposed to our interest are that the enemy will adapt his behavior, within the limits imposed by whatever flexibility he has, to what he knows about the decisions we are making; that he will design his system to keep flexibility and to confront us with uncertainty; and that he will anticipate our doing the same thing.

The second summary point is that in matters like deterrence, limited war, avoidance of inadvertent war, provocation of pre-emptive attack, and so forth, although we assume that the enemy will adapt to our decisions, we must try to design a system that will induce him to adapt his behavior in the ways we want.

I want to make one observation. In both of these cases we are, in a sense, taking the opposite of the view that one should ground one's decisions on the enemy's capabilities rather than on the enemy's intentions. In the kinds of problems I have been discussing, we are necessarily dealing with the enemy's intentions—his expectations, his incentives, and the guesses that he makes about our intentions and our expectations and our incentives. This is patently true in dealing with a concept like deterrence, the whole idea of which is the manipulation of the enemy's intentions by confronting him with a properly designed set of choices. But it is also true of those situations in which we are not trying to deter or to coerce or to persuade an enemy, but simply to out-guess him or to keep from being outguessed. We cannot deal with his capabilities in those cases; his capabilities against the different systems that we may choose depend on how he allocates his resources among the alternative systems available to him, which in turn depends on what he expects us to be doing. The deployment of his capabilities that we should expect is not something we introduce into the beginning of our analysis; it is a conclusion that we reach. When we have looked simultaneously at his problem and ours, and have run through the kind of analysis that he must be assumed to be doing on his side of the problem, we can hope to reach simultaneously a judgment about what is the most reasonable choice for us to make and what is a reasonable choice for him to be making.

This is why so many of the estimates that we need for dealing with these problems relate to intangibles. The problem involves intangibles. In particular, it involves the great intangible of what the enemy thinks we think he is going to do.

Chapter 11

GAMING METHODS AND APPLICATIONS

M. G. WEINER

11.1. The uses of war gaming

War gaming has a long history of military respectability as an educational and training device. It extends back to the time when someone—possibly an oriental general Sun Tzu[1]—attempted to conduct imaginary military operations by representing his own forces and those of the enemy on a map, board, or with scribbles in the sand, and tried to work out the various moves or actions that could be taken by each side. He was, in a sense, constructing a model of the situation. By considering all the military moves that he could make and all the moves that the enemy might make, he sought a way in which he could be most effective against the enemy, despite what the enemy might do to oppose him.

Whether this technique of examining action and counteraction survived because our hypothetical general found that it contributed to his military success, or because it was a useful way of thinking through complex situations, or simply because it was an entertaining pastime is unimportant. The important thing is that it did survive and over the years has undergone many changes and developments.

At the present time war gaming is used in many different ways. Four of the major uses are described below[2].

1. *The use of gaming as a training or heuristic device.* Under this heading are included all those uses in which the play is carried out in the expectation that the simulated environment will create a greater awareness of the multitude of factors and actions that are involved, and will develop an appreciation of these factors or actions in any real world counterpart of the environment.

2. *The use of gaming for self-education.* In this use a situation is established which provides a focus for the experience and judgments of the military and systems analysts. By dealing with specific situations the relevant factors

---

[1] Reported to have said about 500 B.C.: "The general who wins a battle makes many calculations in his temple ere the battle is fought".

[2] Adapted from a classification by Olaf Helmer, The RAND Corporation.

are viewed in a definite context and many of the factors and interrelations that might have been ignored or overlooked are brought under consideration. Many studies involve an initial period in which the analysts engage in crude forms of gaming as a method of getting a feel for the complexity of the problem and of recognizing some of the major aspects that require study.

3. *The use of gaming as a research tool.* The objective of this use, which is generally in the form of an evaluation or a developmental device, is to arrive at specific conclusions with respect to plans, policies, or specific instrumentalities. The example to be developed later in this chapter is a use of this type.

4. *The use of gaming as a stepping-stone toward a better model of the phenomenon being studied.* In this sense, games are used as devices for examining the various factors involved in a situation in the hope that the important aspects can be established and some value assigned to the factors. This use is a preliminary step toward a more precise model which can become part of a much more convenient and valuable theoretical formulation.

The attempts to use gaming as a research device or stepping-stone to theory are relatively recent uses. It is probably premature to try to assess the contribution that war gaming can make as an analytic technique for decisions. It is probably also premature to say that we have a very complete understanding of the different types of games or of the problems to which they can be applied. Even with these reservations, however, we can and do use war gaming as an analytic technique.

11.2.   TECHNIQUES OF WAR GAMING

War games involve setting up a hypothetical situation in which two sides with conflicting interests and objectives interact under a system of more or less definite rules. Under this general format we can consider a number of different methods, some of which may emphasize one aspect of war gaming, some of which may emphasize others. We may consider the different techniques in terms of the following list.

1. Mathematical games.
2. Machine games.
3. Board and bookkeeping games.
4. Games involving human umpiring.

Under the mathematical games are included the games that have been subject to analysis by game theory. In these games each course of action available to one side is matched in a matrix by a course of action available to the other side, and the expected outcome for each combination is specified. The problem for mathematics is to deduce the correct course of action or strategy which each player should employ. In some cases the solutions indicate a single best strategy which each player should choose. In others, however, each player has to choose one of several strategies according to a calculated probability. In this method the rules are absolutely definite and no umpire is required. The method so far has been appropriate to only a limited number of military cases such as some types of fighter-bomber duels.

Another type of mathematical game is one in which a series of choices on allocation of forces is available to each side. One example of this type is an allocation problem in which each side can choose between allocating his air-craft to one of three roles: counterair, counterground, or close support. The problem for analysis is to deduce throughout the campaign the correct alloca-tion for each side. In this situation, as in the preceding one, the conditions must be defined very precisely and the choices available are limited and definite.

Next are games that involve computing machines. An example of this type is an air battle game which traces through the history of each individual attack and the outcome. The rules for each attack must be specified in advance and the machine, using Monte Carlo techniques, plays through a large number of attacks. The analysis can indicate the extent to which some of the factors that have been included are critical to the outcome of the battle.

There are a number of variations on the machine methods which include the addition of one or more human players who decide on the attacks to be made and the forces that will be used, rather than having these specified in advance. The machine then carries out the computations based on the judgments of the players.

A third category includes the board and bookkeeping games. In these games the rules are usually very definite, and they differ from the machine games in that the number of possible actions and their consequences over a period of time become so numerous or interact so much that they exceed any reasonable machine capacity. In a sense these games resemble chess games played on a grand scale. Games in this category have been used to study strategic air campaigns, war planning, and procurement.

Finally, we have games involving humans as umpires and players. In this group the spectrum is very broad, starting with games in which one side plays against an umpire who is the final authority on the outcome of each move and in which detailed rules may or may not be employed.

From this point we get into the two-or-more-sided war games of which there are many combinations and types, including games involving large numbers of players and a large umpiring staff. These games are used in problems involving national and international factors.

Since the games involving human umpiring, decisionmaking, and judgment are the most widely used and offer the greatest flexibility, most of the following remarks on war gaming will be concerned with this type.

11.3. STEPS IN WAR GAMING

Gaming, like any other analytic technique, involves a number of definite steps. We can, somewhat arbitrarily, divide these into

1. Determining the objective or purpose of the game.
2. Preparing the inputs and boundary conditions.
3. Establishing the decision rules and the adjudication mechanism.
4. Playing the game.
5. Analyzing the game.

To illustrate some of the considerations that are important for each of these steps, let us assume that we are going to use war gaming techniques to evaluate the effectiveness of a weapon system.

Determining the objective of the game sets the format for all the subsequent steps. The objective indicates the complexity of the game, the level of detail that will be included, and the magnitude of the play and of the analysis. This is one of those self-evident statements that occur over and over again in the course of gaming operations and other analytic techniques. It seems *particularly true* of gaming because the types of problems chosen are usually fairly broad in scope and allow many possible interpretations by the human participants.

The hypothetical problem we have chosen can be set up for analysis in a large number of ways. We may choose a very well-defined situation at a particular time under very limited conditions. We may attempt to evaluate the weapon system in a specific military situation without regard to preceding events or actions in the situation and without concern for the outcome of the situation on the rest of the military campaign. If we were to do this and present our findings to any reasonable audience they would immediately, and quite correctly, raise questions about the findings. They would point out, among other things, that we had only looked at a single situation, that we could easily have chosen other situations in which the results would have been different, that we had not established the specific situation as being a reasonable one to consider, and that we had not, in fact, been very complete or comprehensive in our investigation.

We might answer by pointing out that the problem we had chosen was a complex one and that we had taken as the objective of our study evaluation of the weapon system under the limited conditions which we had imposed. This might serve to answer our critics on this particular study, but it would provide only a small amount of the information which the decisionmaker might require.

Aware of this possibility, we can consider the problem in a broader way. We might decide to investigate a number of situations, each providing a number of different possibilities for the operation of the weapon system. But, what possibilities? At this point, as with any analysis, we have to consider a large number of alternatives and make an initial judgment on which possibilities are the most important. Two points should be noted. The various situations which we consider represent judgments on the part of the analysts. These judgments may be unavoidable for many reasons, but it should not stop us from recognizing that these are judgments. The second point is that the selection of some of the situations for study, to the exclusion of others, is also a judgment. Each of the possibilities might have been examined in great detail, prior to deciding on which ones are to be gamed, but, at best, the final decision is an educated guess on the part of the analysts. And it is a particular type of guess: it is a guess that the specific situations which have been selected have a more reasonable chance of occurring than the ones that have been eliminated. So it is a prediction about the future. In a sense this is one of the major problems with war gaming. We are forced, because of real limits of time, money, and personnel, to restrict our choices of situations for study. But even if these restrictions were eased, we might find that to explore all the possible situations which could be imagined, either realistically or not, would take such a long time that our weapon system would have become obsolete by the time we had enough analytic data to evaluate it.

Because we have to select some situations rather than others, we are actually making judgments that the situations we have selected are more likely to occur (we may also say "be important", "be more credible", or "be the best range of alternatives", or some other rationale) than some other situations.

We may attempt to justify this by saying that we are not trying to predict that the situations *will* occur, but only to examine the effectiveness of the weapon system *if* they should occur. It rests with the decisionmaker to determine whether they are likely enough to occur to make the results of the analysis useful.

We might try something entirely different. We might move our analysis into a time period in the future which is sufficiently advanced so that even though we require a long period of time to examine a large number of possible situations and factors by game means, we are still capable of ending up with results that the decisionmaker can use. There is a lot of discussion, both pro and con, on the use of war gaming for periods somewhat far removed into the future. At the present time, no clear answer on the applicability of gaming to remote future time is possible. What we do know is that as we move into the future the problems of prediction affect a number of different aspects of the game and increase our difficulties.

These problems of selecting situations to study do get solved. Sometimes the solution is based on the judgment of specialists; sometimes it is based on an arbitrary decision influenced by the resources available to the gaming staff; and sometimes it is based merely on the "pious hope" that the selection is sound.

The next step in gaming is to prepare the inputs. The inputs must be established along with the determination of the objective and the selection of situations to be considered. Three main types can be distinguished: the inputs required to define the locale or context in which the weapons will be used; the inputs required to establish the operating characteristics of the weapons; and the inputs required to establish the effectiveness of the weapon.

In attempting to define the locale or context, several major choices appear immediately. They are related to the original choice of objective but take on new meaning at this point. The choices include such questions as

> Does our primary concern with evaluating the effectiveness of our system lie in grand strategy, detailed strategy, or combat tactics? Or perhaps we may ask whether our concern is with the system in general war, limited war, or both?

> How complex a pattern of political, military, economic, logistic, and intelligence events or conditions should be included?

> To what extent should we limit or constrain the action of each side?

The answers that we give to these questions determine the inputs and boundary conditions of a war game.

If the war game is concerned with a general war situation, the locales are pretty definite—the Soviet Union and the United States. Under these circumstances the inputs will include such things as our force locations, enemy force locations; our targets, enemy targets; etc. At this point we are listing the inputs and can be as exhaustive as our knowledge of the present or programmed position and intelligence will allow. When the play of the game starts we may find that there are some crucial decisions that will be made which influence our use of all of those inputs, such as what our own and the enemy intentions will be, since both of us may have to operate with limited resources or under restrictions as far as target selection, delivery capability, etc., are concerned.

If, on the other hand, the game is concerned with limited war situations, there is a large selection of possible locales, with factors in each locale that will very likely influence evaluation of the effectiveness of our hypothetical weapon system. In addition, the choice of locale will raise problems as to the way in which the situation developed, since the types of actions that will be taken will depend on this development. The types of inputs to be prepared will be influenced accordingly. Factors such as force availability, base availability, logistics feasibility, as well as terrain and weather, must be included. All of this will be against a political background of our own intentions and objectives of our own choosing, as well as self-imposed political and military constraints.

The second type of input—the operating characteristics of the weapons— presents additional requirements. It is not sufficient merely to know hardware characteristics. Many other factors will become important: deployment and employment capabilities, schedules, limitations, tactical procedures, operational requirements, serviceability, maintenance rates, and other similar factors will have to be established. If our weapon system is one of many to be included in the game so that its relation to other weapon systems and forces can be seen, similar inputs will have to be established for the other systems.

A third type of input is required to establish the effectiveness of the weapon. Here again there are several major problems which deserve mention. One is the fact that for many of our weapons we do not have the type of data or information needed. Our experience with combat conditions essentially ceased in Korea, and, although it is possible to make many inferences from tests, simulated exercises, and field studies, we must approach the application of these results to actual combat with some caution. The noncombat conditions are always different, and we have no acceptable and precise way of relating them to combat. Secondly, most of what we do know is in the nature of results or values for particular situations, but in our gaming we may be dealing with situations having characteristics that differ from those to which the available results or values apply.

These are some of the requirements which must be met in preparing inputs. In every case possible, quantitative measures are used, but there are many cases where this is not possible and where reasonable judgments have to be made. In some cases only the very broadest statements are sufficient, while in other cases it is necessary to be as precise and definite as the data and information permit. The amount of detail will differ from game to game, depending on the particular problem being analyzed, but, unlike many other techniques, the uncertainty about how the play of a game will develop makes it difficult to determine the correct detail for all of the inputs in advance. This requires obtaining or developing additional data as the game progresses.

The next step, following preparation of the inputs and related to them, is the establishment of the decision rules and the adjudication mechanism that will be used to enforce these rules. In some cases the rules and the mechanism are prescribed in advance so completely that all the special events or moves in the game can be assessed with little difficulty. In the majority of games in which any degree of complexity exists, this is not possible. The usual method for dealing with the latter condition is an umpiring or control system which decides on all cases where the data or rules are inadequate for the situation. The control function is a way of using judgments to fill in our lack of data or knowledge. The judgments are based on whatever evidence exists, plus as much expert opinion as can be produced. In many cases these judgments are not particularly critical to the outcome of the game, but are necessary to keep the game from bogging down when a situation arises where the data or rules are not complete or clear. In two kinds of cases, however, judgments can be very critical. One case is when the judgment applies to a particular event or situation so important that it affects the entire outcome of the game and the evaluation being conducted. The other case is when the judgment applies to some set of actions or events which occur with such great frequency in the game that they accumulate in a manner that affects the evaluation. Judgments about the effects of a weapon that is used a number of times in the game are in this category. In some situations it is not possible to establish what the effect will be within several orders of magnitude. If the analysis depends very heavily on the judgment, it may be necessary to review the game, taking several different values for the effect, to determine how sensitive the evaluation is to the judgment.

The next step is the play of the game. There are many different techniques for carrying out game play that will not be considered here. However, several aspects related to game play are worth mentioning. In the play of a game where a number of alternative moves exist at any given time, only one alternative can be examined for any given play. Theoretically, a type of gaming could be developed that would explore all the alternatives for all possible values of inputs over large ranges of uncertainty, with many different values being assigned to each factor in the game. At the minimum this would be an expensive undertaking for games involving human decisions.

Generally, however, a decision has to be made as to which of the several possible moves will be chosen. This decision may ultimately depend on the intuition and judgment of the game participants. This is different from the judgments made or the intuition exercised at the start of the analysis. These original judgments are really the assumptions of the analysis. One can examine these initial assumptions and, within limits, modify them so as to explore the results of different assumptions. In the case of game play, the judgments used to elect one alternative rather than another during the play of the game are added to the original assumptions and serve to compound our analysis problem.

Another point in game play concerns the termination of a game. In all our parlor and athletic games we have some form of stop rule, like the "checkmate" of chess or the ninth inning without a tie score in baseball. We know when the game is over and we know who has won. In war gaming we sometimes know neither. It is true that the games come to an end and that this end is sometimes definite. For example, our weapon system might have completely destroyed the capability of the enemy to fight further in any effective military manner. There still may be questions about the long-term solution, but these are not critical to the evaluation of the system. This type of termination is very rare. Usually we are left with a situation in which part of the military capability of both sides has been destroyed, but a residual capability exists making it possible to indicate ways in which military operations could continue and could affect our evaluation.

The most frequent termination of a war game is by an administrative decision that the game will reveal no more significant material for analysis. Although this method of termination may not be completely satisfactory, the present state of our knowledge offers no better substitute.

The final step in gaming is analysis. During the course of a game a large amount of information of many different kinds is accumulated. Each move cycle in the game involves actions taken by both sides. If there are a large number of moves there may be a sizable body of data about the allocations of friendly forces, weapons, and resources; the objective of the allocations; the enemy allocation of forces, weapons, and resources and their objectives; and the outcome of each interplay. If the gaming situation is very broad these military move cycles will be accompanied by logistics, political, intelligence, and economic moves and outcomes. With this much data, different types of analyses can be made.

One type of analysis is an over-all evaluation of the game, showing how various moves contributed to the final outcome. This is sometimes satisfied by a critical narrative of the game outlining the actions and counteractions of each side. The narrative may have several functions. It can provide a synthetic history in which the various conditions, circumstances, and actions affecting the use of the weapon system can be appreciated, or in some cases, re-examined to determine their influence. Or, it may provide a test bed in which, by changing some of the initial assumptions, other alternatives in the use of the weapon system, or perhaps other weapon systems, can be explored.

Related to this over-all evaluation, or in some cases quite independent of it, is an analysis of some particular aspect. In the case of a weapon system it may be the effectiveness of the system under the different conditions that arose during the course of the game. For example, we may be interested in such things as the number of times there was an opportunity to commit the system, the number of casualties produced per unit committed, and the logistics requirements to obtain a given level of effectiveness. In these types of analysis much of the more general material of the game will not be significant.

Another type of analysis is concerned with the factors that influence effectiveness of the system—from political constraints and intelligence requirements to weather and terrain conditions. This type of analysis may be quite independent of the particular moves made, simply examining each of the many situations that developed in terms of weapon effectiveness.

Still a fourth type of analysis is concerned with identifying problems, for example those that arise in the deployment, employment, or operation of our hypothetical weapon system. In these cases the main function of the analysis may be to indicate the problem area so that it can be investigated further and, perhaps, lead to a technical study of ways to overcome it.

The primary point is that a number of different and frequently interrelated analyses can be made, since a war game is generally a source of opinions, attitudes, and judgments about the particular analysis being undertaken, as well as a very rich source of data.

The final point on gaming concerns the validity of the findings. There are two extreme positions on this point that have been taken by people familiar with gaming. One side holds that games are so restrictive in nature, so packed with assumptions and judgments, so limited in the number of possibilities that can be explored, and so artificial that few if any of the findings should be regarded as valid. The other side maintains that games are models in the same sense as many of our other analytic models, that they are full of checks and counterchecks in the actions that take place, that they produce findings not available by any other method, and that the findings have to be accepted as sufficiently valid for the kind of complex situations the games study, if they are to be used as the basis for decision, or at a minimum, to lead to the use of other techniques which can provide additional validation independent of the game.

In general, questions about the validity of game findings are not directed at the methodology used. They are aimed at the types of problems chosen for analysis. These problems usually include many aspects that are difficult to define clearly or measure precisely. They deal with events or choices in the future where the uncertainty of our predictions or estimates may be very great, and they involve situations in which both sides have many possible courses of action that change from time to time during the game. These types of problems are difficult to handle by any analytic technique, and the validity of the findings can be judged only in light of the assumptions made, the factors and criteria established, and the alternatives investigated for a specific problem.

Chapter 12

STRATEGIES FOR DEVELOPMENT

W. H. MECKLING

Formal systematic analysis was first applied to military problems during World War II, when operations research came into its own. These early analyses dealt with problems of military operations—how to get the most out of equipment that was already in being. At the time, many physical scientists and mathematicians felt (as one of them put it) "that relatively too much scientific effort has been expended hitherto in the production of new devices and too little in the proper use of what we have got[1]". The substitution of a highly analytic method—a method employing modern mathematical and statistical techniques—for intuition, or trial and error, it was believed, could provide better answers to many operational problems. These early efforts met with notable success.

After the war, when research and development became of paramount importance, there was a natural urge to put the same powerful methods to work on development decisions. The basic problem of development is how to get maximum results from limited resources. Human ingenuity being what it is, there are always a larger number of systems that might be developed to perform particular missions than we can afford. The military is forced by budget constraints to make difficult choices. Obviously, systematic analysis can make an important contribution to these choices. But having agreed on that, the battle has only begun. The real question is what kind of analysis is appropriate to development decisions.

In answer to this, one of the first things to recognize is that making procurement or operational decisions is a very different business from making development decisions. The problems associated with buying systems that are already developed are not the same as those associated with getting systems under development.

When a procurement decision is required, there is often a good deal of uncertainty about the potential usefulness of the system or systems under consideration, and there may be some uncertainty about how they will perform. Nonetheless, we have a pretty good idea about performance; we

---

[1] P. M. S. Blackett, "Operational Research", *The Advancement of Science,* vol. 5, no. 17, April 1948, pp. 26–38.

know within fairly narrow limits how much the systems will cost, and we are reasonably confident about when they will be available. For purposes of his analysis, the analyst can take these as given. He can systematically compare the various alternative forces he might procure, and on the basis of some appropriate criteria, such as the cost of destroying a fixed target complex, select the optimal force structure. He may still have to contend with serious strategic and political uncertainties, but about the particular parameters—performance, cost, and availability—he has reasonable assurance.

By contrast, when a development decision is required, uncertainty is the keynote—uncertainty about when the newest creations can be available, how much they will cost, and how they will perform. To those who have had even casual contacts with development, the fact of uncertainty hardly needs elaboration. But sometimes we (conveniently) forget how far our predictions have missed the mark in the past. For example, we have found that estimates of cost of production are seldom within a factor of 2 of actual costs, and not uncommonly are off by factors of from 5 to 10. Similarly, slippages in time to operational status of from 2 to 5 years are not unusual. Performance parameters are generally more accurate, but even here differences of 25 per cent from original estimates are not uncommon[2].

What does this uncertainty mean for development decisions? You might simply say, "It's a hard world, but we do have to make choices. All we can do is construct the best estimates possible, and make choices on that basis". In other words all we can do is systematically compare promising systems and, using our best estimates of cost, performance, and availability, choose the one which appears optimal.

But the trouble with this answer is that it ignores an important fact about development, namely, that initial uncertainty can be and is reduced as development proceeds. In fact, reducing uncertainty, or acquiring knowledge, is the whole purpose of development. Systems developments do not directly produce any operational systems. What they do produce is knowledge—knowledge about how particular configurations will work out, which configurations are best, how they can best be produced, and how various components can be put together into a reliable, smoothly functioning whole. Not knowing about these things is the cause of our initial uncertainty about costs, availability dates, and performance. Accordingly, learning about these things as development progresses reduces our uncertainty.

Because uncertainty is reduced as development progresses, the art of making

---

2 Performance estimates tend to be more accurate simply because money and time, the other two variables, are sacrificed to meet original performance requirements. When initial predictions on availability dates, costs, and performance cannot simultaneously be met, something has to give, and usually that "something" is a combination of the first two.

development decisions is one of selecting an appropriate strategy rather than one of selecting the optimal system at the start. Some alternatives can, of course, be eliminated on the basis of early studies, but there are still likely to be two or three among which we are unable to discriminate on the basis of early estimates. The problem then is to adopt a development strategy that will provide the information necessary to make a choice. This is likely to mean initiating a development program that, at first, is consistent with several different end-products. Then, stage by stage, as development progresses, the various alternatives are re-evaluated, and the menu is narrowed to arrive at the final system.

The fact that development produces information about costs, about performance, and about availability dates has important implications for the conduct of systems analyses. The possibility of reducing uncertainty adds another dimension to the decision problem. It is no longer adequate only to ask which among possible alternative *end-products* appears optimal. We must also ask whether it would pay to buy more information, that is, to undertake development up to some later stage, before a final choice is made. Paradoxically, the analysis intended to provide a basis for choice among promising alternatives must also address itself to the question of what choice now is really appropriate.

To illustrate this, consider the following simple example. Suppose the problem is to decide on a course of action with respect to a future ICBM capability. We have narrowed our early list down to two promising alternatives: (1) Missile A, which uses a storable liquid propellant, and (2) Missile B, which uses a solid propellant. To simplify things let us fix the operational dates of the system and fix the capability that must be available. In practice, of course, these will not be fixed. In fact, as I am sure the reader is aware, much of the effort in systems analysis is devoted to examining alternative system capabilities to evaluate their usefulness. But for our particular problem we can take the capability as given, without doing any violence to the argument, and thereby reduce the number of variables to one—namely, costs. What we want then is to achieve the given capability during the given time period at minimum cost—where cost is defined to include all costs of development, procurement, and operation. When confronted with this problem, the decisionmaker is, of course, uncertain about which of the two alternatives will in fact yield the minimum cost. Let us assume, for the sake of a simple example, that his best judgment about probable costs of Missile A and Missile B, based on the information available to him, is summarized in Fig. 12.1. This figure, in other words, portrays his personal estimates of the probable costs of these two missile systems.

In brief, our decisionmaker is convinced that Missile A will cost either $ 8 billion or $ 10 billion and that these two are equally probable. Similarly

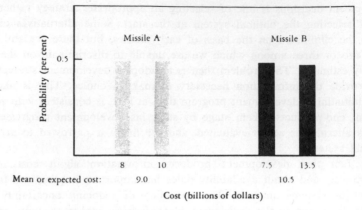

Fig. 12.1   Probable costs of Missiles A and B

he is convinced that Missile B will cost either $ 7.5 billion or $ 13.5 billion, once again with equal probability. If he were pressed, of course, he might say he really believes there is a continuous distribution of costs which the missile could take with corresponding probabilities. But continuous distributions are not readily translated into arithmetic examples, so we have resorted to this fiction to keep our example very simple.

Given the information shown in Fig. 12.1, the decisionmaker might simply say, "I shall make a choice, and the rational choice is to select the system with the lowest expected cost". In other words he might simply choose Missile A on the grounds that if he makes such decisions repeatedly he would expect an average cost of $ 9.0 billion for Missile A as opposed to $ 10.5 billion for Missile B.

Given our decisionmaker's estimates of probable costs, there are four, and only four, possible states of the real world that can exist. These are shown in Table 12.1. The figures in the table represent the four possible combinations of costs for Missile A and Missile B which could occur, given the probable cost estimates shown in Fig. 12.1.

TABLE 12.1

The four possible combinations of costs for missiles A and B

State of the world	Cost of Missile A (billions of $)	Cost of Missile B (billions of $)
S_1	8.0	13.5
S_2	10.0	13.5
S_3	8.0	7.5
S_4	10.0	7.5

S_1 (or state of the world 1) is the case where Missile A costs $ 8.0 billion and Missile B $ 13.5 billion. S_2 is the case where Missile A costs $ 10.0 billion and Missile B $ 13.5 billion, etc. When our decisionmaker is first confronted with the problem, of course, he does not know which of these four situations is in fact true. If he chooses Missile A, that is, if he chooses on the basis of expected costs, and if *either* S_1 or S_2 is the true state of the world, the choice of Missile A will have been best. But if he chooses Missile A, and either S_3 or S_4 is the true state of the world, then the choice of A means he has bet on the wrong horse.

The latter unhappy state of affairs (that is, betting on the wrong horse) he would very much like to avoid, but if he cannot get more information as a basis for his decision, he cannot improve on a straightforward choice of Missile A. It is at this point that the second observation cited earlier about the nature of development becomes relevant. The reason we undertake development is precisely to get information—information that will reduce uncertainty. If our decisionmaker has an opportunity to improve on the reliability of his cost estimates through partial development, he may then be able to improve on the results he would get by simply choosing Missile A.

To illustrate this, let us take the extreme case and see how much it would be worth to him to find out with certainty which of the four situations in Table 12.1 is the true state of affairs. In other words, we are now asking how much our decisionmaker would be willing to pay to determine which of these four actually exists. In order to answer this question let us first suppose he is told which of the four is true. When he is told that either S_1 or S_2 is true, he will choose Missile A just as he did before, because this will give him the lowest cost. But, when he is told that S_3 or S_4 is true he will choose Missile B, because Missile B now gives the lowest cost. Whenever he is told S_3 is true, he will save $ 0.5 billion over what it would have cost to choose Missile A, and whenever S_4 is true he will save $ 2.5 billion over what his cost would have been had he chosen Missile A.

Naturally, at the time he has to make his decision, he never really knows which of the four will turn out to be true. In fact, he regards each as equally likely—to each he has assigned a probability of 0.25 that it will be the one that actually exists. Therefore, his average or expected saving is 0.25 × $ 0.5 billion = $ 0.125 billion plus 0.25 × $ 2.5 billion = $ 0.625 billion, or $ 0.75 billion in all. In other words, knowing which of the four situations actually holds true is worth $ 0.75 billion to our decisionmaker, and if there is any way he can get this information at a cost of less than $ 0.75 billion, it will be rational for him to do so. To be more specific, if he can determine the costs of the two alternatives by carrying both into development, he can afford to spend up to $ 750 million on one of the missiles, even though it is eventually cancelled.

In the real world the problems faced in making development decisions clearly are much more complex than in our simple model, but it is not the purpose of the model to reflect in all of its complexity the real world situation. Nor do I want to leave the impression that RAND is engaged in constructing such models, filling in the appropriate numbers and applying them to development decisions. The purpose of this model and such models generally is to help us understand the essential nature of the development decision problem, so that when a specific analysis is carried out it can be done properly, even when it involves no formal model at all. This particular model shows why, in making development decisions, it is necessary to take into account more than our current best estimates of how particular systems will work out. The alternatives open to the decisionmaker are not limited to choices among particular end-products, that is, weapon systems. To be sure, he will want to compare end-products, but that is only a part of the problem. He will also want to take into account the possibilities of initiating a development program that is specifically designed not only to bring him closer to an operational system, but also to provide information as a basis for a final decision to be made later.

The importance of this for systems analysis can hardly be overemphasized. First and foremost the analyst himself must understand the nature of the problem; he must recognize that choosing the seemingly optimal system now, on the basis of whatever information happens to be available, can lead to far from optimal results. In other words, he must pose the right set of alternative courses of action both for himself and the decisionmaker. Once he has done that, he must provide and analyze whatever information is available and relevant to that set of alternatives. In general, this will mean more than estimating the expected costs of the alternative systems under consideration; it means more than quoting the estimate of $ 9.0 billion for Missile A and the estimate of $ 10.5 billion for Missile B. It is particularly important for him to include these four additional factors in his analysis:

1. How much uncertainty exists.

2. What steps can be taken to reduce uncertainty.

3. How much it will cost to reduce uncertainty.

4. How much uncertainty will be reduced as development progresses.

Unfortunately, in real-life applications, ready answers to these questions are seldom available. For the most part, they must be qualitative, and even where quantitative answers are conceivable, as in point 3, they are themselves subject to great uncertainty. It is worthwhile, however, to discuss each of these in a little more detail.

12.1. HOW MUCH UNCERTAINTY EXISTS

The probability distributions which we used in our little example to reflect uncertainty about costs are purely subjective in the sense that they summarized the "feelings" of the decisionmaker in regard to how much Missile A or Missile B might cost. The problems of trying to construct such distributions for actual systems developments obviously are enormous. Just to mention one, for example: Whose judgment as to the character of these distributions should we accept?

Nevertheless, it is important to get some notion of how uncertain we feel about our estimates, since the amount of effort to be devoted to buying information about various alternatives depends in the first instance on how uncertain we are about these alternatives. If, for example, we had been convinced that Missile A would cost $ 8 billion, with a 99 per cent probability, and $ 10 billion, with only a 1 per cent probability; while Missile B would cost $ 13.5 billion, with 99 per cent probability, and $ 7.5 billion, with only 1 per cent probability, then our enthusiasm for carrying both of these into development would be considerably reduced. It would be reduced because now the probability of an incorrect choice appears small, and the chances of improving our batting average appear negligible.

In the abstract, what we would like to have are complete probability distributions attached to particular estimates. If we are talking about cost estimates, for example, it is important to know whether the probability distributions we attach look like this:

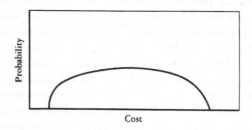

Cost

or like this:

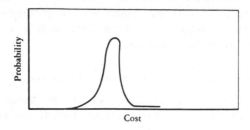

Cost

because our attitude about buying more information would be considerably different in the first case from what it would be in the second. But such precise formulations of our uncertainty are not generally practical.

Even though these uncertainties are subjective, and cannot be formulated precisely, the analyst can get some feeling for this kind of thing, particularly if he has had occasion to see how such estimates have worked out in the past. He or his technical associates can scrutinize the proposed systems to determine what kinds of technical advances they contain, and where the major uncertainties lie. If there is disagreement among technical experts as to feasibility, this a priori implies a good deal of uncertainty. He can also get some feeling for uncertainty by conducting sensitivity studies to determine how sensitive his estimates are to variations in key parameters. What happens to cost if the reliable life of solid propellants is reduced by 50 per cent, for example? Or, what happens to cost if the on-site maintenance required is four or five times greater than expected?

Obviously, this kind of analysis is not a matter of following a prescribed recipe. It relies heavily on the judgment and intuition of the analyst, but that fact by no means completely destroys the usefulness of the analysis.

12.2   WHAT STEPS CAN BE TAKEN TO REDUCE UNCERTAINTY

Once the analyst has an idea of the extent and source of his uncertainty, his next task is to investigate what development steps might be undertaken to resolve these. In our example we used the extreme case where all uncertainty was eliminated, but in the real world there are a whole series of intermediate levels of reduced uncertainty we might try to achieve. These normally would correspond to stages of development for various components or subsystems contained in the system, but they might also involve especially designed tests of prototypes, fuels, materials, etc. If he is to be most useful, the analyst must identify the stages at which additional information will become available and suggest special tests where these appear appropriate.

To illustrate, suppose the cost of one of our missiles depended critically on the reliability obtainable in its guidance system. Having pointed this out, the analyst should then indicate how much more will be known about this at various stages of development; emphasize the need for finding out about reliability very early; or perhaps suggest what opportunities exist, such as construction of test prototypes, for determining with more confidence how serious the reliability problem will be.

12.3.   HOW MUCH IT WILL COST TO REDUCE UNCERTAINTY

Whether it will pay to try to reduce uncertainty before making a final decision depends on the cost of buying information. In our example, it clearly would *not* pay to make certain about the cost of our two missiles, if in order to make certain we had to spend in excess of $ 750 million. On the other hand, as pointed out earlier, there are many intermediate levels of uncertainty it might pay to attain. For example, we could have asked what it would be worth to change the probabilities from 0.5 and 0.5 on each of the respective costs to, say, 0.75 and 0.25. (As a matter of fact, it turns out to be worth $ 125 million to obtain that particular reduction in uncertainty.)

The important point here is that the decisionmaker must be advised of the costs of carrying development to various stages at which additional information becomes available if he is to make the correct decision. Estimates of total system cost alone are not enough. Unfortunately, there will also be uncertainty about these development costs, but once again the fact that we lack complete knowledge does not relieve us from the responsibility of using whatever knowledge we do have.

12.4. HOW MUCH UNCERTAINTY WILL BE REDUCED AS DEVELOPMENT PROGRESSES

The analyst should provide the decisionmaker as best he can with some notion of how much can be learned by carrying development to various stages, for it is the value of this knowledge which must be weighed against the costs to determine whether a choice should be made now. Admittedly, this is a very difficult thing to do. Nice, neat statements, such as "uncertainty is reduced by x per cent after first flight", are not possible. But neither are we completely ignorant. We know from experience that cost estimates improve as development gets closer and closer to the final article. We know fairly well what can be learned about the flight characteristics of an aircraft from early flight tests, and similarly for tests of other types of equipment. Moreover, development programs and testing can be specifically designed to provide critical data if it is recognized from the outset that this is what is wanted.

In requiring that the systems analyst provide answers in his analysis to these four factors, we have already assigned him enough duties to discourage even the most ambitious practitioner. Yet, in many ways, the problems are even more difficult than we have indicated. For one thing, systems development is a sequential process which requires decisions at each step along the way. It is not a matter of deciding at the beginning exactly what will be done up to the date of operation, and then carrying out the plan. What is done in the second stage of development depends in part on what is learned in the first stage, etc. The analyst, therefore, must closely follow the program once it is under way, and follow up his initial analysis with a series of subsequent analyses.

The life of the analyst is further complicated by the sheer diversity of the elements which go to make up a modern weapon system. The level of uncertainty varies from one subsystem to another, and the various elements require different treatment at different stages of development.

Even more important, in actual development decisions, operational dates and performance are never fixed as we have assumed them to be in our example. In fact, trade-offs always exist among the three important parameters of our problem—performance, operational dates, and costs—and, generally, earlier operational dates can only be achieved at the expense of lower performance or greater costs, or both. Deciding what is the best combination of these three is an important part of the whole problem.

Finally, the analyst is also plagued with uncertainties about strategic and political factors[3]. What will be the military posture of the enemy five or ten years hence? What will be the attitude of the public with respect to defense expenditures in the future? What form will future political alignments and commitments take?

In summary, the problem confronted at the initiation of modern weapon system developments is more nearly one of selecting an appropriate development strategy than of choosing the particular end-products. The purpose of development is to increase our knowledge about costs, about how various configurations will perform, and when they are likely to be available. Proper analysis requires that the analyst recognize this fact in his work. He should apprise the decisionmaker of the opportunities that exist for getting and using this knowledge. This is not a simple job, nor one in which main reliance can be placed on analytical techniques — as opposed to intuition, good judgment, and experience. Nor is there a detailed set of rules that will automatically ensure a proper development strategy. Nevertheless, there are more or less intelligent ways of going about the task, and the systems analyst can make an important contribution if he recognizes the nature of the problem and acts accordingly.

---

[3] It is worth noting that uncertainty about future military and political factors very much strengthens the argument for undertaking development of a menu of alternatives. The broader the menu of alternatives from which procurement choices can be made, the more flexible we can be in meeting unexpected military and political situations.

Chapter 13

MATHEMATICS AND SYSTEMS ANALYSIS

E. S. QUADE

To the uninitiated, mathematics may appear to offer the real hope for the solution of problems of systems analysis. Mathematical methods have been reasonably successful in dealing with many complex problems in the physical world and, hence, it is quite natural to hope that, by extension, they might perform equally well in dealing with the broader and even more complex questions which systems analysis tries to answer. It is not only by mere analogy that mathematics might be expected to be pertinent. It is obvious from the outset, and certainly from examples such as that presented in Chapter 3, that systems analysis is concerned with the relationships between a large number of quantities, so that more or less mathematics is bound to be employed.

If one were to make even a casual survey of the literature of operations research—which is identical, insofar as its analytic tools are concerned, with systems analysis[1]—one could easily get the impression that success in this field depends on a thorough knowledge of certain rather special mathematical techniques. In fact, in its rather short life as a named discipline, operations research has so firmly adopted certain tools—linear programming, Monte Carlo, and game theory, to list a few—that together these techniques seem almost to sum to the complete activity.

The difficulties in problem solving range from the philosophical or conceptual to the analytic or mathematical. There is no clear-cut separation, however. The operations research techniques just mentioned are designed to overcome the difficulties at the mathematical or analytic end of the range. And though they are dwarfed by those at the other end, it does not follow that they are not troublesome or significant. For this reason, readers of this book may find it profitable to learn something about the mathematical techniques that have proved extremely useful in dealing with a large and important class of problems. Moreover, even though an understanding of fundamental concepts may be more important than analytic techniques—in part because more elementary methods will ordinarily serve, though less efficiently—new technique frequently leads to a new understanding.

---

[1] And also systems engineering, systems design, systems research, and management science.

The analytic aids associated with operations research and systems analysis range from tools, like a computer or table of random numbers, to broad techniques, like dynamic programming, Monte Carlo, or queuing theory. We will say a few words about some of the more widely used of these techniques, point out their limitations, and describe the part they can reasonably be expected to play in military analysis now or in the future.

13.1. LINEAR PROGRAMMING

Historically, a "program" is a schedule of the quantity and timing of the various actions in a plan. It now often refers to a set of instructions which can be given to a man, or to a machine, that tells what to do next to move toward the objective when a certain stage is reached. If the activity can be represented by a mathematical model, then a computational method may be evolved for choosing the best schedule of actions; this is a mathematical program.

Many economic, industrial, and military activities can be expressed (or at least approximated) by systems of linear equations and inequalities. When this can be done we have linear programming, the best known and most widely used technique of operations research. Its essential features can be illustrated by a simple numerical example.

Suppose that a manufacturer has two factories: the first, A, produces three items of a certain kind in a given period, and the other, B, produces four. Assume that there are three customers, one at M using one item during the period, one at N using 2 items, and one at P using 4 items. Suppose further that it costs \$ 3 per item to ship from A to M; \$ 2 per item from A to N; \$ 1 per item from A to P; \$ 1 per item from B to M; \$ 2 from B to N; and \$ 3 from B to P. (These conditions are illustrated in Fig. 13.1.) What shipping policy should the manufacturer use to minimize the cost of shipping?

One method might be to ship one item from A to each of M, N, and P; one more item from B to N; and finally 3 items from B to P. This would cost

$$(3 \times 1) + (2 \times 1) + (1 \times 1) + (2 \times 1) + (3 \times 3) = 3+2+1+2+9 = \$ 17.$$

But a better scheme would be to ship 3 from A to P and the rest from B. This would cost

$$(1 \times 3) + (1 \times 1) + (2 \times 2) + (3 \times 1) = 3+1+4+3 = \$ 11.$$

Is this best?

Here relatively few cases are possible and it is easy to determine the minimum by enumeration. But if there were several hundred stations and items, discovering the best alternative might take an unacceptably long time. Indeed, in some situations the number of cases might make analysis of all their combinations impossible. Electronic computers, using linear programming,

PRODUCTION   SHIPPING COSTS   CONSUMPTION

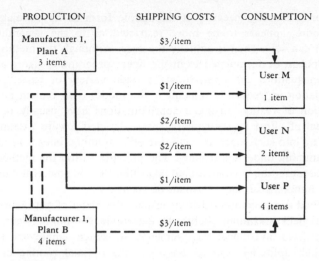

Fig. 13.1   A simple problem in linear programming

have solved problems of this sort, called transportation problems, involving 3200 equations and 600 000 variables. But linear programming gives a systematic and efficient way of finding the best case, or one of the better cases, without the need for examining each possibility separately.

The term "linear" in linear programs refers to the relations that must hold among the various activities for the plan to be consistent with available resources. Thus, in our example, the amounts shipped out of A must be greater than or equal to zero and less than or equal to three. Similar relations hold at B. Mathematically, these relations are linear inequalities. Since the cost of transporting n similar items is n times the cost of transporting one, the equalities as well as the inequalities are linear.

The essence of the technique, when applied to transportation problems, lies in instructing the computer, human or machine, that if substituting one route for another lowers the over-all cost, this same substitution should be repeated as often as is consistent with the constraints as to the number of items which can use that route. The explicit cost calculation of most of the possible routings is avoided, and just enough cases are examined to ensure that no profitable alternative has been overlooked.

Linear programming is also useful in network problems. For example, suppose that a telecommunication network consists of n stations, each of which may send, receive, and relay messages. Suppose further that the stations are joined by communication channels, each with a fixed capacity in messages per unit time. Given these conditions, linear programming can find a routing doctrine that maximizes the number of messages delivered per unit of time.

Linear programming, because of the simple form of its associated mathematical model, appears to be more restricted as to the generality of the problems it can solve than is actually the case. Although the method requires that the problem be formulated to fit the linear programming format, systems of linear inequalities can approximate a wide variety of cases. And while this formulation is frequently difficult if the model is to remain an adequate representation of reality, adequate approximations have usually been found. A great deal of effort by mathematicians is directed toward extending linear programming into such areas as nonlinear programming, integer programming, and programming under uncertainty. The pressure to use the method is great, however, because the computational algorithm is so powerful that systems containing hundreds of equations can be solved.

The method has been applied to determine the blend of petroleum products that would yield maximum profits, to determine the minimal-cost diet that will satisfy fixed nutritional requirements, to assign employees to jobs in terms of their aptitudes, and to determine the optimal routing of messages in a communications network.

13.2. Monte Carlo

Monte Carlo, a second technique used in systems analysis, may be described, roughly, as a method for estimating the answer to a problem by means of an experiment with random numbers. For example, suppose one wishes to determine the probability of winning a game of solitaire—say Canfield. One might attempt to calculate this directly, but would quickly discover that the amount of computation required is staggering. Another approach would be simply to play the game a large number of times, N, count the number of successes, n, and then estimate the probability of winning as the quotient n/N. This estimate would be in error, but the error could be decreased by increasing the number of trials. To speed up this process, the game could be programmed for a high-speed digital computing machine and the trials performed by machine rather than by humans. But even with a fast computer the number of trials required to get a good answer might still be overwhelming since the error may decrease very slowly. In any event, however, a judicious mixture of analysis with random trying is likely to be more effective. And this is precisely what Monte Carlo comes down to.

The origins of Monte Carlo lie in the random sampling investigations of statisticians. The distinction between the two is that the Monte Carlo approach seeks answers to mathematical problems and is dealing with an abstract, rather than with a real, population. This circumstance, because it allows the population to be altered, makes many refinements in technique possible.

During World War II, problems connected with the design of atomic weapons were treated at Los Alamos by the Monte Carlo method. A typical problem was that of determining the number of neutrons escaping through a shield of specified design in which the particles were subjected to random as well as to deterministic influences. To use Monte Carlo, a mathematical analogue of the physical situation was simulated on a computing machine and the path of a particle traced out by using random numbers. In attacking problems of particle diffusion, shielding, and nuclear reactors, the physicists necessarily based their models on the physical process. They were not at all interested in the model as a simulation per se and hence took full advantage of the fact that they were not dealing with a real population. Distortions of the model or its parameters, introduced to cut computation cost by reducing sample size, were regarded as the essence of the method. These mathematical manipulations or "tricks" to reduce the dispersion or variance of the sample are called variance reducing techniques. Thus today we frequently see statements that a sampling computation is not Monte Carlo unless variance reducing techniques are employed.

The use of Monte Carlo is now widespread in operations research, basically because it is the easiest computational method to apply to the large and complicated problems typical of such investigations. These problems often have prominent random elements. They are frequently new and difficult to formulate mathematically. Even if they can be formulated, they almost never have known analytic solutions and the application of the traditional methods of numerical analysis is difficult, if not impossible. In order to apply Monte Carlo methods it is only necessary to be able to model the physical process. Since high-speed machines can take over the laborious part of the calculations, Monte Carlo frequently allows one to substitute brute force for mathematical ingenuity and thought. Furthermore, for a good many problems studied by operations researchers and systems analysts there is no feasible alternative to Monte Carlo—especially if information on the probability distributions of the outcomes is required as well as information about the expected values. Traditional methods of analysis are ordinarily useless in such cases if the problem is at all complicated.

When Monte Carlo is used in operations research, however, it often differs significantly from its use in physics. Here, more frequently than not, the interest lies in preserving the simulation as faithfully as possible, and techniques which reduce sample size are not much used. Aside from the possibility that we don't know how to apply them, there are two reasons why such techniques are generally avoided. First, in most operations research problems, in contrast to those of physics, extremely accurate answers are not required. Lower accuracy is probably inevitable anyway, since the basic parameters in the problem are often only very uncertainly known and the models, no matter how complicated, may be very inadequate. In addition, the analyst is frequently looking for, and only interested in, rather big differences between, for example, a current scheme of operation and a proposed new one. Consequently, sample sizes need not be very large, even when purely random sampling is used. Second, there is usually a great deal of interest in the realistic simulation provided by the model. Variance reducing techniques seriously distort the simulation aspects of the calculations, turning typical observations into rare events and vice versa.

To illustrate the Monte Carlo approach, consider the following drastically simplified servicing process:

Items are assumed to arrive randomly at a servicing facility where they are handled one at a time. Suppose the intervals between arrivals, while random, are such that 40 per cent are 10 minutes long and 60 per cent 20 minutes. Suppose servicing is also random, with 10 minutes required to service 80 per cent of the items and 30 minutes required to handle the other 20 per cent.

It then follows that, per item:

Mean arrival interval:	$0.4 \times 10 + 0.6 \times 20 =$	16 minutes
Mean servicing time:	$0.8 \times 10 + 0.2 \times 30 =$	14 minutes
Mean idle time:	$16 - 14 =$	2 minutes

Our question is: What is the mean waiting time per item?

To tackle the problem, we can use a simulation in which a sequence of random numbers represents the intervals between arrivals and the servicing times. First, the interval between arrivals is determined by the selection of a random digit. If it is a 0, 1, 2, or 3, we assign an arrival interval of 10 minutes; if it is a 4, 5, 6, 7, 8, or 9, we assign 20 minutes. Similarly, to specify the service time associated with the item that arrives after the interval, we select a second random digit. If it is 0, 1, 2, 3, 4, 5, 6, or 7, we assign a servicing time of 10 minutes; if an 8 or 9, we assign 30 minutes.

We can then fill out Table 13.1. We assume the first arrival takes place at time zero. Here R and R' represent random digits.

Thus for the ten samples listed in the table we have a total of 60 minutes waiting time or an average of 6 minutes per item. This example leaves unanswered a great many questions, such as how many samples are needed to give a good estimate of this waiting time. But it does highlight the main features of the Monte Carlo method as it is used in operations research.

There has been an increasing use of Monte Carlo methods as the problems tackled in systems analysis and operations research have become more complicated, and thus sometimes become too difficult for classical analytic and numerical methods. Moreover, the Monte Carlo method has certain virtues

TABLE 13.1

A simple servicing problem

N	R	Time of arrival	Time service starts	R'	Minutes required to service	Time service ends	Number of minutes item waits	Number of minutes facility is idle
1	—	0	0	2	10	10	0	0
2	1	10	10	8	30	40	0	0
3	9	30	40	6	10	50	10	0
4	8	50	50	7	10	60	0	0
5	8	70	70	9	30	100	0	10
6	2	80	100	4	10	110	20	0
7	5	90	110	1	10	120	20	0
8	7	110	120	3	10	130	10	0
9	4	130	130	4	10	140	0	0
10	9	150	150	9	30	170	0	10

beyond being able to treat problems which are difficult to handle otherwise. For example, it always gives good answers if the sample size is large enough, and in many cases of interest to operations researchers—although rarely to physicists—the sample sizes required do not force the employment of techniques that distort the distribution. As a result, it gives supplementary information about such features of the distribution as the range and the variance, as well as what happens on the average. Thus in the solitaire problem mentioned earlier, a Monte Carlo treatment can tell us not only what the probability of winning is, but also about such things as the expected number of cards played or the probability of playing at least a specific number.

While the method is mainly a tool of numerical analysis, its users have discovered that the insight into the physical process simulated in the Monte Carlo study often leads to the construction of a workable analytic model.

13.3. THE THEORY OF GAMES

While linear programming and Monte Carlo are clearly operations research techniques, it is doubtful that the same status should be accorded to the theory of games, especially as a measure of its direct contributions to the solution of specific problems. Nevertheless, in a broader sense, it may have contributed more than any other technique through the changes it has made in the way we now look at problems of conflict.

The theory of games is a mathematical treatment of planning under conditions of conflict. The types of behavior that appear in such situations, of course, have long been observed and recorded. However, aside from some attempts to set up models in which optimal courses of action can be dealt with by the calculus, or, in more sophisticated form, by the calculus of variations, the only mathematical theory so far put forth—and that only relatively recently— is the theory of games. This theory is concerned with the selection of an optimal course of action taking into account not only the possible actions of the planner himself but those of his adversaries as well. The principal modes of resolution are collusion and conciliation.

The name "game theory" may be unfortunate insofar as it suggests that the theory deals only with the conflicts of interest found in parlor games such as poker or blackjack. In fact, it is far more general. Indeed, many of the decision problems which occur in military and economic conflict are similar to those found in such games. Because of this similarity, parlor games form a useful starting point for the study of strategy, particularly as they have rules and moves which are clearly defined.

The theory of games considers the problem of how a participant in a conflict situation can obtain the largest "payoff" under conditions such as the following:

1. The opponents will attempt to discover each other's strategy and at the same time conceal their own.

2. Each participant has only partial control of the outcome.

3. Each opponent may bluff or feint.

4. The opponents may have different amounts of information or intelligence about each other.

5. The participants may be constrained by the elements of chance—that is, by variables not controlled by any of the participants and showing no preferences among the possible outcomes.

All these actions must be taken within the stated rules of the game. Thus, a player may not use espionage or wiretapping to discover an opponent's strategy unless such actions are allowed by the rules of the game.

Game theory does not cover all the diverse factors which enter into behavior in the face of a conflict of interest. There are certain important limitations. First, the theory assumes that all the possible outcomes can be specified and that each participant is able to assign to each a measure of preference, or utility, so that the one with a larger numerical utility is preferred to one with a smaller utility. Second, all the variables which determine the payoff and the values of the payoff can be specified; that is, a detailed description of all possible actions is required.

In the general case, there are conceptual and technical difficulties which make it impossible to determine the optimal course of action. In addition, most military and economic competition exhibits an imperfect conflict of interest, that is, some measure of cooperation by the opponents. On the other hand, the theory is conceptually complete for the special case of two opponents having opposing interests. But even for this case, most actual conflict situations elude full analysis because of the amount of intricate cataloguing and computing they would require.

Only an occasional problem associated with systems analysis has been simple enough to solve by actually computing the game theory solution—and some of these were only marginally related to the real world. Recently, however, advances in our theoretical knowledge have given promise that the situation may be changing. Game theory is now being successfully applied to various tactical problems — such as radar search and prediction, the allocation of defense to targets of unequal value, the study of missile penetration aids, the scheduling of missile fire under enemy pindown, and other problems as diverse as antisubmarine warfare and inspection for arms control.

In contrast to linear programming, which contributes mainly as a tool for solving specific problems, direct uses of game theory are relatively rare. But, as we have said, its contributions to policy analysis are possibly far greater for it tells us how to think about situations of conflict with an intelligent and reacting opponent who may have common as well as opposing interests. As J. D. Williams put the matter in his book, *The Compleat Strategyst*[2],

> While there are specific applications today, despite the current limitations of the theory, perhaps its greatest contribution so far has been an intangible one: the general orientation given to people who are faced with overcomplex problems. Even though these problems are probably for the indefinite future—it helps to have a framework in which to work on them. The concept of a strategy, the distinctions among players, the role of chance events, the notion of matrix representations of the payoffs, the concepts of pure and mixed strategies, and so on give valuable orientation to persons who must think about complicated conflict situations.

13.4. THE COMPUTER

The high-speed computer is sometimes equated with modern decisionmaking. There exists a belief that all that is needed to solve the most difficult problems is a bigger computing machine which is sure to come along. On the contrary, today a computer alone does not solve the problems of interest to military decisionmakers; all that it does is execute that series of instructions, laid out by some mathematician, that may lead to a solution. It is just a tool; it cannot do anything with problems it is not told to do. Solutions by computers are only as good and as sensible as the people who define the problem, state the objective, and choose the criterion can make them.

---

[2] McGraw-Hill Book Company, Inc., New York, 1954.

The next chapter is devoted to a discussion of computers, and points out their limitations as well as their many virtues. Three of these limitations are particularly significant in the analysis of problems of national security. For one, certain intangibles of great importance in planning a nation's security are extremely difficult to quantify—loyalty, morale, resistance to change, the stability of political alliances, and so on. Even the most elaborate models adapted for high-speed computers are not likely to take these factors into consideration with proper emphasis and subtlety. The second limitation is that practical considerations impose many simplifications on a computer representation, requiring the use of aggregate variables and the omission of many details. It frequently requires several years and many people to formulate and program an elaborate model. Thus the model is likely to be not only expensive, but, more importantly, rigid. The assumptions on which a model is based inevitably call for successive corrections as the learning process that parallels the application of the model suggests them, or as changes in the factors which affect national security occur. The learning process is thus frequently hindered rather than enhanced by the use of a computer model. That is the third limitation. For it is in the nature of the process that only selected stages of the computation are readily visible to an observer, while most of the intermediate steps remain hidden in the "black box" of the machine. Hence the direct influence of the variables upon one another, the knowledge of which is crucial in any intuitive reappraisal of a given theory, must generally be inferred indirectly.

We do not want to deny the importance of computers as aids to analysis. They make feasible the application of powerful ideas and techniques which could not even be considered before their advent. Indeed, the new techniques we have just discussed—that is, linear programming and Monte Carlo—are powerful mainly because good computers now exist to put them into operation.

One turns to the mathematician not only for his skill in organizing mass computation but also for his ability to avoid it. With ingenuity, he may be able to substitute simplified for intricate mathematical manipulation and boil down an unworkably large number of cases to a number which, while it may still be large, is manageable.

13.5. THE ROLE OF MATHEMATICS

Except for this brief statement we say nothing about the significance of techniques which, in addition to those already described, go under such names as dynamic programming, queuing theory, and information theory, to mention a few. This is a reluctant omission, for anyone who is to evaluate analyses properly should be able to distinguish between the use of fancy mathematical techniques as window dressing for a possibly bad analysis, and their use as critical ingredients of a first-rate analysis. The omission is made not because the mathematics employed is difficult and can be understood only after thorough training, for to understand broadly the way in which difficult mathematics is used requires no particular mathematical ability. Rather, it occurs because we have chosen to stress other things than specific techniques, which, incidentally, are not the means by which the major difficulties in systems analysis are overcome.

Since we have done little more than barely mention a few mathematical techniques, one may wonder to what extent they are really used in systems analyses. An accurate answer is that they are used extensively in dealing with related, or component, questions but, except in narrowly defined problems, not very much in the determination of the over-all solution.

There are several reasons why this might be so. As explained earlier, before any mathematical technique can be applied to a real-world problem, we must have a quantitative model of the processes involved. In complex situations such as those at the national policy level, only components of the problem can be put in a form in which they can be handled by the standard operations research techniques. The over-all model serves mainly to guide our thinking and not for computation.

Another reason why these tools are not more widely used may be merely that they are new. To quote from an unpublished paper by J. D. Williams, a member of RAND's Research Council, on this subject:

> Now the adoption and use of new tools is not an easy process in any profession. Even in that young, progressive organization known as the USAF there is more than a trace of inertia in these matters. I participated tangentially in the development of the first family of guided missiles; an easy task, it turned out, compared to that of convincing a commander that these rare birds should fly in his theater. The same difficulties arise in science where new tools are capriciously tempered by indiscriminate use of hot and cold water.
>
> You can see why it happens: Someone advances a new idea. If it really is new it is, by definition, unconventional; there is, therefore, a good chance that it conflicts with some of your knowledge or prejudices. There is also a good chance that it isn't obvious, else you would have thought of it yourself. There is a first-rate chance that it isn't correct— you know the adage: most ideas are born in the laboratory, flourish in the laboratory, and die in the laboratory, all within 20 minutes. Now as a reasonable man, should you ignore this idea, or should you try to destroy it, or should you go through the agony of making it your own? It is a sad day when we must do the last. Incidentally, Einstein's first papers were rejected by *Nature*, the leading scientific journal of the day.

An interesting case study of a new abstract tool could be based on the history of the so-called infinitesimal calculus. With this technique in hand, Newton had himself a ball (as my children would phrase it) in the field of mechanics. He was suddenly in a position to give a comprehensive unified account of practically all known phenomena, easily deduced from a few postulates. But there was a little difficulty: The natural philosophers of the day—the astronomers, physicists, and mathematicians— were not fluent in the calculus, did not wish to become so, and moreover were convinced that it was based on nonsense; as a matter of fact, to prove that it is not nonsense has required generations of the most subtle analysis and to this day one or two sensitive spots exist. Newton met the immediate difficulty by deriving his results anew in terms of the then leading scientific tool, namely geometry. We are no longer highly practiced in geometry so his opus, the *Principia,* is almost unintelligible to us. On the other hand, the infinitesimal calculus has run the whole course. There is almost certainly no physical scientist or engineer in this organization [RAND] who does not know it. In fact, I hazard that there are few who know the formal rules of their mother tongues as well as they know those of the calculus.

Another interesting case history concerns the subject now known as mathematical statistics. Gauss erected a magnificent structure known as the theory of errors. This has been part of the ABC's of physical science for generations. It is an almost perfect tool for analyzing data which are basically simple or which are so tightly controlled that the uncontrolled parts are simple. Physicists and astronomers have lived in this Utopia for a hundred years and their happiness is just wonderful. In the meantime, some other people have been very unhappy. Among this unhappy multitude we find the experimentalists in the field of agriculture, who are always plagued by messy data; soil and weather variations are largely beyond their control and the number of combinations of seeds and soil additives (varying in kind and amount) is large. In the last twenty-five years methods of considerable power have been under development, with the result that the experimenters in this field are no longer the unhappiest people on earth. What do the physicists and astronomers think of such new topics as the Analysis of Variance and the Design of Experiments?

Well, they are pretty busy people and Gaussian statistics has always served them well. I will bet that if help is needed in the design and evaluation of a bombing experiment, say, most of you would be more inclined to seek it from the physics department of a university than from the agriculture experiment station; a quarter of a century ago you would have been right but today you would be wrong.

Where do we of RAND stand on modern abstract techniques? Well, it varies. We, as an organization, have been quite active in developing techniques. This means that we have given those of our people who have a bent toward the abstract *carte blanche* to devote their energy to such tasks. They have created quite a lot of stuff, some of which will surely stand the test of time, and more which will provoke something better. Some of what they and others have been devising has found its way into the working repertories of some of our people, but, while I believe our progress is in some sense reasonable, we have a long way to go.

As a unique discipline, systems analysis or operations research is really just emerging. To quote from one military analyst:

My general impression is that the art of systems analysis is in about the same stage now as medicine during the latter half of the 19th century; that is, it has just reached the point at which it can do more good than harm, on the average. Of course, it would be no more sensible to conclude from this that we should not develop and use systems analysis now than it would have been to conclude that we should not use medicine then[3].

In a field such as operations research, people who have been spoiled by the success of earlier mathematical and scientific methods in physics and engineering have a tendency to expect the same level of perfection and the same startling successes. The successes *have* been startling. Many worthwhile results have been obtained and a great many more are to be expected. But the required perfection is still lacking, for something more than mathematics is needed in this field. Certain aspects of mathematics are particularly appropriate to many of its problems; we have named a few. But a great deal of basic research needs to be done; for example, many more algorithms for solving specific problems need to be worked out before these new, high-powered techniques have any chance of supplanting the simplest forms of mathematics—that is, a little probability and statistics, some calculus and geometry—as the working tools of operations research and systems analysis.

---

3   Alain C. Enthoven, Deputy Assistant Secretary of Defense (Systems Analysis), address before the Naval War College, Newport, Rhode Island, June 6, 1963.

Chapter 14

THE USE OF COMPUTERS

PAUL ARMER

My purpose is to discuss computers in the context of systems analysis and not to describe the inner mechanisms of computers. Most of my remarks will concern digital computers, not analogue computers, a distinction I shall explain. An analogue computer is one in which numbers are represented by physical quantities which are then manipulated in the computer. The simplest example of an analogue computer is a slide rule on which numbers are represented by distances. Results are then read by measuring a distance on the rule. Digital computers, on the other hand, represent numbers by a *discrete* setting of a physical quantity like a toothed wheel, an on-off switch, a relay, etc. Simple examples of a digital computer are the ancient abacus and the desk calculator.

I think the best way to set the stage for my remarks is to relate a story. A number of years ago the computing field was somewhat divided over the merits of a particular numerical method. At a computer society meeting, discussion of the subject erupted into a lively debate during which an opponent of the scheme said, "You're playing with fire with your method"—to which a proponent responded, "Man began to play with fire back in the Stone Age, and we'd undoubtedly still be in that age if he hadn't".

The obvious moral is that man should use fire to his advantage; but he must be continually aware that he can be burned. He might also do well to stock up on fire extinguishers. Unfortunately, the computer can be insidious; its burn does not necessarily give rise to immediate symptoms of damage.

14.1. THE USEFULNESS OF COMPUTERS

What are the chief attributes of computers? They are fast, they are reliable, and they can turn out results cheaply, once the problem is running. This, however, is meaningless unless used in comparison with something else. The comparison I will use pits the computer against a human *at the same task*. To illustrate the three attributes, let us take a task at which the computer shines: the calculation of a missile trajectory.

Back in 1949, RAND received a new electronic calculator. One of the first problems put to it was a missile trajectory calculation. Prior to getting it on

250

the machine, the aerodynamicist sponsoring the problem had three cases done by hand. Each case occupied two girls working at desk calculators for about six months; that is, each case involved a woman-year of effort—about $ 5000, including overhead, in those days. On the calculator, each case was run in about three hours at a cost, including machine and operator, of less than $ 100. Thus, we picked up a factor of over 600 in time and about 50 in cost. (Set-up time for the first case on the machine was approximately two weeks at a cost of about $ 500.) More impressive, I think, is the fact that when we reran the three cases done by hand, we found all three had mistakes in them, despite the fact that each had supposedly been checked, step by step, by having one girl go over the work of another.

That was fourteen years ago. The computing machine art has advanced considerably since then. The computer which RAND has had for the past two years would do this same problem in about half a second at a cost of less than 25 ¢ per case. By today's standards it was a trivial problem.

I will not dwell on the advantages of computers in the areas of speed, reliability, and cost. These have, in general, been pushed so hard that computers have been oversold. The fact that a computer can add up a column of numbers as high as the Empire State Building in four seconds at a cost of 20 ¢ may be of academic interest to the analyst or decisionmaker, *but what they really want to know is what the computer can do for them.*

Before leaving this aspect of the field, which has been so glamorized in the popular press, let me summarize what I have said about speed, cost, and reliability by means of Table 14.1.

TABLE 14.1

Speed, cost, and reliability comparisons

Methods	Elapsed time [a]	Cost [a] ($)	Error rate	Set-up time and cost [a]
By hand—1949	6 months	5,000.00	$1/10^3$	None
Computer—1949	3 hours	100.00	$1/10^5$	Two weeks; $ 500
Computer—1956	1 minute	5.00	$1/10^9$	Two days; $ 300
Computer—1961	1/2 second	0.25	$1/10^{12}$	One day; $ 200
Computer—1965	1/200 second	0.01	$1/10^{16}$	One day; $ 100

a Per case of our trivial missile trajectory calculation.

The 1965 figures shown in the table are, of course, speculative, but, based on work going on today, they appear to be quite achievable. All the figures in the last two columns are guesses, and hence subject to considerable error. At the speeds involved for these machines, the number of operations between errors can be large, but the time between errors need not be particularly large.

Let us return to the basic question of what the computer can do for the analyst. It is really just another tool in the analyst's bag of tricks, like a pencil and the back of an old envelope or like a desk calculator. In general, a necessary condition for the use of a computer is that the analyst be able to formulate his problem (or a portion of it) as a mathematical model. This is not a sufficient condition from an economic standpoint, for, as will be discussed later, there are many instances when it will not pay to mechanize a model.

There are certainly advantages in implementing the model with a computer. By utilizing its speed and cost superiority, you can obviously investigate many more cases with a computer than you could by hand. In practice, one normally takes advantage of these factors of speed and cost, not merely in just running more cases of the same model than one would use if doing it by hand, but rather by making the model much more sophisticated. Let me illustrate this by an example. Several years ago an organization got a new computer, the first unit off the production line. Of course, everyone in the computing field was interested in hearing just how much faster the new machine was compared with the old. When asked about this at a meeting, the head of the installation related that they had taken a problem in physics that had been run on the old computer and had run it on the new one. While it had taken an hour per case on the old machine, it took three hours on the new one. As everyone did a double take, he went on to explain that they had been able to use a much more sophisticated model with the new machine.

The moral here is that the computer enables the analyst to examine his problem in more detail than he can by hand methods. For example, the more sophisticated model enables him to optimize over a wider area of the problem and thus avoid suboptimization, provided, of course, that he can construct the more sophisticated model required.

The computer makes it possible for the analyst to do sensitivity studies. This is one of the more important attributes of using a computer—the ability to answer many of the "what if?" questions with comparative ease.

The speed and cost advantages of the computer can be used to the analyst's gain because they enable him to study his problem in a Monte Carlo fashion instead of in an expected-value way, a distinction made in Chapter 4. Also, there are problems involving the analysis or reduction of data for which a computer may be indispensable.

14.2. DISADVANTAGES OF USING COMPUTERS

There are problems where the use of a computer is not profitable, even though a mathematical model does exist. To put any model, even a small one, on the machine involves some set-up time and costs. For small models, if only a relatively few cases are to be calculated, it may be cheaper and faster to do them by hand. Furthermore, the analyst may feel that in doing them by hand he will have a better appreciation for and will have more control over what goes on in the model. Even with medium-sized models, if you are going to run only a very few cases, it may be cheaper to do them by hand than to incur the set-up costs involved in getting the model on the computer. However, as model size and complexity increase, you reach the point where the only way to do even a single case is by machine—you just could not get it done by hand, correctly or incorrectly, in a reasonable period of time.

There is another class of problems that cannot be economically implemented on a machine because the nature of a computer demands that its input must be mechanized; that is, the input must be in a form readable by the machine— on punched cards or magnetic tape, for example. Thus, in cases where the amount of processing of input data is relatively small, it is easier and cheaper to process the data by hand, since machine processing involves comparatively high costs in time and dollars to prepare the inputs. Here is another case where the human is cheaper and faster than the machine.

In general, gaming and simulation problems are typically characterized by the fact that there is a human in the system. That is, if the machine is used in the system, we have a cycle of human processing, machine processing, human processing, machine processing . . . . If we could build a mathematical model of the processing done by the human, we could, of course, mechanize the whole thing. However, for problems of this class, the instances where mechanization can be done are comparatively rare. As to which can and which cannot, this is almost always dependent on the amount of data that would have to be mechanized as input to the computer for each cycle and upon the amount of processing to be done. In passing, I might mention that analogue computers are sometimes quite useful for this class of problems.

14.3. PROGRAMMING THE MODEL

As I have indicated, the successful use of a computer in analysis is intimately tied in with mathematical model making. If you cannot make a model of at least a portion of your problem, then the computer is valueless. *The computer as we know how to use it today cannot help with a problem that you cannot intellectually solve without the computer.* The computer is no panacea. Nor is the fact that a computer has been used in a given analysis the equivalent of the Good Housekeeping Seal of Approval. The results are no better than the model which the computer has implemented. Unfortunately, the fact that a computer has been used in an analysis is frequently used to give an unwarranted aura of authenticity to the results.

The fact that a computer has been used *may* be evidence that the analysis is based on consideration of the problem in detail, and that many possibilities have been examined. But its use bears no testimony whatsoever about the quality of that consideration and examination.

The topic of models, their advantages and pitfalls, is not my province in this chapter, but it is so closely related to that of using computers to implement models that I cannot completely divorce the two. Let me discuss the pitfalls for a minute. A model, for example, may be constructed to reflect accurately the outcome of an air battle, provided the speed of the aircraft involved is subsonic. In other words, the equations in the model involving speed may be such that they give nonsensical results for a battle involving supersonic aircraft. The model-builder may have been quite aware of this at the time and did not care, because he was only concerned with the subsonic case. This illustrates just one of the many dangers in using a model for a purpose for which it was not originally designed—one man's worthwhile model may be another man's trap.

Even when the mathematical model has been designed to handle the general case, implementation of the model on the computer may introduce some loss of generalization. As an example, the computer programmer, for reasons of programming efficiency, may code an air battle model so that the computer routine works only for the subsonic case, knowing that this is the model-builder's area of interest. Subsequent use of the routine may overlook the fact that it was programmed in this way. Consider what happened to us recently when we attempted to use a statistical routine written elsewhere. Although the statistical model involved works for an infinite amount of data, the routine was constructed in such a way that only the first twenty items of statistical information were accepted—all additional data were ignored.

The point here is that the computer routine may embody more assumptions than exist in the model itself. An additional point should be made about assumptions. All models involve assumptions, but with a computer more complex models may be implemented than if one is using hand calculation. But don't be deluded—the assumptions are still there in the more complex model. They have merely been made at a different level of detail. This may be good, but one must not lose sight of the fact that they are there. Some people seem almost mesmerized by the very detail of the calculations.

Associated with the problems of formulating models is the allied problem of writing the computer routine which mechanizes the model. Indeed, these two normally proceed in parallel. However, to focus attention for the moment on the computer programming task, let us assume a finished and polished model. Computer programmers must now spell out in the most painstaking detail (and ultimately, with absolute perfection) the computer instructions that will enable the machine to duplicate the model. It is important to have an appreciation of the work involved, for when one realizes the magnitude of the task, one is less apt to underestimate the time required for it in the complete cycle of problem formulation, programming, running production on the machine, analyzing the results, drawing conclusions, and making decisions. I say less apt, because even experienced programmers often have a considerable optimistic bias in estimating time required to program a given problem.

We often hear the computer described as a giant brain—as being very versatile. In reality, the computer is capable of only a comparatively few basic operations—it can add, subtract, multiply, divide, compare numbers, accept input, and output results. A given computer may be capable of a number of operations which are variations on the above, but its repertoire is still quite limited. To make use of a computer, one must write out a list of instructions (called a routine), which is the task of the computer programmer. Figure 14.1 is a typical short routine. In this case, we have a number stored in the computer, and we want to obtain its square root. I do not intend to go through the example—I present it only to show what a programmer has to write down to get a computer to do something that is relatively simple.

In practice, such routines as the one used to calculate a square root, which are obviously going to be needed by many different programmers for many problems, are written up only once and then added to a library of such routines, from which they may be called by the programmer when he needs

704 SYMBOLIC ASSEMBLY PROGRAM
SQUARE ROOT ROUTINE

Problem No. _____   Programmer _____ Date _____ Page ___ of ___

LOCATION	OPR	VARIABLE FIELD BLANK	COMMENTS		I.D.
SQRT	STO	COMMON	SAVE ARGUMENT SIGN		01
	SSP		N		02
	TZE	SQRT+20	GO TO EXIT IF ZERO		03
	STO	COMMON +1	SAVE N		04
	ANA	SQRT+23	COMPUTE TRIAL VALUE, X		05
	LRS	1	X		06
	ADD	COMMON+	X		07
	LRS	1	X		08
	ADD	SQRT+24	X		09
	SXD	COMMON,4	SAVE RETURN ADDRESS		10
	LXA	SQRT+1,4	SET INDEX FOR 3 ITERATIONS		11
	STO	COMMON+2	SAVE X		12
	CLA	COMMON+1	COMPUTE SQUARE ROOT		13
	FDH	COMMON+2	X N/X		14
	STQ	COMMON+3	X		15
	CLA	COMMON+3	X N/X		16
	FAD	COMMON+2	X+X		17
	SUB	SQRT+23	X DIVIDE BY 2		18
	TIX	SQRT+11,4,1	REPEAT LOOP		19
	LXD	COMMON,4	RESTORE EXIT ADDRESS		20
	LDQ	COMMON	TEST SIGN OF ARGUMENT		21
	TQP	2,4	IF+, SKIP ONE		22
	TRA	1,4	IF−, DO NOT SKIP ONE		23
	DEC	134217728,86570	434560*EXP−127,1/2 *EXP−64		

Fig. 14.1 A short routine

them. This somewhat trivial point does illustrate the fact that most routines
are made up of a collection of subroutines.

In writing out his list of instructions, the programmer must do much more
than just arrange to have the machine carry out the calculations required.
There are housekeeping chores involved in getting the various routines to
mesh and work together; input data must be read, and the results outputted
in some fashion. Restart procedures must be incorporated to handle cases of
machine malfunction so that all is not lost in such an event. Also some degree
of monitoring must be provided for. For instance, suppose you give a missile
trajectory problem, with an error in the formulation, to a desk calculator
operator. A few hours later he comes back and says, "At time equal to 27
seconds the thrust became negative—can that be?" The computer itself will
not provide such service, although the whole calculation may blow up as a
result so that you would know something was wrong, even if you would not
know exactly what. On the other hand, the result of the error in formulation
may not be so obvious; it may, for example, produce a 20 per cent error in
the final result. Consequently, the programmer must build some degree of
monitoring into his routine. That is, he must arrange for his routine to raise
red flags when something happens which should not, as in the case of the
thrust's becoming negative. Our square root routine, for example, does raise
a red flag if the number whose square root we are after is negative. In practice
it is impossible to monitor a computer calculation in the same fashion that
hand calculations are monitored. On the other hand, it is sometimes possible
to build complex checking, which is too laborious to do by hand, into a
computer program.

In worrying about such monitoring, the programmer has learned to ask
many searching questions about the problem. This very probing frequently
uncovers things the model formulator hadn't thought of and accounts for the
fact that, in practice, model building and programming really go hand in hand.
The programmer also knows that there will be many changes made in the
model before it is completed, and he spends a fair amount of his time trying
to make such changes easy to include. Historically, such efforts usually fall
far short of the desired goal, not because he has done a poor job but because
it is so difficult to predict in advance the nature of the changes and their effect
on the model. Changes in a routine almost always call for a programming
effort disproportionate to the size of the change.

In building his routine the programmer tries to anticipate the "what if?"
questions which the model may be asked, and he usually will have most of
them covered. However, life is difficult, and questions will come up that can
be handled only by major revisions in the routine.

After the programmer has written his list of instructions, and they have
been keypunched for entry into the machine, he begins the long process of

AIR REFUELING

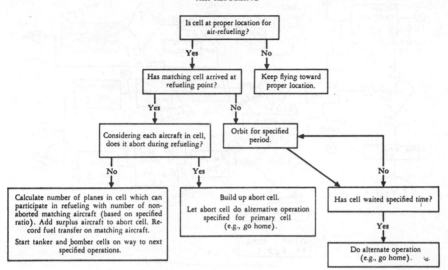

Fig. 14.2 A typical flow chart

debugging his routine. He usually does it by trying to check out one sub-routine at a time. To do this he must often write other routines which put the routine to be tested through its paces. As various subroutines get checked out, he will try groups of subroutines together, and eventually he gets to the point where all of them appear to be working. In referring to the programmer as "he", I have really been speaking in a collective sense. In reality, a number of individuals will be involved in all large programming tasks, each one writing specific subroutines which must be pieced together in the final routine.

I have not yet mentioned one of the earliest steps in the programming task, that of making up a flow chart. A flow chart is essentially a road map showing the route between routines and represents the programmers' "plan of attack" on the problem. Figure 14.2 is an example of a typical flow chart. It might be interesting to note that programmers seldom work from such neat flow charts. Figure 14.3 shows an example of a real working flow chart.

Complete computer routines vary in size from a few hundred to a few hundred thousand instructions. The production of checked-out instructions by individuals varies considerably as well, from about one or two per day to several hundred per day. The cost of a checked-out instruction will likewise vary considerably, say from $.50 to $ 20. The more likely range today is $ 1 to $ 5 per instruction. Thus, large routines can be quite expensive. This does not contradict my earlier statement that one of the chief attributes of

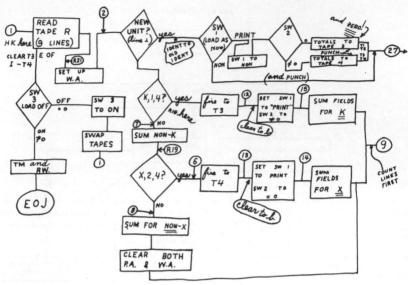

Fig. 14.3   A working flow chart

computers is that they turn out results cheaply. Remember that in the comparison between computers and humans the point was made that computers could turn out results more cheaply than humans *after* the machines have been programmed. One must also distinguish between the cost of programming and the machine costs involved in running the program. In passing, it might be worth pointing out that, since the unit cost is low, the analyst may request copious amounts of work, and thus the total cost may be quite high. He may also overestimate his ability to process the results and find himself unable to cope with the flood of paper which he receives.

14.4. Problem formulation

I have been trying to give you an appreciation of the magnitude of the programming task involved in the use of computers and have really said very little about the magnitude of the task of building the model itself, or, in more general terms, the problem-formulation task. Although model building is not my province, I would like to mention problem formulation for those applications of computers which do not, strictly speaking, involve the implementation of a model in the sense we have been discussing so far.

Problem formulation is usually so intertwined with programming that the two are frequently lumped together. Invariably the amount of effort required is underestimated—frequently grossly underestimated—even when the problem is fairly simple. There are many reasons for this. If personnel familiar with the problem do the programming, they must learn programming. This takes time, and they may never become experts at it. If, on the other hand, programmers have to carry the entire burden of problem formulation, then they have to learn the problem—which again takes time—and they, too, may never really learn it. If a mixed team is used, communication becomes a problem; each has to learn the other's language, which takes more time. The technique of using personnel familiar with the problem to do the programming has worked successfully in a number of business data processing applications. The approach using programmers to carry the formulation burden is pretty much untried. The mixed team approach is fairly widely used, and I personally believe it is the best. However, I think that there is an important point which should be made about this approach. For large systems, I believe that it is very important *for the man familiar with the problem to learn the programmer's language and to learn about programming and about machine limitations*. The man with the problem, when it is a large one, cannot just hand it to the programmer and tell him to solve it.

Another reason for underestimating the magnitude of the task of introducing a new computer application is that the computer method frequently represents a completely new approach somewhat foreign to the old way of doing the problem. Here, the conservatism of individuals and the inertia of organizations often make the introduction of changes difficult and sometimes impossible.

Of all the factors contributing to the size of the task, I believe that deciding in detail just what problem you are going to solve is the point that gives the most trouble. For example, a bank official whose procedures were recently mechanized stated that 65 per cent of the data processing group's effort went to deciding in detail what problem they were solving.

Let me give several examples to illustrate the fact that long lead times are involved and to point out the reasons for them.

Possibly the most infamous example in the data processing field involved a manufacturing concern which set out to mechanize its payroll. It was a payroll involving group incentives and individual incentives and was, consequently, a fairly complicated payroll, but still just a payroll. The firm had its own experts, the computer manufacturer supplied a number of knowledgeable individuals, and, just to be safe, a firm of public accountants was hired as consultants. They thought they had the problem well in hand. Some two years later, after writing several hundred thousand instructions, they all threw in the towel. To be fair, this group was pioneering, and there was much to be learned. Today, the machine involved is really paying its way in an inventory-control application as well as processing the payroll efficiently. Unfortunately, people and organizations in this field are not very good at learning from others' mistakes, and, consequently, there have been many similar instances since. Even today some organizations are making the same mistakes all over again and are headed for the same result.

The second example involves a public utility. Here the approach was quite intelligent and deliberately slow, but still they underestimated the size of the job. They began studying their problem in 1953. A year later, the company decided that it could justify a computer on economic grounds and selected a particular machine. Experts immediately began problem formulation and programming. Two and a half years later the utility got its computer and began the job of converting the manual system to the machine. They planned on a nine-month conversion period, but it actually took them 14 months. Originally it had been estimated that 30 000 program instructions would be required. When the job was finished there were 42 000 instructions: they had underestimated the amount of individual judgment being used in the handling of exceptions and had discovered the importance of programming many checks and controls (the red flags mentioned earlier). In addition, they had to write 20 000 instructions to take care of the conversion. A number of new people had to be added during the conversion because they really had three systems in operation during this period—the old system, the new one, and the conversion operation. In order to install a computer that would eventually reduce the work force, the company had to increase temporarily its work force by 60 people. In the process of installing a computer, clerical work groups and many company policies were changed. A great deal of reorganization resulted from the conversion.

The point is this: For large systems, *the largest single factor contributing to long lead times is most probably the computer program itself, even when fairly complex hardware must be developed and produced.*

14.5. THE LANGUAGE MISMATCH

Why is it that programming is such a lengthy task? Is there any hope for shortening it? I suppose that the chief cause is the mismatch between the language of the computer and that of the human. As we have seen, the computer must be instructed in precise detail. Contrast this with instructions you might give an engineering aide, like "Please integrate this function from zero to one". Also, the engineering aide works with a large background of information and common sense. The aide knows, for example, that missile thrust should not go negative.

Progress is being made on the language mismatch between computers and humans. The sample routines shown in Figs. 14.1 and 14.4 do not represent actual machine language, which is strictly numeric. The instructions on the sheet shown in Fig. 14.1 will first be processed by a routine called an assembly

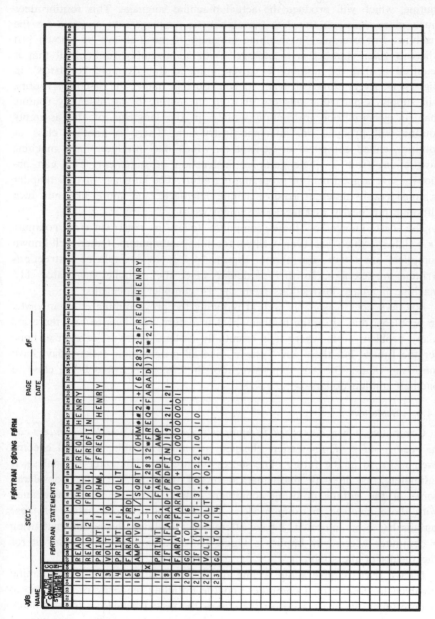

Fig. 14.4 An example of instructions written in FORTRAN

routine, which will produce the actual machine language. This routine does much more than just translate the alphabetic language into numeric for the machine. For example, in machine language it must always be known just where a given number is in storage. With an assembly routine, all that is required is that the number be given a name (for example "COMMON" in Fig. 14.1). Every time you want it, you use that name; the assembly routine will supply a particular address. It is in the nature of an assembly routine that, in general, one instruction written in the language of the assembly routine will produce one machine instruction. There is another class of routines, called compilers or generators, which may produce many machine instructions from a single compiler instruction or statement. This can obviously save a good deal of programming effort. The language of the compiler is considerably different from machine language (and more like our own although not nearly as alike as we might wish).

The best known of these compilers today is FORTRAN (for FORmula TRANslator), which has been written for many computers. Other well-known compilers are COBOL and ALGOL. Figure 14.4 is an example of instructions written in FORTRAN. In this particular case, the compiler generated 113 machine language instructions from the 14 compiler statements.

FORTRAN does reasonably well at reducing the programming effort involved in problems that are quite mathematical in nature. Needless to say, there are many problem areas where it is essentially useless. There is, of course, hope for the future, but these new systems, like all progamming tasks today, have long lead times. They are expensive, too, the cost of FORTRAN being close to one-half million dollars.

14.6. SUMMARY

Computers, when *compared to humans doing tasks to which computers can be readily adapted,* are faster, cheaper, and more reliable, and will become even more so in the future. The successful use of a computer in analysis is intimately tied in with mathematical model building. We have considered some of the pitfalls in using computers, which are also closely associated with those involved in using models. The possibly insidious nature of these pitfalls has been indicated. I have attempted to debunk the notion that using a computer necessarily implies a Good Housekeeping Seal of Approval for the results of the study.

I have tried to give some feeling for the magnitude of the programming involved in the use of a computer and the unfailing tendency of everyone to underestimate it. The reason for the size of the task, I believe, is the mismatch between the language of the human and the language of the computer. I have touched upon the effort under way to do something about this language mismatch.

In discussing the magnitude of the programming task, I have provided several examples, not in the implementation of models but in the business data processing field. In data processing there are additional reasons for the magnitude of the task. Problem formulation and definition are more difficult, for example, and the conversion to electronics frequently involves changes in policy and group reorganization. Since, in many cases, the only precedent is an existing manual system, an additional problem is the lack of knowledge about the detail required to treat exceptions and to provide adequate controls.

I have presented a fairly negative attitude because I believe that in many ways computers have been oversold. They are not oracles; they are not a panacea. The computer cannot help you with a problem that you cannot intellectually solve without it.

On the other hand, I do not want to undersell the computer. In clerical procedures, it is obviously bringing about a revolution. In the area of analysis, coupled with model building and the new advanced mathematical techniques (including all the concepts that can be lumped under the term operations research), computers enable the analyst to study problems in a way heretofore impossible.

I have purposely not done any prophesying about getting computers to accomplish tasks that require intelligence, not because I do not believe that such applications are coming, but because I believe that they are far enough in the future as to be inappropriate for this discussion.

In closing, let me return to the analogy of playing with fire—we can do tremendously good things with computers, but we must not let the application run away with us.

Chapter 15

COSTING METHODS

G. H. FISHER
and the
STAFF OF THE RAND COST ANALYSIS DEPARTMENT

15.1. INTRODUCTION

In Chapter 6, M. W. Hoag discussed the relevance of cost in systems analyses. The present chapter is concerned with how cost is to be estimated and taken into account in such an analysis.

Before turning to a discussion of cost-estimating techniques, a few comments should be made about the general type of costing method the systems analyst might need in a particular study. It may seem trite to say that the type of method needed "depends on the problem", but this is clearly the case. Furthermore, even for a given problem, the method used at one stage in the analysis may differ from that used at another stage. For example, in the preliminary phases of a systems study there may be a very large number of alternatives to be considered. The problem is to screen these alternatives with a view to weeding out the obviously unattractive ones. Numerous quick optimization runs may be required to do this; and for these preliminary calculations, only very gross cost inputs usually are needed. Here, the need is for a costing method that is flexible, not too demanding on manpower and time, and one that stresses consistency rather than a high degree of accuracy. Later on in the analysis, when the number of interesting alternative systems has been reduced to manageable size, more refined—and hence more time consuming—costing methods may be used.

In choosing among alternative military systems or force structures, why do we make cost estimates? The short answer is that cost is an element of choice we cannot ignore. To choose wisely, we must know the cost of the proposal and be able to compare it with the costs of other proposals. We must also know the benefits of the choice, and be able to compare them with the benefits of the alternative possibilities. The intelligent weighing of costs and benefits is at least as important in military management and decisionmaking as in any other sector of government activity or in private business enterprise.

Good cost estimates for weapon and support systems are becoming increasingly important, not only because the new system proposals are often extremely costly, requiring a substantial share of the nation's resources, but

264

also because there are so many systems competing for consideration. More and more it is recognized that a proposed system cannot be judged unless both its costs and its capabilities are estimated and compared with those of alternative proposals. Both costs and capabilities are difficult to assess, particularly when we try to look several years ahead, but the assessment must be made in advance if it is to provide a basis for choice, now, among competing proposals.

This suggests that the matter of *uncertainty* is a very real problem in cost analysis of future military systems and forces. Here, the problem is especially severe because the system and force proposals being analyzed may, and usually do, change as the future unfolds. These changes may stem from many sources: a change in enemy capabilities or intentions, failure of a particular system configuration to attain the desired performance levels, a change in specified performance requirements necessitating redesign of a system's hardware and/or operational concept, and so on. Over and above uncertainties of this type are those inherent in the cost-estimating process itself: errors in basic data, errors in cost-estimating relationships used to prepare cost estimates, extrapolation errors, and the like. One of the central problems in cost analysis today is to develop new methods for dealing with the types of uncertainty mentioned above. So far, only slight progress has been made; and, for this reason, very little is said in this chapter about how to treat the problem of uncertainty. We hope that research now under way at The RAND Corporation and elsewhere will produce useful results in the not-too-distant future.

The purpose of this chapter is to describe briefly methods of cost analysis which are being developed under Project RAND for use in estimating weapon and support system and total force costs.

A weapon system is defined by Air Force Regulation 80-1 as follows:

> Weapon System. Composed of equipment, skills, and techniques the composite of which forms an instrument of combat, usually, but not necessarily, having an aerospace vehicle as its major operational element. The complete weapon system includes all related facilities, equipment, materiel, services, and personnel required for the operation of the system, so that the instrument of combat can be considered as a self-sufficient unit of striking power in its intended operational environment[1].

Support system and control system are similarly defined and are becoming increasingly important in terms of cost. While this is recognized in the present chapter, we do not deal with them in as much detail as we should like. Much of our work in developing methods of cost analysis for these systems is still

---

[1] Air Force Regulation no. 80–1, "Research and Development, Definitions of Terms", August 28, 1959.

tentative and does not permit definitive presentation.

In comparing the costs of military systems, we prefer to speak of "cost analysis" rather than "cost estimation", because the identification of the appropriate elements of cost—the analytical breakdown of many complex, interrelated activities and equipments—is so important a part of the method. Weapon systems cost analysis is much more than an estimate of the cost of the weapon itself. Weapon procurement cost may be relatively small compared to other necessary costs, such as base facilities, training of personnel, and operating expenses; and these other costs may vary greatly from system to system. Moreover, in comparing and programming future systems as far as five or ten years ahead, the costs of research and development must be taken into account. Recent experience indicates that research and development costs are rising relative to the other costs, and may be expected to rise further as technological change accelerates. In comparing alternatives, therefore, it is necessary to estimate the cost of the complete system, including directly related support costs, over the whole time period from the beginning of its development to its activation and on through its subsequent operation while still in the active inventory.

What specifically do we mean by cost? In an economic sense, the cost of something means the resource drain on the economy caused by the attainment of that something. Thus the economic cost of national security is measured by the resources allocated to the accomplishment of that objective.

In analytical work, for example in weapon systems analysis, we most generally use *dollar* cost as a measure of economic resource cost. For most purposes dollar costs are a sufficiently meaningful measure of the resources needed to develop, procure, and operate a weapon system. Moreover, in fixing our attention on the weapon system as a whole, we need some way of representing a sum of many dissimilar resources—manpower, missiles, base installations, training schools, etc. These items can best be aggregated in terms of the dollars that will buy them. Thus, systems analysts and military planners generally find it convenient to represent total resources by dollar cost. In generating the dollar cost—in weapon systems cost analysis—the major components of the system are, of course, described in terms of categories of physical resources. This description of physical resources is often extremely useful in itself, in calling attention to major differences between systems, and in identifying unrealistic choices, such as systems that would exceed the possible supplies of a given resource—say, technical manpower.

In using dollar cost, questions naturally arise about possible changes in the price level in future years. However, if we reflect on the purpose of the analysis, it appears that changes in price level usually will not significantly affect the result. What is wanted is a method for broad comparison of costs of competing systems in a given year or over a period of years. As inflation or deflation will presumably affect the costs of the various systems in essentially the same way, it is convenient to assume a stable price level or a "constant dollar". In any case, if there is special interest in the effects of price-level changes, it is usually easiest to begin with cost estimates in terms of constant dollars and then to modify them in accordance with the expected course of future prices.

Moreover, even in the best systems analysis, other future uncertainties are very large. Systems will be subject to many unforeseen changes in configuration as they advance through future years from research and development through procurement to operational use. The effects of these changes have cost implications which are almost sure to be greater than the effects of any probable change in the general level of prices. The methods of cost analysis described here seek meaningful comparisons among systems, recognizing that in long-range projections only the dominant differences can be used to distinguish one proposed system from another. We do not aim at an accuracy of detail such as would be required for estimates for the procurement of specific items or the recruitment and training of personnel to be used in, say, next year's military budget.

Although possible changes in the future price level may be relatively unimportant in systems analysis, the incidence of cost from year to year may be an important consideration in programming systems into future force structures, particularly when tight ceilings are expected on the over-all budget. The annual incidence of costs—the time-phasing of costs—therefore is an important concept in our cost analysis system. It is not always sufficient to describe the cost of a system by means of a single figure representing total expenditure at the end of a long period of years. Successive annual totals (sometimes referred to as cost streams) may be computed for each system under consideration. Comparing the future cost streams of competing systems is somewhat more difficult but often more useful than comparing simple "lump sum" costs.

Closely related to the time-phasing of system costs is the concept of incremental costing. A new generation of weapons can often use, or use in part, the facilities created for earlier generations. When B-52's came into use, many existing base facilities could be used by the B-52 wings. In calculating the cost of base facilities for the B-52 system, it was therefore necessary to include only the additional (and in this case relatively small) expenditures necessary to adapt the facilities for the new use. Incremental costing can significantly affect choices where one of the competing systems can take advantage of existing military assets.

Until recently the choice among weapons was a somewhat isolated procurement decision. But in the last decade the choices—and the problems of military planning—have become much more interconnected. Among the reasons for this may be mentioned the increasing rapidity of technological change, the greater complexity of the new systems, the length of time required for their development and production, and their greater dependence upon other weapon and support systems within the same service and in the other services as well.

These interdependences are recognized in the RAND concept of total activity cost. Under this concept a proposed system is examined in terms of units of combat capability placed in a complete operational context. In the Air Force these units are typically wings, squadrons, or sites. For a B-52 wing, for example, costs include not only the "hardware", personnel, and basing costs easily identified at the wing level, but also the costs of necessary supporting activities, such as Air Training Command replacement training and Air Force Logistics Command depot maintenance associated directly with the B-52 system.

From what has already been said about the significance of time-phasing in systems cost analysis, it will be apparent that there are advantages in clearly identifying costs as they occur in natural time sequence. Before a new system can be procured, it must be developed, and this involves a series of research and development costs. When the new system is adopted and is being introduced into the active inventory, there are expenditures for procurement, basing, initial training, etc. Finally, there are annual operation expenses. These natural time divisions are identified as separate categories in the RAND costing structure.

Estimates of the total cost of a system are developed by a process of analysis and synthesis. Major categories and subcategories of resources are identified and grouped, and their dollar costs estimated and summed. Subtotals are developed which represent the estimated system costs for (1) research and development, (2) investment, and (3) operation.

These three major categories are discussed later. At this point it need only be said that systems cost analysis is not a mechanical operation. It requires judgment, skill, and objectivity on the part of the analyst. The analyst must take particular care with those elements of cost that are specially sensitive to differences in system characteristics or methods of operation, for these are often the key to differences in total cost between competing systems. It should be emphasized, too, that the primary purpose of cost analysis is comparison: to provide estimates of the comparative or relative costs of competing systems, not to forecast precisely accurate costs suitable for budget administration. Comparison is aided by consistency in method: by ensuring the similar treatment of similar items of cost in different systems. Consistency also requires that each system be given the benefits derivable from existing assets.

So far we have spoken as if systems cost analysis were limited to comparisons of individual systems. In the past this was often true, although what has already been said above about incremental costing and time-phasing of costs should suggest that alternative systems cannot be fully compared without taking into account the other systems and nonsystem elements which constitute the existing (or projected) "total force structure".

If the total force is costed both with and without the addition of a particular system, the difference between the two total costs is the cost of the system. Here the comparison of costs between two competing systems is a comparison of the additional or "marginal" costs incurred in each case in adding the new system to the total force. This type of study requires, therefore, a more complete and profound analysis of costs than is necessary for system comparisons carried out, as it were, in isolation.

There are good reasons for regarding cost analysis of the total force structure as one of the main goals toward which research in military cost analysis should be directed. We rely on and pay for the effectiveness of the total force. The military services are attempting to achieve the most effective over-all "mix" of weapon systems and other systems for a given cost, or the least cost for a given total effectiveness—in short, the most efficient use of *all* the resources which the nation allocates to defense.

From this point of view, individual weapon systems cost analysis is an example of what is called lower-level "suboptimization" in systems analysis. It is the seeking of efficiency in the small, while total force structure analysis aims at efficiency in the large[2].

It must be admitted that there are difficulties involved in carrying out the effectiveness analysis of alternative total force structures. But, even if the total effectiveness of the various possible combinations of systems should be largely a matter for subjective judgment, it is still imperative to know what the costs are likely to be.

15.2. COST ANALYSIS OF INDIVIDUAL SYSTEMS

This section, concerned with cost estimation for individual systems, simplifies the problem by looking at each system as if it were more or less isolated from other systems within the total force structure. It fixes attention on the various elements, within and directly related to the system, which must be taken into account in the cost analysis process. As we have already indicated, this is but one approach to the cost analysis of an individual system. The system cost may also be derived, through total force cost analysis, as the marginal cost involved in adding the system to the force structure. While the advantages of the latter approach are more and more recognized, it is

---

[2] See C. J. Hitch and R. N. McKean, *The Economics of Defense in the Nuclear Age,* Harvard University Press, Cambridge, Mass., 1960, pp. 125–133.

not always possible to carry out a total force analysis; and, if a quick, gross comparison of several rather similar systems is required, the total force method may be unnecessarily refined for the purpose. Moreover, many of the basic methods of costing are the same whether we look at isolated systems or aggregations of systems. The present discussion therefore provides a foundation for total force cost analysis.

The first thing an analyst must do is to make sure that he understands the system with which he is working. He should begin his work by gathering sufficient descriptive material and data. The degree of detail of this information depends upon the nature of the system, and part of the skill of the analyst lies in selecting and seeking out the specifications he needs. The list in Table 15.1 is typical, and gives an idea of the complexity of the analyst's task. Of course, many of the specifications will be uncertain approximations, especially for systems whose operational use lies far in the future. For these, a range of likely values should be obtained rather than a single value.

TABLE 15.1

System specifications and assumptions (examples)

I. Primary equipment specifications (if possible by major components, e.g., airframe or structure, propulsion, guidance).

   A. Performance specifications
      1. Examples for airframes
         a. Speed
         b. Combat radius
         c. Climb
         d. Ceiling
         e. Range
         f. Load
      2. Examples for electronics
         a. Frequency
         b. Continuous vs. spasmodic operation
         c. Functions to be performed and speed of computation
         d. Accuracy (e.g., in terms of deviation over time and/or drift rate, discrimination capability, etc.)
         e. Jamability
      3. Examples for engines
         a. Rating
         b. Specific fuel consumption
         c. Operating temperature

   B. Weight data

   C. Other physical data
      1. Examples for airframes
         a. Size data (e.g., fuselage length, wing area, wing span, etc.)
         b. Construction characteristics

(1) Sheet and stringer
(2) Sandwich, waffle, etc.
(3) Foamed metal
(4) Welded vs. riveted
(5) Castings, forgings, extrusions, weldments, etc.
 c. Basic metal types (with respect to items in b, above)
 d. Tolerances (with respect to items in b, above)
2. Examples for electronics
 a. Volume
 b. Type of construction technique (tube, transistor, modular)
 c. Number of tubes or transistors
 d. Number of stages
 e. Power requirement
 f. Antenna diameter (for radars)

D. Who the manufacturer is or is likely to be.

II. Ground support equipment specifications analogous to those listed under I.

III. Operational concept specifications or assumptions and related matters.
Examples are:

A. Force size
B. Geographical deployment (especially overseas vs. zi)
C. Dispersal scheme
D. Activity rates
E. Fixed or mobile system and description thereof
F. "Hard" or "soft" system, and psi specification if hard
G. Organizational concept: wing, group, etc., and number of squadrons per wing or group
H. Alert capability and related manning concept
I. Degree of system automation, stated by function if possible, in relation to manning and GSE requirements
J. Number of years the system is to be in the operational inventory
K. Training concepts; and in the case of missile systems: (a) number of missiles to be used in initial training, (b) number of live firings for "proficiency" training purposes per year
L. Logistics support concepts, especially regarding depot maintenance (AMC depot, or contractor?). Is there to be a "central support" area?
M. Permanent or temporary facilities?
N. Tenant or nontenant operation?
O. Main aspects of the development program, especially number of vehicles in the test inventory.

In addition to the information in such lists, the analyst needs a basic frame of reference, generally applicable to all systems, and specifically designed for cost analysis. In our experience, the following characteristics are desirable in a set of cost analysis categories:

1. Provision should be made for segregating total cost into the three major time-phases:

 a. research and development

    b. investment (procurement and placing in operational use), and

    c. operation (cost of operation over a period of years).

2. The set should be as all-inclusive as possible so as to preclude the omission of significant elements of cost.

3. The cost categories should be designed in a way that will facilitate determination of those elements of the system that have the greatest impact on total cost, and that are most sensitive to changes in hardware characteristics or variations in operational concept.

As a result of experience with a variety of analytical schemes, we have developed the framework of cost analysis categories given in Table 15.2. Here, various cost elements are grouped under the three major categories which represent the phases in the life cycle of a typical weapon system.

TABLE 15.2

Cost analysis categories for individual systems

I. Research and development costs
   A. System development
   B. System test and evaluation
   C. Other system costs

II. Investment costs
   A. Installations
   B. Equipment
      1. Primary mission
      2. Specialized
      3. Other
   C. Stocks
      1. Initial stock levels
      2. Equipment spares and spare parts (initial)
   D. Initial training
   E. Miscellaneous
      1. Initial transportation
      2. Initial travel
      3. Intermediate and support major command

III. Operating costs
   A. Equipment and installations replacement
      1. Primary mission equipment
      2. Specialized equipment
      3. Other equipment
      4. Installations
   B. Maintenance
      1. Primary mission equipment
      2. Specialized equipment
      3. Other equipment
      4. Installations
   C. Pay and allowances

    D. Training
    E. Fuels, lubricants and propellants
       1. Primary mission equipment
       2. Other
    F. Services and miscellaneous
       1. Transportation
       2. Travel
       3. Other (including maintenance of organizational equipment)
    G. Intermediate and support major command operating cost (only exceptionally included in cost analysis of individual systems)

Figures 15.1 and 15.2 show in simplified form the cost history of a typical weapon system. In Fig. 15.1 the costs for each of the three basic categories are represented by smoothed curves, overlapping somewhat, but typically displaying successive maximums. Figure 15.2 shows the same data for successive fiscal years in a bar graph on a slightly different scale. The height of the bar shows the total yearly expenditure for all three categories.

In the discussion that follows, it is helpful to keep these figures in mind. Chronologically, we should begin with a description of research and development costs, proceed to investment, and end with operating costs. However, because of the very nature of research and development activities with their long lead times and elements of uncertainty, the costing of this category presents special difficulties. It is less routine and more speculative and draws heavily on professional insight and judgment. It would be an advantage to the reader, if he is not already experienced in cost analysis, to approach the problems of research and development costing after he has been introduced to investment and operating costing. This is the plan of exposition we have adopted here.

Investment Costs

Investment costs are those one-time outlays required to introduce a new capability into the operational force, after the required equipment has been developed and tested to an acceptable level of reliability. This new capability may be represented by a new weapon system or a modification of an existing one—for example, a new air-to-surface missile introduced into an existing strategic bombing system. Investment costs are also generated in the non-systems part of the Air Force. Initial outlays for additional personnel facilities at Headquarters SAC and for a new warehouse at an Air Force Logistics Command depot are illustrations of such investment costs. In what follows, we shall describe each of the investment costs listed in Table 15.2[3].

---

[3] Space limitations preclude discussion of how costs are estimated in each of these categories. For such a discussion, see David Novick, *System and Total Force Cost Analysis.* The RAND Corporation, RM-2695, April 15, 1961, Chapter 2, from which much of the above material has been quoted verbatim.

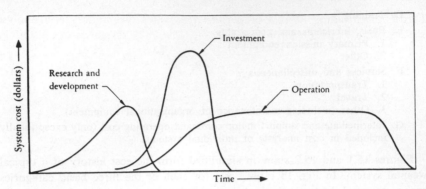

Fig. 15.1 System costs time-phasing (idealized curves)

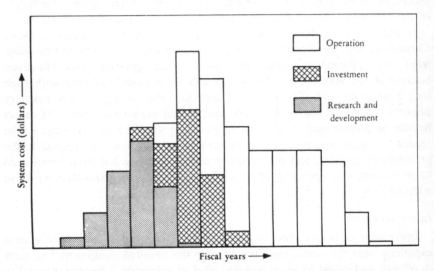

Fig. 15.2 System costs time-phasing (by fiscal years)

Installations. Introduction of a new weapon system into the Air Force inventory usually implies a substantial investment in installations. This is particularly true if additional bases have to be constructed, but, even if a new weapon is phased-in on an existing base structure, some investment in facilities is usually necessary. Runways may have to be lengthened, launch pads constructed, new maintenance shops provided, additional personnel facilities built. Whether new installations are constructed or existing ones modified, the costs are included under the heading of installations.

A good starting point for detailing the elements of this category is the Air

Force nomenclature for real property[4], with which the military cost analyst should make himself thoroughly familiar. The main headings are listed in Table 15.3.

TABLE 15.3

Basic property nomenclature

Operational facilities
    Airfield pavements
    Fuel dispensing facilities
    Communications and navigational facilities
    Land operational facilities

Training facilities
    Training buildings
    Training ranges and drill fields

Maintenance facilities
    Aircraft
    Guided missiles
    Automotive
    Weapons
    Ammunition
    Electronics and communications
    Other

Supply facilities
    Liquid fuel storage
    Ammunition storage
    Cold storage
    Covered storage
    Open storage

Hospital and medical facilities
    Hospital buildings
    Laboratories and clinics
    Dental clinics
    Dispensaries

Administrative facilities
    Administrative buildings
    Administrative structures, underground
    Other

Housing and community facilities
    Family housing
    Troop housing

---

[4] Air Force Manual no. 93–2, *Real Property Standard Codes and Nomenclature*, July 1, 1960.

Community facilities
    Personnel support and services
    Morale, welfare and recreation (interior)
    Morale, welfare and recreation (exterior)

Utilities and ground improvements
    Electrical facilities
    Heating facilities
    Sewage and refuse facilities
    Water facilities
    Roads and sidewalks
    Railroads
    Ground drainage and fencing
    Fire and other alarm systems
    Miscellaneous facilities

Land

Equipment. Expenditures for equipment are often the largest of all the investment outlays in dollars required to establish a new Air Force combat capability. An extremely wide variety of equipment is needed—varying from missiles, mission aircraft, and prime radars and the associated ground support equipment, to stoves and tables used in mess halls.

Our procedure summarizes the initial equipment costs for a combat squadron under the following main categories: (1) primary mission equipment, (2) specialized equipment, and (3) other equipment. Investment in equipment for the direct support of the system at the support major command level is included in the miscellaneous category II E.

The *primary mission equipment* category represents the initial cost of the primary mission equipment assigned to combat organizations. It includes the total cost of the equipment itself (including all government-furnished equipment), but excludes initial spares and spare parts. These latter items, although procured along with the equipment, are accounted for under stocks (category II C). Since the unit cost of any particular item of equipment depends, to a considerable extent, upon the number of items produced, the cost-estimating process for primary mission equipment must be an integrated one embracing not only the deliveries of equipment to the combat organization, but also items of equipment accounted for in other cost categories. The RAND procedure therefore provides for simultaneous estimation of the cost of the equipment assigned to various cost categories, such as research and development, primary mission equipment, support major command investment, initial training (for missiles), equipment replacement, and annual training. Usually, equipment cost estimates are built up by summing the costs of major components by cost element for each component. Examples of major component structures are given in Table 15.4, and cost element structures in Table 15.5.

TABLE 15.4

Equipment components (examples)

Component structure for a ballistic missile
(or similar aerospace vehicle)

Airframe
 Structural
  Leading edges
  Body skin (including tankage)
  Structural members (frame)
 Sub-systems (electrical)
 Controls (electromechanical)
Power Plant
 Liquid rocket
  Pump drive assembly
   Turbo-pump
   Gas generator
  Thrust chamber
  Propellant lines and fittings
  Vernier and exhaust system
  Frame or mounting structure
  Accessory power supply
 Solid rocket
  Casing
  Nozzle
  Propellant
Guidance
 Inertial
  Inertial measurement unit
   Platform
   Accelerometers
   Gyroscopes
  Computers
  Control central & associated
   electronics
 Radio command
  Decoder
  Beacons
  Antenna
Payload
 Nose cone
  Shell
  Arming and fuzing
  Warhead

Component structure for a prime radar

Antenna and wave guide
Transmitter
Modulator
Pulse compression equipment

Receivers
Power supply equipment
Miscellaneous
 Velocity filter
 Moving target indicator group
 Cabling
 Other

Component structure for a bomber aircraft

Airframe
 Wings
 Fuselage
 Empennage
 Miscellaneous
Propulsion system
Electronics
 Bombing navigation & missile guidance
  system
 Defense electronics system
 Mission and traffic control system
 Other
Offensive missile (ASM)
 Airframe
 Propulsion
 Electronics
Defense missile (if any)
Miscellaneous

Component structure for fighter aircraft

Airframe
 Wings
 Fuselage
 Empennage
 Miscellaneous
Propulsion system
Electronics
 Fire control system
 Mission and traffic control system
 Other
GAR or other type of missile
 Airframe
 Propulsion
 Electronics
Miscellaneous

TABLE 15.5

Cost elements of equipment components
(Applicable generally to items of major equipment)

Manufacturing	Material
Direct labor	Overhead
Material	Production engineering
Raw materials	Direct labor
Purchased parts	Material
Subcontracted items	Overhead
Manufacturing overhead	Engineering changes
Fixed	Publications
Variable	General and administrative expense
Tooling	Profit
Direct labor	Industrial facilities (if required)

The *specialized equipment* category includes items of support equipment which are specialized to the primary mission equipment. For many future systems (especially ballistic missile and satellite systems) the cost of specialized equipment may be large. In some cases, it is already the largest single element in system investment cost. Because of the nature of specialized equipment, its components vary considerably from one system to another. Three examples are given in Table 15.6.

TABLE 15.6

Specialized equipment (examples)

1. For a ballistic missile system:

   Launching
   Missile handling
   Control
   Checkout
   Power and pressurization
   Cabling and communications
   Special transport vehicles (mobile systems only)
   Special maintenance equipment
   Special simulation equipment (for training purposes)

2. For a satellite reconnaissance system:

   Launching
   Checkout
   Training
   Readout
   Maintenance
   Communications tie-in network

3. For a high-performance fighter aircraft system:

> Aircraft servicing equipment
> Special trucks and trailers
> Missile servicing equipment
> Special maintenance and test equipment
> Specialized simulation equipment

The cost of all initial equipment not included in the two previous categories is included under the heading *other equipment*. This category contains such items as tactical unit support aircraft (if bought from current production), general purpose vehicles, construction equipment, materials-handling equipment, general purpose communications and test equipment, mess hall equipment, special flying clothing and similar individual equipment, and general purpose maintenance equipment.

Stocks. The continuing and effective operation of a system is in large measure dependent on the ready availability of certain supplies. Air Force combat and support organizations must have on hand supplies of fuels, lubricants and propellants, maintenance supplies and parts, spare aircraft engines, etc.

The costs incurred in establishing these initial inventories at the time a combat unit is formed are included under the investment category called stocks. RAND's concept of stocks is a broad one. The term is defined to mean not only initial inventories on hand with the combat unit, but also the unit's pro rata share of supplies at the Air Force Logistics Command depots and the supplies in the pipeline from manufacturing plant to depot.

For convenience in computation and presentation, the category has been broken down into two subcategories: initial stock level of supplies and fuels, and equipment spares and spare parts.

Initial training. These costs cover:

1. Formal training necessary to bring each man up to the level of skill required for his occupation with the new system. This includes direct costs (pay and allowances of students, pay and allowances of instructors, etc.), indirect costs (pro rata share of pay and allowances of support personnel, base support costs, training command overhead, etc.), and pro rata share of depot maintenance costs for courses using trainer aircraft.

2. Missiles consumed in live firings during the initial training of personnel for a new weapon system. The cost of these missiles is computed by the integrated primary equipment costing method referred to previously.

Miscellaneous investment. This category includes the following items:

1. Initial transportation: the cost of transportation of all initial supplies and equipment, except aircraft and materials used in construction of base

facilities. Aircraft are assumed to be transported under their own power, and construction cost factors used to compute the initial cost of installations include an allowance for first-destination transportation.

2. Initial travel: the cost of transporting personnel and their dependents to the operating bases when a system is phased in to the active force.

3. Intermediate and support major command investment cost: investments made at the intermediate and support major command level which can be *specifically* identified with the particular system under consideration. Examples are the following:

The initial cost of simulation equipment (including initial spares) to be used by the Air Training Command in direct training support of a given system.

The initial cost of primary mission equipment (including initial spares) to be used by the Air Training Command in direct training support of a given system (for example, the F-102's assigned to the ATC to support the F-102 program, both for initial and replacement training).

Investment in new equipment and/or facilities at Air Force Logistics Command for depot maintenance support of a given system.

Operating Cost

Operating costs are those recurring annual outlays needed to operate and maintain USAF activities after they have been initiated into service.

Our analysis deals with these costs in the major categories discussed below.

Equipment and installations replacement. This category includes the cost of annual attrition of primary mission equipment, the annual replacement cost of specialized and "other" equipment, and the outlays for replacement (in kind) of worn-out base facilities.

Maintenance. Here, we accumulate the cost of maintaining the primary mission equipment (including depot maintenance), the specialized and "other" equipment, and the outlays required for materials and contractual services for maintenance of base facilities. (Pay of military personnel engaged in maintenance activities at the base level is not included here, but is accumulated under the pay and allowances category.)

Pay and allowances. This category includes basic pay (including longevity), cash subsistence allowances, cash quarters allowances, general officer personnel money allowances, hazard pay, maintenance clothing allowance, overtime and cost-of-living allowances for civilians, dislocation allowance, retirement deductions, and income taxes withheld, plus a supplemental cost which includes lump-sum payments, FICA charges, subsistence, permanent change of station travel, and temporary duty travel for military personnel.

Training. Annual training cost is made up as follows.

1. The cost of training replacements for personnel leaving an Air Force unit because of discharge, resignation, return to inactive status, etc.
2. The cost of any missiles and fuel consumed in periodic live firings for training purposes. (Missiles are costed by the integrated procedure previously described.)

Fuels, lubricants, and propellants. The annual cost of fuels, lubricants and propellants for the primary mission equipment and unit support aircraft is accumulated under this category.

Services and miscellaneous. This category includes a large number of small items of operation cost, the aggregate of which is typically a small proportion of the total annual operation cost for a weapon or support system. Since the aggregate cost is relatively small, it is estimated by major component only, using gross estimating methods. The major components are:

1. The annual cost of transporting to the base the replacement equipment and the supplies consumed during that year.
2. The annual cost of transportation of military personnel and dependents incident to normal peacetime turnover.
3. Other services and miscellaneous operating costs, including the cost of materials, supplies, and contractual services for such functions as base administration, flight service, supply operations, food and medical services, and operation and maintenance of organizational equipment.

Research and Development Costs

According to the logic of our division of costs, this category must include all costs necessary to bring a system to the point where it is available for introduction into the active inventory. We have employed this comprehensive definition since our initial efforts in the late forties and early fifties. To avoid confusion it should be pointed out that in the past this usage has been considerably broader than some of the specialized meanings conventionally associated with the phrase in an Air Force context.

Through 1957, for example, the Air Force funded development aircraft and test missiles as items of production hardware rather than R & D. Test facilities were funded out of general installations money, much of test site maintenance out of base operations, and a number of smaller elements currently classified as items of R & D by the Air Force were funded elsewhere. Thus, in 1957, while RAND's broader definition of R & D totaled about $ 3 billion, the Air Force's narrower usage showed a $ 600–700 million figure.

Since 1957, the Air Force's definition of R & D has expanded to where it now includes all the incremental costs required to accomplish a given R & D program, except military personnel, and some R & D base installation costs. Thus for fiscal year 1963 the R & D expenditures as defined by the

Air Force totaled some $ 3.6 billion and RAND's some $ 4.2 billion for the same year.

Concurrent with increased spending for research and development, the size of operational forces has tended to decrease. Thus, as a proportion of total weapon system cost, research and development has taken on a new importance. In addition, an increasing number of weapon systems are either developed and never put to operational use (for example, Navaho and Goose) or phased out after very limited operational procurement (for example, Snark and Jupiter). The increasing length of time required for weapon development, the accelerated rate of technological progress, and the nature of our competition with the Soviets, have all contributed to unexpectedly early project termination.

The implications for military budget management and programming are clear. Better and longer-range research and development cost estimates are needed both for evaluating individual weapon system proposals and for estimating the funding requirements of projected total force structures.

A word of caution is in order at this point. The nature of research and development makes the cost-estimating task a difficult one. The existence of a research and development program itself implies that a proposed system is expected to have a previously unattained performance level or a combination of properties never before incorporated in a single system. Its final configuration and perhaps even its successful development are uncertain. The design, the methods of fabrication, and the manpower, material, and facility requirements cannot be described precisely at the time a project is started. All these uncertainties indicate the need for analysis to produce, not a single figure, but a range of reasonable values.

Table 15.7 displays the major categories used at RAND for analysis of research and development costs. The structure shown is intended for systems built around an aerospace vehicle, but it is adaptable for electronic command and control and other support systems. Basically, the table distinguishes between system costs (Categories I, II, and III) and nonsystem costs (Category IV). The latter are dealt with as part of total force cost analysis.

TABLE 15.7

Research and development cost categories

I. *System development*

A. Preliminary study and design

B. Design engineering: the scientific and engineering services conducted within a contractor's own facilities, including development testing of subsystems and combinations of subsystems. For a ballistic missile development program this includes design and development work on all subsystems together with special instrumentation and ground equipment for launch, checkout,

and control. Wind tunnel, structural, environmental, and reliability tests may be needed
   C. Hardware fabrication: breadboard models, mockups, and special test articles; special jigs, dies, fixtures, and other tooling required primarily for development and development testing
II. *System test and evaluation*
   A. Vehicle fabrication: the complete system produced for the test inventory; equipment spares; and pro rata shares of new industrial equipment and facilities required for plant expansion
   B. Captive test operations
   C. Flight test operations: including fuels and propellants used, data reduction, analysis, and reporting
   D. Test equipment: such as launchers, checkout consoles, handling devices, guidance and computer systems for use at test sites; instrumentation; and equipment spares
   E. Installations: design and construction of test facilities
III. *Other system and development costs*
   A. Depot maintenance and supply support
   B. Miscellaneous
IV. *Research and other nonsystem activities* (used in total force cost analysis)

15.3. COST ANALYSIS OF TOTAL FORCE STRUCTURES

In our discussion of cost analysis for individual systems, we have already touched on problems that required the particular system to be treated in relation to other systems and nonsystem activities. A new system may use base facilities already in being. It may employ personnel already trained, and it may embody the results of basic and applied research carried out by the Air Force without reference to specific systems. In this section, we take these relationships explicitly into account.

In its more general sense, total force cost analysis refers to the costing of many different "mixes" or combinations of systems and nonsystem activities, so that the total costs of various real or hypothetical force structures can be compared. In addition to its inclusive character, total force cost analysis emphasizes the specific timing of requirements for funds and other resources. In its more limited sense, total force cost analysis refers to the costing of particular systems in the context of a force structure otherwise more or less fixed. The cost of a system thus becomes a marginal cost—the change in the total cost caused by the addition of the system to the force structure.

Force Composition and Assumptions

Total force composition is expressed in terms of the number of squadrons (or other appropriate unit) at the end of the fiscal year for each of the weapon and support systems making up the total structure. As in individual system cost analysis, a prime objective is to identify with each system the costs of all the activities generated by it.

Physical specifications of systems, numbers of squadrons, etc., are only part of the data required. In addition, there is the kind of information referred to earlier as concept specifications or "assumptions". Differences in assumptions (for example, about live-firings in missile training) can lead to very large differences in cost estimates. Assumptions include information about concepts of system deployment, training, and operation. In total force analysis, they also include relevant information about mission and Air Force organization and policies. Thus, in dealing with the total force, the analyst must draw upon a much wider universe of information than for individual system cost analysis carried out in isolation.

Incremental Costing and Long-Term Programming

Total force cost analysis aims at incremental costing in its fullest sense. The availability of existing resources is taken into account in estimating the additional resources required to add a new system to the force. Changes in the existing force structure (for example, the phasing-out of a weapon system) may make resources available for new systems being phased in. These resources may be of any kind, but especially important are trained or partly trained personnel, and installations and equipment usable directly or after modification. In total force cost analysis, all resources are taken into account simultaneously as well as all the systems and other activities which are competing for these resources.

Figure 15.3 illustrates this principle in the simple case of two systems which (we will assume) can make use of the same bases, crews, and other resources. B-47 squadrons are part of the existing force, and B-58 squadrons

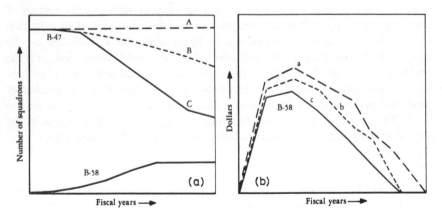

Fig. 15.3   Incremental costs and phase-in phase-out relationships

are being phased in. Figure 15.3a shows three hypothetical patterns of B-47 phasing. Curve A corresponds to a constant number of B-47 squadrons during the whole period under consideration. Curve B corresponds to a gradual phase-out of B-47's, and curve C to a rapid phase-out. The curve at the bottom of the chart represents a hypothetically programmed phase-in of B-58's.

Figure 15.3b shows the associated time-phasing of investment costs for the B-58 system. Curve a (corresponding to curve A) is the upper limit of costs, with all bases having to be built from the ground up, all personnel having to be trained from the beginning, etc. Curve b illustrates costs with B-47 bases available for modification, but crews requiring full training. Curve c illustrates costs with maximum carryover of resources: bases available for modification and crews requiring only transitional training. Aircraft, ground equipment, and stocks are therefore the main elements of cost represented by curve c.

Total force cost analysis provides for incremental costing by establishing a framework within which all the resources available and the needs of the various systems can be considered simultaneously at successive intervals of time.

In practice, the fiscal year is the unit of time employed, and estimates are developed for each fiscal year of the programmed period. The period considered is usually a long one—five or ten years or more—because of the long "lead-time" required for the development and procurement of modern systems. It now takes some five to ten years or more to move from idea to operational hardware[5]. Long-range planning and programming of systems must therefore take such periods into account. In the Air Force, long-range plans and programs often cover a period of ten years or more.

Mission and Other Levels of Cost Analysis

Between the individual systems on the one hand, and the total force on the other, we may distinguish an intermediate grouping, that of the major missions of the Air Force: strategic, defense, and tactical. Certain nonsystem activities, such as SAC Headquarters, which are closely identifiable with a major mission, are combined with the appropriate weapon systems to make up the total cost of the mission.

Nonmission activities such as those parts of support major commands (Air Force Logistics Command and Air Training Command, for example) which cannot be allocated to systems or missions, are also analyzed and the costs estimated. Thus, totals are provided for each weapon or support system,

---

[5] See David Novick, *Lead-Time in Modern Weapons*, The RAND Corporation, P-1240, December 26, 1957.

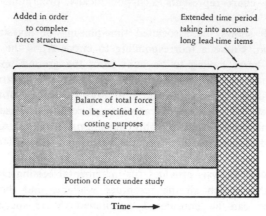

Example

Study: Strategic forces for five years

Costed: Total force for eight years

Fig. 15.4   Mission cost analysis as part of total force cost analysis

for each mission, for all nonmission activities, and for the Air Force as a whole. Total force cost analysis also makes possible the cross-classification of costs, in order to provide subtotals for specialized support activities such as logistics and training, and for the major budget series or appropriation "programs".

Users of cost estimates frequently have need of analyses at the mission level or other level or grouping below the total force. Figure 15.4 depicts schematically the relation between such an analysis and the total force cost analysis which is its context. In some cases, a suitable total force cost analysis will be already available, so that the lower-level analysis may be accomplished by selection and cross-classification. But, if a suitable total force cost analysis is not available, both the portion of the force under study and the balance of the total force are specified and extended for several years beyond the period under study.

Sensitivity, Timeliness, and Clarity

In emphasizing their inclusiveness, we should not lose sight of the fact that total force costing methods must be sufficiently refined to reflect the cost implications of significant changes in structure. These changes are not only in materiel: very important are changes in the assumptions about deployment, dispersal, alert status, activity rates, training, manning, logistics, etc. While sensitivity is required, it cannot be bought at the price of an extremely detailed analysis. For one thing, great detail is impossible for estimates extending five or ten years into the future. For another, too much detail will slow up the progress of the analysis and make it impossible to provide estimates when they are most needed. A method of analysis that requires two or three months for calculation of a single cost estimate is inadequate for most Air Force needs. What should be aimed at is a method that will enable the analyst to produce estimates within a much shorter time and that will enable changes in already costed force structures to be estimated in a day or two.

Simplification and mechanization are important aids to rapid estimation. The cost model must be simpler than the real world if procedures are not to be encumbered by the mass of detail involved in a force structure calculation. On the other hand, too great simplification will result in cost models too insensitive for meaningful use. The solution is to be found in generalized cost-estimating equations and statistical techniques rather than in a mechanical "bookkeeping" approach. Even so, a great deal of bookkeeping and detailed calculation is involved, and a high degree of mechanization is required. For this purpose a large-memory, high-speed, digital computer is employed at RAND[6].

The computer printouts provide a wealth of information which must be summarized and presented in a suitable manner. From the beginning, the methods used should aim at the production of results significant in themselves and easily interpretable. Estimates should be accumulated in a way that facilitates presentation in terms of fiscal years, missions, systems, appropriation costs, and cost categories and their principal elements. So important is the method of presenting results that we have devoted a section to it later on.

Cost Categories Reconsidered

In total force cost analysis the basic cost categories used are the same as those described previously for individual weapon systems, and the costing of subcategories is carried out in very much the same way. Some differences may exist because of the greater use of electronic data processing in total force cost analysis, but the principles are the same. Many of the key inputs are hand-calculated, however, and the computers only "bookkeep" the results.

Up to a point, the total force cost is an aggregation of the costs of individual systems, calculated to take into account integrated procurement and inter-relations among systems. In addition, total force cost analysis takes into account and provides cost estimates for the elements of supporting systems and nonsystem activities which do not enter directly into system costs. We

---

[6] The computer program cannot be discussed here. For a description, see Novick, *op. cit.*, pp. 76–93.

will discuss these here, following the pattern outlined in Table 15.2, beginning with investment.

Investment Costs: Intermediate and Support Major Commands. Intermediate command investment costs include such things as SAC radar evaluation and electronic countermeasures units. These are charged to the strategic mission as a whole rather than to individual systems.

Support major command investment costs include such items as (1) the initial cost of the U.S. Air Force Academy and new facilities there and at the Air University; (2) the initial cost of new trainer aircraft (and related initial spares) assigned to the Air Training Command for general Air Force training; and (3) the initial cost of new general purpose storage facilities at AFLC depots. All of these are charged as investment costs to the Air Force as a whole.

Operating Costs: Intermediate and Support Major Commands. The intermediate command cost category includes (1) the headquarters of air divisions and numbered Air Forces; (2) the headquarters of tactical major commands (for example, SAC, ADC, TAC, USAFE); and (3) various noncombat organizations which serve a tactical major command as a whole (for example, personnel processing squadrons, radar calibration units, and statistical services squadrons). The cost of intermediate command operation is computed as an entity for each of the major Air Force missions.

The support major command cost category includes the Air Force Logistics Command (excluding depot maintenance costs charged to systems) and the Air Training Command (excluding training costs charged to systems). It also includes Headquarter USAF, Headquarters Command, Continental Air Command, USAF Security Services, Air University, U.S. Air Force Academy, Air Force Accounting and Finance Center, and Air Reserve and Air National Guard programs. (MATS is not included, because it is treated as a separate "mission".)

Research and Development Costs: Research and Other Nonsystems Activities. This category includes all "nonsystems"-oriented R & D activities. (Systems-oriented R & D costs are identified to the systems to which they pertain.) Examples of nonsystems research and development activities are basic and applied research, test instrumentation, and development support[7].

15.4. Cost sensitivity analysis

Cost sensitivity analysis attempts to answer the following questions: How does the cost of a system vary as a result of changes in the configuration of

---

[7] For a more detailed discussion see Novick, *op. cit.*, pp. 74–76.

the system? To what elements (considering operational assumptions as well as hardware specifications) is the total cost of the system especially sensitive or insensitive? Similar questions may be asked with respect to total force structures.

In a recent study carried out at RAND, a proposed system was costed for 36 different configurations, in which the following elements were varied within certain ranges: force size, warhead weight, type of propulsion, squadron size, fixed or mobile operation, degree of dispersal, activity rate, and logistics support concept. Even with force size held constant, the other variations in configuration produced a range of system costs varying from a minimum of $ 10 billion to a maximum of $ 21 billion. Repetitive costing, with some elements of the configuration held constant and others varied singly or in groups, soon revealed the elements to which costs were sensitive or insensitive.

Except for this repetition or iteration, cost sensitivity analysis is basically no different in method from cost analysis as already described. It benefits, of course, from techniques that facilitate repetition, such as the generalized cost-estimating relationships discussed under investment costs, and it is facilitated by electronic data processing. As in other analyses, consistency is important in cost sensitivity analysis, and the analyst should be careful to avoid any methodological bias in favor of a particular system.

Examples of Cost Sensitivity Analysis

Perhaps the best way to describe cost sensitivity analysis would be to give some examples of its use, both in individual system and total force cost analysis. So that security restrictions will not inhibit our choice of examples, the systems are not always identified and the charts are presented without numerical values. Nonetheless, we believe that they will effectively illustrate some of the basic principles of cost sensitivity analysis.

Figure 15.5 shows sensitivities and insensitivities revealed by costing various configurations of a ballistic missile system.

1. The system cost is relatively insensitive to increases in payload; that is, a considerable increase in payload can be obtained for relatively small increases in cost. The explanation is that a number of the expensive components of the system change little with increases in gross weight of the missile (for example, guidance and control systems, ground support equipment, and installations items associated with fire control and flight vehicle guidance).

2. The system cost is relatively sensitive to type of propellant used. The explanation is that the use of solid or storable liquid propellants eliminates the need for the expensive storage and transfer facilities and equipment required by cryogenic propellants.

3. The system cost is relatively sensitive to the automation of the ground

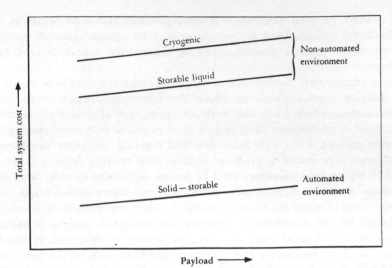

Fig. 15.5 Missile system cost vs. payload for various types of propellants and ground environments (fixed number of ready missiles)

environment. The explanation in this case is that an automated environment requires less launch-site checkout equipment and personnel and personnel facilities.

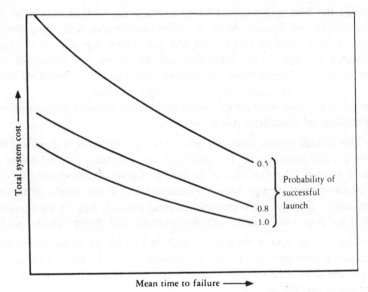

Fig. 15.6 Missile system cost vs. mean time to failure for various probabilities of successful launch (fixed number of launched missiles)

Figure 15.6 illustrates a missile system's cost sensitivity to the reliability of its components, as measured by the probability of a successful launch and by the average length of time a weapon could remain on alert status without maintenance (that is, "mean time to failure"). Very significant reductions in system cost would result from improvements in these characteristics, and the potential savings might justify additional innovation costs aimed at improved component reliability.

Figure 15.7 illustrates a boost-glide system which is initially quite sensitive to increases in the weight of the warhead. The cost curve shows that the sensitivity decreases with increasing warhead weight, so that after a point we could buy substantial increases in weight for only moderate rises in system cost. Figure 15.8 displays (on a slightly different scale) the major elements of cost which contribute to the total cost curve shown in Fig. 15.7. From this breakdown, it is apparent that the cost of the operational flight vehicles is the most important element in the total cost curve, although other elements also contribute to its change of slope.

Figure 15.9 illustrates a case in which the total cost of a system initially decreases and then increases as one of the system characteristics is altered toward higher values. The system includes a number of satellites in orbit. As their altitude is increased, the cost of the system falls markedly at first, primarily because the change in altitude makes it possible for fewer satellites to do the job; this saving is later counterbalanced by the increasing costs of other components: the larger boosters, more sensitive instrumentation, and more powerful communication equipment needed for the greater altitudes.

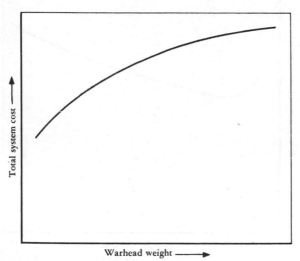

Fig. 15.7   Boost-glide system cost vs. warhead weight (fixed ready vehicle force)

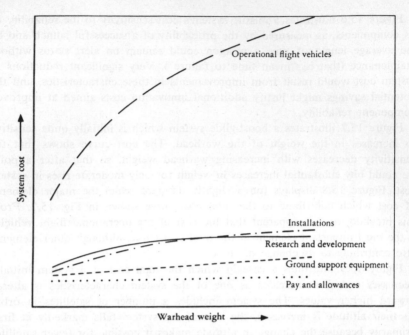

Fig. 15.8   Major elements of cost in Fig. 15.7 (shown on a slightly different scale)

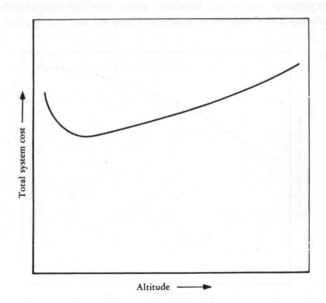

Fig. 15.9   Satellite system cost vs. altitude (fixed job to be done)

Table 15.8 illustrates cost sensitivity analysis applied, not to a single system, but to the group of systems making up the strategic mission. In a recent RAND study, seven variations of a basic strategic mission were investigated as part of a total force cost analysis. Force structure changes were proposed as shown in the "Number of Squadrons" panel and the cost implications were shown in the "Total Expenditures" panel. (For security reasons, only a few numerical results are given here.)

Uses and Advantages of Cost Sensitivity Analysis

The systems analyst may be only touching the surface of the cost-effectiveness problem unless he studies, not only alternative system proposals, but also alternative configurations for each of the systems under analysis. For this purpose, he requires the results of a cost sensitivity analysis giving a range of estimates corresponding to various system specifications and assumptions. This is as true for the more subjective long-range military planning and programming as it is for the formal systems analysis with effectiveness specified and alternative systems described in concrete detail.

In total force structure studies, the cost of a given structure is of vital interest, but it is likely to be only a starting point for further investigations as the original structure is adjusted to bring it within given budgetary limits while maintaining an acceptable level of effectiveness. In this iterative process of structure adjustment, total force cost sensitivity analysis gives valuable insights into the choices available.

Cost sensitivity analysis is a useful technique for dealing with problems of uncertainty, the more so because conventional statistical methods for deriving confidence limits and other criteria of uncertainty cannot be applied generally to cost estimates. In studying proposed future systems, numerous uncertainties must be recognized together with their impact on system costs. For example, there are uncertainties about the size of the system force, the future price levels, and the configuration of the system (hardware specifications and operational assumptions). Studies of systems historical data have shown that perhaps the most important reason for differences between early estimates and final costs is that the configuration of the system ultimately obtained differs considerably from that envisaged early in the program. Cost sensitivity analysis deals explicitly with cost differences related to differences in system configuration, and it therefore can provide a range of system costs which is likely to be a more realistic guide than a single, most probable cost.

15.5. PRESENTATION OF RESULTS

It is not enough that the analyst should produce timely and reliable cost estimates. The data are so numerous, the results so complex, and their various

TABLE 15.8

Force structure cost sensitivity analysis for the strategic mission
(Base case and seven alternative plans)

	Base Case				Case 1				Case 2				Case 3				Case 4				Case 5				Case 6				Case 7			
Weapon System	FY1	2	3	4	FY1	2	3	4	FY1	2	3	4	FY1	2	3	4	FY1	2	3	4	FY1	2	3	4	FY1	2	3	4	FY1	2	3	4
Number of Squadrons at End of Fiscal Year																																
B-52	x	x	x	x					On air alert												Procurement cuts				Rapid phase out							
B-47	x	x	x	x																												
B-58	x	x	x	x																												
B-X	x	x	x	x									Earlier phase-in				Later phase-in															
SM-65	x	x	x	x	Increased				Increased				Increased				Increased				Increased				Moderate increase				Moderate increase			
SM-68	x	x	x	x																												
Missile X	x	x	x	x																												
Missile Y	x	x	x	x																												
Etc.																																
Total Expenditures, Strategic Mission (Billions of Dollars)																																
B-52																																
B-47																																
Etc.																																
Total*					—	0.3	1.0	0.1	0.1	0.7	1.5	0.4	—	0.5	1.4	0.7	—	0.3	1.2	0.1	0.5	1.1	0.4	(1.5)	0.9	1.7	0.9	(0.5)	0.3	0.8	1.8	(0.1)

* Differences from base case. ( ) denotes negative quantity.

applications still so little understood generally, that the analyst's work is only half done unless he presents his conclusions so that they can be understood readily and made use of quickly. Presentation of results cannot be reduced to a few rules to be followed mechanically. Presentation is a form of inter-pretation requiring the professional skill and attention of the cost analyst. He must understand and keep in mind the needs of systems analysts and Air Force planners and programmers. These needs will influence not only the method of presentation, but also, to some degree, the analyst's choice of cost model and costing techniques.

In discussing cost sensitivity analysis, we have already illustrated some graphical methods for presenting estimates characterized by a range of a series of values arising from uncertainties about system performance (for example, Fig. 15.6) or developed by varying the configuration of a system (for example, Figs. 15.5, 15.7, and 15.9). Table 15.8 displays a tabular method of comparing alternative mission structures built around the same basic elements. This type of table can be adapted for many uses and is employed at RAND for total force studies as well as studies of mission structures.

In the following discussion, we will describe briefly or refer to a number of other formats and methods of presentation that have been found useful.

A summary of costs like that shown in Table 15.9 is often useful in itself and also serves as a convenient method to record results for incorporation in later studies.

TABLE 15.9

Presentation of system costs by cost categories
(Format for a missile system)

	Estimated cost
I. *Research and development costs*	
System development	
Preliminary study and design	$ xx
Design engineering	xx
Hardware fabrication	xx
System test and evaluation	
Vehicle fabrication	xx
Captive test operations	xx
Flight test operations	xx
Test equipment	xx
Installations	xx
Other systems research and development costs	
Depot maintenance and supply	xx
Minor modifications	xx
Miscellaneous	xx
Total research and development cost	$ xxx

II. *Investment costs*

Installations			xx
Equipment			
Primary mission			xx
Specialized			xx
Other			xx
Stocks			
Initial stock levels			xx
Equipment spares and spare parts			xx
Initial training			
Formal training			xx
Missiles consumed in initial training			xx
Miscellaneous			xx
	Total investment cost		$ xxx

III. *Operating costs*

	3 years	5 years	7 years
Equipment and installations replacement			
Primary mission equipment	$ xx	$ xx	$ xx
Specialized equipment	xx	xx	xx
Other equipment	xx	xx	xx
Installations	xx	xx	xx
Maintenance			
Primary mission equipment	xx	xx	xx
Specialized equipment	xx	xx	xx
Installations	xx	xx	xx
Pay and allowances	xx	xx	xx
Training	xx	xx	xx
Fuels, lubricants and propellants	xx	xx	xx
Services and miscellaneous	xx	xx	xx
Total annual operation cost	$ xxx	$ xxx	$ xxx

IV. *Total system costs*

Research and development + investment + operation for 3 years $ xxxx
Research and development + investment + operation for 5 years $ xxxx
Research and development + investment + operation for 7 years $ xxxx

If the costs of research and development, investment, and operation differ significantly among alternative systems, it is important to present estimates for several periods of operation, say three, five, and seven years. The cheaper system, in the short run, may be the more expensive in the long run, if it has greater operating costs. The choice between systems therefore may turn on the projected period of operation. If the time-phasing of cost estimates is of particular interest, presentations based on Figs. 15.1 and 15.2 may be used.

Table 15.10 illustrates a typical format used in presentation of the summary results of a total force cost exercise. Sometimes the summary is presented in

TABLE 15.10

Illustrative format for presenting summary of total force structure cost estimates

Missions and System	Force Structure — Number of Squadrons (end of fiscal year)							Manpower Requirements (thousands of people) — Military							Civilian							Expenditures (or "Total Obligational Authority") (millions of 1962 dollars) — Research and Development							Investment							Operation							Total Expenditure						
	'61	'62	'63	'64	'65	...	'70	'61	'62	'63	'64	'65	...	'70	'61	'62	'63	'64	'65	...	'70	'61	'62	'63	'64	'65	...	'70	'61	'62	'63	'64	'65	...	'70	'61	'62	'63	'64	'65	...	'70	'61	'62	'63	'64	'65	...	'70
STRATEGIC																																																	
B-47																																																	
B-52 (incl. GAM)																																																	
B-58																																																	
KC-135																																																	
CAMAL																																																	
SM-65																																																	
SM-68																																																	
SM-X																																																	
DYNASOAR																																																	
Etc.																																																	
Other Strategic																																																	
Total Strategic																																																	
DEFENSE																																																	
F-101, 102 (incl. GAR)																																																	
F-104, 106 (incl. GAR)																																																	
IM-99																																																	
IM-X																																																	
AEW (RC-121, EC-X)																																																	
BMEWS																																																	
Anti-ICBM																																																	
Etc.																																																	
Other Defense																																																	
Total Defense																																																	
TACTICAL																																																	
F-104, 105																																																	
F-X																																																	
TM-76																																																	
TM-X																																																	
Troop Carrier																																																	
Etc.																																																	
Other Tactical																																																	
Total Tactical																																																	
MISCELLANEOUS																																																	
MATS																																																	
Other Unallocated																																																	
Total Miscellaneous																																																	
GRAND TOTAL																																																	

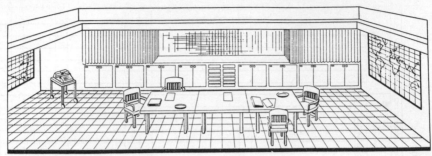

Main working area, showing sliding blackboards

Back wall for display and storage

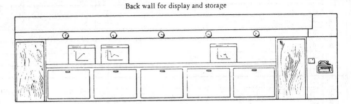

Fig. 15.10   Room for display and discussion of total force cost analysis

a more detailed form: for example, investment costs may be broken down into installations, major equipment, initial stocks, initial training, etc.; and operating costs may be shown in terms of maintenance, pay and allowances, replacement training, fuels, lubricants and propellants, etc.

Presentation of total force cost estimates is a particularly difficult task because of the large volume of data involved. For initial presentation, RAND relies at present on a combination of blackboards for summary data and computer printouts for detailed data. The aim is to present results in a meaningful manner as soon as possible. Later, when the cost implications have been thoroughly considered, and, if necessary, force structures adjusted and system proposals revised, cost estimates are placed in more permanent form in typed reports with charts prepared by the graphic arts department.

RAND makes use of a specially designed room for the development, presentation, and discussion of total force costs. Figure 15.10 shows a sketch of that room. Basic tabular data are posted on sliding blackboards using a format similar to that shown in Table 15.10. Multiple sets of blackboards are arranged so as to facilitate rapid posting, flexibility, and comparison of results. Storage area for computer runs is provided in the drawers and cabinets below the blackboard area. A permanent blackboard and chart rack, along with chart storage area, is contained in the back wall shown in the lower half of Fig. 15.10. Our experience indicates that a facility of this kind is of great assistance in total force cost analysis and in successful presentation of its results.

15.6. CONCLUDING REMARKS

In conclusion, the importance of the basic cost-estimating technique should again be emphasized. It is easy to get carried away by elaborate display boards and other fancy display devices. But without a reasonably good cost-estimating method, there is really no basis for considering the use of sophisticated presentation devices. To produce results useful in planning and programming deliberations, the cost-estimating method must, as a minimum, stress the following major characteristics.

1. Total activity cost concept oriented toward identification of meaningful "end product" activities—for example, weapon and support systems.
2. Distinction among R & D, investment, and annual operating costs.
3. Incremental costing.
4. Time-phasing of systems and forces and the related costs.
5. Emphasis on those system cost components that are relatively most important and that are particularly sensitive to changes in weapon characteristics or methods of operation.
6. Emphasis on consistency of method in costing alternative weapon proposals.
7. Recognition of the problem of uncertainty.

Chapter 16

PITFALLS IN SYSTEMS ANALYSIS

E. S. QUADE

Problems for systems analysis are frequently important, urgent, and difficult. For instance, consider the problem of determining a strategic force posture. It is important not only from a military point of view but equally from an economic one, since the vast expense of modern missile and aircraft systems makes efficiency imperative. It is urgent, for it must be solved before we can have national security. It is characterized by the number and diversity of the factors involved, which embrace engineering, economics, politics, and psychology as well as military science; by the need to commit funds, under conditions of great uncertainty, for the development and location of weapons far in advance of the time they will become operational; and by the necessity for taking into account the will and intelligence of the enemy. These things, together with the comparative newness of this entire approach to policy determination, create an environment full of pitfalls for the analyst.

This chapter calls attention to the kind of errors that are sometimes found in systems analyses, in particular those carried out to aid long-range military planning. A knowledge of what pitfalls may lie in his path should help the analyst to avoid them and the user to discover any errors into which they may have led [1].

The errors are of two kinds: simple mistakes or blunders, and fallacies.

Blunders are largely due to ignorance, stupidity, or carelessness—corresponding to errors in arithmetic or, in these days of computers, to coding errors. There are few precepts to tell us how to avoid blunders. Besides the empty statement that only smart, well-trained, and careful people should be used as systems analysts there is little practical advice one can give. To discover errors before it is too late, careful checking and qualitative evaluation of the reasonableness of the results are helpful. Nevertheless, humans just make mistakes and experts turn out to be wrong.

---

[1] For an additional discussion, see Herman Kahn and Irwin Mann, *Ten Common Pitfalls,* The RAND Corporation, RM-1937, July 1957. Many of the ideas of this chapter originated in their work. See also Bernard O. Koopman, "Fallacies in Operations Research" and "Comments by C. J. Hitch", *Operations Research,* vol. 4, no. 4, August 1956.

Since fallacies, on the other hand, represent a false idea or an error in logic, we have more hope for their elimination. Why do we have fallacies? One reason, mentioned earlier, is the lack of theory. However, we do have a certain amount of experience and a few precepts based on common sense which should permit us to avoid some of the more flagrant fallacies.

The fact that an error or fallacy has been found in a particular analysis does not necessarily invalidate all the work, for it may be repaired. And the very fact that someone can point out where an analysis went wrong strongly confirms the validity of the method.

Experience indicates that we find our pitfalls by falling into them. To avoid them, we not only need guidance to keep us on the right path, but warning to tell us when we have strayed. Since in Chapter 8 I separated the activities involved in analysis into four stages, I will discuss the pitfalls under the same headings.

16.1. FORMULATION

A real pitfall is the failure to allocate and to spend a sufficient share of the total time available deciding what the problem really is. As said earlier, the problems faced by the systems analyst frequently belong to that class in which the difficulty lies more in deciding what ought to be done than in deciding how to do it.

Rather than be guided primarily by what the sponsor believes or states is the best approach, a good systems analyst will insist on formulating his own. It is a pitfall to give in to the tendency to "get started" without a lot of thought about the problem.

The first systems analysis this author worked on is an example where thinking about the general problem and asking a few questions might have been well worthwhile. The analysis was being carried out to help in the design of strategic bombers for the mid-1950's. One moot question was whether or not to put a tail turret on the bombers. My assignment was to determine how the correlation between aiming points in air-to-air machine gun fire—something always present because the shots were not aimed independently—lowered the probability of hitting an attacking fighter. I saw an interesting problem and started right to work. Several months later, after we had found a satisfactory approximation and checked it by a Monte Carlo simulation I saw an early version of an air-to-air guided rocket. It suddenly dawned on me that by the time the bombers under study became operational, they wouldn't have an opportunity to fire back at fighters with machine guns. Asking a few questions and thinking about the more general aspects of the problem might have saved a lot of work.

The most serious error likely to be made in problem formulation is to look at an unduly restricted range of alternatives. Although narrowing our range of choice certainly makes the analysis easier, we may pay a high price for the labor we save if some of the excluded alternatives are better than those remaining.

Accepting a problem posed in a certain way is sometimes equivalent to excluding alternatives from consideration. There is a tendency, when a problem is first observed in one cell of a business or military organization, to try to find a solution that is also completely contained in the cell. An administrator ordinarily attempts to solve his problems within the boundaries of his responsibilities. He is likely to pose his problem in such a way as to bar from consideration, or to dismiss as impractical, alternatives or criteria that do not seem familiar or do not fit into the chain of steps by which policy has been made in past years in the field in question. Problems, however, do not respect organizations. The analyst must try to consider everything pertinent to the analysis, including the possible reorientation of the entire activity. A most important qualification for a systems analyst is his ability to see this fact. It is not always obvious. For example, several years ago a committee was appointed to review the air defense situation. They were told that the objective of air defense was to make the United States invulnerable to surprise attack by maintaining an adequate capability for shooting down enemy aircraft and missiles. This was not a fruitful assignment for it made air defense seem hopeless. The real task was not to prevent ourselves from being destroyed in some specific manner but from being destroyed in any way whatsoever. All the possible ways in which air defense might contribute to national security needed to be examined, not just the one that seemed obviously to be the direct means. When this is done, air defense turns out to have other roles, equally important—such as to provide early identification of an attack and thus tactical warning for U.S. offensive forces. It is foolish to design a weapon system against a specific enemy tactic rather than against the enemy himself.

Sometimes analysts content themselves with applying some mechanistic test to alternatives suggested by others. This is unfortunate because the invention of new alternatives, new weapons systems, and new ways to accomplish military objectives has proved frequently to be the analyst's most constructive and valuable role. The diverse and multiple ways in which military ends can be achieved are often not realized because the alternatives do not always appear as obvious substitutes. They may not look alike or have the same specific function. Thus, to protect civilians against air attack, shelters, "shooting" defenses, counterforce attack, and retaliatory striking power are all alternatives.

Thus, the possible alternatives may be too numerous to be examined individually. Many may have to be eliminated by assumption. This must not be done arbitrarily, but by preliminary analysis. Such assumptions should be regarded as flexible in the sense that they may be relaxed or removed if it appears that their presence is an unduly controlling factor. For example, the analysis mentioned earlier, an attempt to determine the requirements for an optimum long-range bomber, began with a strict requirement by the sponsor that both the payload and range exceed certain minimum values. We considered different cruise and target speeds, altitudes, engine types, number of engines, etc., but because of the restrictions on range and payload, found that certain "interesting" configurations were excluded. By arguing the virtues of refueling and the possibility that improved weapon technology could reduce the need for payload capacity, we managed to get the restriction lifted. If we hadn't, the type of plane later considered "best" would have been excluded.

It is also easy to fall into the pitfall of trying to do too big a job. Many factors tend to lead the analyst in the direction of increasing the amount of work that he is going to try to do. Turning out a good analysis requires spending a lot of time thinking of questions that can be usefully answered in the time available.

The determination of objectives and criteria requires great care. Quoting from C. J. Hitch[2],

> How does an operations researcher typically go about choosing criteria—choices to which the results of his analysis are typically far more sensitive than the choice of mathematical models, to which inordinate study and debate are usually devoted? In some cases he casually takes the first criterion that pops into his mind and dashes on to the less important but more congenial aspects of his job. In some other cases he falls back on one of what Professor Koopman calls operations research's "procedural fallacies"[3]:
>
> *Authorititis*—letting the customer (probably a general or admiral) choose the criterion, even though this involves letting the customer "ask the question" or "define the problem", a responsibility no self-respecting scientist would abdicate to his customer, for good reasons, when he is on his own familiar ground as scientist; or
>
> *Mechanitis*—putting his machines to work as a substitute for hard thinking. Because he lacks any rationale for choosing a good criterion, the operations researcher writes down all the objectives he wants to accomplish and

[2] "Economics and Military Operations Research", *Review of Economics and Statistics,* vol. XL, no. 3, August 1958, p. 204.

[3] Professor Koopman, a mathematician, refers to the choice of "figures of merit" and "measures of effort". In my terminology the former are objectives, the latter costs, and the criterion usually some relation between them (difference, ratio, maximization or minimization of one with the other as constraint, etc.). See Bernard O. Koopman, "Fallacies in Operations Research", and "Comments by C. J. Hitch", *Operations Research,* vol. 4, no. 4, August 1956.

all the costs he wants to avoid, links them in various permutations to form criteria and lets the machine optimize for each criterion in turn. Then either he bases his recommendations on some form of majority vote (this might be called the fallacy of misplaced democracy—all criteria are inherently equal) or he combines the fallacy of mechanitis with that of authoritis, passing all results on to the customer who, thoroughly confused by a welter of apparently equally plausible solutions, has to make the choice.

Mr. Hitch goes on to talk about particular criteria errors:

A particularly common and vicious form of ratio criteria is the one that maximizes an objective divided by some single valuable input, when other valuable inputs are required. It is apparently altogether natural for the noneconomist to optimize on the scarcest or most valuable resources, treating other inputs as if they were free goods. More frequently than not operations research studies of nuclear bombing systems have maximized destruction per gram of fissile material—completely ignoring far more costly delivery system inputs, and getting weird results. It is seldom that all but one input can be regarded as free, with no alternative uses. An economist would not fall into this trap. The ignoring of some cost elements may in turn be regarded as a special case of another extremely common criterion error—the neglect of effects, which may be either harmful or beneficial, on other military or national objectives. The typical operations research study dealing with strategic air problems simply ignores important impacts of bomber deployment on air defense, as well as possibilities of jointly supplying some tactical offensive power along with the strategic[4].

The point is that the only way to choose criteria is to undertake analysis; the pitfall is to believe the contrary.

It is Mr. Hitch's contention in the article quoted that a rudimentary grounding in elementary economic principles is most urgently needed in systems analysis and operations research, more than knowledge of elaborate quantitative techniques.

Operations research essentially involves using "cost" (in some sense or another) as a guide to the efficient choice among alternative objectives. In the traditional military "requirements" approach, cost considerations are excluded until requirements have been established by "military judgment on the basis of needs". In this latter use cost serves only to indicate how much can be achieved, not what can be achieved and how it should be done.

The costs considered in evaluating future alternatives should be the "in-

4 "Economics and Military Operations Research", *Review of Economics and Statistics,* vol. XL, no. 3, August 1958, p. 206.

cremental" costs, that is, the net additional resource drain that would be incurred because of the choice of each particular alternative. When a proposed system can use facilities purchased for an earlier system, such facilities are free to the weapon system still under consideration. Therefore, in comparing systems it is an error to compute the costs as if no other systems exist. If a new system can use existing facilities or equipment, but other proposed alternatives cannot, it naturally achieves a cost advantage. Capabilities leading toward the attainment of objectives, other than that toward which the study is directed, must also be taken into account. If certain cost-effectiveness comparisons had been taken at face value, no modern Navy carrier would exist. In comparing alternatives for limited-war roles, these studies took no account of the carrier's central war capability in a comparison with weapons systems that had almost no capability in other roles.

It is putting the cart before the horse to search for an objective in terms of which to compare weapon systems. The objective must come first. If it does not, we run the risk of analyzing ways in which the possible weapon systems can best be used to implement the wrong objective.

Something must always be left out, otherwise problems are too big. For example, the decision to use a particular radar on a new jet fighter should fundamentally rest on the military worth of the available alternatives. It is futile to try to make this choice by considering all possible wars in which this equipment might be used. Yet, even though it may be beyond the analyst's capability to do a complete job, he can at least do some thinking about the larger problem. The dangerous path is to reduce the problem by fixing factors which, if sufficient thought had been given to the larger problem, would have been allowed to vary.

As an illustration, we might consider a decision made by the missile planners of ten years ago, torn by conflicting requirements for range, altitude, speed, payload, accuracy, and reliability. To simplify their problems, the common solution was to specify accuracy and payload—with the result that missiles which now look the most promising were effectively excluded from consideration. This was because the accuracy and the payload demanded were much beyond the capability of the engines. These requirements, however, became obsolete with the development of lighter nuclear weapons before the alternative missiles were operational.

The pitfall in development analysis is to concentrate technical competence and military expertise on the problem of recommending for development the system that will be most effective in the environment expected to exist at some future time. For in spite of our efforts, the future will remain broad and uncertain and the specific system selected may find itself faced with a completely different environment. The real problem is to provide a menu of alternatives to confront a spectrum of future events.

Along with the failure, in the rush to get started, to realize the importance of a searching analysis of what the problem should be, it is easy to fall into the pitfall of unconscious adherence to an attention bias or to "party line"—"fanaticism" in Herman Kahn's list of pitfalls. He calls it "the most important single reason for the tremendous miscalculations that are made in foreseeing and preparing for technological advance or changes in the strategic situation" [5], and describes the situation as follows.

> Almost all organizations are subject to fashion; some are even monolithic. An idea gets popular and everybody hops on the bandwagon. Sometimes, it is only a question of having vested interests or being obviously partisan. Mostly though, it's just the way people (including scientists) are. Very few people can hold tentative opinions about questions they are interested in, particularly if their colleagues have made up their minds. Even the most independent members may be swept off their feet by the intellectual tide. It may be a little worse in classified work but the other fields are not immune.

> Several things can be done to alleviate the situation:
> 1. Get a competent and honest staff.
> 2. Make the effective discussion groups for the important ideas fairly large.
> 3. Encourage independence of thought among individuals as much as possible. In particular be tolerant of lone wolves and mavericks.
> 4. Provide for frequent and effective outside criticism and refereeing.

> Still in spite of everything that is done, there will be a party line. This is probably the most important single reason for the tremendous miscalculations that are made in foreseeing and preparing for technological advances or changes in the strategic situation.

> One of the main advantages in having at least some Systems Analysis done by independent civilian organizations is that their non-military nature—and more importantly, *their freedom from staff responsibility*—make them a little more capable of withstanding pressures for intellectual conformity.

All military systems have been traditionally conservative with respect to new weapons and methods. This is reflected in a standard "party line"—to seek refinements and improvements in an ongoing proven system rather than a new one. This means resistance to novel and more advanced technology and to methods that disturb tradition.

The history of strategic bombing studies since World War II illustrates the workings of this influence. In World War II, the bombing problem was to penetrate the defenses, bomb accurately, and return. The bomber's concern[6] was with enemy fighters, antiaircraft guns, and missiles—not with enemy bombers. For years, even in studies for time periods after the Soviets were expected to have nuclear weapons, no serious attention was paid to the fact

---

5   Kahn and Mann, *op. cit.*, p. 42.
6   See Chapter 7.

that our bombers might be attacked on the ground, and we did not plan such an attack on theirs. Requirements and specifications for future bombers hardly considered the problem of surviving the enemy offense. This was not stupidity but an attention bias. For instance, in the Navy-SAC controversy over the B-36 in 1949, the Navy questioned the B-36 on every basis they could think of, including moral ones—except its vulnerability on the ground. RAND strategic bombing studies, even after the seriousness of the problem of bomber survival on the ground had been pointed out, continued to concentrate on such questions as speed, altitude, low vs. high penetration, supersonic dash, bombing altitude, small vs. large planes, and what targets to select. The Russians and the British took even longer than we did to recognize ground vulnerability, and some people think the French have not yet really absorbed the idea. It took the searching, detailed analysis of the Base Study (Chapter 3) and its extensive briefings to attract major attention to the problem.

It is difficult to overemphasize the importance of a careful formulation. It should identify the subproblems involved, isolate the major factors, develop a vocabulary for dealing with them, sketch out the relationships between the variables as they appear, and even arrive at a tentative set of conclusions. The idea is to make clear the structure of the analysis. But more importantly, it offers a concrete hypothesis for others to probe.

The setting forth of possible conclusions or recommendations at an early stage helps to guide the analysis. Also, such a consideration may turn out to be useful if the sponsor wants preliminary guidance on policy or off-the-cuff judgments prior to completion of the analysis.

Once we recognize that analysis is iterative and that a single cycle of formulation, search for the facts, and model building is unlikely to be adequate, we realize that the pitfall lies not in forming a preconceived or early idea about the solution, but in being unwilling to discard such an idea in the face of new evidence.

16.2. SEARCH

"Search" is the name we have given to the investigation that determines the facts or evidence on which the analysis is to be based and seeks to discover alternatives other than those that are immediately obvious. Here we note several possible sources of error.

One lies in the acceptance of "official" figures. The historical reasons for designing a new system are embodied in the planning factors and tactics used in official studies. But conditions change and it should be a major duty of the study to review these figures. For example, it is futile to base a study solely on intelligence estimates of specific future enemy capabilities. We cannot even predict the capabilities of our own military establishment ten years from now, even though we know our resources and plans. It is well to remember that one of the important functions of the information-gathering procedure is that of rejecting information.

Uncertainty about enemy capabilities can lead to yet another pitfall. While it is clear that to base the conclusions of a study on the "most probable" estimate of enemy capabilities is not enough, it is equally an error to base it on the "worst possible". The worst possible case may not only be extremely unlikely but call for systems so expensive that totally different alternatives may have to be sought.

One frequent pitfall is the completely mistaken technical notion or fact.

> Anyone who has spent any time at all in this field has had the following disturbing experience. He consults his own people and gets a very flat statement from them on what the technical situation is or can be. He then goes to another organization that is also technically competent. There he finds out that the situation is at best controversial, or even that his own people are completely wrong. This should not be treated as a disaster causing one to lose all faith in the competence of the people (though it is clearly not confirmatory evidence of their competence), but as a fairly normal occurrence which can be expected to happen occasionally [7].

For example, the analyst may learn that a cheap and simple countermeasure exists which renders almost worthless the system that the analyst has indicated as preferred. It is clearly a pitfall to expect a man or organization who created a system to discover its faults. The suggested way to avoid such surprises is to consult as many sources and experts as possible, asking the advocate of a particular point of view how his critics would attack it. For such an approach to be of value, it is important that people with an adverse opinion of the worth of the system be consulted. It is hard to get an engineer to display much ingenuity in tearing down a technically brilliant design that he has been working on for years.

Sometimes errors occur because the analyst fails to communicate effectively with the professional people on whom he must rely. For example, in the previously mentioned analysis undertaken to choose a next-generation bomber from among the thousands of possible designs, the number of engines unexpectedly appeared as a most significant factor in bomber survival. Since we felt sure that the aircraft designers had some flexibility as to the number of engines, we went to people who supplied the designs to determine what penalties would be incurred if the number of engines were increased. Then we found out that while they had worked out the total thrust required for each of the designs, they had no rule for and had not specified the number of engines. The people who gathered the data for the attrition model had obtained the number of

---

7   Kahn and Mann, op. cit., p. 49.

engines by counting those shown on a diagram that indicated the pertinent features of each configuration. It then turned out that the artist who drew the illustrations had decided that without engines the figures didn't look like aircraft and simply drew in the number of engines that looked suitable to him for the shape and size of the wing! A possible way to avoid this type of pitfall is to have someone on the analyst's team who is at least a lay expert in all the important fields with which the study is concerned; however, sharp limits of time and money may make this impossible.

It is not necessarily true that if enough factual research in a subject area is carried out a valid generalization will somehow automatically emerge.

As Kahn and Mann state:

> The Systems Analyst must have high standards for the quality of the technical work that goes into the study but the standards should not be so high that they are self-defeating. If he insists on checking every fact with every possible person who could have any opinion on the subject, then he would never finish the study. He must do enough cross-checking to convince himself that, in all probability, he has the correct facts, and then he takes his chances. This means that once in a while he will be misled and will look foolish, but one cannot do effective work in this field unless one is willing to take this risk [8].

16.3. EXPLANATION

It is a pitfall to become more interested in the model than in the real world. Technical people with specific training, knowledge, and capability like to use their talents to the utmost. It is easy for analysts whose basic training is in mathematics to focus attention on the mechanics of the computation or on the technical relationships in the model rather than on the important questions raised in the study. They may thus find out a great deal about the inferences that can be drawn from the model, but very little about the question they set out to answer.

A model is but a representation of the real world. More must be left out than can be included. Consider, for example, the model in Appendix B. Conceptually, we try to represent a series of wars in which we send our missiles over enemy territory, let them be shot at, and then determine how much damage they do. Everything is then restored to its original condition and another experiment tried with a different strategy or system. The actual operation is certainly unfeasible, and *any* such exercise with real equipment is unfeasible. We are almost completely restricted to hypothetical experiments consisting of pen-and-paper or computer exercises.

There are dangers in oversimplification in the model, although in a general

---

[8] Kahn and Mann, *op. cit.*, p. 51.

sense it pays to be simple. Formulas involving large numbers of symbols—possibly so complicated to write down that they are much easier to use when broken down into several pages of computational procedure—may seem to be more accurate than approximate relations. But the human mind is limited. There are only a few concepts that can be held simultaneously in mind. Long formulas or relationships so involved that it is impracticable to reduce them to a single expression are likely to convey no meaning at all, while a simple, though possible approximate relation may be easily understood. Through human fallibility a major error may invalidate the more complicated expression and yet, in general complexity of formulation, pass unnoticed. In uncomplicated expressions serious error is apt to become obvious long before the computation is completed because the relationships may be simple enough for us to see whether the behavior of the model is going to be reasonably in accord with intuition. The most convincing analysis is one which the nontechnician can think through.

I once worked on a systems analysis in which we used a very complicated model for bomber attrition in a strategic bombing campaign. Figure 16.1 displays the equations for a small part of that model, and one of the simpler parts at that. These equations make up a submodel for computing the expected number of bombers that survive the gun and missile defenses during the approach by the bombers to a defended target. This submodel was inherited from an earlier study; we had not built it ourselves. We had similar submodels for the other survival probabilities.

$$m^* = R_t MP_{\mathrm{SAI}} \cdot$$

$$E^*_{\mathrm{AAGM}} = E_{\mathrm{AAGM}}\left(1 + \frac{1}{25}\sqrt{m^* - 2}\right) \qquad \text{if } m^* > 2.$$

$$E^*_{\mathrm{HAA}} = E_{\mathrm{HAA}}\left(1 + \frac{1}{5}\sqrt{m^* - 2}\right) \qquad \text{if } m^* > 2.$$

$$a = S_p + \frac{50 - H}{47\sqrt{S_p}} W_t \qquad \text{if } 35 \leq H \leq 50.$$

$$U = \frac{2}{4.5m^*}\left(216E^*_{\mathrm{HAA}} + 7.5E^*_{\mathrm{AAGM}}\right).$$

$$P_{\mathrm{SLD}} = \exp\left(-\lambda U a^{\%}\right)\left[4\exp\left(-3A^{\%}_e \lambda U\right) - 3\exp\left(-4A^{\%}_e \lambda U\right)\right]$$
$$\cdot \left[2\exp\left(A^{\%}_p \lambda U\right) - \exp\left(-2A^{\%}_p \lambda U\right)\right]\exp\left(-\frac{12\lambda S_p E_{\mathrm{AABR}}}{4.5m^*}\right).$$

$$E_{Bk} = m^*(1 - P_{\mathrm{SLD}}).$$

Fig. 16.1   Submodel of bomber survival probability against local defenses

We used this model to compute a great many cases. To our embarrassment, someone looking over the numbers after most of the computation had been finished noticed a peculiar feature, namely, once the number of attackers got large, the number shot down decreased (even though no attempt was made to destroy the defenses)! It took intense investigation to discover that this absurdity arose from an assumption about the defense firing doctrine which was no longer sensible when the number of bombers became as large as the number we were investigating. We found a more suitable assumption, but, our suspicions aroused, probed further and then abandoned the whole construction. The point is, the formulation was too complex for us to understand until almost too late. There is another point here, too; it is an error to use someone else's model unless you thoroughly understand its implications and limitations.

The people for whom analysis is undertaken should become aware of another aspect of big computing projects. Almost invariably the time required to set up the computing program for large problems is underestimated. Instead of taking a few months it may take a year or longer. Ideas change fairly rapidly in the field of military analysis, and questions that people now think are important become unimportant. The large-model man always runs into the danger of having to spend most of his time looking for ways to make the computing machine better approximate some relatively trivial aspect of the real world rather than studying the problem he set out to solve. He thus learns a lot about programming and very little about military decisions. For these reasons, we said earlier, we should turn to the mathematician as much for his ingenuity in escaping mass computations as for his skill in organizing them. Indeed, the role of the big model in systems analysis has been more to verify and to work out details, and to prepare for presentation ideas that were already fairly well understood than to discover solutions. There is a good chance that ideas originated and the analyst became convinced of their validity through very rough and elementary calculations.

Another dangerous pitfall lies in forcing a complex problem into an analytically tractable framework by emphasizing ease of computation. Compromises must always be made in model building, but this is not the direction in which to go. It is almost always better to sacrifice workability in order to represent the process being modeled more adequately.

Another pitfall consists of trying to use more complicated techniques than the data warrant. The story of how, in World War I, Colonel Leonard P. Ayres, Chief Statistical Officer of the U.S. Army, decided when to issue the first draft call is pertinent[9]. The first registration for the draft occurred in June 1917, and registered 500 000 men. Very shortly there were grave differences of opinion as to when the first call should be issued. The Chief of Staff asked Ayres if there was any statistical method by which to ascertain when the draft should be called. Ayres said "Yes", and then set out to figure how to find it. The problem was to match the number of men to the equipment available. He

---

9   Colonel Leonard P. Ayres, *The Uses of Statistics in War,* The Army Industrial College, May 4, 1940.

collected all the information he could about everything that might be a controlling factor, subjected it to thorough analysis, but did not get any answer. Finally, he looked at the problem in another way and said, "What are the minimum essentials? What do recruits absolutely have to have?"—and then passed in a report saying the draft should be called the first week in September without explaining how he worked it out. Nobody asked.

The draft call worked out very well. How did he arrive at an answer? He computed the day on which there would surely be in every camp one pair of breeches for every expected recruit—the one item he regarded as absolutely essential.

Another pitfall is the effort to set up a complete model which attempts to treat every aspect of a complex problem simultaneously. What can happen is that the analyst finds himself criticized because the first model he has selected has left out various factors related to the situation being investigated. He is vulnerable to these criticisms if he doesn't realize the importance of the point made about models in Chapter 4: *the question being asked as well as the process being represented determines the model*. Without attention to the question, he has no rule for guidance as to what to accept or reject; he has no real goals in view and no way to decide what is important and relevant. He can only answer criticism by making the model bigger and more complicated. This may not stop the criticisms, for something must always be left out. The size of the model is then determined not by what is really relevant but by the capacity of the computing machine.

One approach to designing a model is to attempt to reduce the real system to a logical flow diagram. The danger of this approach is that the model may tend to be too detailed and that components of the real process will be included that contribute nothing to the question to be answered. For this reason, it is advisable to design the model around the questions to be answered rather than as an imitation of the real system.

The failure to put sufficient emphasis on the question in the design of the model leads to another pitfall: the belief that there are "universal" models—one model, say, to handle all questions about a given activity. For example, it has been proposed (even to the extent of writing a study contract) that a general computer model for strategic air war be set up to supply weapons designers with a systematic evaluation of their design concepts and to enable the Department of Defense to evaluate the worth of alternative "design solutions" developed by competing contractors.

One argument for such a model notes that "the choice of assumptions, the forecast of the future, and the methods of analysis have a marked influence on the performance and physical characteristics of the weapon system set forth as preferred or optimal"; therefore, a uniform framework would mean that "the results obtained by the various contractors would be comparable since the effects due to variation in the assumptions they might have chosen to form their models would have been eliminated". This may indeed be the case, but will the end result be desirable? A rigidly specified framework may mitigate one sort of undesirable bias by making it difficult for an analysis to be used to rationalize conclusions already otherwise derived by the contractors; but only at the severe risk of introducing other biases.

The most fundamental objection is that such uniform framework necessarily conceals or removes by assumption many extremely important uncertainties, therefore tending to lead to designs that disregard the value of hedging against those uncertainties. Another is that if such a model were used to indicate which design to buy, emphasis would soon focus on how to make the design look good in terms of the model, not on how to make it look good against the enemy. Also, even if efforts were made to keep the model "up to date", this would turn out to be impossible, for the analyst must be able to modify his model in the terminal stages of his study to accommodate information acquired during the early phases. Indeed, in a problem involving the struggle between nations, there are so many factors of shifting importance, and such radical changes in objectives and tactics are likely, that most models are obsolete before the recommendations from the study can become accepted policy.

Systems analysis is concerned with problems whose essence is uncertainty. Uncertainties whose probability of occurrence is more or less objective or calculable can be handled in the model by Monte Carlo or other methods. The treatment of such uncertainty is a considerable practical problem, however, and a challenge to the analyst. The pitfall for model-builders lies in accepting this challenge to the neglect of the real uncertainties. These typically involve forms of ignorance that cannot be reduced to probabilities, and their consequences can be devastating. The objective in system studies is not to learn what can happen in a given situation with a specific probability as the consequence of physical fluctuation, but to design or operate the system so that any fluctuation is unimportant.

Since a full Monte Carlo investigation may seriously expand the analysis, it is frequently better first to carry out a simple expected-value treatment, deferring a full investigation of fluctuation phenomena until the qualitative aspects of the problem are fully understood. It may then turn out to be unnecessary to perform these more complicated calculations since consideration of the real uncertainties may make trivial the effect of any statistical uncertainty.

When planning in the face of a large variety of uncertainties, it is an error not to keep in mind that some improbable event or combination of events may occur. For example, before Pearl Harbor the Japanese used war gaming techniques to analyze the possibilities of success. They must have considered that any sequence of events which would give the United States warning would lead to failure. Yet, by a strange and unlikely turn, we *did* get warning. Just as strangely we ignored it! Such a combination of events, or at least all the billions of them that *might* have arisen, could not have been considered. Such events or sequences, remarkable when considered singly, are characteristic when the number of possibilities is large.

A serious pitfall is to ignore uncertainty or to try to remove it by assumption. Systems analysis, as well as any other attempt to answer the same questions, must necessarily face uncertainty squarely, treat it as an important element in the problem, and take it into account in formulating recommendations.

16.4. INTERPRETATION

The decisionmakers to whom an analysis is presented almost always have information that may not be known to the analysts. As an example from the military, the question occasionally arises whether under some very special desperate circumstances, men in the ranks can be counted on to carry out a maneuver that means certain death. The generals who use the analysis may be the best source of information on this type of question.

The analyst must be prepared to have his recommendation modified by considerations that the clients alone can apply to the problem or by other differences in judgment. For one thing, the analyst may not know the value system of the men who are going to use his analysis for decision. It is a serious pitfall for the analyst to concentrate so completely on the purely objective and scientific aspects of his analysis that he neglects the subjective elements or fails to handle them with understanding.

Since the analyst knows his study will be subject to scrutiny, interpretation, and possibly further analysis, he should make his subjective judgments known. Trust is essential because the client has to take the analysis and recommendation of any study team in a large part on faith. The client usually cannot repeat the study, will very seldom have the time to review it in meticulous detail, and will be influenced by it depending on his belief about how the analyst reached his conclusions. He cannot hope to master the variety of specialized skills that frequently go into a complicated analysis. At best he can acquire enough background to identify really incompetent or patently biased work. Faith in the analyst's purely technical and scientific competence is not sufficient; what is required is a similar confidence in his subjective judgment. Trust requires disclosure; the client must know either how the analyst has disposed of the subjective elements in the study or whether he has merely accepted and used the client's judgments. If he does this latter uncritically, the analyst is not using the full potentialities of analysis.

No decisionmaker can absorb all the information prepared for his attention nor can he remember all he pays attention to. But what he considers and retains may be the key to what he decides. This, in turn, depends on the way it is presented and his confidence in the men and organization from which it comes—in particular, on what kind of response he gets to his questions. There should, therefore, be a general admonition to the analyst to keep his consumer relations good. If they are not he can never win acceptance for his analysis. In his presentation he must answer questions carefully and avoid expressions of condescension or a style of communication too didactic for his client's taste.

In a comparison of systems, it is a pitfall to put much faith in the values of the *variables* which determine the strategy associated with the best system, for the model was probably designed only to discriminate between systems. Thus a cost-effectiveness analysis that indicates missile A as the preferred missile will also indicate that to obtain the maximum effectiveness (for a given cost) with missile A, a specific number of missiles should be fired on a certain target. But that number may be of doubtful validity, since the particular model may have suppressed certain factors important for this very point but not for the over-all comparison.

Sometimes a mathematical model used in evaluation problems indicates a preference for extreme strategies, such as the prescription to throw all resources into one action over an initial period of time and then suddenly switch all of them to another action. For example, one tactical study indicated that for the first few days all offensive aircraft should be used against the enemy air forces and then suddenly, for the rest of the campaign, everything should be used in close support of troops. No war has ever been fought in this way, and one should be extremely dubious about such an extreme strategy. This may be the correct solution for the model, but a model cannot reflect all of the smoothing-out factors present in the real world. Troops not opposed by enemy aircraft cannot be expected to follow the model's equations. This does not mean that such calculations are of no value, but that modifying circumstances must be considered before such solutions can be offered as operational guidance. Too neat a solution, particularly if it goes against established experience and intuition, should be viewed cautiously.

Administrators sometimes feel that one of the worst characteristics of systems analysts and operations researchers is that they want to make basic changes in a study after the work is half done. This results in a great deal of "wasted work" and means that deadlines are not going to be met.

It is, of course, quite true that making a major change in a study at a late stage means that much of the early work is not used, and because such a change may involve a great deal of additional work, that deadlines may not be met. For these reasons, some analysts when they are one-half, two-thirds, or three-fourths through the study may not pause to evaluate what they have done thus far. A periodic reappraisal is valuable, however, because as the study progresses the analyst broadens his understanding of its scope and purpose.

Stocktaking that results in junking a major portion of the work indicates that a reappraisal was especially necessary.

A practice that can lead to serious error is suggested by the following statement: "If several alternatives have similar cost and effectiveness and if these results are quite sensitive to the values assigned the inputs, some other basis for decision must be found". This may amount to saying that if after honest analysis we are fundamentally uncertain about which of several alternatives is best, the issues should then be resolved on the basis of some specious side criterion not originally judged adequate to discriminate. This implies that unique optimization results are not to be trusted, and therefore that they should not be trusted. On the contrary, the point to stress is that the decision must be made on the basis of forthright recognition of the fundamental uncertainty.

Without question, an analyst is in a position to bias the conclusions of a study, for example, by judicious selection of the alternatives for examination and of the variables he chooses to include in his model. Doing this deliberately to impose his personal preferences is certainly unethical.

Along this line are pitfalls which are almost impossible for the analyst to avoid. For example, as a person responsible for predicting the outcomes of on-going processes or trends, he may frequently be liable to severe punishment for being wrong, but rarely rewarded for being right. This does not always encourage him to say what he thinks is the best thing to do. Suppose, for instance, he is an investment analyst and he thinks his boss can make a killing by buying certain stock. Say, if the boss invests $ 100 000 in this stock the chances are three to one he will lose it, but there is one chance in four that he will increase it tenfold. Suppose there is another investment available which has a 100 per cent chance of bringing in $ 10 000. His expected gain from the first investment is $ 175 000 in contrast to $ 10 000 from the second. Suppose also that the boss is rich enough to afford the loss of $ 100 000 several times. It may be extremely difficult for the analyst to tell him just point blank to make the investment that will maximize his expected gain. After all, three times out of four the boss will take the terrible loss and as a result may fire him. This illustration shows that courage has its place in this field as well as in others.

It is sometimes assumed that whoever understands the engineering details and is able to design the computation is also fit, without further study, to carry out the analysis as a whole. This is like saying that whoever is fit to build a house is fit to design one. The builder and the architect may have many of the same abilities and their training may be almost the same, but skill in one field does not necessarily mean skill in the other.

Out of context, these "pitfalls" we have mentioned seem so obvious that one wonders how they could have led to error a first time, let alone be repeated. One has only to examine actual analyses to find that they are still present. Our hope is that as theory develops they will occur less frequently.

Part Four

SUMMARY

In addition to summarizing the points made earlier, this last chapter attempts to indicate the limitations of systems analysis and its alternatives. For emphasis, the summary is presented as two lists. The first collects many of the principles or precepts suggested in earlier chapters as essential to good analysis. The second cites questions that anyone who is expected to act on the basis of another's analysis (or even the analyst himself) might ask to clarify his thinking about or uncover weaknesses in a study.

Chapter 17

RECAPITULATION

E. S. QUADE

Systems analyses are undertaken to provide policy guidance, usually for decisions in which rigorous quantitative analysis can only provide part of the solution. The man who expects to act on the basis of someone else's analysis needs more than confidence in the qualifications of the analyst to assure himself that the work is competent. To act wisely he needs, at the very least, to understand the important and fundamental principles involved. The executive or decisionmaker does not ordinarily have the time or frequently the training necessary to work through all the aspects of the analysis and to understand those that he cannot accept intuitively. Therefore, he must resort to questioning the analyst. With these questions he attempts to make sure that the study has been conducted according to generally accepted principles of good analysis, that the analyst has properly communicated the necessary doubts, and that, if the conclusions are not acceptable to common-sense reasoning, he understands why.

To help the man who must act on the results of analysis, we have assembled two lists. The first of these collects principles or precepts that are compatible with good practice in analysis involving problems of decision. The second lists questions that a user might ask to clarify his thinking about or uncover possible weaknesses in a systems analysis[1].

Unfortunately, even if these lists were firm, they could not be guaranteed to be very helpful. Of course, no one would expect to find a device suitable for mechanical evaluation of a complicated analysis "by the numbers". As for the principles presented, these generalizations are not unrestricted or universal like the laws of physical science. No one can say with assurance, "Follow these principles and you can't go wrong". One *can* say that they are more true than false (although in some cases even this may be a matter of opinion). They are presented as common-sense propositions, not as a list of rules or dicta that might substitute for thinking or for knowledge gained by experience and education.

---

[1] Donald M. Fort of RAND suggested that such a list might be useful and contributed some sample questions.

17.1. PRECEPTS

1.   The design of the analysis is crucial. A large share of the effort by the *leaders* of a project must be invested in thinking about the problem, exploring its proper breadth, trying to discover the objectives of the systems or operations under consideration, and searching out good criteria for choice. It is useful to know as much as possible about the background of the problem— where it came from, why it is important, and what decision it is going to assist. Problem formulation necessarily involves a great deal of judgment and intuition about the scope, the degree of detail, and the level of optimization, but this is a field for analysis as much as the rest of the study.

2.   The decision about what to analyze and what to treat by assumption is a significant one. If an assumption begins to take on overwhelming importance, then it should be re-examined.

3.   The investigation may require many cycles or passes at the problem. Any analysis that attempts to make use of scientific methods is essentially an iterative process. Thus it may happen that the first set of assumptions and model can do no more in a real-world problem than help to decide how to continue.

4.   Setting forth possible conclusions early in the study is essential to the guidance of later analysis, but the analyst must stand ready to discard his early notions about the solution in the face of later evidence.

5.   Detailed treatment usually should come late in the study, when it can be important in discovering misconceptions and mistakes. Early in the study, it is generally a mistake to spend much time on relatively well-understood details or complicated models. To turn up ideas, a rough treatment of many models is better than a careful and detailed treatment of one.

6.   Systems analysis should try to create as well as to eliminate alternatives. The invention of new alternatives can be much more valuable than exhaustive comparison of given alternatives, none of which may be very satisfactory. The job of the systems analyst is thus not only analysis but also design. His analysis should suggest new alternatives or changes in given ones that will make the preferred system or operation more satisfactory.

7.   The systems analyst should spend at least as much time trying to make the decision problem less agonizing as trying to decide what the decision should be. This requires attention to design, not merely to evaluation. As a result of suggested modifications, a single alternative may stand out, or perhaps choice among competing alternatives will be seen as a matter of indifference. A model or a theory that represents the performance of the competing alternatives— however useful it may be—is not all that the policymaker wants.

8.   In all analysis, the use of models is inevitable. In systems analysis, because the problems are complicated, models are frequently detailed and

elaborate, requiring the investment of many man-hours. However, it is the question—not the model—that is important. The analyst must be more interested in the real-world problem than in the idealized model he uses to compare the alternatives. He must be more interested in practical questions that demand answers than in the intellectual and mechanical gadgets used to get solutions.

9. For most phenomena there are many possible representations; the appropriate model depends as much on the question being asked as on the phenomena about which it is asked. There are no "universal" models; no one model can handle all questions about a given activity.

10. Compromises are necessary in model building. When there is a choice, it is almost always better to sacrifice workability for a more adequate representation of the process being modeled.

11. In economic, military, and industrial problems, a clearly defined mathematical formulation is fundamentally difficult. But after this formulation is complete, sophisticated mathematical techniques may frequently be useful in obtaining the best solution. No matter how difficult the equations or complicated the analyses, some sort of approximation can always be made.

12. Computations with models and machines are frequently valuable not because they prove results, but because they lead to more and better analysis at the intuitive level.

13. A computing machine can help only in problems that the analyst knows conceptually how to solve by himself.

14. Military decisionmaking must rely mainly on using a great many partially formulated and largely intuitive judgments by experts in the field. By introducing a precise structure and terminology the model is primarily an effective means of communication, and through a feedback process helps the experts arrive at a clearer understanding of their subject matter. Completely objective decisionmaking is an ideal and should be so recognized.

15. In conflict situations, the effect of the enemy's or the competitor's decisions on those of the analyst, and vice versa, must be taken explicitly into account. This requires analysis of the enemy's or the competitor's systems and operations. Countermeasures and counter-countermeasures must be considered.

16. A study that attempts to influence policy must make a convincing comparison of alternatives. This implies that the analysis may have to be done in two parts: one to find out what to recommend and a second to make the recommendations convincing.

17. Alternatives—policies, systems, or courses of action—must be compared in the same contexts. That is, the objectives, costs, and risks of a first alternative must be compared with those of a second in a context that includes everything pertinent to both.

18.   Systems analysis should be systems oriented. Emphasis should be placed on the simultaneous consideration of the major relevant factors, even if this requires use of a crude and imprecise model or unaided (but explicit) judgment. Rather than reduce the problem to component parts by deliberately neglecting their interactions, the analyst tries to extend the systems boundaries as far as necessary to determine which interdependences are important, and then studies the total complex system.

19.   The type of problem systems analysis is designed to handle usually calls for an interdisciplinary team consisting of persons with a variety of knowledge and skills. This is not merely because a complex problem is likely to involve many diverse factors which cannot be handled by a single discipline. An even more important reason is that a problem looks different to an economist, to an engineer, or to a sociologist, say, and their different approaches to the problem contribute to finding a solution.

20.   Insofar as possible, a systems analyst should try to use the methods of science and to establish the same traditions. He should be objective and quantitative; all his calculations, assumptions, data, and judgments should be made explicit and subject to duplication, checking, criticism, and disagreement.

21.   It is necessary to look for ideas and new alternatives as well as for facts and relationships. Unless we have ideas and alternatives, there is nothing to analyze or to choose between. But ideas are easy to kill at the start before one knows enough about them to evaluate them.

22.   Inquiry can never be complete. The decisionmakers responsible for action must get along without all the additional analysis that, given more time, could have been done. They must add considerations that the analysis could not or did not have time to deal with.

23.   Analysis is as applicable to problems of research and development as it is to other problems of choice. However, the parameters for comparing the performance of several systems are subject to great uncertainty—as is always the case when research is involved and usually when development is under way. Analysis is then likely to be more useful in pointing out where further information would be particularly valuable and how to get it than in evaluating or specifying the "best" system. But analysis alone cannot locate all the theoretical and empirical knowledge required; experiment and development cannot be replaced by systems analysis.

24.   Real uncertainty that cannot be removed by further analysis is always present in any study of the real world. It must be explicitly treated and analyzed to determine its consequences.

25.   In a complex real-world problem, full optimization over the entire scope of the problem is ordinarily beyond the capability of analysis; hence decisions

must be reached through judgment based on incomplete optimizations or sub-optimizations. To lessen the possibility of introducing error by an incomplete optimization, it is necessary to (a) check for consistency of criteria and objectives between the present level of optimization and possible higher levels of optimization; (b) consider the value of the resources or alternatives used for other objectives; and (c) estimate at least roughly how the operation or system being investigated helps or hinders other operations or systems.

26. Costs are a guide in choosing among alternatives and risks. It is important to cost alternatives in some appropriate sense, however approximately, prior to choice. Otherwise, we cannot know which alternatives will contribute most toward the attainment of the objectives.

27. The traditional, conventional, or plausible way of carrying out a task is not the only way. Usually a great variety of ways, each with its particular advantages and disadvantages, benefits and costs, certainties and risks, can be weighed by analysis. Even if the analysis cannot produce a convincing comparison of the relevant alternatives—say, because no satisfactory criterion can be found—the preparation of a list of alternatives, together with their consequences, and the possible recognition or discovery of new ones makes the effort worthwhile.

28. It is an error to assume that anyone who understands the engineering or operational details and can carry out the computation is also fit, without further knowledge or training, to design the investigation as a whole.

29. In broad policy questions, an alternative cannot be preferred merely because it is the lowest-cost choice in a single cost-effectiveness comparison. Even at best, such a comparison can reflect only the most probable future circumstance. A preferred alternative should also go a long way toward achieving the objectives in less probable or even in many improbable situations —and we would even like it to offer a good chance to attain many of the lower priority objectives always present.

17.2. QUESTIONS

Many systems analyses and operations research studies are reported to the sponsor in an elaborate briefing or an impressive brochure that can conceal as well as reveal the analysis. Is there any way that the recipient of such a report can guard against the possibility of bias or error and be sure that he understands the implications of the study? Not with certainty, unless he can follow the work in detail. However, one traditional way that helps is to ask questions of the analyst.

Of course, no list of general questions can be prepared, independent of the particular analysis, to guarantee a good evaluation, but such a list may at least remind the client and the analyst of considerations otherwise overlooked.

Although specific questions about points made in the study are likely to be more effective, the following general questions may help both the analyst and the evaluator.

1.   Does the project leader appear to have a fair background knowledge of the subject area? If he doesn't, is there some compensating reason why he should be leading the project?

2.   Does the preliminary formulation show an understanding of what needs to be done to fill in the gaps in our knowledge? Does the proposed approach look promising?

3.   Is the process an organized one? Is there a timetable showing what substudies are to be done and when? Is there a cost estimate? Is there an awareness of who should be working? Or is this a study where it is better to forget about organization?

The next question could be asked early as well as late in the analysis.

4.   What is the purpose of the analysis? Is it to determine the one best course of action? Or is it merely to provide information which, although not adequate as a sole basis for choosing the best course of action, might be helpful in making the choice? Or is it to justify a particular action in which the analyst or the client has a vested interest? (A manufacturer may only be trying to show how his particular design fits into an operational context, using the systems analysis mainly to determine whether there is some important factor missing in his design. In that case, the analysis should not be used to select one design for development, excluding other possibilities.)

5.   Who is doing the analysis? While disinterest does not guarantee objectivity, interest, on the other hand, can definitely lead to shortsightedness. And an analysis by an agency with access to competitive data should be more reliable than one by a single contractor who cannot really do more than make a good case for his product.

6.   What decision is the analysis concerned with? Can the analysis help with that decision?

7.   Who must make the decision? Is it to be made by a single individual or agency? If not, does the analysis distinguish among matters to be decided upon by different individuals or agencies?

8.   When must or should the decisions be made? Does the analysis distinguish between matters that require decisions soon and others for which final commitments can be postponed?

9.   What alternative decisions about courses of action are considered in the analysis? Have any been ignored?

10.   Does the analysis ignore any related factors that should be considered

jointly with the problems in the analysis? If so, could consideration of such joint decisions currently affect the conclusions of the analysis? For example, consider an analysis to determine a choice of missiles for the strategic force. If aircraft are also to be used in the force, the number and type of aircraft with the same mission must certainly be affected by the choice of missiles, and hence should be considered at the same time.

11.   Are all the alternative actions considered in the analysis really possible? If not, could the elimination of the unattainable alternatives conceivably affect the conclusion? For example, some alternative actions that are perfectly feasible in an economic or a military sense are impossible because of political, cultural, or policy considerations unknown to the analyst.

12.   Does the analysis ignore any consequence of the decision that should be considered in making the decision?

13.   Are the assumptions explicitly stated? Are there alternative assumptions not explicitly considered in the study which might be just as reasonable? Are the assumptions unusual in any important respects? Is it possible that some plausible assumptions might invalidate the conclusions? If some conditions could change the conclusions, are they indicated?

14.   What is the basis for the preliminary elimination of inferior alternatives in the analysis? Is the elimination based on a formula, on judgment, or on both? If formulas are employed, what are the constraints? If judgment, who is exercising it and what aspects are taken into account?

15.   Do the decisionmaking criteria appear reasonable? Are they consistent with higher level criteria? Are there other criteria that would also appear reasonable? Are the conclusions sensitive to the criteria?

16.   Does the systems analyst fully disclose his subjective judgments? Where judgment is used, is the logic behind the opinion made explicit?

17.   Does the analysis lose effectiveness by passing the buck to the decisionmaker? That is, does the analysis fail to go far enough in eliminating inferior alternatives?

18.   Are the results of the analysis presented in a useful form, with the conclusions spelled out so that they are meaningful to the recipient?

19.   Are the limitations of the analysis, as well as its good features, pointed out clearly and candidly?

20.   Does the analysis provide some relatively simple rules for computation or for any scheme that the decisionmaker can use to eliminate inferior actions himself? Can he do this by judgment, or is some formula that is buried in the study required? For instance, are the relevant outcomes shown for each alternative under various possible circumstances?

21. Are the conclusions intuitively satisfying? Does the study support the conclusions? If the conclusions appeal to the intuition, does this appear to be a case where the conclusions could have been reached anyway on the basis of intuition? If the conclusions are intuitively unappealing, does this appear to be a case where intuition has been shown to be unreliable? Or, on the other hand, is this an indication that the analysis may be unreliable, perhaps because it has ignored some subtle and analytically intractible considerations which an intuitive approach would have taken into account?

22. If there are special cases in which the conclusions are known, are these conclusions consistent with the general ones?

23. Is the significant problem being considered, or is a related problem really the significant one?

24. Does the analysis allow for uncertainties about the correct form of relationships in the model, or for the future environment, or for probabilistic uncertainties, as well as for uncertainties in the parameter values employed? Does the analysis distinguish between these types of uncertainty?

25. What contingencies were considered? Have any obvious ones been ignored? If probabilities are assigned to various contingencies, are they intended to represent subjective or objective probabilities? If subjective, whose? Is there any question as to the legitimacy of assigning probabilities to some of the contingencies? Are the numerical values questionable?

26. Are enemy or competitor reactions explicitly taken into account?

27. If development proposals are being evaluated, how do they compare on the basis of commonly used "rules of thumb" as to (1) the number of places in the design where "breakthroughs" are assumed; (2) the number of points in the design at the present limit of the engineering state of the art; (3) the number of proven components in the design; (4) the quality control and management control proposed; (5) past performance on similar designs by the contractors in question?

28. Were the assumptions of the model made explicit?

29. Is the model adequate?
   a. Does the model represent correctly the known facts and situations?
   b. When the principal parameters are varied, do the results remain consistent and plausible?
   c. Can the model handle special cases in which there is some indication about what the outcome should be?
   d. Does the model assign causes to known effects?

30. Does the study give consideration to other possible models?

31. Are the recommendations made with full recognition of the uncertainties involved?

17.3. IN RETROSPECT

In general, these lectures have dealt with the problem of what can and what should be done by systems analysts, engineers, and scientists—including social as well as physical scientists—to help people who must make decisions in the face of *real* uncertainty. It is this uncertainty that makes the problems difficult. A long-range military problem is comparable, for example, to the problems of the owner of a racing stable who wants to win a horse race to be run many years hence, on a track not yet built, between horses not yet born. To make matters worse, the possibility exists that when the race is finally run the rules may have been changed, the track length altered, and the horses replaced by greyhounds. Yet, in spite of such uncertainty, analysis can help.

What are the limitations of analysis? C. J. Hitch, Assistant Secretary of Defense (Comptroller), in an address before the U.S. Army Operations Research Symposium at Duke University (March 26, 1962) championed the use of operations research at the level of the Department of Defense. He remarked,

> ... there will always be considerations which bear on the very funda-mentals of national defense which are simply not subject to any sort of rigorous, quantitative analysis. It is not even possible to draw a line between those which are and those which are not—the gamut encompasses a wealth of considerations which are *more* or *less* subject to analysis. Thus, there will necessarily be some questions which are outside the scope of our analytical technique. For this reason alone, we cannot expect a panacea. It is as if some of the digits had been left off the input keyboard of our computer. As an example, I might mention considerations of the morale of our forces. How do you quantitatively distinguish between men who are highly motivated, and those who are demoralized? In fact, how do you quantitatively predict what it is that motivates or discourages a man? And which man? The fact that we cannot quantize such things (and there are many other similar examples) does not mean that they have no effect on the outcome of a military endeavor—it simply means that our analytical techniques cannot answer every question.

> That such is the case is widely recognized, particularly by those in the military profession who have had to live with these realities. But does that mean that all analysis becomes meaningless? I think not. Every bit of the total problem that can be confidently analyzed removes one more bit of uncertainty from our process of making a choice. While I can hardly believe that any significant military problem will ever be wholly susceptible to rigorous analysis, I feel just as certain that analytical techniques can allow us to make significant choices with a very real increase in confidence.

> On the second point—that such techniques constitute a potential hazard as well as a potential benefit—there is a well-known human tendency to

believe the printed word. By the same token, in the design of military forces, there is a tendency to associate analysis with credibility—particularly if the magic word "computer" is mentioned. In fact, of course, the Machiavellian analyst can "prove" the most outrageous theses. But he is not the major threat—such analyses are subject to rebuttal by equally clever opponents. The real threat lies not so much in deliberate deceit as it does in our own imperfections—inadvertent omission of important factors—the pyramiding of erroneous analyses on an unsuspected fallacy —subconscious desires to substantiate one's previously committed position, and so on.

It is easy to exaggerate the degree of assistance that analysis can offer to a policymaker. Using value judgments, imprecise knowledge, and intuitive estimates of enemy or competitor intent, gleaned either from specialists or from the policymaker himself, a study can assess the implications of choosing one alternative over another and thus help the decisionmaker make a better decision than would otherwise be made. But the man who has the responsibility must interpret such assessments in the light of his own knowledge, values, and estimates. And the decision becomes his own.

Some difficulties prevent full optimization through objective analysis—such as contradictory objectives, the necessity for dependence on subjective judgment, the uncertain implication of costs over time, inaccurate or missing data, and the freedom of action available to the enemy. These can be compensated for to some extent by the policymaker; for example, by temporizing decisions, decisions to postpone commitment of funds even when such postponements mean higher costs, preference for decisions in which more money will be spent in later time periods, duplication of research and development effort, and the preference for flexible and multipurpose systems. Advising such actions when they are appropriate is the role of analysis, and the knowledge that they are possible can make the job easier.

How then can we summarize the danger of reliance on systems analysis, operations research, cost-effectiveness analysis, etc., in defense decisions? First, since certain factors fundamental to national defense problems are not subject to rigorous, quantitative, computer-based analysis, they may possibly be neglected, deliberately set aside, or improperly weighted when a decision is based on such analysis. Second, the analysis may, on the surface, appear so scientific and quantitative that it may be assigned a validity not justified by the many subjective judgments involved. But better analysis and careful attention to where analysis ends and judgment begins should overcome these dangers.

Systematic quantitative analysis of military questions often falls short of being scientific research because predictions ordinarily cannot be verified and the urgency of military problems forces the substitution of intuition for verifiable knowledge. But, in contrast to other aids to decisionmaking, it extracts everything possible from scientific methods, and its virtues are the virtues of those methods. *Furthermore, its limitations are shared by its alternatives.* And if we exclude intuitive or "unbuttoned" judgment, then in a sense these alternatives are also analysis, but less systematic and quantitative.

One alternative way to handle a problem is to turn it over to an "expert". His considered opinion can be very helpful if it results from a reasonable and impartial examination of the facts, with due allowance for uncertainty, and if it is made *explicit*. For if it is explicit, others can use his information to form their own considered opinion. But an expert is even more valuable if his knowledge and opinions can be used in association with other experts. The analytic approach, with its models and games, is essentially a device for providing a framework for the systematic exploitation of experts.

Another alternative way to handle a problem is to turn it over to a committee. Now although there is no real reason why a committee should not engage in systematic analysis, this is not likely to happen. Committees usually accept the problem as defined in advance. Given a problem, however, the very first thing that should be done is to determine carefully what the problem really is—not just study how to make it go away. Committees are much less likely than experts to make their reasoning explicit since their findings are usually obtained by bargaining. A group, more often than not, strives for a consensus, for an acceptable compromise and for unanimity in place of originality, precision, and efficiency.

Answers obtained from experts or from a committee depend largely on subjective judgment. Moreover, it is difficult to determine the consensus of these judgments—and impossible to obtain one in some cases—although techniques exist for just such a purpose[2].

What can we say about the future of systems analysis and operations research in defense and national security problems?

Resistance by the military to its use in broad problems of strategy is gradually breaking down. With regard to systematic, quantitative analysis in general, the military is in an evolutionary flux, like industry in the throes of automation. Military planning and strategy has always involved more art than science; what is happening is that the art form is changing from an *ad hoc,* seat-of-the-pants approach based on intuition to one based on quantitative analysis. The military itself has changed. In the old Air Force, a man flew, or fixed aircraft that flew. Today the ratio of staff to fliers is increasing to the point where the force appears to be turning completely into staff and support personnel. With this change the computer is becoming increasingly significant—as an automaton, a process controller, a service trouble-shooting technician, a complex informa-

---

2 For example, the DELPHI technique explained in Chapter 8.

tion processor, and as a *decision aid*. But the computer is no more than a tool to expedite analysis; even in narrow military contexts considerations not subject to rigorous, quantitative computer-based analysis are always present. Big decisions cannot be the automatic consequence of a computer program, of cost-effectiveness analysis, operations research, or any application of mathematical models, or of systems analysis.

For broad studies, involving force posture and composition or the strategy to achieve foreign policy objectives, intuitive, subjective, even *ad hoc* study schemes will continue to be used—but supplemented to an increasing extent by systematic quantitative analysis. And as ingredients of this analysis, in recognition of the need for judgment, a greater use of "scenarios", gaming, and techniques for the systematic employment of experts can be expected.

These essays have tried to demonstrate the necessity of abstraction and show its nature in dealing with any complex problem of the real world; to explain, in simple language, what a model of a problem is; and then to show, by examples, the usefulness which explicit models can have despite their inability to be realistic in all details. The alternative methods to answer questions of decision without explicit analysis also necessarily involve models. However, the models involved there, because they are implicit, are more likely to be dangerously inadequate.

The analytic method, in contrast to its alternatives, provides its answers by processes that are reproducible, accessible to critical examination, and readily modified as new information becomes available. As has been pointed out, however, more is involved than the collection of information and its manipulation in mathematical models. But, whatever approach is used, asking the right questions, inventing ingenious alternatives, and skillfully interpreting the results of the computations and relating them to the many nonquantifiable factors are all part of the analytic process. These steps may prove more helpful in decision-making than thousands of machine computations or a thorough knowledge of sophisticated mathematical techniques.

At the very least, systems analysis can provide a way to choose the numerical quantities related to a weapon system so that they are logically consistent with each other, with an assumed objective, and with the calculator's expectation of the future. But systems analysis, rather than simply supplying solutions that correctly follow from sets of arbitrarily chosen assumptions, aspires to solutions that experience will confirm.

It is our hope that this book has achieved the following purposes:

First, that it has created a favorable attitude toward the use of systems analysis as an aid to decisionmaking. In particular, we would like it to

... persuade a lot of people, including a good many military planners and commanders, that it is appropriate and useful to approach military problems in a "scientific" spirit of inquiry; that the "maxims of war" are not immutable and sacrosanct, but relative, conditional upon circumstances, and subject to analysis; and that even systematic quantitative analysis by civilian scientists can on occasion be helpful in making "strictly" military decisions[3].

Second, that it has instilled just the right amount of skepticism in those who believe that systems analysis or operations research can solve every problem— and just the right amount of belief in those who feel that it can solve none.

The central theme of this book has been that while model building, which is to say quantitative analysis, can assist the decisionmaker, it must be tempered with experience, judgment, and intuition. Analysis cannot entirely replace other approaches, but it *can* help build a framework in which they operate more profitably. It is no magic device to eliminate all uncertainty from decisionmaking, and the systems analyst does not believe that he can read the future or that his models will prove a sure guide to tomorrow. He does believe, however, that to solve successfully the problems of this hazardous world, it is necessary to use all the available resources of experience, of judgment, of intuition—and of analysis.

---

[3] C. J. Hitch, "Economics and Military Operations Research", *Review of Economics and Statistics,* vol. XL, no. 3, August 1958, pp. 199–209.

APPENDIXES

The subject of the analysis described in Appendix A is in considerable contrast to those of the other lectures. In the lunar base problem treated here, experiment and observation must remove many of the uncertainties before any analysis can be used, if ever, to determine an optimum way to put a base on the moon. In the meantime, analysis along these lines can help organize our thinking about a lunar base, determine where some of the problems lie, and suggest directions for research. This appendix also shows how the structure of an analysis of a complex problem can be described in nontechnical language.

We hope that the example in Appendix B is more typical of the systems analysis done in the past than of that to be done in the future.

Appendix A

AN INTRODUCTION
TO THE LUNAR BASE PROBLEM

E. W. PAXSON

In this chapter we consider the problem of establishing a lunar base and illustrate the type of considerations which would have to go into a systems-analytical treatment of such a problem.

A.1. BASES ON THE MOON—PRO AND CON

"Lunar base" in this account means a manned base. We shall not argue the question of whether or not man should be in space. The fundamental philosophical argument is that the basic biological nature of man will force him to such exploration. A variant on a von Kármán definition is also to the point. In comparison with machines, man is a highly flexible servomechanism made cheaply and quickly by an unskilled but enthusiastic labor force.

The proponents of military operations on the moon argue that missile and reconnaissance bases sited there would distribute the enemy's target system clearly in space and also in time, since a missile directed against lunar bases would spend some thirty hours in transit and would be readily detected. Consequently, simultaneity of terrestrial and lunar attack and hence surprise would be made very difficult. This is a deterrence argument. It is also argued that missiles could be launched readily from the moon under one-sixth earth gravity and be guided to targets on earth in the event of war. Also, presumably, the earth would be under continuous observation with a resolution of 50 to 100 feet. The opponents of military bases on the moon consider it inane to take missiles all the way to the moon simply in order to shoot them back. They also argue that at far less cost a highly dispersed system of hardened bases could be set up on the earth.

Setting aside questions of military value, research scientists consider the moon an excellent laboratory. Low gravity, stability, and lack of atmosphere are usually put forth as the primary values. Presumably, experimental work done on the moon would accelerate not only space technology but developments in many aspects of earth technology. Here again, opponents believe that all

332

these advantages could be achieved at a much lower total cost by placing laboratories in space stations orbiting the earth.

Economically, no one considers the extraction and processing of materials on the moon for shipment to earth a paying proposition. However, the moon would serve as an excellent communications relay point and as a meteorological observation post. Tourism is remotely possible, though expensive. The economic arguments are also countered by the orbiting space station proposal.

A final persuasive proposition is the notion that colonies on the moon are essential for future space exploration. In a colony, as distinguished from a base, extraction of materials, production of fuel and power, and fabrication of objects are carried out. Such fabrication, extended to the reproduction of people, is clearly the cheapest way to get men on the moon. Of course, arguing for space exploration and justifying colonies on the moon on this basis replaces the "lunar bases" in the preceding discussion with "planetary bases".

For our purposes, it is not necessary to take sides. It appears much more appropriate to perform a paper analysis of the entire problem. This is not only cheap but, in its own right, supplies information of major value bearing on decisions about lunar bases.

Assuming that an analysis will be performed, one common feature appropriate for a systems model can be abstracted from the military, scientific, economic, and colonial arguments above. In every case the problem is to achieve useful productive man-machine output hours on the moon over and above the effort required for housekeeping. In the military case this clearly means reconnaissance time and missile alert time; in the scientific case, research hours. The interpretation is obvious for the economic and colonial aspects. Consequently, since every systems analysis must have a preliminary criterion, we offer the following formulation: *For any given total sum of money to be expended over a given number of years, what method of setting up, maintaining, and operating a lunar base maximizes the total useful output?*

A.2. SOME ELEMENTS OF ROCKET TECHNOLOGY

For all engines a common index of performance is the specific fuel consumption. This is "the pounds of fuel per hour consumed per pound of thrust achieved". This statement, viewed as a fraction, can be turned upside down and restated as "pounds of thrust achieved per pound of fuel consumed per hour". If we go further and consider pounds of fuel consumed per second as more appropriate for the rapidly exhausted rocket tanks, we end up with a specific impulse. It should be noted that dimensionally the "pounds" in fuel consumed cancel the "pounds" in thrust achieved. Hence, dimensionally, specific impulse is expressed in seconds. For example, a specific impulse of 300 sec is read in complete form as 300 lb of thrust for each pound of fuel per second burned at the rear end.

With this interpretation it is clear that although specific impulse is measured in seconds it has nothing to do with burning time. The latter will be determined by the total amount of fuel carried and burned. If, for example, we are burning 500 lb of fuel per second and are working with a specific impulse of 300 sec, we are getting 150 000 lb of thrust at every instant during the burning time. If 30 tons of fuel are carried, this burning time is two minutes. Now the mass of the rocket in burning changes rapidly because of the great fuel consumption. This decreasing rocket mass times the acceleration at any instant during burning is equal to the constant thrust of 150 000 lb. Consequently, the acceleration of the rocket is not constant but is, in fact, increasing. The velocity the rocket achieves at burnout is proportional to this constant instantaneous thrust and so is proportional to the specific impulse. If fuel of a higher efficiency could be used, so that the specific impulse became 400 sec instead of 300, then, with everything else the same, burnout velocity would be one-third higher. It is for this reason that specific impulse is such a key efficiency index in discussing rocket performance.

There is another reason why specific impulse is a key index. If we fix the desired velocity at fuel burnout, then, simply by increasing the specific impulse, we can decrease the percentage of gross weight which must be carried as fuel and hence, in effect, have a higher payload. This relation is illustrated in Fig. A.1.

At the present time, the specific impulse attainable with chemical fuels is probably no more than 300 sec. Consequently, according to Fig. A.1, with

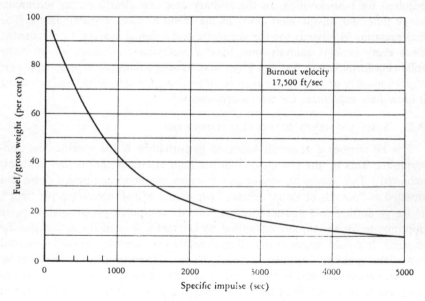

Fig. A.1   Fuel as percentage of gross weight

present rockets, more than 80 per cent of the gross weight is in fuel. The thermodynamic limit on specific impulse for chemical fuels is 400 sec, achieved with hydrogen; for impulses in excess of this, other propulsion systems must be considered. A nuclear system could give specific impulses in the range of 500 to 1500 sec and, in the future, ion rockets ejecting very low mass particles at very high speed may achieve 2000 to 10 000 sec.

What appears to be needed in the propulsion business is a highly efficient nuclear-to-electrical powerplant supplying some fraction of a megawatt per pound of propulsion system. This possibility is clearly far in the future. At present, 10 or more tons are needed per megawatt produced.

The preceding discussion dealt implicitly with single-stage rockets. In multi-stage rockets the lower larger sections are detached after their useful purpose has been served, since otherwise inert weight would penalize further accelera-tion. The cigarette is an ideal example of continuous staging, provided the ashes are removed continuously. Practically, continuous staging would require that the engine and fuel containers be consumed concomitantly as fuel, but this is not yet feasible. As an example of the value of stages, the table below indicates how the ratio of gross weight at take-off to final payload weight decreases as the number of stages increases, for a specific impulse of 300 sec and a burnout velocity equal to escape velocity from the earth.

Stages	Gross weight per payload (1b)
2	600
3	200
4	160
5	140

According to this table, as the stages exceed four the returns become marginal. Even this is chimerical. Hardware penalties result from equipment to connect and to separate stages. Hence, it is likely that the curve implied by this table is flat in the vicinity of three or four stages and then increases.

In their own right, larger vehicles offer certain advantages. Certain com-ponents, such as control equipment, will not increase in weight as the vehicle grows larger. Fuel containers are increasing in volume by something like the cube of a linear dimension, whereas the area, hence the weight, is only in-creasing as the square. In fact, a generalization could be made to the effect that the "best" number of stages is one more than the least number that is required.

It may appear that there are other potential improvements in structure technology. With present design, fuel weight is about nine times the dry weight of the vehicle less payload. Suppose this ratio could be increased to nineteen, using stronger but lighter structures, powerplant, and fuel tanks. This would be equivalent to an increase in specific impulse of only 10 per cent, from 300 to 330 sec. In summary, it is perfectly clear that major R and D effort should be devoted to improving efficiency by obtaining greater specific impulses.

A.3. VARIOUS SYSTEMS

With the above material as a background, let us now consider some of the possible ways to develop vehicle systems for setting up, maintaining, and operating lunar bases. The first possibility envisages a vehicle that takes off from the earth, lands on the moon, takes off again from the moon, and returns a payload to the earth.

Breaking this system down into its parts, suppose first that we wished to get one pound of playload from the earth to the moon. We can use a four-stage rocket whose last stage is retrograde or braking to permit a soft landing on the moon. We establish first the velocity potential which must be available at the earth's surface for this initial half of the mission. The velocity potential is expressed as if it were the total burnout velocity which must be achieved. However, because of the retrograde fourth stage, this will not be the case— hence the phrase "velocity potential". The following table shows roughly the various velocities required, totaled to yield the velocity potential.

Feet per second	Reason
+ 37 000	Escape earth
— 1 000	Earth rotation (fixed eastward)
+ 3 500	Gravity losses
+ 500	Atmospheric drag losses
+ 8 000	Deceleration for lunar impact
48 000 (velocity potential)	

Escape velocity from the earth can be thought of as the velocity an object would achieve falling from a very remote distance to the earth's surface under the increasing gravitational field of the earth. In effect, this fall must be reversed. Next, if we fire east, then, depending on the latitude, we gain something like 1000 ft/sec because of the earth's rotation at the launch site. During the time of burning we must accelerate the weight of the rocket against the earth's gravitational field, and we must also make allowance during this burning phase for the drag of the earth's atmosphere. One of these last two velocity require- ments will increase at the expense of the other, depending on the angle of passage through the atmosphere. But the total is likely to be about 4000 ft/sec. Finally, the retrograde fourth-stage requirement is 8000 ft/sec, representing the escape velocity from the moon. For a four-stage rocket with this velocity requirement, the gross weight at take-off per pound of payload delivered soft on the moon is about 1000 lb if the specific impulse is 300 sec.

The second half of the mission requires us to get each such pound of payload back to the earth. This means that a three-stage rocket made up of what was left from the retrograde fourth stage must leave the moon with one lb of payload. Here the velocity potential required is about 18 000 ft/sec, of which 8000 is lunar escape velocity; the remainder is required to decelerate from near-earth's escape velocity to a satellite velocity which would allow for an atmospheric braking upon return to the earth. There will be, of course, additional requirements in heat dissipation materials. At the moon the gross weight at take-off, per pound of payload, will be about 11 lb. Therefore, to return one lb to earth, 11 lb will have to be taken to the moon. Consequently, it is the product of gross weight at earth by gross weight at moon which gives the total gross weight required for the 1-lb mission. This is 11 000 lb. If the mission is to deliver one ton to the moon and then return it to earth—a plausible payload consisting of a small crew and the ecological equipment needed to survive in space—the gross weight at take-off from the earth would be 11 000 tons. This is a formidable vehicle.

Let us now suppose that fuel is available on the moon, that upon landing we can, in effect, drive up to a filling station. In this case, for the same mission—a one-ton payload on a round trip—the gross weight at earth launch would be only 2000 tons. This saving illustrates that in making a systems analysis of lunar bases, detailed consideration must be given to transporting extractive and processing equipment to the moon for fuel production there.

Transit time to the moon depends very critically on velocity potential as illustrated below.

Burnout Velocity (ft/sec)	Transit Time (days)
40 000	2.4
41 000	1.3
42 000	1.0

These will be hard landings on the moon, perhaps appropriate for certain cargo rockets. From the point of view of manned spacecraft, the longer the transit time the greater the requirement for ecological equipment and perhaps the greater the exposure to radiation and meteoric hazards. To lower the transit time, however, implies an increase in gross weight to achieve the higher burn-out velocity. This is a trade-off which must be built into the analysis.

The above calculations are not only rough but also do not tell the whole story. Consider, for example, the problem of the space artillerist who wants to hit the visible face of the moon with a rocket from the earth. Stringent accuracy requirements are placed on him. He must err no more than 40 ft/sec one way or the other in speed and no more than one-fourth degree in angle. It is evident that further allowances must be made in fuel carried, and hence in gross weight, to permit vernier corrections in the vicinity of the moon. It will be remembered that the Russian Mechta missed the moon by about 3000 mi whereas Pioneer IV missed by 37 000 mi.

As promised, a more detailed formulation of the model for the earth-to-moon direct system will be given. But, there are competing possibilities which clearly must be considered as part of a total analysis. One such system sets up an earth satellite platform from which vehicles are launched to the moon and which accepts these vehicles on return. Figure A.2 illustrates such a system. Analysis of this system will be complicated since a full study of methods of setting up and pricing-out space platforms as a major system charge must be made.

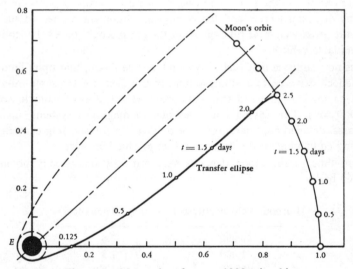

Fig. A.2   Moon shot from a 1000-mi orbit

A third system of considerable promise assumes that in addition to a platform orbiting the earth, a second platform orbiting the moon is etablished. Chemically fueled rockets are used at both the earth and the moon for round trips to the respective space platforms. Between the platforms a nuclear tug is employed. The lunar platform simplifies the rendezvous or trapeze artist's problem for the tug and for a vehicle coming from the moon. In the future, this nuclear tug might have a specific impulse of 1300 sec and gross no more than 10 000 lb. Of course, the system charges in this case will be great. The real advantage will appear only upon amortization of system cost over long-term operation of lunar bases. If only for this reason, the calendar time interval of base operation as a parameter of the study must be permitted to take on large enough values to demonstrate the possible economic gains in such a tug system.

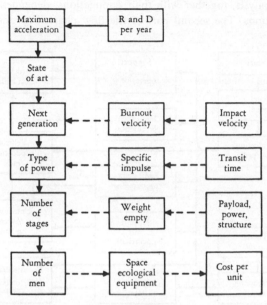

Fig. A.3   R and D

We can now summarize in Fig. A.3 the factors about rocket technology that will enter into the complete analysis as variables partly under design control. For example, we expect future generations of rockets to employ propulsion systems with higher specific impulses. Achieving such improvements will, of course, depend on the state of the art, which in turn will depend directly on the R and D effort expended. Since we are analyzing a dynamic system in which various generations of vehicles will be phased out in favor of following ones, it will be an important question to balance out the economic gains in delaying production in favor of increased research and development.

Within each generation of vehicles there are other design options important to a systems analysis. Transit time and the number of men or amount of cargo to be carried per vehicle are examples. For any generation and any engineering choice of vehicle specifications, a cost per unit will emerge which will also depend, because of an experience curve, on the total number in the production run for a given generation. This, in turn, indicates a trade-off in the analysis between production runs and the number of generations.

A.4. The direct system—the model

Figure A.3 initiates a flow chart formulation of a model for the earth-to-moon-and-back direct flight system of realizing lunar bases. Such flow charts are nothing but systematic means of presenting in verbal terms the various factors in an analysis, together with their connections, dependences, and some of their interactions. The second part of the flow chart, Fig. A.4, shows some

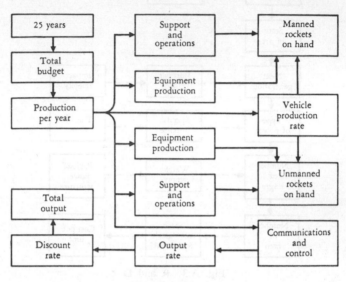

Fig. A.4   Terra

of the factors for terrestrial events. In the upper left-hand corner of Fig. A.4, we find the total time interval under consideration. This should be a parameter. (Twenty-five years is chosen only as an example.) The second fundamental parameter of the analysis is the total budget to be made available for any such total time period. The idea of total budget is important in dynamic systems analyses of posture planning over time. We may well find major gains if we have under our control the determination of a budget stream adding up year-by-year to a total budget, as opposed to expenditure under political constraints determining how much can be spent year-by-year. Of course, constraints other than political ones restrict the possible expenditures per year. There are limits on acceleration in R and D because of personnel and facilities and the competing requirements for them. Equally, because of production lead times, there are constraints on annual expenditure for production. The main point, however, is that the analysis proposes to study various allocations of the total budget year-by-year and the division between R and D and production for each year.

Annual production money will be spent not only on fabrication of manned and cargo rockets at various rates and of various generations, but must also be diverted to meet major charges for support and operations, communications and control, and for equipment that will be needed on the lunar bases. All these things must be kept in balance and hence the analytical form of the model will specify the proportionate shares of production funds that must be diverted, not only year-by-year but at the right years in relation to these other categories. It is worth emphasizing that the decisions we are juggling here are not the decisions made by an executive at his desk. They are, rather, various allocation possibilities which the analyst sets up and computes without prejudice.

Up to this point we have considered the engineering factors in the problem and some of the aspects of budget allocation. Figure A.5 shows the operational

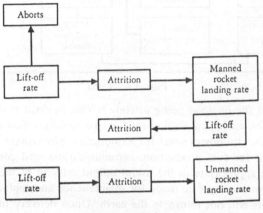

Fig. A.5   Cisluna

phase of the model, which again represents various possible decisions made and results computed by the analyst. He must, for example, within the limitations of available vehicles, available bases, and suitable times for launch, choose various lift-off rates for the manned and cargo rockets. Proper allowance must be made here for aborts and attrition. These allowances are not likely to be trivial.

The main problem in mission planning is scheduling. The right things must arrive at the moon in the right order and in the right proportions. This is equivalent to the problem of planning an invasion. Ships are loaded in reverse order for correct unloading and are scheduled to hit beaches in the right sequence.

We can now assume that the operational choices made in the mission schedule have succeeded in placing men and cargo on the moon. Figure A.6 shows some of the balance or trade-offs to be considered at the moon.

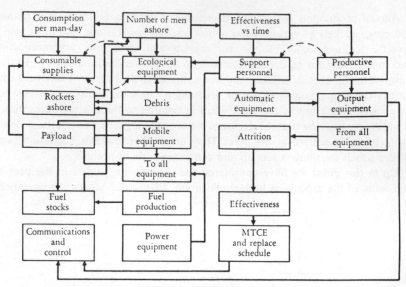

Fig. A.6   Luna

First, look at the payload being delivered. This payload is divided into consumable supplies, ecological equipment for base build-up, fuel stocks for return missions, mobile equipment used for exploration, powerplant equipment, perhaps equipment for fuel production, communications and control equipment, and equipment appropriate to the useful output mission of the base. It will be noted that allowance must be made for maintenance and replacement.

Cargo rockets will not return to the earth. Upon delivery of their payloads, the resulting debris must be put to use. In fact, because of the great expense of delivering a pound to the moon, one measure of the efficiency of the planning will be the size of lunar junk piles. If there is a junk pile, the planning was bad. It follows that cargo rocket design must allow for subsequent use of such structures in ecological and other equipment roles.

The men on the lunar beach at any time will be divided into support and production categories. There may be a balance sought between automatic or unattended equipment and manned equipment. There may be periods when the base operates completely unattended. This possibility minimizes the ecological requirements for the lunar base. The question of length of tour for personnel is of analytic importance because of the requirements that rotation places on additional flights back to earth. This is also a psychological problem because personnel effectiveness falls off with length of tour.

There is a balance between the degree of ecological self-sufficiency aimed for and the amount of consumable supplies brought in. It is possible, for example, to farm hydroponically on the moon, producing a diet of algae and fungi.

Presumably this diet could be enlarged by bringing aboard rabbits and letting them eat the algae and fungi.

One other major balance to be built into the model is the relation between fuel produced on the moon and fuel brought to the moon. In the cargo delivery scheduling, extractive and processing equipment for fuel would be a major item. The analysis must show the worth of such a penalty under amortization.

The question of how many bases there should be and their location on the moon is not shown in Fig. A.6. Additional bases may well be needed not only for the useful output mission implied by lunar occupation but also for exploration and extractive missions. Multiplication of bases, however, aggravates the questions of ecological equipment, power equipment, mobile equipment, and communication and control. But this is another necessary part of the total model.

The total flow chart for this particular system is shown in Fig. A.7. On it we can follow back to the earth the useful output from operation of the lunar base. This effort, at expiration of a certain length of time and after the threshold for support and housekeeping is exceeded on the moon, will appear as an output rate considered valuable back at the earth.

This output, monthly or otherwise, should not simply be added up to give the total return of the system in question. It is probably wise to subject it to a discount rate. It can be argued that research results from the moon achieved in the near future are more valuable than delayed results. Early results may not only lessen the expense of future space technology but may also bring earlier economic returns on the earth. This represents, in effect, increased value which may be capitalized. One balances the value of such early returns against the increased cost of achieving them in the earlier time periods while the state of the art is still primitive. In the military sense the discount rate may be viewed as a weighting factor to be attached at given calendar dates to lunar bases to represent their value. A military value may be that we consider unilateral occupation of the moon by peoples other than ourselves as threatening; or, we may simply choose to attach great value to points made earlier in the psycho-social game. In any event, it is evident that assigning a discount rate is largely arbitrary, that this should be done with great caution, and that various possibilities for it should be considered. The results of an analysis may be thrown violently one way or the other by the choice.

Figure A.8 summarizes the combinatorial choices which the system analyst must take, feed into his model, and compute.

The computation of such models will be made most difficult by lack of hard data in a large number of categories. The thickness of lunar dust and the presence or absence of a lunar ionosphere are only two samples from a large number of unknowns. Nevertheless, it is argued that nothing is lost by initiating a paper analysis. It is quite feasible to bracket unknown parameters in many cases. In fact, in its own right, this is a sensitivity analysis that should be made in any event.

1. CHOOSE — TIME, BUDGET, SYSTEM.
2. ALLOCATE BY YEARS — R AND D/PRODUCTION.
3. CHOOSE — VEHICLE PARAMETERS (EACH GENERATION).
4. BALANCE — SUPPORT/OPERATIONS/COMMUNICATIONS/EQUIPMENT.
5. CHOOSE — LIFT-OFF SCHEDULES.
6. BALANCE — LUNAR SUPPORT EQUIPMENT.
7. SUBMODEL — BASE PATTERN/FUEL PRODUCTION/SUPPLY VS. ECOLOGICAL/AUTOMATIC VS. ATTENDED EQUIPMENT.
8. CHOOSE 2–7 TO MAXIMIZE TOTAL USEFUL OUTPUT.
9. RETURN TO STEP 1 AND REPEAT.

Fig. A.8   Decision pattern

It is also an advantage to do the paper analysis as early as possible so as to uncover the dominant major factors in the problem. This determination is of value in directing and channelling research and development work. It is frequently possible to establish such dominance even in the face of major uncertainties and without the need of a highly detailed and extensive computing program. This may well be the case in the problem under discussion.

The final formulation of a model, for any of the possible systems mentioned to realize a lunar base, should undoubtedly be preceded by one-sided or Robinson Crusoe gaming. This is a paper simulation of the entire exercise designed to bring out perhaps unexpected requirements induced by catastrophe, major or minor, and the like. This, in fact, would be an excellent way to pool the skills of the various experts needed to carry out a study of this nature and would be the best way to build a model with some pretense to completeness, as opposed to the preceding flow charts.

The lunar base analysis introduced in this account is only one part of a total space program and an analysis of such programs. A total program involves preliminary operation of manned and unmanned probes, orbiting innumerable satellites, and perhaps constructing space stations. The total program must also involve extensive research and development in numerous subareas. Such areas include cislunar data; selenological data; astromedicine and biotechnical systems; precise navigation, guidance, and communications; extractive, power, and processing equipment; vehicle design (considering salvage and lunar refabrication); hydroponics; and control equipment, including computers and robots. We should also go as far as possible on earth with full-scale simulation "in the metal" of a lunar base to bring out some of its human and mechanical problems. Above all, research and development in the area of propulsion systems to increase specific impulse is essential.

A MISSILE COMPARISON

E. S. QUADE

B.1. PROLOGUE

One way to give an appreciation of systems analysis is to work through a sequence of examples of different types. The purpose of this appendix is to present an example of a cost-effectiveness comparison simplified to such an extent that the reader can duplicate the analysis.

This example is a fictitious one. However, it resembles the kind of analysis frequently prepared to influence weapon choice[1]. Such studies are not always as well conceived and executed as the example of Chapter 3. The systems analysis here. for example, is deficient in numerous respects. In fact, to simplify the presentation a number of factors that would be given extensive consideration in any real analysis are suppressed. For example, no analysis of the predicted performance of the missiles is included; this at least would be part of an actual analysis. Arguments to support performance predictions and estimates of their accuracy are among the most important factors in a comparison of missile systems. Other factors are not considered that should be—damage to ground installations by enemy action is one of these—but such factors are frequently omitted in real analyses.

Two points might be re-emphasized. First, regardless of its deficiencies, some of which are always present, analysis such as this is usually much better than no analysis at all. Second, because of the nature of the subject matter, the time available, and the context, systems analyses are "good" only in a relative sense. Further examination can always lead to improvement.

B.2. THE EXAMPLE

Assume the following hypothetical situation:

As a consequence of a design competition, two proposals for "next-generation" strategic missiles have been submitted.

The military requirements of the competition specify that the missiles

---

[1] As part of the original lecture course, a similar study was presented as a briefing on the afternoon of the first day. The students were asked to criticize the analysis during workshop sessions. On the final day, their criticisms, plus others supplied by the faculty, were discussed. This example might serve the same purpose.

are to be capable of attaining a certain minimum range and are to be fired, within twenty minutes after being put on alert, from hardened underground bases. These bases are to be located on the North American continent. The two contractors submitting the designs have, as expected, come up with different schemes for the unspecified characteristics, such as propulsion and guidance. This, in turn, leads them to indicate different costs of production and different estimates of accuracy and reliability.

A decision is to be made to develop one of two proposed missiles, the AZTEC or the GRIFFON[2]. The problem is to decide which proposal to support.

We further assume that some analytic group is asked to conduct an evaluation to assist in arriving at a decision.

Although these hypothetical missiles are essentially similar vehicles, both designed to satisfy the same set of military requirements, it is not immediately clear how such factors as a greater accuracy for one should be weighed against a more reliable propulsion system for the other. Moreover, a decision cannot be made properly on the basis of technological considerations alone. Many factors concerned with costs, operations, and logistics are involved— some of which can be quantified, others handled differently or even ignored. All the ingredients must be searched out, the inessential ones eliminated, and the rest brought together into a logical framework in terms of which the various alternatives (for there may be others than the two being explicitly considered) can be examined and a best one chosen. This is the process of systems analysis.

The kind of analysis asked for can take many different forms. We will outline the steps in one approach by presenting it in the form of an informal report, adding questions and answers to bring out points that might otherwise be overlooked.

Let us suppose that the project leader or principal investigator is giving an informal review of his work to the management of his organization to get advice on how to continue. His presentation might be the following.

B.3.   A MISSILE COMPARISON

Our first problem was to decide what evidence would be convincing to the people who must make the decision[3]. It is immediately clear that the superiority

---

[2]   Chapter 12, "Strategies for Development", makes the point that such decisions are, when all the facts are considered, seldom called for at such an early stage.

[3]   This may sound like salesmanship, but if the analyst is going to attempt to substitute another set of values for those held by the decisionmakers, he has an almost impossible task.

of one missile over the other cannot be decided on the basis of performance alone—even if no uncertainties of prediction existed. All our estimates indicate that the GRIFFON, even though it has a more refined and accurate guidance system, will be considerably cheaper to produce. On the other hand, the AZTEC, because fuel storage is easier and its guidance system less complicated and more rugged, will certainly be cheaper to maintain in a state of operational readiness.

To choose between these missiles we must compare them in a context that takes into account these diverse features. To do this, we must somehow model the future environment in which they will be used.

The decision to develop and, by implication, eventually to procure one or the other of these two missiles has already been made. We can take advantage of this fact in our analysis by comparing the two systems as if other types of weapon systems did not exist. We recognize that this is not quite correct, but to consider other vehicles as alternatives would complicate the analysis immensely.

No one can tell us today precisely what the mission of a missile force will be five or seven years from now, when these missiles can be operational. Before we carry out an analysis, however, we need a precise statement of what the missile system is expected to accomplish. It must, of course, be consistent with the general objectives of our military posture. First, we would like to make thermonuclear war unlikely. But, *if* it comes we are interested in limiting damage to ourselves and our allies and in obtaining a favorable military and political outcome. At the same time we would like our missile system to help us achieve our foreign policy objectives. Certainly, as one goal, we hope to convince the enemy that if they attack us they will suffer devastating damage to their civil society. We have chosen to evaluate our missiles in terms of this latter mission, which we think approximates deterrence. That is, we assume that the role of these strategic missile systems is to stand alert, in a hardened posture, making it apparent to the enemy that if he launches an initial surprise attack on this country, the system will respond, destroying such a large portion of his population and industrial centers that he will not consider the attack worth the consequences. What is really important here is not only that we have a high degree of confidence in the capabilities of the system but that the enemy have it as well; the communication of this confidence to the enemy may well depend on the choice of systems. Since these systems are so similar, however, we have not investigated this factor.

Unfortunately for the purposes of analysis, the contribution of a ready missile force to deterrence cannot be precisely measured. It is difficult to decide which aspects are important and how much they contribute. Consequently, we were forced to define the objective even more narrowly, hoping it would remain a satisfactory approximation. The objective for each system is to acquire and maintain the capability of destroying, with a high degree of confidence, at least 80 of the enemy's 100 largest population centers after he makes the first strike. One point should be noted. The target system used for the comparison is not to be construed as a recommended target objective for a strategic campaign in the event that deterrence should fail, nor the number of targets considered or the percentage of destruction required to imply an estimate of the magnitude or type of the strategic bombing effort required for all-out war. The system was chosen merely as a representative base (in range and distribution) upon which the capabilities of the two weapon systems might be compared.

We decided that the system capable of carrying out this mission with the lowest total expenditure of Department of Defense funds should be recommended. Since neither missile is very far advanced in development, not much money has been spent as yet, so there is no great problem of "sunk" funds to influence our choice.

To make the criterion for comparison of these competing systems even more definite, we decided to compare the minimum system costs for each system to accomplish the objective just stated.

The system cost is taken to be the total dollar investment required to develop and procure the system and maintain it in a state of operational readiness for a four-year period. It includes the cost of such items as fissile material, crew training, practice missiles, base construction, hardening, etc. The system cost is, of course, sensitive to such things as the size of the salvo or number of missiles that can be fired at the same time, the rate of fire, and the state of alert.

Each of these missile systems can be based underground and hardened to an equal degree. In the analysis, we have assumed that the bases for both systems are dispersed and hardened to the same standards—making the necessary allowance for differences in dollar costs to do this, of course. Consequently, for the purpose of comparing the two missile systems, we felt justified in further assuming that the effects of enemy attacks on our ground installations could be neglected.

The choice of 100 as the number of targets, 80 as the number to be destroyed, and four years as the cost-base period was arbitrary but does not favor either system appreciably. We did not know this at the start, but later computations using other figures made this apparent.

The cost of maintaining a missile on a launcher ready for firing goes up rapidly with the increase in crews and equipment required to attain either a shorter alert period or a higher rate of fire during combat. An increase in the number of such "ready" launchers tends, on the one hand, to increase the system cost because launching facilities are expensive in comparison with the missiles themselves. On the other hand, it tends to decrease the system cost because larger salvos can be fired and hence a smaller percentage of the salvoed missiles is lost to enemy defenses on each salvo. This phenomenon occurs because the defenses tend to become saturated[4]. To compare these two missile systems, we need to determine for each system the proper number of "ready" launchers required to keep costs at a minimum.

The operational plan we have adopted is essentially the following. The missiles are to be located at dispersed and hardened bases on the North American continent; one missile is to be held on each launcher in ready status. In our cost computations we have arbitrarily used a 20-minute alert period as standard. This is possible with either design although the cost is not equal. After the order to fire is given, as many missiles as possible are to be fired immediately. The launchers are then reloaded and the salvo is repeated.

Enemy defenses against these missiles are assumed to be (1) a control and warning network capable of detecting and tracking a large number of incoming missiles, and (2) a limited number of antimissile installations. Since the terminal phase is the same for both missiles, we have assumed that any antimissile missile that works against one will be equally effective against the other. But, because the effectiveness of an antimissile missile five years from now is anybody's guess, we have made the defense strength a parameter. Although this parameter is assumed to be the same for both missiles, its value affects the optimum salvo size, which is *not* the same for both systems; therefore, the comparison is affected.

To prepare a mathematical model by which a comparison of the system costs of these two missiles can be computed, the steps in a strategic campaign involving them must be thought through and simulated[5]. We first set out to build a complete war-game model and program it for the large digital computer, using Monte Carlo techniques to simulate the behavior at the various attrition barriers. However, we ran into considerable difficulty with this program and are not yet ready to compute. Since the time remaining to us is short, we have decided to go ahead with a simplified version of the detailed model, which uses the average or expected value at each stage in the com-

---

[4] Saturation occurs when such a large number of missiles reach the enemy defenses that all his antimissile weapons are engaged and hence some missiles get through without being fired at.

[5] The purpose in presenting the detail in this campaign is to help clarify the meaning of the term "model". The one presented here is drastically simplified in the interest of illustration. Note some of the unrealistic features: All the complications of defense and damage are compressed into a single parameter; no account is taken of geography, countermeasures, uncertainty of parameters, statistical fluctuation, etc.

putations. We expect eventually to use the full-scale operational gaming model to verify these values.

The sequence of events that a particular missile used in a strategic campaign may pass through is extremely uncertain. Any one of several things may happen to the missile: It or its launching facilities may be destroyed in the enemy's first strike; it may fail at countdown and not be ready for firing at the scheduled time; it may have to be destroyed after takeoff; it may miss the target or hit it and fail to explode; or it may complete its mission successfully. Yet, assuming we know the average values of such uncertain parameters as reliability and accuracy, while the fate of a particular missile cannot be predicted, the fraction of the cases in which each contingency occurs can be forecast with greater and greater accuracy as the number of missiles involved increases. Moreover, we also assume that the fate of an individual missile is essentially independent of the fate of any other. Since the number of missiles involved in these campaigns worked out to be of the order of 600 or more, use of the average or expected value in our computation seems quite adequate. While this is perhaps too great a simplification, it enables us to present early results.

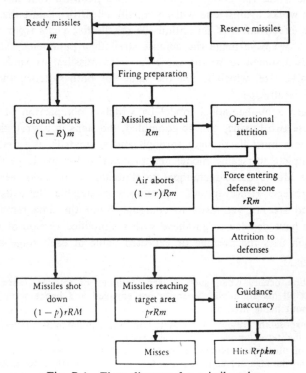

Fig. B.1   Flow diagram for missile salvo

The missile campaign (Fig. B.1) starts with a number of missiles, denoted by m, ready on launchers and standing by on 20-minute alert. When the order to fire is received, final preparations and the countdown begin. It is inevitable that some missiles will not pass all checks and be ready to fire by the scheduled firing time. Any missile that cannot be fired within 15 minutes of the scheduled firing time and is repairable is held for the next salvo (these we call "ground aborts"). Ground aborts are held and not fired singly because enemy defenses are assumed to be essentially 100 per cent effective against a single missile.

Some percentage of the missiles that are fired abort and must be destroyed. The percentage actually fired is represented by R and the fraction of those that are fired and do not abort by r. These two fractions cannot be represented by a single factor because the ground aborts can be repaired and used on a later salvo, while an air abort is a missile expended[6].

We assume there exists a "kill potential", A, which is a measure of enemy defense strength and of the offensive missile vulnerability. This number represents roughly the expected number of missiles that would be shot down by enemy defenses under saturation conditions. The probability that a missile will survive the defenses can then be approximated, for large values of m, by $p = 1 - A/Rrm$. If the number of missiles entering the defense is less than A, all are assumed shot down and $p = 0$. The values of A are assumed to be the same for both missiles. We have parameterized this, using $A = 30$ as a basic case.

Not all the surviving missiles do damage to the target, however. Any function measuring the probability that a target is destroyed by a missile that reaches the target area through all the attrition barriers must depend for its value upon the characteristics of the target, the yield of the weapon delivered, the accuracy of delivery, and the "measure of destruction" at which we choose to call a target destroyed. We adopted destruction of 75 per cent of the target's urban construction as an adequate standard.

Cost estimates for the missile also include the cost of the weapon. We have assumed, of course, that the use of the largest yield weapon consistent with the payload characteristics of the missile leads to the lowest system cost.

The probability of destruction for each target was computed as a function of delivery accuracy obtainable with the particular guidance system employed. For each weapon system a mean value, k, of the various probabilities of destruction for the separate targets was then computed; this was used for all targets interchangeably. The value of k depends on the yield of the warhead as well as the delivery accuracy. In our notation, then, the expected number of destroying hits per salvo can be expressed as $Rrpkm$.

---

6 The percentage that aborts on the ground but cannot be repaired and must be destroyed is included in the computation with the air aborts rather than with the ground aborts.

Since these missile systems provide no means of reconnaissance or damage assessment, to obtain a high confidence that at least 80 of the 100 targets have been destroyed, it is necessary to "overkill", that is, obtain an average of more than one hit per target. Calculations indicate that when the expected number of destroying hits per target reaches two, the assurance that 80 or more of the 100 targets have been destroyed will reach approximately 95 per cent. In our computations we repeated salvos until the expected number of hits per target reached two. The number of repetitions thus gave us the required number of salvos, N.

Knowing the number of salvos, the number of missiles expended per salvo, and the costs involved, we are able to express the over-all system cost for the campaign as

$$C = C_L m + R C_M N m + C_M (1-R)m,$$

where

$C_L = $ the cost, exclusive of the missile itself, of maintaining a missile ready on a launcher;

$m = $ the number of missiles maintained ready on a launcher;

$R = $ the ground reliability factor;

$C_M = $ the cost per missile;

$N = $ the number of salvos.

The first term, $C_L m$, represents the cost of keeping m missiles ready; the second term, $R C_M N m$, represents the cost of the missiles actually fired in N salvos; and the last term, $C_M (1 - R)m$, represents the cost of the missiles that ground abort on the last salvo and are not fired. These cost coefficients include the pro rata share of the costs associated with each weapon system for such items as development, procurement, investment in real estate, and maintenance over the four-year period. They also depend critically on the desired rate of fire and concept of operation.

The values used in our computations are shown in Table B.1.

The mathematical and logical manipulations carried out in this weapon system study necessarily reflect a fairly high degree of abstraction with respect to the real world. In attempting to understand the basic forces at work through the device of a model rather than through actual warfare, the quantities chosen to represent the real world must cover a whole range centered on the "best estimates", so that the sensitivity of the over-all result can be expressed relative to the individual parameters.

Uncertainties in the best estimates for these parameters may arise from (1) random variations; (2) measurement errors; (3) rough approximations of complex features; (4) inability to analyze some factors, such as human performance during thermonuclear war; (5) the actions of the enemy.

Since these uncertainties can be large, small differences between numerical results should not ordinarily be considered significant unless they can be supported by arguments indicating that these differences are in the right direction.

TABLE B.1

Comparison of parameter values and costs of the two missile systems

Item	Missile system	
	GRIFFON	AZTEC
Parameter values		
Ground reliability, R	50%	85%
Inflight reliability, r	80%	80%
Enemy kill potential, A	30 missiles	30 missiles
Mean probability target destroyed by a delivered missile, k	85%	66%
Cost values (millions of dollars)		
Cost per missile, C_M	16.0	22.0
Cost per launcher [a], C_L		
$t = $ 2 hr [b]	75.0	51.0
$t = $ 4 hr	56.6	38.7
$t = $ 6 hr	52.5	35.1
$t = $ 8 hr	50.2	33.8
$t = $ 10 hr	48.6	33.1

[a] Cost of maintaining a missile ready on a launcher to fire within 20 minutes after order.

[b] t is the time required to repeat a salvo.

Let us compare the system cost of these two missiles in terms of firing interval and total length of time required to carry out the required target destruction.

The first comparison, Fig. B.2, shows system cost plotted as a function of the firing interval, t, the number of hours required to reload and fire a second salvo[7]. Since considerably fewer personnel and less equipment are required

[7] *Note for the non-mathematically inclined reader.* To compute the curves of Fig. B.2, it is necessary to determine the minimum value of the system cost, C, for each missile at the values of t listed in Table B.1. To do this by successive

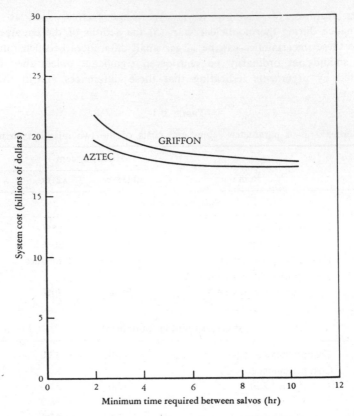

Fig. B.2   System cost as a function of firing interval

___

approximation, we try out a series of values of m in the equations

$$C = C_L m + R C_M N m + C_M (1 - R)m,$$

$$N R r p k m = 200,$$

where the values of the constants C_L, R, C_M, r, k, and A are listed in Table B.1 and $p = 1 - A/Rrm$.

As a sample computation, consider the case of the AZTEC with $t = 6$. We have

$$C = 35.1\,m + 18.7\,Nm + 3.3\,m,$$

$$200 = 0.45\,Nm \left(1 - \frac{30}{0.68\,m} \right).$$

Then for $m = 200$, we have $200 = 90\,N\,(1 - 0.22)$ or $N = 2.85$ and C (for $m = 200$) = $7020 + 10{,}680 + 660 = \$\,18{,}360$ million or $\$\,18.4$ billion. Similarly, for $m = 150$, C = $\$\,17.5$ billion and for $m = 100$, $C = \$\,18.7$ billion. A glance at the curve shows that the minimum occurs somewhere near $m = 150$.

To the reader with a knowledge of differential calculus, it is clear that the value as this interval is increased, C_L and hence the system costs go down. This comparison indicates some, but very little advantage for the AZTEC. However, comparison in terms of the firing interval is not very significant. We are not interested in the firing interval except insofar as it affects the duration of the campaign and thus our ability to fight and win the war.

Figure B.3, which shows system cost plotted as a function of the total time required to carry out the destruction of the 80 targets with the required confidence, indicates a somewhat greater superiority for the AZTEC. For

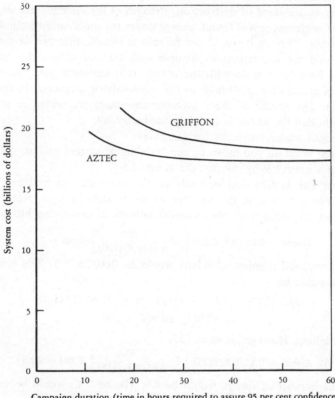

Campaign duration (time in hours required to assure 95 per cent confidence
that 80 of the 100 largest enemy cities have been destroyed)

Fig. B.3   System cost as a function of campaign duration

of m leading to the minimum value of C can be found by differentiation. This is not accidental. The equations were deliberately chosen so as to make this possible— something unlikely to happen in any real analysis.

To obtain the curves of Fig. B.3, the campaign duration is computed by multiplying the firing interval by the number of salvos.

example, at an expenditure of $ 20 billion the curves indicate that the AZTEC could do the job in half the time.

The degree to which a conclusion is sensitive to variations in the estimates or assumptions is important. Certainly a recommendation that the AZTEC should be preferred cannot be made if a combination of parameters equally or nearly as probable as the one assumed does not support that recommendation.

To test for sensitivity the costs were also computed using the same model but making reasonable variations in the basic inputs, such as number and hardness of the targets, standard of destruction, strength of the enemy defenses, etc. No reversal of preferences was found, except under the most extreme combinations of parameters. Though it would not be safe to assume that two or three parameters would not simultaneously assume such extreme values, the causes that affect one have little to do with the others. It is therefore quite unreasonable to assign a probability at all high to the possibility of a reversal in the general conclusion. The results of these investigations therefore served to strengthen our opinion that the AZTEC is certainly the better bet.

The project leader now calls for questions.

Question: What do you mean by the "minimum" system cost at, say, a firing interval of 4 hours? Why not just the system cost?

Answer: The system cost depends on the salvo size as well as the firing interval. For example, if the number of ready launchers, m, were 100, we would have, for the AZTEC, the expected number of destroying hits per salvo:

$$Rrmpk = 0.85 \,(0.8)\,(100) \left[1 - \frac{30}{0.85\,(0.8)\,(100)} \right] (0.66) = 25.$$

Then the required number of salvos would be $200/25 = 8$. The system cost for $t = 4$ would be

$$38.7 \,(100) + 22 \,(0.85)\,(8)\,(100) + 22 \,(0.15)\,(100)$$
$$= 3870 + 14\ 960 + 330$$

or $ 19.2 billion. However, if $m = 135$,

$$Rrmpk = 0.85 \,(0.8)\,(135) \left[1 - \frac{30}{0.85\,(0.8)\,(135)} \right] (0.66) = 40.8$$

and N, the number of salvos, would be 4.9. The cost, C, would become

$$38.7 \,(135) + 22 \,(0.85)\,(4.9)\,(0.35) + 22 \,(0.15)\,(135)$$
$$= 5224 + 12\ 370 + 445$$

or $ 18.0 billion.

This is about the best we can do for $t = 4$. However, the salvo size close to the value that yields the minimum is not very critical. Figure B.4 shows that, for this particular case, the cost is close to the minimum from $m = 120$ through $m = 160$.

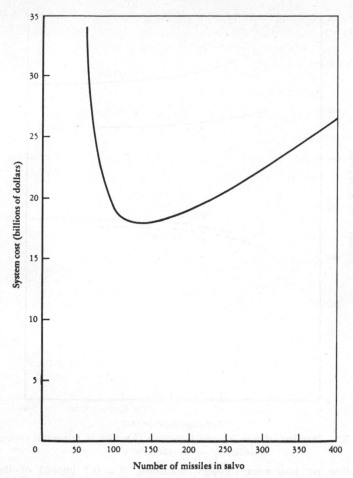

Fig. B.4   Cost versus salvo size (AZTEC, $t = 4$)

Question: Are there large differences in the number of missiles required by the two systems?

Answer: No. The GRIFFON requires both more missiles and launchers than the AZTEC for a campaign of the same duration, but the difference is hardly significant. Figure B.5 shows the estimated number.

Question: I don't understand the ground abort factor. Looking at the cost equation, it appears to me that lowering the value of R would reduce the cost, not raise it.

Answer: This is not the case. If R is smaller, fewer missiles get off and the expected number of targets destroyed per salvo goes down. Let us repeat the

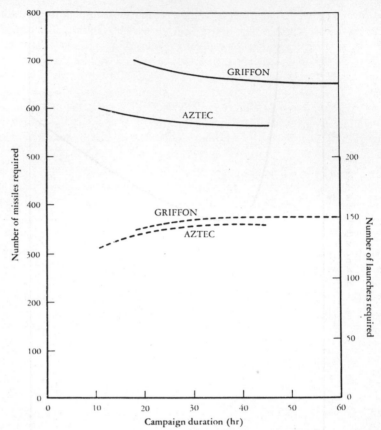

Fig. B.5   Number of missiles and launchers required at minimum system cost
(missiles ———; launchers – – – –)

calculation we just went through, assuming $R = 0.7$ instead of the value
$R = 0.85$, which is our best estimate. This gives us, for $m = 135$,

$$Rrmpk = 0.8\,(0.7)\,(0.35) - 30\,(0.66) = 30.1;$$

hence $N = 6.67$. Again using $t = 4$, we get

$$C = 135\,(38.7) + 22\,(0.7)\,(6.67) + 22\,(0.3) = \$\ 19.9\ \text{billion.}$$

Question: Such a value for R would reverse the curves, would it not?

Answer: Not quite. For this value, the minimum system cost occurs at
$m = 154$. Here the cost is $ 19.7 billion and the time requirement to complete
the campaign is 22 hours. This point still would be below that on the GRIFFON
curve.

Question: Might it not be more sensible to plan to achieve the required
destruction with a single salvo?

Answer: It might indeed, but it would cost more. According to our estimates, using the AZTEC it would take 490 missiles to get the required 200 hits. On the average, it is expected that 74 remain on the ground, 83 are destroyed after take-off, 30 are lost to enemy action, 103 miss, and 200 hit. When there is no requirement to provide a rapid second-salvo capability, the cost of maintaining a ready AZTEC missile drops to about $ 29 million. The over-all system cost with $m = 490$ goes up to $ 24 billion. For the similar case with the GRIFFON, the cost of maintaining a ready missile becomes $ 39.3 million and the corresponding system cost to carry out the required destruction with a single salvo would be about $ 37 billion. The number of missiles required would be 663.

Question: Did you consider something like a salvo and a half? Say, instead of maintaining 663 GRIFFONS in a ready state, why not just enough so that the initial salvo plus a second salvo made up of ground aborts would do the job? Since you expect about 50 per cent to ground abort, these missiles could be used to pick up the targets the first salvo failed to get.

Answer: Yes, this works out fairly easily. Used in this way, 500 would do the job. With 500 ready, on the average, 250 would fire and 200 penetrate to the defenses. Of these, 170 would reach the target area and we would expect 145 hits. For a second salvo, we would then use the 250 which stayed on the ground. Of these, 125 would be expected to fire, 100 to penetrate, and 70 to reach the target. We would thus expect 59 hits or a total of 204. The cost would then be 500 (39.3 + 16) or about $ 27.7 billion.

Question: What action do you think we should recommend on the basis of this work?

Answer: Certainly, if development turns out as we have estimated it will, the AZTEC should be the preferred weapon. The point is, it is too early in the development to be sure. We should make this point and not only say that we prefer the AZTEC but also that both proposals should be continued until we are certain this new propulsion system will work.

Question: How confident are you of these results?

Answer: Considering the uncertainties in some of the estimates, fairly confident. The one really critical factor is the reliability of the AZTEC propulsion system. If the fraction of ground aborts were to go up to around 30 per cent instead of the 15 per cent which we estimate to be probable, then the GRIFFON would show about the same cost. The AZTEC scheme is fundamentally more reliable. There should be fewer air aborts as well, although we assumed 20 per cent for both (in an a fortiori argument). Moreover, if certain improvement in bomb technology came into being in this time period, there should be about a 40 per cent increase in the effective damage radius which can be obtained with the warheads. This would raise k from 0.85 to 0.98 for the GRIFFON and from 0.66 to 0.88 for the AZTEC. In turn, this reduces the cost and the campaign duration by about 7 per cent for the GRIFFON, but by more than twice that for the AZTEC (again in an a fortiori argument).

Our confidence is not based on these numerical comparisons alone. We are well aware that by changing the *model* as well as by errors in the estimates these curves might even be reversed. The point is that working with these missiles in this way has taught us a great deal about them. We are convinced that, as improvements are made, the AZTEC will improve relative to the GRIFFON.

B.4. EPILOGUE

Since the example we have presented is, after all, a hypothetical study about fictitious missiles, it hardly seems sensible to argue too seriously about the validity of the results. Our example suffers somewhat from its fictitious nature, but we hope it illustrates both the failings and the virtues of the systems approach.

What are some of these failings? Because a systems analysis ordinarily deals with the future, as simulated in our hypothetical example, the assumptions are open to challenge. The choice of a strategy or course of action may have to be made (as in the example) on the basis of differences that seem insignificant in the face of uncertainties that exist in the estimation of parameters and the description of environment.

One can always point out possible ways to improve the analysis of the problem. But though it is always easy to do a "better" analysis, it is hard to do a good one.

The objective of an analysis of this type is to help someone decide policy or take action; it is not merely to educate the analyst. It should take little analysis to establish the desirability of developing a missile with promising reliability characteristics, if for no other reason than its use as a hedge against the uncertain future. A good case can be made for allocating funds purely to push development to the stage at which it is possible to predict what the missile's properties will really be—in other words, to buy information. The purpose of putting money into the AZTEC program is not to get a greater operational capability for the strategic force at an early date; if it were, then all the complications of the broad analysis involved in problems of force composition would enter. But the analysis, as formulated in the example, went little beyond comparing the relative military worth of particular development end products, under the assumption that their properties would be essentially as predicted at a stage when the uncertainties involved were very great. The comparisons exhibited are a typical end product of past systems analyses. They tell, given certain assumptions, how much must be spent to do a given job provided things work out as expected. But, to govern policy, some information about risks is needed also.

It is difficult to attribute positive results to a hypothetical study, but since numerous past studies have been like this one in form, we can talk about the virtues of such real studies instead. These have not only thrown light on the questions they were designed to answer but have also produced a good many valuable by-products. Some of these are listed below.

1.   As a result of the organized systematic approach necessary to formulate an analytic study, facts previously unknown or neglected may become obvious. For example, the attempt to formulate the computational model in one early missile investigation showed that no operational plan had even been considered. In the attempt to model one, it became apparent that the logistic problems were so formidable that another alternative could be chosen on this basis alone. Thus, the analytic approach, even before the computation stage, points up the necessity for clearly formulating objectives and focuses attention on those parameters upon which the optimization depends.

2.   Military models even less sophisticated than our example emphasize things many people have found hard to believe. For instance, such models have won acceptance for the fact (always evident in principle) that measures to make missiles less vulnerable might pay off even at the sacrifice of numbers, accuracy, and payload. Moreover, only a few years ago, the ballistic missile was thought to be invulnerable on the ground. Systems analysis has done a great deal to change this belief.

3.   The policy of looking at many factors simultaneously has led to the exposure of overly stringent, and sometimes unrealistic, design requirements— for example, accuracy requirements for bomb fuses. Systems analysis helps to make clear which factors are important and which are not, frequently re-orienting development effort.

4.   A systems analysis provides an excellent environment for thinking up substantially more effective ways to use any weapon system being investigated. Attempts to "beat the model", that is, to find ways to improve the relative standing of particular alternatives, have resulted in inferential or intuitive leaps. Ideas for new hardware or for new ways to operate the old have appeared in this way. For example, an early study of bombers made a great contribution by stressing the importance of air-refueling. What now seems obvious was first made obvious by its presentation in a systems context.

BIBLIOGRAPHY

The literature of operations research is currently growing at an extremely rapid rate. This bibliography lists some works of general and technical value in the field. In addition, the following publications sponsored by the Operations Research Society of America list further references.

A Comprehensive Bibliography on Operations Research, John Wiley & Sons, Inc., New York, 1958.

A Comprehensive Bibliography on Operations Research, John Wiley & Sons, Inc., New York, 1963.

International Abstracts in Operations Research, Operations Research Society of America, Mount Royal and Guilford Avenues, Baltimore, Md. (Published quarterly.)

General

Ackoff, R. L. (ed.), *Scientific Method*, John Wiley & Sons, Inc., New York, 1962.

Ackoff, R. L. and P. Rivett, *A Manager's Guide to Operations Research*, John Wiley & Sons, Inc., New York, 1963.

Hall, A. D., *A Methodology for Systems Engineering*, D. van Nostrand Company, Inc., Princeton, N. J., 1962.

Helmer, O. and N. Rescher, "On the Epistemology of the Inexact Sciences", *Management Science*, October 1959, pp. 25–52.

Hitch, C. J. and R. N. McKean, *The Economics of Defense in the Nuclear Age*, Harvard University Press, Cambridge, Mass., 1960.

Kahn, H. and I. Mann, *Techniques of Systems Analysis*, The RAND Corporation, RM-1829-1 (DDC No. AD-123512), December 3, 1956.

Kahn, H. and I. Mann, *Ten Common Pitfalls*, The RAND Corporation, RM-1937, July 1957.

McCloskey, J. F. and J. N. Coppinger (eds.), *Operations Research for Management*, vol. II, The Johns Hopkins University Press, Baltimore, Md., 1956.

McCloskey, J. F. and F. N. Trefethen (eds.), *Operations Research for Management*, vol. I, The Johns Hopkins University Press, Baltimore, Md., 1954.

McKean, R. N., *Efficiency in Government Through Systems Analysis*, John Wiley & Sons, Inc., New York, 1958.

Peck, Merton J. and Frederic M. Scherer, *The Weapons Acquisition Process: An Economic Analysis*, Harvard University Press, Cambridge, Mass., 1962.

Wellington, A. M., *The Economic Theory of the Location of Railways*, John Wiley & Sons, Inc., New York, 1877.

Wilson, E. Bright Jr., *An Introduction to Scientific Research*, McGraw-Hill Book Company, Inc., New York, 1952.

Technical

Ackoff, R. L. (ed.), *Progress in Operations Research,* vol. I, John Wiley & Sons, Inc., New York, 1961.

Charnes, A. and W. W. Cooper, *Management Models,* vols. I and II, John Wiley & Sons, Inc., New York, 1961.

Churchman, C. W., R. L. Ackoff and E. L. Arnoff, *An Introduction to Operations Research,* John Wiley & Sons, Inc., New York, 1957.

Dantzig, George B., *Linear Programming and Extensions,* Princeton University Press, Princeton, N. J., 1963.

Davis, M. and M. Verhulst (eds.), *Operational Research in Practice,* Pergamon Press, New York, 1958.

Dresher, M., *Games of Strategy: Theory and Applications,* Prentice-Hall, Inc., Englewood Cliffs, N. J., 1961.

Goode, H. H. and R. E. Machol, *System Engineering,* McGraw-Hill Book Company, Inc., New York, 1957.

Hertz, D. B. and R. T. Eddison (eds.), *Progress in Operations Research,* vol. II, John Wiley & Sons, Inc., New York, 1964.

Kaufman, A., *Methods and Models of Operations Research,* Prentice-Hall, Inc., Englewood Cliffs, N. J., 1962.

Luce, R. D. and H. Raiffa, *Games and Decisions,* John Wiley & Sons, Inc., New York, 1957.

Morse, P. M. and G. E. Kimball, *Methods of Operations Research,* John Wiley & Sons, Inc., New York, 1951.

Myer, H. A. (ed.), *Proceedings of a Symposium on Monte Carlo Methods,* University of Florida, John Wiley & Sons, Inc., New York, 1956.

Saaty, T. L., *Mathematical Methods of Operations Research,* McGraw-Hill Book Company, Inc., New York, 1959.

Sasieni, M., A. Yaspan and L. Friedman, *Operations Research: Methods and Problems,* John Wiley & Sons, Inc., New York, 1959.

Williams, J. D., *The Compleat Strategyst,* McGraw-Hill Book Company, Inc., New York, 1954.

A-bomb:
development unknown to B-36 planners, 107
effect on strategic bombing assumptions, 109—110
Absolute scale:
of objective or cost, 85—86
A fortiori analysis:
as basis for recommendation, 173
Air base construction:
fiscal 1952 authorization, 26
Air base planning:
critical location factors, 29, 30
factors affecting decisions, 26
Air bases:
Air Force construction requirements, 112
design constraints, 114
distances to Russian targets, 30
overseas operating vulnerability, 46—48
summary of defense and expected damage, 54—56
types of systems (diagram), 28
vulnerability of U.S. operating, 43—45
See also Base operation systems; Overseas operating bases; Overseas refueling bases; Strategic Air Bases Study
Air Battle Model:
amplified from Strategic Operations Model, 79n
Aircraft:
cost index, 191—193
versus cruising speed, 190—191
subsonic, turbojet-powered cargo, design and cost study, 189—193
See also Bombers; Fighters; Nuclear-powered aircraft; Penetration fighters; Vertical-takeoff aircraft
Aircraft design:
factors affecting flight radius, 30—31
Air defense:
roles in national security, 302
Air-defense system:
problem of design, 9—10

Air Force:
Development Planning Objectives and General Operating Requirements, 111—112
genesis of intercontinental mission, 106—111
nomenclature for real property, 274—276
See also Intercontinental mission
Airplanes:
and fissile material as allocated inputs, 93—99 passim, 101
Air-refueling:
difference between peacetime and atomic wartime requirements, 142
effect on B-36 development, 108
Air strikes:
intercontinental routes, with air-refueling (diagram), 37
Russian defense deployment (diagrams), 39
three penetration routes, 38
Air war:
simulation by model, 78—79
ALGOL, 262
Allocation:
of inputs, 93—99
Alternatives:
appropriate costing of, 322
comparison of, 320
elimination of, 164
evaluated by decisionmaker, 324
invention of, 319
omission of, 162
pitfalls in exclusion of, 301—303
problem of choosing, 160
in systems analysis, 155
See also Objectives
Analogue computers. See Computers
Arms control:
application of systems analysis to, 105
perplexities involved in decisions, 104
relevance of minimax analysis to design, 131
Assumptions:
in computer programming, 254

in design of analysis, 319
effect on decisions, 105
in eliminating alternatives, 302
about enemy behavior, Chap. 10
evaluated by decisionmaker, 324, 325
in model building, 168
in problem formulation, 161—162
producing absurdity, 311
of rational behavior of heads of state
  and military commanders, 131
simplification by, 168
in total force cost analysis, 284
Atomic weapons:
  use of Monte Carlo in design prob-
    lems, 240—241
Attrition:
  affected by designed flight radius, 31
  effect on strategic bombing analysis,
    130
  limitations of models, 133
  1956 Russian strike against U.S.
    targets, 43—44
  reduction by supersonic speed, 141
  rendezvous problems in multiple re-
    fuelings, 33n
Authority:
  as source of objectives, 121—122
Aviation medicine:
  importance in high-altitude flights, 75
Ayres, Col. Leonard P.:
  decision in World War I draft call,
    311—312
Aztec:
  and Griffon, hypothetical missiles,
    compared, 345—361

B-29:
  and the B-36, interservice contro-
    versy, 108
  in 1943, 107
  in 1951 strategic bombing force, 25
B-36:
  and the B-29, interservice controversy,
    108
  factors influencing design, 107—110
    passim
  history of, 106—111
  interservice controversies and inves-
    tigation, 125
  jets added to design, 135
  1949 Navy-SAC controversy, 307

in 1951 strategic bombing force, 25
post-World War II considerations,
  108—110
specifications, 107
B-47:
  alternative systems for basing, 55,
    56—57
  cost of campaigns (graph), 40
  costs for increments of radius, 33
  flight radius design questions, 31
  minimum-penetration routes pre-
    ferred, 38
  prototype in 1951, 25
B-50:
  in 1951 strategic bombing force, 25
B-52:
  cost of base facilities, 267
  in design stage in 1951, 25
B-58:
  "supersonic dash" in design, 141
Base operation systems:
  contingency planning, 142—147
  cost of base defense, 42
  inferiority of exclusively air-refueled,
    41
  routes preferred, 38
  programmed for 1956, 27—28
  See also Overseas operating bases;
    Overseas refueling bases
Battle of Britain:
  British assumptions about German
    objectives, 132
Blackett, P. M. S.:
  quoted, 227
Blackstone, Sir William:
  on excessive penalties and proba-
    bility of crime, 128-129
Bombers:
  air- versus ground-refueling, 32—37
  attrition in multiple refuelings, 33n
  component structure for (table), 277
  cost versus combat radius (graph), 32
  development analysis, 14
  flight radius, 30—31
  formation operations analysis of
    World War II, 14, 19
  in 1956 base operation system, 27—28
  nuclear-powered, 114
  types of base systems (diagram), 28
Bombing systems:
  air-refueled multistage, 33

Bombsight procurement:
example of criteria selection, 84
Boost-glide system:
cost sensitivity to warhead weight, 291
Break-even analysis:
as basis for recommendation, 173
Budget:
as a constraint in criteria selection, 86
Burnout speed:
as a performance parameter, 183
of single-stage rocket, 185
and specific impulse, 334
of two-stage rocket, 185

Calculus:
case study of new abstract tool, 248
Civil defense:
considered in developing strategic force, 120
COBOL, 262
Cold war:
policy of deterrence, 119
Combat radius:
and combat losses, 31
and cost of bombers (graph), 32
effects on system weight or cost, 33
extended by refueling bases, 33
See also Flight radius
Common law:
excessive penalties and probability of crime, 128—129
Communications:
between space ships, 186—187
Complexity:
as problem of analysis, 105
Computers:
aid to intuition and understanding, 80
an analytic tool, 252
and application of linear programming and Monte Carlo, 246
assumptions in programming, 254
attributes of, 250
capabilities of, 255
as central element of model, 78
compilers (generators), 262
and decisionmaking, 245—246
disadvantages of, 252—253

distinction between analogue and digital, 250
estimate of time involved in running problems, 254
and gaming and simulation problems, 253—258
human factors affecting results, 77
IBM 704, 78
increasing significance of, 328—329
the language mismatch, 260—262
limitations in problems of national security, 246
machine language, 260—262
and optimization, 252
pitfalls in model building, 254
problem formulation, 258—260
programming the model, 253—258
and sensitivity studies, 252
size and cost of routines, 258
speed and cost superiority, example, 250—251, 252
in systems analysis, 65
tool of operations research, 238
a typical short routine, 255—256
used to determine optimum values, 76
in war gaming, 219
Conflict:
introducing uncertainties in analysis, 152
Conflict system design:
application to national defense and arms control, 105
appraisal of ends and means, 121—122
assumptions about enemy behavior, Chap. 10
consideration of enemy objectives and capabilities, 129—135
continual evaluation of objectives, 116
contribution of models, 169
derivation and modification of objectives, 120—122
deterrence as objective, 122—129
development problems, 133—134
distinguished from model building, 104
enemy resource constraints, 133
exploitation of difference between peace and atomic war, 141
functions of inventiveness, 140

guidelines for strong design, 141
high-confidence objectives of U.S. and
    enemy, 135—136
history of B-36, 106—111
hypothetical missiles, Aztec and Grif-
    fon, compared, 345—361
interdependence of objectives, 117
likelihood of irrationalities and ra-
    tional behavior, 131—133
limitations of game theory, 130
objectives and constraints in,
    111—117
precepts, 319—322
reducing uncertainty, 229
term explained, 129n
uncertainties as to enemy capabilities
    and intentions, 133, 134
uncertainty and the framing of work-
    able objectives, 136—139
Consumers' research:
type of analysis function, 81, 90
Context:
of systems analysis, 20—21
Contingencies:
evaluated by decisionmaker, 325
Contingency analysis:
defined, 172—173
Contingency planning:
base operation systems, 142—147
See also Hedging
Cost analysis:
categories for individual systems
    (table), 272—273
cost elements of equipment com-
    ponents (table), 278
cost sensitivity analysis, 288—293
equipment components, examples
    (table), 277
framework of cost analysis categories,
    271—272
incremental costing, 267
of individual systems, 269—282
investment costs, 273—280
major characteristics, 299
operating costs, 280—281
preliminary calculations, 264
presentation of results, 293—299
presentation of system costs by cost
    categories (table), 295
primary purpose, 268
problem of uncertainty, 265

research and development cost cate-
    gories (table), 282—283
research and development costs,
    281—282
selection of descriptive material and
    data, 270
specialized equipment, examples
    (table), 278—279
system costs time phasing (graphs),
    274
system specifications and assumptions,
    examples (table), 270—271
time phasing of costs, 267
of total force structures, 283—288
weapon systems, Chap. 15
See also Total force cost analysis
Cost-effectiveness analysis, 9
Costs:
accuracy of estimates, 228
considered in choice of alternative,
    161
cost sensitivity analysis, 288—293
defined, 266
determining criteria, 81—82
estimates evaluated by decisionmaker,
    323
fixed inputs, multiple objectives,
    93—97
fixed inputs, one objective, 92—93
a guide to choice among alternatives,
    322
as a guide to choice of objective, 304
impact of alternative courses, 87
as imposed constraint, 161
mathematical expression of, in hypo-
    thetical missiles comparison, 352
ratio of achievement-of-objective to,
    85
relevance to systems analysis, 92
selection for consideration, 99
sources of error in criteria selection,
    86
"spill over" to other operations, 98
in systems analysis, 155
variable input supplies, 97—102
wrong concepts of, 88
See also Dollar cost; Investment
    costs; Money costs; Operating
    costs; Production costs; Real costs;
    Research and development costs;
    Total activity cost

Cost sensitivity analysis:
applied to strategic mission, 293, 294
electronic data processing, 289
examples of, 289—293
iterative process, 293
problems of uncertainty, 293
uses and advantages of, 293
Cost streams, 267
Counter-countermeasures:
in conflict situations, 320
Counterforce campaigns:
in defense of SAC, 60—61
Countermeasures:
in conflict situations, 320
Criteria:
applied to wrong problems, 89—90
choice of, in problem formulation, 157
in choosing alternatives, 160
cost and objectives as factors, 82
dangers of incomplete, 95
determination of, 303—304
dominance in comparing tests, 90
effect of development policies on selection, 89—90
effect of procurement policies on selection, 89—90
effect of suboptimization, 83—85
evaluated by decisionmaker, 324
example, bombsight procurement, 84
example, machine gun procurement, 84—85
overdetermined tests, 88—89
and problems of measurement, 82
rules for choosing, examples, 160—161
selection of, 18—19
some common errors, 85—90
in systems analysis, 155
test of preferredness, 81
time as a factor in selection of, 88
ways to avoid errors, 90—91
See also Proximate criteria

Dam construction:
as example of effect of budget constraint, 101
Decision:
based on analysis, evaluated by decisionmaker, 323
See also Development decisions

Decisionmakers:
and computers, 245—246
as consumer of systems analysis, 11
continual evaluation of objectives, 116
as factor in war gaming, 220
included in model, 76—77
and missile development decision (model), 229—232
questions to clarify evaluation of analysis, 322—325
and systems analysis, 318
value of systems analysis to, 104
Decisionmaking:
allocation of, 83
as an art, 176
Defense:
active, for overseas operating bases, 50—51
of air bases and neighboring cities, 117—118
broad objectives in developing strategic force, 120
combined active and passive for overseas bases, 51
deployment of forces, 22
of operating bases, study conclusions, 54—56
of overseas refueling bases, 52—54
passive, for overseas operating bases, 48—50
of strategic missiles, 118
of a strategic wing, 113
See also Air defense; Civil defense; National defense; Passive defense
Defense deployment:
Russian, against air strikes (diagrams), 39
Delphi technique:
in systems analysis, 163
Department of Defense:
multiplicity of decision alternatives, 104
Design:
of the analysis, 319
defense contractors' problems, 112—117
requirements and trade-offs, 193
selection of performance requirements, 135
See also Conflict system design

Deterrence:
  and assumptions about enemy behavior, 199
  cold war rationale, 119
  considered in contingency planning, 147
  effectiveness dependent on plausibility, 128—129
  effect of Strategic Air Bases Study on U.S. policy, 62—63
  high-confidence measures of U.S. and enemy, 135—136
  invulnerability of SAC, 124
  1951 U.S. objective, 25
  as objective in intercontinental mission, 122—129
  overlapping the objective of waging war, 127
  policy clarified by systems analysis, 126
  role of strategic missile systems, 347—348
  and strategy choice, 214—215
  tests in comparing policies, 90
  traffic violations, example, 123, 128, 129
  value of mutually unsatisfactory strategies, 135—136
Deterrence policies:
  time dimension as a factor, 88
Development decisions:
  cost of reducing uncertainty, 234—235
  differentiated from procurement or operational decisions, 227
  establishment of degree of uncertainties, 233
  importance of uncertainties, 228
  responsibilities of analyst, 232
  selection of appropriate strategy, 229
  trade-offs among parameters, 236
  uncertainty factors considered in analysis, 232
  uncertainty reduced in course of development, 235—236
  ways to reduce uncertainties, 234
Development policies:
  effect on criteria election, 89—90
DEW:
  evaluation of, 210
Digital computers. See Computers

Disasters:
  systemic, extra-systemic, and political, in contingency planning, 144—145
Distant Early Warning. See DEW
Doglegging:
  to avoid enemy defense, 37
Dollar cost:
  changes in price level, 266—267
  as a measure of economic resource cost, 266
  in weapon systems cost analysis, 266
Dominance:
  in comparing tests for criteria, 90
Dominant system:
  in choosing preferred strategy, 17
Dynamic programming:
  aid to intuition, understanding, 80
  technique for submodels, 168
  tool of operations research, 238

Einstein, Albert:
  first papers rejected, 247
  his equation ($E = mc^2$), 182
Enemy defense:
  assumptions about enemy behavior, Chap. 10
  cost to U.S. of penetrating, 37—41
  deployment against air strikes (diagrams), 39
  effect on U.S. offensive systems, 130
  effect on U.S. programs, 62
  against missiles, 349
  operations analysis of, 38—39
  three penetration routes, 38
  uncertainties, 57—58
Enemy offense:
  assumptions about enemy behavior, Chap. 10
  effect on second-strike capability, 126
  effect on U.S. programs, 62
  1950 capacity against U.S. strategic force, 125
  omission from earlier strategic studies, 130
Enemy reactions:
  evaluated by decisionmaker, 325
Energy:
  released from rocket fuel, 182
Energy release divided by annihilation energy ratio:
  state-of-the-art parameter, 183

Engineering:
 differentiated from systems analysis, 152
Enthoven, Alain C.:
 quoted, 155, 249
Escalation:
 considered in development of strategic force, 119
Escape velocity:
 from the earth, 336
 from the moon, 337
Expected outcomes:
 in choosing preferred strategy, 17

Fighters:
 component structure for (table), 277
 penetration. See Penetration fighters
Fire control systems:
 design problems, 113
First-strike capability:
 considered in contingency planning, 146
 and development of second-strike capability, 125
Fissile material:
 and airplanes as allocated inputs, 93—99 passim, 101
 requirements in air-refueled system, 36
Flight radius:
 design factors, 30—31
 See also Combat radius
Flyaway kit:
 design of, 151
 difficulties of input data on contents, 164
Flying saucers:
 Martian analysis, 74—75
Force composition and development:
 analytic techniques in decisions, 14
 assumptions about enemy behavior, Chap. 10
 factors of uncertainty, 26
 in total force cost analysis, 283—284
 use of expert intuition in analysis, 23
FORTRAN, 262
Fuel-weight to gross-weight ratio:
 effect of increase in specific impulse, 334
 and rocket burnout speed, 185
 state-of-the-art parameter, 183

Games:
 value of, as models, 166
 See also Mathematical games; War gaming
Game theory:
 aid to intuition and understanding, 80
 application to tactical problems, 245
 contribution to operations research, 243—245
 insight on deploying defenses, 22
 limitations of, in analysis, 130
 in model building, 18
 tool of operations research, 237
 See also Mathematical games; War gaming
General Operating Requirements:
 hypothetical, for bombers, 111—112
Griffon:
 and Aztec, hypothetical missiles, compared, 345—361
Gross-weight to payload ratio:
 effect of increase in number of stages, 335
 round trip to moon, 337
 for soft landing on moon, 337
 of three aircraft, 191
 typical of transportation systems, 186
Ground refueling:
 difference between peacetime and atomic wartime requirements, 142

Headquarters USAF:
 briefed on strategic air bases, 24
Hedging:
 in B-36 development, 111
 B-36 after Hiroshima, 108
 B-36 in 1941, 106—107
 B-36 in 1943, 107
 B-36 in 1945, 108
 considered in developing objectives, 139
 See also Contingency planning
Helmer, Olaf:
 quoted, 150
High-confidence measures:
 minimax as response to assumed opposing strategy, 135
 as a powerful deterrent, 135—136
Hitch, Charles C.:

quoted, 161, 303—304, 326—327, 329—330
Human mind. *See* Intuition; Judgment

IBM 704:
  used in air war model, 78
IBM 709:
  used in air war models, 79n
ICBM. *See* Missiles
"Ideal kill potential":
  in Rand analyses of air defense, 137
IL-28:
  U.S. bases within flight radius, 61
Incremental costs:
  in evaluating future alternatives, 305
  and phase-in phase-out relationships (graphs), 284
  in total force cost analysis, 284—285
Indochina:
  probability of use of U.S. nuclear weapons, 128
Infinitesimal calculus:
  case study of a new abstract tool, 247—248
Inputs:
  allocations of, 93—98
  alternative combinations of, 93—94
  assumed to be free, 99
  determined by judgment, 164
  effectiveness of the weapon, 223
  establishment of, in war gaming, 222
  locale or context, 222
  of missiles comparison model, 66
  operating characteristics of the weapon, 223
  substitution, 94—98
  variable, 97—102
  weighted, 99—100
Intelligence information:
  affecting enemy behavior and ours, 204
Interceptor armament:
  evaluated in systems context, 20—21
Intercontinental mission:
  as example of divergence of objectives, 123—129
  genesis of, 106—111
Intuition:
  analysis tools as aid, 80
  in analysis of uncertainties, 234
  conditioned by assumptions, 105

  in detecting errors, 310
  effect on computer results, 77
  in evaluation by decisionmaker, 325
  in military decisionmaking, 320
  in play of games, 224
  in problem formulation, 319
  in problem solving, 21—22, 72
  and scrutiny of constraints, 116—117
  in selection of criteria, 90
  as source of objectives, 121—122
  supplemented by systems analysis, 329
  in systems analysis, 154
  utilized through simulation, 167
Investment costs:
  defined, 273
  equipment, 276—279
  initial training, 279
  installations, 274
  miscellaneous investment, 280
  other equipment, 279
  primary mission equipment, 276
  specialized equipment, 278
  stocks (supplies), 279
  in total force cost analysis, 288
"It's-Hotter-in-the-Combat-Zone Principle," 141

Joint optimization:
  Atomic Energy Commission and customers, 98, 99
Judgment:
  in analyses, 153
  in analysis of uncertainties, 234
  of analyst, evaluated by decisionmaker, 324
  based on optimization, 322
  in cost analysis, 268
  in determining inputs, 164
  as factor in war gaming, 220, 221
  in interpretation and recommendation, 314
  in interpretation of rules of war games, 224
  in military decisionmaking, 320
  in model building, 77
  in play of games, 224
  in preparing inputs, 223
  in problem formulation, 162, 319
  reliance on, 176
  supplemented by systems analysis, 329

in systems analysis, 154

Kahn, H., and I. Mann:
quoted, 80, 173, 306, 308, 309
Korea:
probability of use of U.S. neclear weapons, 128

Linear programming:
aid to intuition and understanding, 80
application to network problems, 239
application to transportation problems, 239
application of, 240
extensions of, 240
in petroleum and transportation industries, 106
technique of operations research, 238—240
tool of operations research, 237
Locality costs:
in air base planning, 29, 30
Location costs:
in air base planning, 29
Low-confidence measures:
as exploitation of uncertainty, 136
inert strategies in developing, 135
value of, 136
Lunar base problem:
additional bases, 343
composition of payload delivered to moon, 342
direct flight system—the model, 340—344, 577—587
effect of research and development, 339
formulation of analysis problem, 333
pros and cons, 332—333
research and development (diagram), 339
Robinson Crusoe gaming, 344
satellite platforms, earth and moon, 338
some elements of rocket technology, 333—336
tour of duty for personnel, 342
transporting extractive and processing equipment, 337
various vehicle systems, 336—339

Machine gun procurement:
example of criteria selection, 84—85
Machine language:
assembly routine, 262
Mann, I., and H. Kahn:
quoted, 80, 173, 306, 308, 309
Massive retaliation:
effectiveness dependent on plausibility, 128—129
Mathematical games:
limited application in war gaming, 218
Mathematical program:
defined, 238
Mathematics:
game theory, 243—245
linear programming, 238—240
Monte Carlo, 240—243
role of, 246—249
in systems analysis, 65
Methods and procedures:
a fortiori analysis, 173
basis for recommendations, 174
break-even analysis, 173
contingency analysis, 172—173
cost of inquiry, 165
Delphi technique, 163
explanation by models, 165—173
formulation of problem, 156—164
gaming, Chap. 11
interpretation of solution, 173—176
operational gaming, 163
problem of choosing alternatives, 160
problem of choosing objectives, 159—160
reliance on expert judgment, 162—163
rules for choosing criteria, examples, 160—161
scientific method, 150
search for relevant data, 164—165
sensitivity analysis, 172—173
stages of analysis, 156
diagram, 158
MiG:
U.S. bases within one-way flight range, 61
Military planning:
pitfalls in systems analysis, Chap. 16
Military worth:
effect on input allocation, 93

maximization of, 82
Minimax system:
  in base operation systems, 144
  in choosing preferred strategy, 17
  matching of move and countermove, 131
Missile-defense system:
  problem of choosing, 8
Missiles:
  aborts, 351
  bases on moon, pros and cons, 332
  calculation of a trajectory for, 250—251
  comparative costs of campaigns, 71—72
  component structure for (table), 277
  cost of accuracy requirement, 72—73
  cost of maintaining launching facilities, 348—349
  cost sensitivities and insensitivities, 289—291
  cost sensitivity to component reliability, 291
  effect of reliability increase, 72—73
  enemy defenses against, 349
  exclusion of alternatives by specifications, 305
  flow diagram for salvo, 350
  hypothetical comparison, 345—361
  kill potential, 351
  measure of destruction, 351
  mission of force, 347—348
  model demonstrating development decision, 229—232
  model used in computing comparisons, 66—67
  over-all system cost for campaign, 352
  overkill, 352
  probability of target destruction, 351
  saturation of defense, 349
  strategic, defense of, 118
  targets per salvo, 73
Model building:
  aggregation of quantifiable factors, 70—72
  assumptions, 168
  compromises in, 320
  computer applications, 258
  and computer programming, 253—258

determination of relevant variables, 71
distinguished from conflict system design, 104
factors to be considered, 166—169
human judgment in, 77
omission of factors, 69—70
omission of variables, 169
pitfalls, 254
  in compromises, 311
and programming, 257, 258—259
quantifiable factors, 69—73, 169—170
and the real world, 73—77, 79
reduction to logical flow diagram, 312
relevant factors, 68—69
round trip to moon, direct flight system, 340—344
rules for, 285
uncertainties, 170—172
Models:
  air attrition, 133
  in aviation medicine, 75
  capabilities and limitations, 79
  computer example, 78—79
  and computers, 253—258
  dangers in oversimplification, 309—310
  defined, 68, 165
  design of, 168
  detailed treatment deferred, 319
  in development decisions, 232
  evaluated by decisionmaker, 325
  features of, 75—76
  function of, in analysis, 103
  in hypothetical missiles comparison, 349—356
  mathematical example, missiles comparison, 66—67
  of missile duels, empirical content, 130
  Monte Carlo type, 78
  obsolescence, 313
  in petroleum and transportation industries, 106
  pitfalls connected with, 309—314
  primary function of, 167
  and the real world, 80
  relative importance of, in analysis, 319—320

round trip to moon, direct flight system, 340—344
simulation, 166—167
solutions indicating extreme strategies, 315
in systems analysis, 155
tailored to fit the question, 74—76
testing by experiment and workability, 168—169
time parameters, 18
"universal," 312—313, 320
value of games, 166
vulnerability of a runway, 140
See also Model building; Strategic Operations Model
Money costs:
affected by regulatory measures, 100
in estimating production costs, 100
as measures of real costs, 100
and real costs, 92
substituted for real costs, 99
Monte Carlo:
aid to intuition and understanding, 80
applications in operations research, 241
and design of atomic weapons, 240—241
distinguished from random sampling, 240
illustration of method, 241
technique of operations research, 240—243
techniques in machine war gaming, 219
tool of operations research, 237
used in operations research and physics, 241, 243
Moon base. See Lunar base problem
"Multiple-Use Principle":
in contingency planning, 145

National defense:
application of systems analysis to, 105
considered in developing strategic force, 120
National security:
importance of strategic force posture to, 300
roles of air defense in, 302

Network problems:
and linear programming, 239
Newton, Sir Isaac:
and acceptance of infinitesimal calculus, 248
"New toolism":
occupational disease of operational researchers, 106
"Nth country":
effect on design of strategic forces, 126
Nuclear-powered aircraft:
design problems, 114—116
Nuclear reactions:
and released energy, 182—183
Numerical analysis:
limitations of, in operations research, 241, 242

Objectives:
achievement of, ratio to cost, 85
changed by systems studies, 157
continual evaluation of, by decision-makers and analysts, 116
derivation and modification of, 120—122
of design, 313
determination of, 303—304
in war gaming, 220—221
determining criteria, 81—82
in development of the B-36, 111
effect of analysis, 126
elimination of, 159
of enemy, 129
impact of alternative courses, 87
interdependence of, 117
maximization of military worth, 82
methods of determining, 136—139
of missile force, 347—348
problem of choosing, 159—160
selection of, 18—19
source of error in criteria selection, 86
in systems analysis, 155
See also Alternatives
Operating costs:
equipment and installations replacement, 280
fuels, lubricants, and propellants, 281
maintenance, 280
pay and allowances, 280

services and miscellaneous, 281
in total force cost analysis, 288
training, 281
Operational gaming:
in systems analysis, 163
Operational variables:
effect on models, 67—68
of missiles comparison model, 67—68
Operations analysis:
and derivatives, 3
essential elements, 13—14
in World War II, 6, 13
Operations research:
analytic tools, 237—238
handicapped by novelty, 247—249
assumptions about enemy behavior,
Chap. 10
contrasted to systems analysis, 7
cost as a guide to choice of objective,
304
distinguished from systems analysis,
153—155
dynamic programming, 167
and engineering, 151—153
future use in national security problems, 328—329
game theory, 243—245
hypothetical missiles, Aztec and
Griffon, compared, 345—361
limitations and value of, 326—328
linear programming, 238—240
mathematical technique, 167
methods of science, 150
Monte Carlo, 240—243
need for elementary economic principles, 304
optimization in component studies,
167
queuing theory, 167
and science, 149—150
simulation, 166—167
See also Systems analysis
Optimization:
in component studies, 167
possibility of error, 322
"shadow prices" as by-product of, 97
See also Joint optimization
Optimization procedures:
reason for the inadequacy of, 80
Outputs:
of missiles comparison model, 66

Overseas operating bases:
active defense, 50—51
allocation of budget, 60
compared with overseas refueling
bases, 41—42
cost of operations, 41—42
passive defense measures, 48—50
vulnerability, 46—48, 52—54
Overseas refueling bases:
compared with overseas operating
bases, 41—42
cost of operations, 41—42
defense of, 52—54

Parking lot:
policy, as example of criterion choice,
160
size and pricing policy criteria, 98
Passive defense:
changes within a base, 50
multiplying operating bases, 48—49
relocation of operating bases, 49—50
of strategic bases, 117
of a strategic wing, 113
See also Defense
Pearl Harbor:
example of improbable combination
of events, 313—314
hindsight recommendation on aerial
reconnaissance, 135
U.S. deployment of reconnaissance,
1941, 131—132
Penetration fighters:
in ground-refueling system, 62
programmed for 1956, 35
Penetration problem:
and specifications for nuclear aircraft,
116
"supersonic dash" solution, 141
Performance parameters:
burnout speed, 183
defined, 179
in development analyses, 228
speed, 179—184
Petroleum industry:
linear programming in, 106
Philippine bases:
U.S. assumptions before Japanese
attack, 132
Pitfalls:
in explanation by models, 309—314

in formulation of problem, 301—307
in interpretation of solution, 314—316
in search for relevant data, 307—309
Preference schemes:
in contingency planning, 147
Problem formulation:
for computers, 258—260
evaluated by decisionmaker, 323
Procurement policies:
effect on criteria selection, 89—90
Production costs:
relevance to variable inputs, 97
substitution of estimated money costs, 100
Programming:
assumptions in, 254
building the routine, 255
debugging the routine, 258
estimate of time required, 254
loss of generalization, 254
making up the flow chart, 256—258
and model building, 257
monitoring in the routine, 255
pitfalls in model building, 254
size and cost of routines, 258
a typical short routine, 255—256
See also Computers
Project leader:
evaluated by decisionmaker, 323
Property:
Air Force nomenclature, 274—276
Proximate criteria:
inevitability of, 82—83
source of errors, 85

Quantification:
assumptions about enemy behavior, Chap. 10
extent of, 25
in model building, 169—170
Queuing theory:
technique for submodels, 168
tool of operations research, 238

Radar:
component structure for (table), 277
Radar equation, 188
Radar problem, 188
Radiation dose:
as constraint in bomber design, 112, 114

RAND Corporation:
approach to systems analysis, 79
determination of cost coefficients, 71
example of war game, 76—77
"ideal kill potential" in air defense analyses, 137
lectures on systems analysis methods, V, 11
Martian counterpart of, on flying saucers, 74—75
methods of cost analysis, Chap. 15
position on modern abstract techniques, 249
presentation of total force cost estimates, 298—299
role in developing systems analysis, V
Strategic Operations Model, 78—79
study of moves and countermoves, 131
See also Strategic Air Bases Study
RAND costing structure. See Total force cost analysis
Random numbers:
tool of operations research, 238
Real cost:
allocations of inputs to minimize, 93
alternatives for derivation of, 99
defined, 92
fixed inputs, multiple objectives, 93
of input considered zero, 95
inputs specific to one use, 92
and money costs, 92
Recuperation:
after A-bomb attack on air base, 51
Refueling:
air- versus ground-, 32—37
air- and ground-, comparative costs, 34
graph, 35
Refueling bases:
to extend bomber radius, 33
sensitivity to first strike, 126
See also Overseas refueling bases
Regulatory measures:
relevance to operations researchers, 100
Reliability:
choice of appropriate criterion, 196
discussion of consequences of engine failure, 193—196

effect of increase in, 72—73
as technological consideration,
193—197
Research and development:
difficulties of costing, 273
effect on lunar base problem, 339
estimation of time and cost, 184
rising costs of, 266
selection of development strategy, 236
value of analysis in, 321
post-World War II, 227
See also Development decisions
Research and development cost:
categories (table), 282—283
defined, 281
implications for military budget management, 282
in total force cost analysis, 288
uncertainties, 282
Rockets:
acceleration of, 334
burnout speed, 334
as performance parameter, 181
chemical fuels, 334—335
continuous staging, 335
escape velocity, 336
fuel, 334
fuel weight relative to gross weight,
182
ion, 335
nuclear-to-electrical powerplant, 335
specific impulse, 185, 333
staging to improve performance, 185
state of the art of performance, 184
technology, 333—336
lunar base problem, 339
velocity potential, 336
See also Burnout speed; Energy;
Energy release divided by annihilation energy ratio; Escape velocity;
Fuel-weight to gross-weight ratio;
Gross-weight to payload ratio;
Nuclear reactions; Specific impulse;
Speed; Staging; Velocity potential
Russia. See Soviet Union

SAC:
briefed on strategic air bases, 24
counterforce campaign, 60—61
defense of, 123—124, 138
deterrent effect, 124

evacuation plan, 45
future force composition, 19
modifications of evacuation plan, 46
1951 status, 25—26
preservation of, a high-confidence
objective, 135
vulnerability, 52, 54, 63
projected for 1956, 43
Satellite platforms:
earth and moon, 338
Satellites:
cost sensitivity to change in altitude,
291
Savage, L. J.:
quoted, 152—153
Scaling laws:
communication between space ships
as illustration, 186—187
limitations of, 189
reasons for usefulness, 186
used in nuclear or chemical explosions, 188—189
used in nuclear weapon testing, 189
Scarcity value:
by-product of optimization, 97
of capital funds for government
project, 101
in determining measure of efficiency,
99
Science:
and operations research, 150
Second-strike capability:
development of, as objective in planning, 125
problem not considered in 1950, 124
Secrecy:
as problem of analysis, 105
Selection and use of strategic air bases.
See Strategic Air Bases Study
Sensitivity analysis:
defined, 172—173
"Shadow prices":
as by-product of optimization, 97
Shielding:
nuclear aircraft, 114, 142
Simulation:
defined, 166
Soviet Union:
1951 air defenses, 25—26
See also Enemy defense; Enemy
offense

Space exploration:
  analysis needed for many programs, 344
  chemical reactions as energy source, 183
  conversion of nuclear energy, 183
  value of colonies on the moon, 333
Space platforms. *See* Satellite platforms
Specific impulse:
  defined, 184
  efficiency index in rocket technology, 333—336
  relationship to energy-release parameter, 184
  research and development needed, 336
Speed:
  energy released from fuels, 182
  and nuclear reactions, 182, 183
  as performance parameter, 179—184
  See also Burnout speed
STAGE:
  amplified from Strategic Operations Model, 79n
Staging:
  principle defined, 185
State-of-the-art parameters:
  energy release divided by annihilation energy ratio, 183
  fuel-weight to gross-weight ratio, 183
  in technological considerations, 184—186
Statistics:
  development of new techniques, 248
Strategic air bases:
  selection and use of, Chap. 3
Strategic Air Bases Study:
  adaptability of recommended system, 62
  allocation of funds, 59
  alternatives considered, 27—28
  cited, 114n
  comparison of basing systems, 56—57
  conclusions on vulnerability (quoted), 55—56
  cost of base vulnerability, 42—56
  cost of increasing flight radius, 30—37
  cost of overseas base systems, 41
  cost of penetrating enemy defense, 37—41
  cost of a summer campaign, 34
  counterforce campaign, 60—61
  in developing second-strike policy, 125—126
  effect on deterrence policy, 127
  effect on objectives, 126
  estimated savings to U.S., 24—25
  evaluated as a systems analysis, 62—63
  feasibility of preferred system, 59
  flexibility and campaign time, 59—60
  impact on strategic bombing "party line" adherence, 307
  intermediate criteria, 138
  limitation of problem, 26
  matching of move and countermove, 131
  plan of analysis, 30
  preferred system, preliminary, 30
  preliminary analysis, 26
  preliminary findings held tentative, 124
  research philosophy, 26
  Russian area defenses analyzed, 40
  Russian industrial-target complex, 61—62
  uncertainties in enemy capability, 57—58
Strategic Air Command. *See* SAC
Strategic bombing:
  analysis affected by attrition, 130
  effect of nuclear weapons on policies, 125
  1950 concept of, 125
  1950 operations program, 124
  post-World War II conception, 109—110
  studies revealing pitfall of "party line" adherence, 306—307
  World War II requirements, 109n
Strategic force:
  broad objectives in development of, 119—120
  defense of, 118, 123—124
  1950 mission, 124
Strategic force posture:
  importance of determining, 300
Strategic missiles:
  defense of, 118
Strategic Operations Model:
  amplified by Hq USAF, 79n

description of, 78—79
inputs, 78
output, 78—79
Strategies:
optimal, nonoptimal and inert, 134
Suboptimization:
advantages and disadvantages,
83—85
and criteria, 83—85
illustrated, 84
necessity for, 159
See also Subproblems
Subproblems:
effect on criteria selection, 83—85
solutions essential in analysis, 85
See also Suboptimization
Substitution:
of inputs, 94—98
rates, in production, 100
"Supersonic dash" capability:
in design of B-58, 141
Systems analysis:
analytic tools, 237—238
approaches to problems, 79
as an art, 153
assumptions about enemy behavior,
Chap. 10
blunders, 300
contrasted to operations research, 7
and the decisionmaker, 318
of defense and bombing systems,
1950, 125
defined, 4, 103
and development decisions, Chap. 12
differentiated from engineering, 152
distinguished from operations research, 153—155
effect of error on validity, 301
effect on objectives, 126
elements of, 13—14, 65
and engineering, 151—153
essence of, 167
failings and virtues, 360—361
fallacies, 301
future use in national security problems, 328—329
growth, nature, and uses of, 2—12
hypothetical missiles, Aztec and
Griffon, compared, 345—361
importance of problem formulation,
307

in industrial enterprises, 4
interdisciplinary orientation, 163
iterative character of, 158, 159, 166
limitations and value of, 326—328
in military context, 4
need for elementary economic principles, 304
objective of, 360
precepts, 319—322
recommendation modified by client,
314
responsibilities of analyst, 232
and scientific experimentation, 169
scope a reasonable compromise, 85
stages of, 156
state of the art, 249
value to decisionmakers, 104
value of periodic reappraisal,
315—316
during World War II, 227
See also Conflict system design;
Methods and procedures; Operations research; Technological considerations

Tankers:
attrition in multiple refuelings, 33n
in 1956 base operation system, 28
Targets:
effect on input combinations, 93
Russian, distances from U.S. bases,
30
value assigned in systems analysis, 69
Technological considerations:
optima and constraints, 189—193
performance parameters, 179—184
reliability, 193—197
scaling laws, 186—189
state-of-the-art parameters, 184—186
summary, 197
Test of preferredness:
in choosing alternative, 155, 160
as the criterion problem, 81
devising of, 81
"Thermonuclear-War-Is-Not-Peace
Principle", 141
Time:
as a factor in deterrence policies, 88
importance to analyst, engineer,
scientist, 151

Time phasing:
  explicit treatment of, 18
Timing:
  affecting enemy behavior and ours,
    204
Total activity cost:
  defined, 267
  estimates by analysis and synthesis,
    268
  three major categories, 268
  See also Total force cost analysis
Total force cost analysis:
  approach to individual system,
    269—270
  basic cost categories, 287—288
  digital computer employed at RAND,
    287
  force composition and assumptions,
    283—284
  generalized equations and statistical
    techniques, 287
  inclusive character of, 283
  incremental costing and long-term
    programming, 284—285
  investment costs, 288
  major missions of the Air Force, 285
  mission cost analysis as part of
    (figure), 286
  operating costs, 288
  research and development costs, 288
  sensitivity, timeliness, clarity,
    286—287
  See also Total activity cost
Trade-offs:
  in operations research and in systems
    analysis, 154
Traffic control:
  as example of deterrence, 123, 128,
    129
Transportation industry:
  linear programming in, 106
Transportation problems:
  and linear programming, 239
  solved by computers, 239
Traveling salesman problem:
  solved by intuition, 21

Uncertainties:
  always present, 321
  B-36 history exemplifying multiplicity
    of, 110

central problem in systems design,
    136
  challenge and pitfall, 313
  concealed by "universal" model, 313
  conceptual, 170
  in cost analysis, 265
  dealt with by cost sensitivity analysis,
    293
  in development decisions, 228
  effect of ignoring, 86—87
  in enemy defenses, 57—58
  enemy as source of, 200
  as to enemy's capabilities and in-
    tentions, 133, 134
  in estimates for parameters, 352—353
  evaluated by decisionmaker, 325
  explicit treatment of, 15—17
  factors considered in analysis, 232
  important element in the problem,
    314
  in model building, 170—172
  as problem of analysis, 105
  a problem of fact, 139
  in problem formulation, 164
  real, 171
  reduced as development proceeds,
    228
  specifications variables, 113—114
  statistical, 170—171
  in Strategic Air Bases Study, 27
  strategic and political factors, 236
  technical and operational parameters,
    172
USSR. See Soviet Union
Utility:
  complete ordering of preferences un-
    realistic, 147

Vandenberg, Gen. Hoyt S.:
  and the B-36, 107, 108
Variables:
  selection of, 15
Variance reducing techniques:
  in Monte Carlo, 241
Velocity. See Speed
Velocity potential:
  earth to moon, 336
  moon to earth, 337
Vertical-takeoff aircraft:
  consequences of engine failure,
    193—196

War:
  likelihood affected by strategy choice, 211
War gaming:
  aid to intuition and understanding, 80
  analysis of the game, 225—226
  establishment of rules, 223—224
  example, 76—77
  general war situation, 222
  in hypothetical missiles comparison, 349
  limited war situation, 222—223
  in model building, 18
  play of the game, 224
  spirit of, 77
  steps in, 220—226
  techniques of, 218—220
  termination of a game, 225
  used by Japanese before Pearl Harbor, 313—314
  uses of, 217—218
  validity of the findings, 226
Warning systems:
  1956 adequacy, 43—44
  for strategic forces and cities, 117
Weapon systems:
  cost analysis, Chap. 15
  defined, 265

procurement alternatives affecting criteria selection, 89—90
research and development cost, 282
typical cost history of, 273
Weather:
  effect on base operations systems, 143
Wellington, Arthur Mellen:
  quoted, 1
Williams, J. D.:
  quoted, 245, 247—249
Wohlstetter, Albert J.:
  quoted, 5
  strategic air bases study project leader, 24
World War I:
  statistical determination of draft call date, 311—312
World War II:
  importance of high sortie rates, 60
  operations analyses in, 13
  operations research in, 227
World War III:
  importance of high sortie rates, 60
  role of B-36, 108

Zone of the Interior:
  in 1956 base operation system, 28

SELECTED RAND BOOKS

Arrow, Kenneth J., and Marvin Hoffenberg. *A Time Series Analysis of Interindustry Demands.* Amsterdam: North-Holland Publishing Company, 1959.

Bellman, Richard. *Adaptive Control Processes: A Guided Tour.* Princeton, N.J.: Princeton University Press, 1961.

Bellman, Richard (ed.). *Mathematical Optimization Techniques.* Berkeley and Los Angeles: University of California Press, 1963.

Bellman, Richard, and Stuart E. Dreyfus. *Applied Dynamic Programming.* Princeton, N. J.: Princeton University Press, 1962.

Brodie, Bernard. *Strategy in the Missile Age.* Princeton, N. J.: Princeton University Press, 1959.

Buchheim, Robert W., and the Staff of The RAND Corporation. *The New Space Handbook: Astronautics and Its Applications.* New York: Vintage Books, A Division of Random House, Inc., 1963.

Dantzig, G. B. *Linear Programming and Extensions.* Princeton, N. J.: Princeton University Press, 1963.

Dorfman, Robert, Paul A. Samuelson, and Robert M. Solow. *Linear Programming and Economic Analysis.* New York: McGraw-Hill Book Company, Inc., 1958.

Dresher, Melvin. *Games of Strategy: Theory and Applications.* Englewood Cliffs, N. J.: Prentice-Hall, Inc., 1961.

Edelen, Dominic G. B. *The Structure of Field Space: An Axiomatic Formulation of Field Physics.* Berkeley and Los Angeles: University of California Press, 1962.

Ford, L. R., Jr., and D. R. Fulkerson. *Flows in Networks.* Princeton, N. J.: Princeton University Press, 1962.

Harris, Theodore E. *The Theory of Branching Processes.* Berlin, Germany: Springer-Verlag, 1963.

Hitch, Charles J., and Roland McKean. *The Economics of Defense in the Nuclear Age.* Cambridge, Mass.: Harvard University Press, 1960.

McKean, Roland N. *Efficiency in Government through Systems Analysis: With Emphasis on Water Resource Development.* New York: John Wiley & Sons, Inc., 1958.

McKinsey, J. C. C. *Introduction to the Theory of Games.* New York: McGraw-Hill Book Company, Inc., 1952.

Williams, J. D. *The Compleat Strategyst: Being a Primer on the Theory of Games of Strategy.* New York: McGraw-Hill Book Company, Inc., 1954.